SOLVING BUSINESS PROBLEMS USING

SQL

A DEFINITIVE GUIDE FOR BEGINNERS WHO WANT TO BE PROFICIENT IN DATABASE DESIGN AND WRITING SQL

HAFIZUR RAHMAN

Published by:
Hafizur Rahman
Email: solvingbusinessproblemwithsql@gmail.com

Table of Contents

Acknowledgements

My immeasurable appreciation and deepest gratitude goes to all who directly or indirectly contributed for publishing this book.

Special thanks goes to Aaron Martin for his editorial suggestions which make the book more readable to the beginners.

Thanks also to Sadman Rahman for his contribution to Lesson 3 and overall review of the book.

Finally, thanks to wife, daughter and friends for encouraging me to write my ideas and experiences in this book.

Introduction

What Is SQL?

Structured Query Language (SQL) is the standard language for communicating with most relational database systems. SQL is involved in some shape or form any time a computer is used to make a transaction or search a database. All such interactions fall into one of the following categories:

- A Desktop application (e.g. an order processing application)
- A Web application (e.g. an order processing web application)
- A direct transaction request to a relational database

Whenever an order is placed on an e-commerce site or money is withdrawn from an ATM machine, this transaction must be stored somewhere. That "somewhere" is called a database. A database can be as simple as an Excel spreadsheet file with a list of products on it, or it can be in the form of a complex relational database that stores, categorizes, and allows users to manipulate data in remarkably sophisticated ways.

Figure A.1 shows some the generic model for any business application that uses a relational database:

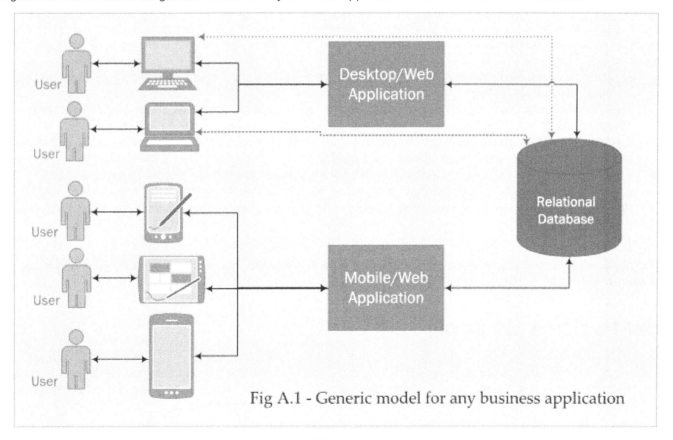

Fig A.1 - Generic model for any business application

As you can imagine, a business will accumulate a lot of data over time. Transactions are made, employees come and go, vendors add or discontinue products, etc. All of these interactions need to be recorded, stored, and managed, and the accumulated data can add up fast! It simply isn't practical to store vital business information in a simple file format anymore. That's why most of today's business applications—whether they are web-based or internal, on a desktop computer or mobile device—are using a relational database to store and manipulate their information. SQL is the language that these databases are built with and SQL is the most widely used language for adding, updating, or retrieving data stored in a database.

Why Should You Learn SQL?

As we just discussed, so many of the digital interactions we've come to rely on nowadays are powered by SQL. There's a strong chance that your company couldn't even perform its basic day-to-day activities without the aid of a SQL-based relational database. The desktop or web application you're using needs SQL whenever it sends transaction requests to a relational database. The same is true whether you're on a Mac, PC, smartphone or tablet. And as a developer, you may be using tools such as ASP.NET, PHP, Java or ColdFusion, but when you're designing a user interface you need to execute SQL within your code to send user inputs and receive results from the database.

Whether you are a database administrator, developer of web or mobile applications, or you are engaged in a similar business applications role, a good understanding of SQL is essential for communicating with modern database systems. The point is that, if you are working with databases, you definitely need to know SQL.

Who Is This Book For?

This book is for anyone who has little to no knowledge about databases or SQL and would like to become an expert in it. The lessons and practice scenarios in this book are designed to teach a total beginner how to build a complete database from scratch using SQL. For those of you who are not novices, we recommend this book as a valuable resource for:

- Application developers who want to learn how to write SQL on their own rather than rely on a database developer to do it for them
- Application developers who want to become a solution designer/architect by becoming proficient in database design and SQL
- Data analysts, data architects, report analysts or report developers who have to answer a lot of business questions and want to use SQL to answer those questions
- Application users who want to go the extra mile and find answers to their own questions using SQL
- Anyone who is an expert in one database tool and wants to become an expert in another database tool
- Business users or project managers who would like to know how to talk to technical people (such as those mentioned above)
- Anyone who can write SQL but doesn't know how to design a database from a business case

In short, if you want to take a more active role in how your database powers your business, the SQL skills taught in this book will give you an advantage in your career.

How to Use This Book

The best way to learn database design and SQL is to work through business examples that you can apply in the real world. That's why this book poses realistic design obstacles and real-world solutions to teach database design and SQL. The scenarios you will find in this book are common for businesses that use a database to power their day-to-day activities.

Throughout this book, you'll be working to develop and improve a database for our fictional company, *SaleOnYourOwn.com*. Creating and manipulating SQL statements for this e-commerce website case study will help you understand:

- How to transform a business case into a relational database model
- How to do the day-to-day data manipulation

- How to write proficient SQL to deliver day-to-day business reporting

We will use standard SQL based on ISO (International Organization for Standardization) standards, which have been implemented in most popular relational database management systems (RDBMS). In some cases, the implementation may differ between vendors, but we will show you side-by-side examples in two popular database management systems to show their similarities and differences: Microsoft SQL Server and MySQL.

As we cover the various SQL topics in these lessons, you'll be asked to write SQL statements along with the book to explore SQL database concepts and practice solving business problems. We have included the necessary SQL statements you'll need at the beginning of each lesson via Google Docs. As you are exploring SQL features via examples and solving business problems, you can either type the SQL statements out yourself, or you can simply copy the code sample directly from Google Docs and paste it into your relational database management system. Regardless of the method, when you run the statement to perform the task you should see the same result, but we encourage you to try writing the SQL statements by yourself for the practice business problems, then check your solutions with the ones in the Google Docs.

What Exactly Is This Book Going to Teach?

This book is aimed at users across a wide range of experience levels from total beginner to intermediate (and some advanced users). To that end, we aren't going to throw you to the wolves, so to speak, if you're not familiar with SQL at all. Instead, the first few lessons focus solely on the fundamental database design concepts that beginning users need to understand. We realize that there will be some users who will want to skip this and jump right into the SQL topics that are relevant to their level. If that sounds like you, take a moment to acquaint yourself with the section summaries below to decide where you want to start.

Without further ado, here are the five different sections of the book and what you'll learn in each:

Section A: Transforming Business Cases into Relational Databases

If you're a SQL novice, you need to understand the concepts behind it to use it effectively. In the first few lessons, we'll start by giving you a basic vocabulary of database design & SQL. Next, we show you how to design a logical data model and explain physical database design. Finally, we discuss manipulating data within the database. You'll follow a step-by-step process to design a database for *SaleOnYourOwn.com*. With this hands-on experience, you should be able to design a working database from a business case by yourself.

If you don't have access to a database or your computer/laptop does not have any database tools installed on it, *Lesson 3* will show you where to get the tools you need (and how to install them). You'll also learn how to add new data into a database table, how to modify an existing data from a database table, and how to delete erroneous data from a database table.

In terms of SQL commands, you will learn how to use the *INSERT*, *UPDATE* and *DELETE* statements in this section.

Section B: Retrieving Business Insights from a Single Table

Section B will show you how to generate reports and solve business problems that require retrieving data from a single table.

You will also learn some valuable uses for the *SELECT* statement in this section.

Section C: Retrieving Business Insights from Multiple Tables

Here, we'll show you how to generate advanced reports that require retrieving data from multiple tables. You'll also see how to solve some common business problems involving multiple tables.

You will learn how to use a *SELECT* statement with the *INNER JOIN*, *OUTER JOIN* and *UNION* operators in this section. You will also learn how to save your *SELECT* statement with a name for future uses by creating a database view.

Section D: Programming with SQL

This section will show you how you can use multiple SQL statements with conditional statements to build a routine to implement complex business rules. You will learn:

- How to create a batch/routine of SQL statements
- How to run the routine on an ad-hoc basis
- How to store the routine in the database as a procedure
- How to run the stored procedure
- How to store the routine in the database as a trigger to run it automatically after a data manipulation event

Section E: Database Administration

In the last section of the book we will show you some basic administrative practices such as how to improve your database's query performance using indexes. We'll also show you how to backup and restore your database.

Section A

Transforming Business Cases into Relational Databases

Lesson 1
A Basic Vocabulary of Database Design & SQL

Lesson Objective

Knowing the ins and outs of databases is essential if you want to design an optimized database that ensures the data integrity of your vital business information. In this lesson, you will learn the basic concepts of database design, SQL, and data modelling.

Here are the specific vocabulary terms and concepts we'll be covering:

Databases	Relational database management system (RDBMS)
Data modelling	Primary, foreign, candidate & surrogate keys
Entities and entity classes	The relationship between two entity classes
Attributes	Normalization
Tables, rows, and columns	The process of data modelling

Database Concepts

To understand how databases are used for business applications, let's start by looking at how a successful retailer would have stored and managed its data in the early days before computer systems. In this example, our retailer keeps a run-of-the-mill file cabinet with all its business data on paper. In the file folder are the three primary types of records the retailer keeps:

Products Catalogue – The catalogue includes a list of all products, their vendor names, current unit costs and stock quantities.

Payables File (Vendor Invoices) – This includes all invoices received from vendors. Each invoice includes vendor name, address & contact details, items details with prices and quantities, invoice date and few other pertinent details.

Receivables File (Customer Invoices) – The receivables file includes all invoices issued to the customers. Each invoice includes the customer's name, address & contact details, items details (including prices and quantities), the invoice date and few other details.

When a vendor delivers products to the retailer, an employee must physically take the relevant files out of their folders to add the details for any new products to its *Products Catalogue* and increases stock quantities for everything the vendor has delivered (see the example in Fig 1.1).

The retailer also receives an invoice from the vendor that it

PRODUCTS CATALOGUE

XYZ Electronics Shop

6123 Flinders St, Melbourne VIC 3000
Phone: +61 3 12345678   Fax: +61 3 12345678

PRODUCT NAME	VENDOR NAME	UNIT COST PRICE	STOCK QUANTITY
50 Inches Samsung LED TV	ABC Electronics Supplier Ltd 9600 Firdale Avenue, Edmonds, Washington, USA Email: abcSupply@SaleOnYourOwn.com	$1,500.00	25
60 Inches Sharp LCD TV	PQR Electronics Supplier Ltd 5000 Melbourne Rd, Williamstown, Victoria, Austra Email: pqrSupply@SaleOnYourOwn.com	$1,550.00	12
23 Inches Acer LED Screen	ABC Electronics Supplier Ltd 9600 Firdale Avenue, Edmonds, Washington, USA Email: abcSupply@SaleOnYourOwn.com	$120.00	20
21 Inches Acer LCD Monitor	PQR Electronics Supplier Ltd 5000 Melbourne Rd, Williamstown, Victoria, Austra Email: pqrSupply@SaleOnYourOwn.com	$110.45	10
24 Inches Acer LED Monitor	PQR Electronics Supplier Ltd 5000 Melbourne Rd, Williamstown, Victoria, Austra Email: pqrSupply@SaleOnYourOwn.com	$110.45	5

Fig 1.1 - A section of products catalogue

adds it to its payables file. When the retailer pays to the vendor, someone must search for the invoice in the payables file and mark the invoice as paid.

The process is similar when a customer buys one or more products. When a sale is made, the customer receives one copy of the invoice and the retailer's copy must be filed. The retailer then decreases the stock quantity in its products catalogue. However, if the payment isn't made right away, a copy of the customer's invoice goes into the receivables file. When the customer pays for the order, an employee searches for the invoice in the receivables file and marks as 'payment received'. You can see two invoice examples in Fig 1.2 and Fig 1.3. Note that we will be comparing these two invoices a little later, so it may be helpful to bookmark them so you can refer back to them easily.

Ideally, all these important files are carefully organized and stored in a dedicated place where the retailer knows it can easily find it. In reality, errors are bound to be made, and it's far too easy for files to get lost, damaged, stolen, or simply stored in a disorganized manner. It's not the most efficient system, especially considering the bookkeeping required to manage every order that comes in, every vendor that adds or removes a product, every stock quantity, etc. The more products, more customers, more sales orders, etc., the more work is required to manage it.

INVOICE

XYZ Electronics Shop
Best Price Guaranteed

DATE 15/10/2016
Order ID 20160001
CUSTOMER ID TOM001

BILL TO Tom Robert
5001 Sydney Rd
Melbourne VIC 3000, Australia
EMAIL TomRobert@SaleOnYourOwn.com

SHIP TO Tom Robert
5001 Sydney Rd
Melbourne VIC 3000, Australia

DESCRIPTION	PRICE	QUANTITY	TOTAL AMOUNT
50 Inches Samsung LED TV	$1,500.00	1	$1,500.00
23 Inches Acer LED Screen	$120.00	2	$240.00
TOTAL			$1,740.00

Make all checks payable to XYZ Electronics Shop. Thank you for your business!
6123 Flinders St, Melbourne VIC 3000   Phone: +61 3 12345678 Fax: +61 3 12345678

Fig 1.2 - A sample invoice for customer 1

INVOICE

XYZ Electronics Shop
Best Price Guaranteed

DATE 19/10/2016
Order ID 20160002
CUSTOMER ID RIC001

BILL TO Rick Smith
7007 Friars Rd
San Diego, California, USA
EMAIL RickSmith@SaleOnYourOwn.com

SHIP TO Tom Robert
5001 Sydney Rd
Melbourne VIC 3000, Australia

DESCRIPTION	PRICE	QUANTITY	TOTAL AMOUNT
50 Inches Samsung LED TV	$1,500.00	1	$1,500.00
21 Inches Acer LCD Monitor	$110.45	1	$110.45
TOTAL			$1,610.45

Make all checks payable to XYZ Electronics Shop. Thank you for your business!
6123 Flinders St, Melbourne VIC 3000   Phone: +61 3 12345678 Fax: +61 3 12345678

Fig 1.3 - A sample invoice for customer 2

So then, let's take a look at what the retailer's data collection and storage system would look like if they upgraded to a more modern system. The whole file cabinet is now a database. As our retailer modernizes its filing system, each of the three files become distinct entity classes, also known as tables, while each type of information within each file can now be referred to as an attribute or a column for the entity class (table). Finally, all the information on a single invoice or a single product can now be referred to as an entity occurrence or a row. It's helpful to imagine a simple database as a combination of tables, with each table looking like a common spreadsheet (such as a products catalogue) where the vertical columns of this table are each particular category (the product name) and the horizontal rows are the actual data (the product's actual name data, like "50 inch Samsung LED TV").

Fig 1.4 shows how business data can be stored in a file cabinet vs. a database:

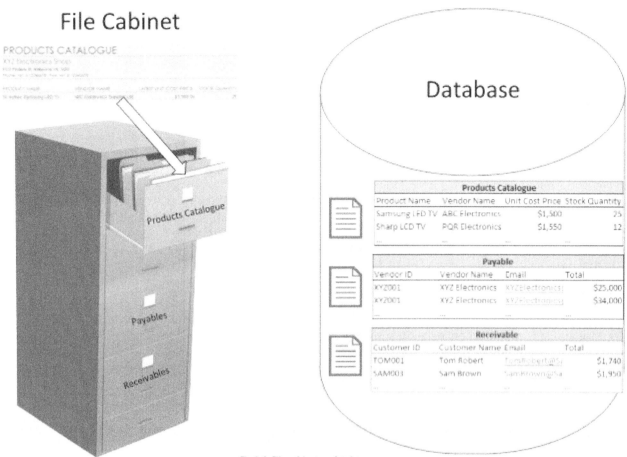

Fig 1.4: File cabinet vs database

Of course, this is not a relational database—yet. Our retailer has replaced its paper files and file cabinet for a computer with a bunch of spreadsheet files that still need to be manually updated. Our retailer's employees will probably come up with a database table such as the one shown here in Fig 1.5:

Order ID	Order Date	Customer ID	Customer Name	Billing Address	Shipping Address	Email Address	Item 1				Item 2				Order Total
							Description	Unit Price	Quantity	Total Price	Description	Unit Price	Quantity	Total Price	
20160001	15-Oct-16	TOM001	Tom Robert	5001 Sydney Rd, Melbourne, Victoria, Australia	5001 Sydney Rd, Melbourne, Victoria, Australia	TomRobert@SaleOnYourOwn.com	50 Inches Samsung LED TV	1500.00	1	1500.00	23 Inches Acer LED Screen	120.00	2	240.00	1740.00
20160002	19-Oct-16	RIC001	Rick Smith	7007 Friars Rd, San Diego, California, USA	7007 Friars Rd, San Diego, California, USA	RickSmith@SaleOnYourOwn.com	50 Inches Samsung LED TV	1500.00	1	1500.00	21 Inches Acer LCD Monitor	110.45	1	110.45	1610.45
20160003	26-Oct-16	RIC001	Rick Smith	7007 Friars Rd, San Diego, California, USA	7007 Friars Rd, San Diego, California, USA	RickSmith@SaleOnYourOwn.com	60 Inches Sharp LCD TV	1550.00	1	1550.00					1550.00
....	....	....	....	....	....	....	....	....	....	....	....	....	....	....	....

Fig 1.5: Customer's Sales Orders (Invoices)

There are several issues with this type of database. Notice that customer *Rick Smith* has placed two orders. Let's assume that his items have not yet been shipped, and he has suddenly moved to a new address. He notified the retailer of his new billing and shipping addresses, but the employee who updated this data in the system didn't notice that there were two orders and therefore didn't change the second one. As a consequence, *Mr. Smith* will receive items from the first order at his new address, but the second order will end up at his old address.

Another issue with this table is that it only supports a maximum of two items for each order. If a customer wants to buy three or more items, someone needs to manually add four new columns for each product. This can be a tedious exercise, especially for a business with lots of transactions. As you can see, this digital database is just as tedious as the file cabinet version when it comes to managing orders, vendors, customers, etc.

These are the sort of problems that a well-designed relational database can avoid. In a properly designed database, any time a customer wants to change his details (e.g. his address), no more than one row ever needs to be changed—even if he has placed thousands of orders! In today's digital world, the concept of a database, entity class and attribute remain the same, but the techniques for storing and retrieving data have improved quite a lot. Business users can now do in-depth analyses within just a few minutes whereas the same activity used to take months or years. As a result, users expect to have a more robust range of data available to them. For example, business users may want to analyse data based on age groups, but the above spreadsheet would prove inadequate since it doesn't include the customer's date of birth. As you can imagine, in order to streamline your data manipulation processes, a relational database is a must! On that note, let's dive into database and design principles next.

Databases

A database is basically a vast collection of facts (facts are often referred to as 'data') organized in such a way that is optimized for addition, modification, deletion and retrieval. The database, therefore, is like a container (usually one or more files) that contains all of a business' facts in an organized way. Within the database, data are divided into a broader logical grouping called schemas (e.g. by department or by application), then within schemas, they are divided into subject-based tables which contain rows and columns.

Fig 1.6 shows a typical representation of the different components within the database:

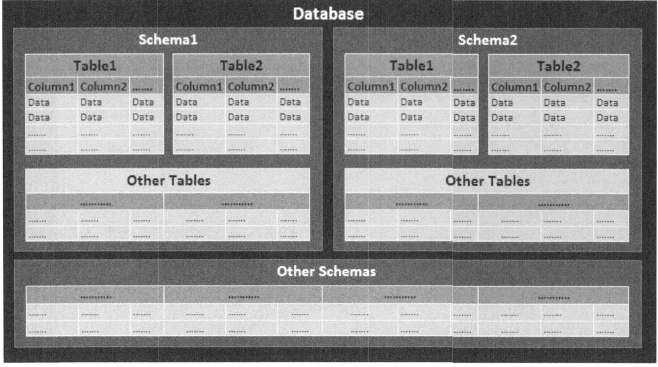

Fig 1.6: A typical database diagram

Please note that not all database systems support multiple schemas within a database. In those cases, both the schema and the database represent a single container.

Data Modelling

When you want to design a database to store facts for your business, you need to plan it out first specifically, you need to decide how to organize the facts you're storing. The process of organizing the facts within a database is called *data modelling*, and the result of data modelling is called a data model (it is often a graphical representation of facts). There are different types of data models; but the relational model is the most widely used database model for day-to-day operation for almost every business around the world. The relational model was first invented by Dr. Edgar F. Codd in 1970. It is based on set theory and first predicate logic. In a relational model, business facts are grouped by entity classes and their attributes, as well as how entity classes related to each other. A database created using the relational model is often called a relational database.

The *Entity-Relationship Diagram (ER Diagram)* is the most widely used data model for relational database design. In a relational database, we implement the entity class as a table and the attribute as a column. Business facts are stored in one or more tables, and each table contains one or more columns. For the remainder of this book, the terms entity class/table, attribute/column, and fact/data will be used interchangeably.

Data modelling starts at the logical level, which is platform-independent and referred to as logical data modelling. The result of data modelling is a logical data model, which is then converted into a physical data model. This physical data model is platform dependent (i.e. the RDBMS, storages subsystem etc.).

Relational Database Management Systems

A *Relational Database Management System (RDBMS)* is a type of software that is used to create and maintain one or more databases. Some of the most popular RDBMSs are:

- Microsoft SQL Server
- MySQL
- Oracle
- DB2
- PostgreSQL
- Microsoft Access

You will learn the principles, techniques, and concepts of relational database design in this lesson, but you won't need to install an RDBMS just yet. In the next lesson, you will use these techniques to complete an ER diagram for our business case. After that point, you will need a RDBMS to actually create your database from the ER diagram. Since there is so much to cover, we will only teach Microsoft SQL Server and MySQL. It's perfectly fine if you choose to use another RDBMS, but be aware that some of the sample codes may not work, so you'll need to refer to your RDBMS's documentation.

Entities and Entity Classes

In a relation model, an *entity* is anything that is relevant to the database you are designing. It can be objects, persons, activities or abstractions, for example. If you are designing a database for the fictional retailer we discussed earlier, an example of a physical object could be a *50 Inches Samsung LED TV* or a *23 Inches Acer LED Screen* that is currently in-stock in the storeroom. Meanwhile, an example of a person representing an entity would be *Tom Robert* or *Rick Smith* (both are customers of the retailer). Finally, examples of abstractions would be *the invoices (sales orders) given to customers Tom and Rick*. These are all individual occurrences of entities.

All similar entities in a database are grouped together as entries of an *entity class* or *entity type*. Even though *Tom Robert* and *Rick Smith* are different men, both are customers of the retailer, both pay for their purchase orders and both receive goods from the retailer. Therefore, both *Tom* and *Rick* are occurrences of the same entity class *Customers*; and both *50 Inches Samsung LED TV* and *23 Inches Acer LED Screen* are occurrences of the entity class *Products*. In the data model, we usually identify an entity class by its subjects (as mentioned above, subjects can be physical objects, persons, activities or abstractions).

Attributes

Different entity occurrences within an entity class store similar facts. Let's look at some facts our fictional retailer is storing for its customers. As a reference, you can find this information on customer invoices 1 & 2 that we showed earlier in the lesson (Fig 1.2 & Fig 1.3).

First Set of Facts: Tom was born on 11th February 2000 and Rick was born on 2nd June 1992. Here, both customers have entries under name and birth date.

Second Set of Facts: Tom lives at 5001 Sydney Rd, Melbourne VIC 3000, Australia and Rick lives at 7007 Friars Rd, San Diego, California, USA. Here both customers have a mailing address.

Third Set of Facts: Tom's email address is TomRobert@SaleOnYourOwn.com and Rick's email address is RickSmith@SaleOnYourOwn.com. Here both customers email addresses are listed.

If you review the above three sets of facts you can conclude that each occurrence of the *Customers* entity class will have a name, birth date, mailing address and email address. These are all different characteristics of the entity class, and we will often refer to them as *attributes* when we're discussing these facts relate to a database.

Facts vs Entities vs Entity classes vs Attributes

It is essential to have a clear understanding of entity occurrences, entity classes and attributes before you start to model your data. *Facts* are any data that you are interested in storing in your database. Let's review the facts used in the attributes section:

1. Tom was born on 11th February 2000
2. Rick was born on 2nd June 1992
3. Tom lives at 5001 Sydney Rd, Melbourne VIC 3000, Australia
4. Rick lives at 7007 Friars Rd, San Diego, California, USA
5. Tom's email address is TomRobert@SaleOnYourOwn.com
6. Rick's email address is RickSmith@SaleOnYourOwn.com

All the above facts are related to the retailer's customers. So, they should be grouped together under the subject, *Customers*, which is an entity class.

Facts 1, 3 and 5 are about a customer, Tom. The combination of facts can be represented as Tom was born on the 11th February 2000, he lives at 5001 Sydney Rd, Melbourne VIC 3000, Australia, and his email address is: 'TomRobert@SaleOnYourOwn.com'. This combination of facts is an entity occurrence of the *Customers* entity class. Similarly, the facts 2, 4 and 6 are about another customer, Rick. His personal information and address information fall into the same attribute categories as Tom's, but they obviously have different data. In short, both Tom and Rick are entities that share similar attribute. You could say that each has the characteristics born, lives and has an email address. The noun forms of these characteristics are date of birth, mailing address and email address. These are the attributes of the *Customers* entity class.

So, you can summarize the definitions of the entity class, entity and attributes like so:

Entity: All the facts for a particular occurrence of a subject (object, person, activity or abstraction) grouped together to form an entity (sometimes called an entity occurrence).

Entity Class: All the facts for all occurrences of a particular subject (object, person, activity or abstraction) are grouped together to form an entity class or entity type.

Attribute: An attribute is a characteristic that describes all the occurrences of a particular subject (object, person, activity or abstraction).

How This Relates to Our Business Case Database

For a further understanding of the concepts and vocabularies of data modelling and database design, it will be helpful if we use our fictional retailer to demonstrate a real-world business process. Our retailer is preparing to launch an e-commerce website, *SaleOnYourOwn.com*, and so they need to migrate all their business processes into a database. We already have a basic framework for the tables, columns, rows, etc., but we still need to develop a logical model that will be functional and designed based on best practices. The next series of topics will use more examples from our retailer demonstrate these database design concepts.

We know that customers can place orders to buy products. So, *Customer*, *Product* and *SalesOrder* are three subjects related to the customer's order processing system. *Vendors* are supplying products to the retailer for sale. So, *Vendor* is another subject related to customer's order processing system. Therefore, they are the entity classes. If you carefully review the earlier discussion as well as the product catalogue and sample invoices, you can easily identify the attributes of the entity classes like so:

For our purposes, the attributes of the *Customers* entity class will be *CustomerID*, *CustomerName*, *DateOfBirth*, *MailingAddress* and *EmailAddress*. Attributes of the *Products* entity class will be *ProductName*, *VendorName*, *UnitPrice* and *StockQuantity*.

The same goes for the attributes of the *Vendors* entity class and the *SalesOrders* entity class, as you can see in Fig 1.7.

In the entity diagram, the commonly used notation for an entity class is a two-part rectangle where the entity class name stays in the upper part and attributes are in the bottom part. Therefore, the entity diagram for these four entity classes may look like Fig 1.7.

Customers	SalesOrders	Products	Vendors
CustomerID	SalesOrderID	ProductName	VendorName
CustomerName	OrderDate	VendorName	MailingAddress
DateOfBirth	CustomerID	UnitPrice	EmailAddress
MailingAddress	BillingAddress	StockQuantity	
EmailAddress	ShippingAddress		
	ProductName		
	ProductUnitPrice		
	ProductQuantity		
	ProductTotalAmount		
	OrderTotalAmount		

Fig 1.7: Entity diagram without keys identified

Tables, Rows, Columns and Keys

Entity class, entity and attribute are the elements of logical database design. The physical implementation of an entity class, entity and attribute are the table, row and column respectively. Fig 1.8 shows a typical representation of a

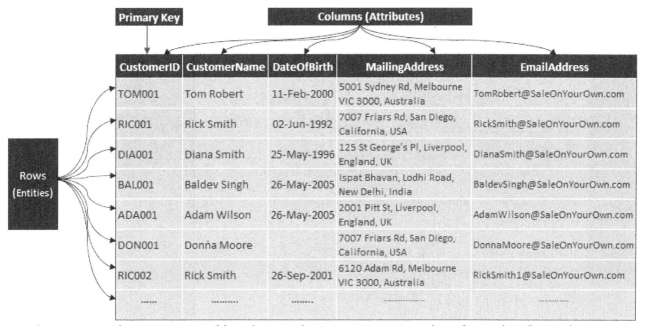

Fig 1.8: A sample Customers table using a unique customer ID as the primary key for each entry

Customers table. You'll see Tom and Rick's data listed here, along with several other customers who have bought from our retailer.

Note that table names must be unique within a database or schema and column names must be unique within a table. You can use same column name in two different tables, but you can't use the same column name within a table. Notice that each of the attributes of the *Customers* entity class represents a column in the above *Customers* table.

Since each column stores a specific characteristic of the subject, it stores a specific type of data. Therefore, each column has an associated data type (e.g. integer, string or date etc.). Whichever RDBMS you use will prevent you from adding the wrong type of data into a column.

Functional Dependencies between Columns (Attributes):

Within each table, value in each column, functionally depends on at least one other column or more. It functions much like the mathematical function, $f(x) = y$. In this case, y depends on x. When the value of x changes, the value of y may change as well, but when the value of x remains unchanged, the value of y must remain unchanged as well. As per the sample data in the *Customers* table from Fig 1.8, we can draw a diagram to show how the *CustomerName*, *DateOfBirth*, *MailingAddress* and *EmailAddress* columns all depend on the *CustomerID* column i.e. $f(\text{CustomerID}) = y$, as you can see in Fig 1.8(a):

$f(CustomerID)$							
EmailAddress	TomRobert @SaleOnYou rOwn.com	RickSmith@ SaleOnYour Own.com	DianaSmith @SaleOnYou rOwn.com	BaldevSingh @SaleOnYou rOwn.com	AdamWilson @SaleOnYou rOwn.com	DonnaMoore @SaleOnYou rOwn.com	RickSmith1 @SaleOnYou rOwn.com
MailingAddress	5001 Sydney Rd, Melbourne VIC 3000, Australia	7007 Friars Rd, San Diego, California, USA	125 St George's Pl, Liverpool, England, UK	Ispat Bhavan, Lodhi Road, New Delhi, India	2001 Pitt St, Liverpool, England, UK	7007 Friars Rd, San Diego, California, USA	6120 Adam Rd, Melbourne VIC 3000, Australia
DateOfBirth	11-Feb-2000	02-Jun-1992	25-May-1996	26-May-2005	26-May-2005		26-Sep-2001
CustomerName	Tom Robert	Rick Smith	Diana Smith	Baldev Singh	Adam Wilson	Donna Moore	Rick Smith
	TOM001	RIC001	DIA001	BAL001	ADA001	DON001	RIC002	*CustomerID*

Fig 1.8(a): Other columns' dependencies on CustomerID

Notice that for every *CustomerID* value we have only one value for *CustomerName* column:

$$f(TOM001) = Tom\ Robert$$
$$f(RIC001) = Rick\ Smith$$
$$f(DIA001) = Diana\ Smith$$
$$f(BAL001) = Baldev\ Singh$$
$$f(ADA001) = Adam\ Wilson$$
$$f(DON001) = Dona\ Moore$$
$$f(RIC002) = RickSmith$$

You can say based on this that the *CustomerName* value is dependent on *CustomerID*. Similarly, you can also notice that for every value of *CustomerID*, we have only one value for both *MailingAddress* and *EmailAddress* columns. Therefore, both *MailingAddress* and *EmailAddress* are also depended on *CustomerID*. Also notice that, for every value of *CustomerID*, we have only one value for *DateOfBirth* column. The only exception here is *CustomerID DON001* where no value exists that means the date of birth for *DON001* is unknown (when the value is unknown we do not need to check the dependencies):

$$f(TOM001) = 11 - Feb - 2000$$
$$f(RIC001) = 02 - Jun - 1992$$
$$f(DIA001) = 25 - May - 1996$$
$$f(BAL001) = 26 - May - 2005$$
$$f(ADA001) = 26 - May - 2005$$
$$f(DON001) = No\ Value$$
$$f(RIC002) = 26 - Sep - 2001$$

Therefore, you can also say that the *DateOfBirth* value is dependent on *CustomerID*. So, you can conclude that all other columns in the *Customers* table depend on *CustomerID* column.

Fig 1.8(b) shows the other columns' dependencies on the *DateOfBirth* column:

Fig 1.8(b): Other columns' dependencies on DateOfBirth

Notice that for the value of *DateOfBirth 26-May-2005*, we have two values for *CustomerID* column: *ADA001* and *BAL001*. Therefore, you can say that *CustomerID* is not depended on *DateOfBirth*. Similarly, for the value of *DateOfBirth 26-May-2005*, we have two values for each of the columns *CustomerName*, *MailingAddress* and *EmailAddress*. Therefore, you can say that none of columns *CustomerName*, *MailingAddress* and *EmailAddress* depend on *DateOfBirth*.

Primary Keys

Primary keys are handy for managing the data in a given table. For instance, if *Rick Smith* relocates from Australia to UK, you need to modify his mailing address. Similarly, if *Diana Smith* is no longer one of your customers, you need to delete her from the *Customers* table. So, how do you identify them? You need a column (or combination of columns) that stores unique values for each row of the table. In the above *Customers* table the *CustomerID* column stores unique values for each row (because no two customers share the same ID: even if we have two customers with the same name *'Rick Smith'* they have different *CustomerID*).

So, we can easily identify *Rick Smith* by his ID *RIC002* or *Diana Smith* by her ID *DIA001*. In this case, the *CustomerID* column is called the *primary key* for the *Customers* table. Therefore, *a primary key is a column (or set of columns) that uniquely identify each row within a table*. It is used as the identifier of each row within a table. The best practice is that every table must have a primary key. We recommend not using any column as a primary key for a table if data in the column or set of columns can be changed. You will see why later in this lesson. If a set of columns (i.e. multiple columns) uses as a primary key, it is called as *composite primary key*. If you define a column (or set of columns) as a primary key, RDBMS will not allow any duplicate value in that column (or set of columns). Therefore, the primary key will enforce table-level data integrity by not allowing duplicate values.

Candidate Keys (aka Alternate Keys)

A table can have more than one column (or set of columns) that uniquely identify each row. Each of them are candidates for becoming the primary key of the table, and they therefore are known as candidate keys or unique keys for that table. One candidate key becomes the identifier for each row, aka the primary key (see above). In the *Customers* table, you have two unique keys: *CustomerID* and *EmailAddress*. *CustomerID* becomes the primary key and *EmailAddress* remains a candidate key. The candidate key is often called an *alternate key*.

Surrogate Keys

In some cases, a table may have a unique key while retaining the option to change the data inside. In other cases, a table may not even have a unique key. In these cases, an artificial key (a column which does not have any meaning to the business) should be created to function as the table's primary key. This artificial key is called surrogate key. A *surrogate key* usually is an auto-number, and all mainstream RDBMSs support it.

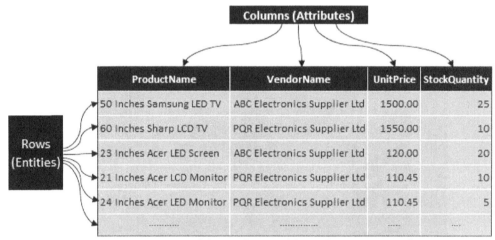

Fig 1.9(a): Products table without primary key

In Fig 1.9(a), we show you how to implement the *Products* entity class (as mentioned in Fig 1.7) as a table called *Products* and add some sample data into it.

Notice that the *Products* table has 4 columns, but none of them is a good candidate for a primary key because the *VendorName*, *UnitPrice* and *StockQuantity* columns can have duplicate values. *ProductName* may not have duplicate values, but the user may want to modify the name for a product in future. So, we need to add a surrogate key (an auto-

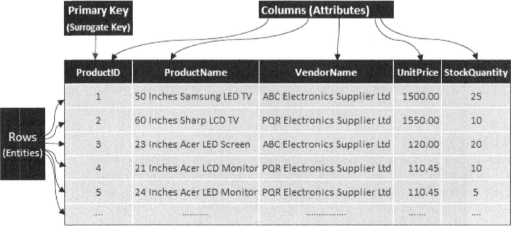

Fig 1.9(b): Products table with surrogate key as primary key

incremental integer as artificial key). Let's call it *ProductID*. You can see the new table with the *ProductID* primary key in Fig 1.9(b). Similarly, if you add a surrogate key (*VendorID*) to the *Vendors* entity class, the *Vendors* table may look like Fig 1.9(c) below:

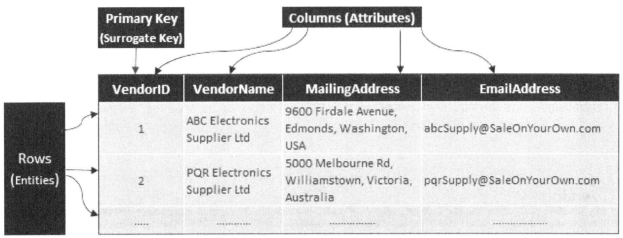

Fig 1.9(c): Vendors table with surrogate key as primary key

In the real world most of the attributes' values can be changed. Therefore, the business user sometimes uses a meaningful business key (like a *CustomerID*) as the primary key, but most of the time uses the surrogate key (like *ProductID*) as the primary key for an entity class (table).

Foreign keys

When you use the *primary key* of another table within a table, it is called a *foreign key*. A *foreign key* is used to establish a relationship between two tables. Here's an example. If you look at Fig 1.9(b) and Fig 1.9(c), *Products* table has a column *VendorName* that represents the vendor who is supplying the products. Let's assume *PQR Electronics Supplier Ltd* has merged with *LMN Suppliers Ltd* and has started trading as *LMN Suppliers Ltd*. So, *PQR Electronics Ltd* no longer exists. You have changed the *VendorName* in the *Vendors* table and also changed the *VendorName* from *ProductID* 2 & 4, but forget to change the name from *ProductID* 5, as seen in Fig 1.10(a) here:

Products

ProductID	ProductName	VendorName	UnitPrice	StockQuantity
1	50 Inches Samsung LED TV	ABC Electronics Supplier Ltd	1500.00	25
2	60 Inches Sharp LCD TV	LMN Supplier Ltd	1550.00	10
3	23 Inches Acer LED Screen	ABC Electronics Supplier Ltd	120.00	20
4	21 Inches Acer LCD Monitor	LMN Supplier Ltd	110.45	10
5	24 Inches Acer LED Monitor	PQR Electronics Supplier Ltd	110.45	5
....	....	....	....	....

Vendors

VendorID	VendorName	MailingAddress	EmailAddress
1	ABC Electronics Supplier Ltd	9600 Firdale Avenue, Edmonds, Washington, USA	abcSupply@SaleOnYourOwn.com
2	LMN Supplier Ltd	5000 Melbourne Rd, Williamstown, Victoria, Australia	pqrSupply@SaleOnYourOwn.com
.....	....	....	....

Fig 1.10(a): Vendor's name has been partially changed from

PQR Electronics Supplier Ltd **to** *LMN Supplier Ltd*

A few days later, a business user needs to email vendor for more supply of *ProductID 5* but cannot find the vendor's email address. This is because *ProductID 5* has become an orphan product (because the associated vendor *PQR Electronics Ltd* is no longer exists). Here's the solution: if you use the *VendorID* column instead of *VendorName* in the *Products* table, then you would only need to change the *VendorName* in the *Vendors* table and everything else should be consistent. This kind of streamlined organization is the primary principle of the relational model. If *table A* depends on *table B*, you have to use the primary key of *table B* as a column in *table A* to link two tables. When you use the primary key of another table within a table, it is called a foreign key. A foreign key is used to establish a relationship between two tables. When you establish a primary key – foreign key relationship, RDBMS ensure the data integrity between two tables.

Fig 1.10(b) and Fig 1.10(c) show the primary key and foreign key relationship between the *Vendors* and *Products* tables before and after the vendor's name changes, respectively:

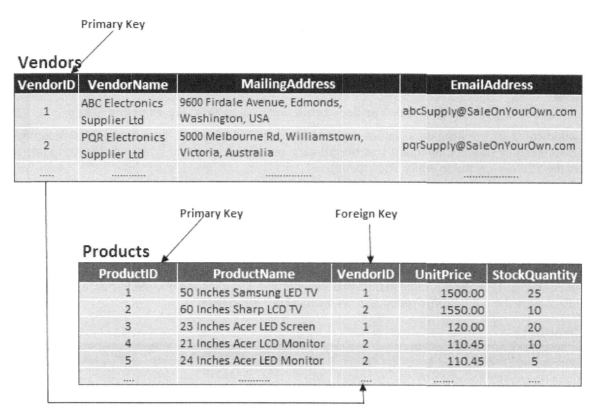

Fig 1.10(b): Relationship between Vendors and Products tables with data before vendor's name change

Primary Key

Changed from PQR Electronics Supplier Ltd to LMN Supplier Ltd

Vendors

VendorID	VendorName	MailingAddress	EmailAddress
1	ABC Electronics Supplier Ltd	9600 Firdale Avenue, Edmonds, Washington, USA	abcSupply@SaleOnYourOwn.com
2	LMN Supplier Ltd	5000 Melbourne Rd, Williamstown, Victoria, Australia	pqrSupply@SaleOnYourOwn.com
.....	....	....	....

Primary Key   Foreign Key

Products

ProductID	ProductName	VendorID	UnitPrice	StockQuantity
1	50 Inches Samsung LED TV	1	1500.00	25
2	60 Inches Sharp LCD TV	2	1550.00	10
3	23 Inches Acer LED Screen	1	120.00	20
4	21 Inches Acer LCD Monitor	2	110.45	10
5	24 Inches Acer LED Monitor	2	110.45	5
....	....	....	....	....

Fig 1.10(c): Relationship between Vendors and Products tables with data after vendor's name change from **PQR Electronics Supplier Ltd** to **LMN Supplier Ltd**

Notice that, in a properly designed table, you only need to change one data value.

Relationships between entity classes (tables)

We have already identified the keys for *Customers*, *Products* and *Vendors* entity classes. *SalesOrders* is the only entity class for the customer's order processing system that we have not yet identified keys for. Let's do this now before starting our discussion on the relationship between entity classes. If you replace *ProductName* with *ProductID* and add some sample data from Fig 1.5, the *SalesOrders* table may look like Fig 1.11(a):

Primary Key   Foreign Key   Foreign Key

SalesOrderID	ProductID	OrderDate	CustomerID	BillingAddress	ShippingAddress	ProductUnitPrice	ProductQuantity	ProductTotalAmount	OrderTotalAmount
20160001	1	15-Oct-16	TOM001	5001 Sydney Rd, Melbourne, Victoria, Australia	5001 Sydney Rd, Melbourne, Victoria, Australia	1500.00	1		1740.00
20160001	3	15-Oct-16	TOM001	5001 Sydney Rd, Melbourne, Victoria, Australia	5001 Sydney Rd, Melbourne, Victoria, Australia	120.00	2		1740.00
20160002	1	19-Oct-16	RIC001	7007 Friars Rd, San Diego, California, USA	7007 Friars Rd, San Diego, California, USA	1500.00	1		1610.45
20160002	4	19-Oct-16	RIC001	7007 Friars Rd, San Diego, California, USA	7007 Friars Rd, San Diego, California, USA	110.45	1		1610.45
20160003	2	26-Oct-16	RIC001	7007 Friars Rd, San Diego, California, USA	7007 Friars Rd, San Diego, California, USA	1550.00	1		1550.00

Fig 1.11(a): SalesOrders table with key identified

In Fig 1.5, each sales order is stored within a single row and repeated description, unit price, quantity and total amount for each item (products) in separate columns, but if the customer wants to place an order with 3 products you need to add 4 more columns. That is why, in *SalesOrders* table we have included only 4 generic attributes for items called *ProductID*, *ProductUnitPrice*, *ProductQuantity* and *ProductTotalAmount* and have added new row for each item. Now that the *SalesOrderID* has become non-unique, one order may include multiple products (e.g. first and second rows have same *SalesOrderID*). But the combination of *SalesOrderID* and *ProductID* becomes unique. So, let's call them composite primary key. *ProductID* and *CustomerID* are the primary keys of *Products* and *Customers* tables respectively. Therefore, they are foreign keys for the *SalesOrders* table. Let's mark primary keys as *PK*, foreign keys as *FK* and candidate (alternate) keys as *AK*. At this moment the entity diagram may look like Fig 1.11(b):

Customers	
PK	CustomerID
	CustomerName
	DateOfBirth
	MailingAddress
AK	EmailAddress

SalesOrders	
PK	SalesOrderID
PK, FK	ProductID
	OrderDate
FK	CustomerID
	BillingAddress
	ShippingAddress
	ProductUnitPrice
	ProductQuantity
	ProductTotalAmount
	OrderTotalAmount

Products	
PK	ProductID
	ProductName
FK	VendorID
	UnitPrice
	StockQuantity

Vendors	
PK	VendorID
	VendorName
	MailingAddress
AK	EmailAddress

Fig 1.11(b): Entity diagram with keys identified

One-to-many relationships

In the relational data model, we divide data into subject-based entity classes (tables). This means that two entity classes can be related to each other. Consider the two facts below:

> *ABC Electronics Supplier Ltd.* sells *50 Inches Samsung LED TV*
> *ABC Electronics Supplier Ltd.* sells *23 Inches Acer LED Screen*

Each of the two facts shown above are a combination of two pieces of data: one instance retrieved from the *Vendors* entity class and one from the *Products* entity class. The phrase "*ABC Electronics Supplier Ltd.*" is pulled from the *Vendors* table that you see in the diagram above, while the two different product phrases are pulled from the *Products* table ("*50 Inches Samsung TV*" and "*23 Inches Acer Screen*"). This is therefore an example of a *one-to-many relationship* because, as is so often the case, this one *vendor* sells many *products*.

In the ER (entity relationship) diagram, we often refer to this kind of relationship as a verb phrase of facts, in this case sell. If you look at Fig 1.10(b), you can notice that *VendorID* 2, PQR Electronics Supplier Ltd (one instance of *Vendors* entity class), relates to 3 products (three instances of *Products* entity class). That is each instances (rows) of *Vendors* entity class can have multiple associated instances (rows) of *Products* entity class, but each instances (rows) of *Products* entity class can only have one associated

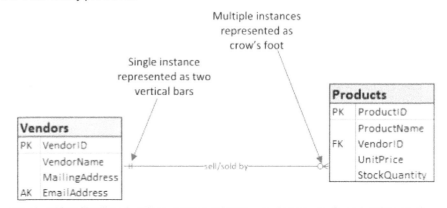

You can read the diagram from Vendors to Products as "One vendor can sell zero, one or more products" or from Products to Vendors as "One product can only be sold by one vendor"

Fig 1.11(c): ER diagram – One to many relationship

instance (row) of *Vendors* entity class. This type of relationship between two entity classes is called one-to-many relationship and can be represented in the ER diagram like Fig 1.11(c).

A one-to-many relationship can be drawn by connecting one entity class with another entity class through a solid line with single instance (parent entity class or table) as two vertical bars and a multiple instance (child entity class or table) as a crow's foot. You can see how these two small symbols are used to show the relationship between the *Vendors* and *Products* entity classes shown in Fig 1.11(c) above. A single instance will be connected with primary key and the multiple instances will be connected with a foreign key. Therefore, this is a one-to-many relationship, specifically a primary key – foreign key relationship.

Notice that in Fig 1.11(c) we do not read the relationship as "One vendor can sell many products"; instead, we read the relationship as "One vendor can sell zero, one, or many products." We would hope that all our vendors are active in the system, but we can't exclude vendors that don't fall into this common category. A brand-new vendor may not have started selling products yet, for example. Note that, while it's possible to have a vendor in the system that isn't selling products, it's not possible to have a product without an associated vendor who is selling it. This is the one-to-many relationship. You can think like a parent-child relationship: every parent can have zero, one or many children, but every child must have a parent.

One-to-one relationships

When each instance (row) of an entity class has only one or zero related instance of another entity class, the relationship between these entity classes is called a *one-to-one relationship*.

To demonstrate, let's assume the company is currently running a promotional sale. Every customer under this sale will be entered into a drawing, and one lucky customer will win a lifetime 30% discount. To set up this promotion in your database, you will need to add two more attributes in the *Customers* entity class: *DiscountPercentage* and *PromotionName*. Obviously, only one customer will have values for these attributes, so you will be wasting storage space if every single customer has these attributes. It may seem like a minor issue, but trust us when we say that you should keep your database as small and efficient as possible.

In the scenario just described, we would usually create another entity class (let's called it *CustomerSpecialDiscounts*) with *CustomerID* as its primary key, then create a relationship between the *Customers* and *CustomerSpecialDiscounts* entity classes by their primary keys (i.e. their *CustomerID*s). This relationship uses *Customers* as the parent entity class and *CustomerSpecialDiscounts* as the child entity class. Here's what this one-to-one relationship might look like in an ER diagram (Fig 1.11(d)):

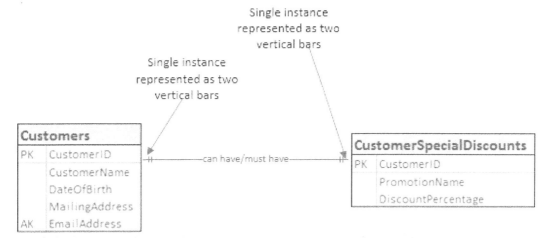

You can read the diagram as "One customer can have zero or one special discount" or "One special discount must have one associated customer"

Fig 1.11(d): ER diagram – One to one relationship

Many-to-many relationships

When one instance (row) of a first entity class can have multiple related instances (rows) of a second entity class and one instance of a second entity class can also have multiple related instances (rows) of the first entity class, then the relationship between these two entity classes is called a *many-to-many relationship*.

The *Customers* and *Products* entity classes share a many-to-many relationship and can be represented in the ER diagram in Fig 1.11(e).

Notice that we call this an unresolved many-to-many relationship. The reason it's "unresolved" is because, although these two entity classes have primary keys, they do not have foreign keys to establish relationships between them (note that the foreign key *VendorID* in the *Products* table relates it to the *Vendors* table, not the *Customers* table, and the *Customers* table has no foreign key at all).

You can read the diagram as "One customer can purchase many products and One product can also be purchased by many customers"

Fig 1.11(e): ER diagram – Unresolved many to many relationship

So then, how should we solve this problem? If you try to establish the relationships by adding *CustomerID* as a foreign key to the *Products* entity class and *ProductID* as a foreign key to the *Customers* entity class, both entity classes become unusable because these primary keys include duplicate values. To visualize this scenario, see Fig 1.11 below:

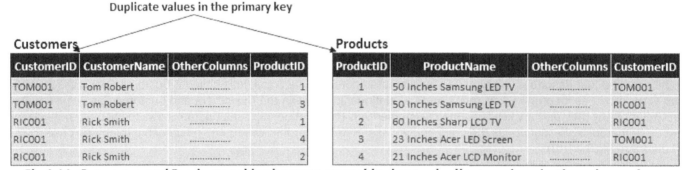

Fig 1.11: Cutomers and Products tables become unsuable due to duplicate values in the primary keys

To resolve this issue, in most cases you should be able to find another entity class that sits between the two entity classes and serve as an intermediary between these. In this case, the *Customers* entity class is related to the *Products* entity class via the *SalesOrders* entity class. One customer may place multiple orders, and one product may be included in multiple orders. So, *Customers* and *SalesOrders* have a one-to-many relationship, and *SalesOrders* and *Products* have a many-to-one relationship. This will resolve the many-to-many relationship by creating two one-to-many relationships.

Fig 1.11(f) represents the resolved many-to-many relationship. You can see how we created two one-to-many relationships, and you should be able to identify which customers are buying a particular product or which products are

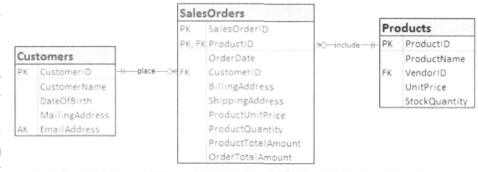

You can read the diagram as "One customer can place orders for many products and One product can be included in many customer's orders"

Fig 1.11(f): ER diagram –Resolved many to many relationship

being bought by a particular customer. This will become very important in later lessons when we start writing SQL statements to answer business questions about customers and sales orders.

So then, what if you do not have an intermediate entity class to use in a case like this? Then you must create an abstract entity class with both primary keys as its attributes. To show you an example, let's set aside our order processing system for a moment and discuss the relationship between *Customers* and *Accounts* entity classes in a bank. One customer can have multiple accounts (e.g. savings account, checking account, loan account etc.) and one account can also be associated with multiple customers (e.g. a joint account). So, *Customers* and *Accounts* are related with a many-to-many relationship. To create this relationship for the bank's database, you would need to create another entity class, let's call it *Customers Accounts* like Fig 1.11(f1):

You can read the diagram as "One customer can have one or many accounts and one account
can be associated to many customers"

Fig 1.11(f1): ER diagram –Resolved many to many relationship

Normalizing our ER diagram

By now you have learned most of the vocabulary of data modelling and database design and we have already identified the relationships between entity classes of *Customer's Order Processing System*. If you put everything together, our ER diagram will look like the one you see in Fig 1.11(g):

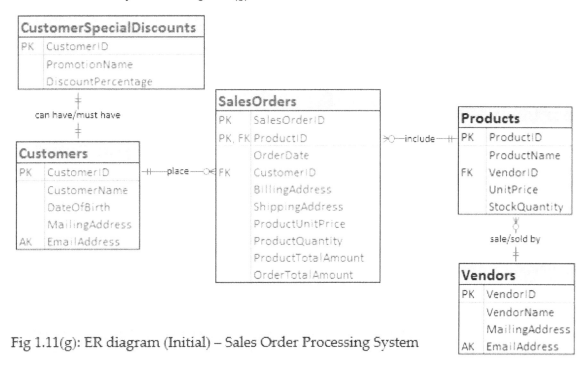

Fig 1.11(g): ER diagram (Initial) – Sales Order Processing System

After you have identified all the entity classes, attributes, keys and relationships, you will have an entity relationship model like Fig 1.11(g) that can store all business data need to be stored, but the data model may still have some hidden problems like data redundancies and/or insert/update/delete anomalies. If you carefully look at the *SalesOrders* table in Fig 1.11(a) from our earlier model, you will notice several problems that we'll discuss next.

SalesOrderID	ProductID	OrderDate	CustomerID	BillingAddress	ShippingAddress	ProductUnitPrice	ProductQuantity	ProductTotalAmount	OrderTotalAmount
20160001	1	15-Oct-16	TOM001	5001 Sydney Rd, Melbourne, Victoria, Australia	5001 Sydney Rd, Melbourne, Victoria, Australia	1500.00	1		1740.00
20160001	3	15-Oct-16	TOM001	5001 Sydney Rd, Melbourne, Victoria, Australia	5001 Sydney Rd, Melbourne, Victoria, Australia	120.00	2		1740.00
20160002	1	19-Oct-16	RIC001	7007 Friars Rd, San Diego, California, USA	7007 Friars Rd, San Diego, California, USA	1500.00	1		1610.45
20160002	4	19-Oct-16	RIC001	7007 Friars Rd, San Diego, California, USA	7007 Friars Rd, San Diego, California, USA	110.45	1		1610.45
20160003	2	26-Oct-16	RIC001	7007 Friars Rd, San Diego, California, USA	7007 Friars Rd, San Diego, California, USA	1550.00	1		1550.00

Fig 1.11(a): SalesOrders table with key identified

Non-atomic values in a column

Atomic values are an important concept when it comes to database normalization, as you will soon learn. We will only discuss atomic/non-atomic values briefly in this book. For our purposes, you should know that an atomic value is any piece of data that cannot be divided into a smaller piece of data.

For example, both the *BillingAddress* and *ShippingAddress* columns you see above store full addresses including the street, city, zip/postal code, state/province and country. Is the full address atomic or non-atomic in this example? The answer depends on your business. If your business always asks for the whole address, then this design should be fine (if for example this data will be used only to print invoice). However, if your business has any reason to retrieve data for a particular country, state/province, city, etc., then the *BillingAddress* and *ShippingAddress* columns are non-atomic. Examples might be if a business user ask you questions like *"Give me a list of all the sales orders from Australia"* or *"How many customers do we have in New York,"* etc.). For answering these questions, we need country and city columns that are not readily available. Therefore, you need to write some extra code to answer these questions. However, if the columns have atomic values (i.e. country and city values are stored in separate columns), you won't need to write any extra code to retrieve the data. This will have a positive overall impact on your database's performance.

Redundant values in a column

Both the first and second sales orders have two rows (copies) of data in the *SalesOrderID*, *OrderDate*, *CustomerID*, *BillingAddress*, *ShippingAddress* and *OrderTotalAmount* columns. If you want to modify an attribute's value but forget to modify all copies of that attribute's value (for example you have changed *BillingAddress* for the first row but not the second), then you'll end up with conflicting data (an update anomaly) in the column. Multiple copies of the same data/facts need more time to store and update, which will slow performance for your system in addition to wasting storage space.

Insert/Delete Anomalies

To understand insert and delete anomalies, let's assume that, in your design, you did not identify *Products* and *Vendors* as two separate entity classes and instead put both in a single entity class (table) as you see in Fig 1.11(h):

Deleting rows for a vendor will delete the related products as well					
ProductName	**ProductUnitPrice**	**ProductStockQuantity**	**VendorName**	**VendorMailingAddress**	**VendorEmailAddress**
50 Inches Samsung LED TV	1500.00	25	ABC Electronics Supplier Ltd	9600 Firdale Avenue.....	abcSupply@SaleOnYourOwn.com
60 Inches Sharp LCD TV	1550.00	10	PQR Electronics Supplier Ltd	5000 Melbourne Rd......	pqrSupply@SaleOnYourOwn.com
23 Inches Acer LED Screen	120.00	20	ABC Electronics Supplier Ltd	9600 Firdale Avenue.....	abcSupply@SaleOnYourOwn.com
21 Inches Acer LCD Monitor	110.45	10	PQR Electronics Supplier Ltd	5000 Melbourne Rd......	pqrSupply@SaleOnYourOwn.com
24 Inches Acer LED Monitor	110.45	5	PQR Electronics Supplier Ltd	5000 Melbourne Rd......	pqrSupply@SaleOnYourOwn.com
			EFG Electronics Supplier Ltd	6000 McDonald Rd......	efgSupply@SaleOnYourOwn.com

Without a product a vendor details will not be inserted

Fig 1.11(h): Insert/Delete Anomalies

Let's say you want to temporarily blacklist the *ABC Electronics Supplier Ltd*. You deleted all of this vendor's rows from the table, but by doing so you also deleted all of its products from the list as well (the *50 Inches Samsung LED TV* and the *23 Inches Acer LED Screen*). Because of this error, you will need to re-enter them if *ABC Electronics Supplier Ltd.* starts selling products again. In short, one group of data was deleted by accident when a different group of data was deleted, and this is called a *delete anomaly*.

On the other hand, you want to insert a new vendor, *EFG Electronics Supplier Ltd.*, but you do not have any of its product details yet. Because products and vendors aren't separate entity classes in your current model, you can't insert this vendor due to insufficient data. This is called an *insert anomaly*.

The main problem here is data redundancy and data integrity. We need to organize our data in such a way so that it will reduce redundant data and improve the integrity of the database. The process of doing this is called database normalization (or just normalization). Normalization happens at the table level, but it will reduce the overall redundancy and integrity of data for the whole database. Dr. E. F. Codd introduced a set of rules for normalization which are called normalization rules. Later, Raymond F. Boyce and few others made more contributions to the normalization rules. These rules are called *First Normal Form (1NF)*, *Second Normal Form (2NF)*, *Third Normal Form (3NF)*, and *Fourth Normal Form (4NF)* and so on.

At what stage in the design process should we do the normalization? Most of the time, designers choose to convert an entity relationship model into relational tables first, then normalize the tables, but some designers choose to normalize the entity relationship model, and then convert it to relational tables. Both ways have their advantages and disadvantages, and in this book we will mention both if it's relevant. Note that for simplicity we will simply refer to entity class/table as a table. Let's dive into Normal Forms now.

First Normal Form (1NF)

A table is in First Normal Form (1NF) if it satisfies both of the conditions below:

1. The table must have a key (primary key)
2. Every column of the table must store atomic values:

Composite values and a repeating group of values are two types of non-atomic values can violate the 1NF.

Composite valued columns: Whether a value is composite or not that depends on how it is being used. For example, in the *Customers* table, the *CustomerName* column can be atomic if your business almost always uses customer's name in full, but if your business frequently uses *FirstName* and *LastName* separately then the

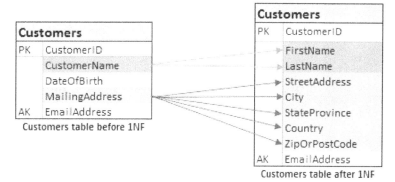

Fig 1.12(a): Confirm 1NF by splitting composite columns

CustomerName column becomes non-atomic composite attribute (combination of the *FirstName* and *LastName* attributes). Similarly, *MailingAddress* is a combination of the *StreetAddress*, *City*, *StateProvince*, *ZipOrPostCode* and *Country* attributes. To fix the composite column, we will split it into multiple columns that store atomic values.

Specifically, we split the customer's mailing address into unique pieces of information that cannot be broken down any smaller. This will satisfy 1NF. Fig 1.12(a) demonstrates this process.

Repeating group valued columns: Sometimes the value of an attribute (column) will occur repeatedly. For example, your company wants to store customer phone numbers, and you have added a *PhoneNumber* column in the Customers table. But when customer data starts coming in, you realize that some customers only have a home phone, some of them have a home phone, work phone, and mobile phone, and so on. In your current setup, you have no choice but to store them with commas (,) as separated values like you see in Fig 1.12(b):

Primary Key | | | Alternate Key

Customers

CustomerID	Other Columns	PhoneNumber	EmailAddress
TOM001	....	(03)111111111,(0400)1111111,(02)111111111	TomRobert@SaleOnYourOwn.com
RIC001	....	(312)333-333333,(312)444-444444	RickSmith@SaleOnYourOwn.com
DIA001	....	(7123)2222222	DianaSmith@SaleOnYourOwn.com
RIC002	....	(03)222222222,(0400)2222222,(02)222222222	RickSmith1@SaleOnYourOwn.com

Fig 1.12(b): *Customers* table with *PhoneNumber* column as repeating group

If you know you will be storing a limited number of phone numbers, then you can split the PhoneNumber column into multiple columns (*HomePhone, MobilePhone* & *WorkPhone*) that will satisfy 1NF as you see in Fig 1.12(c):

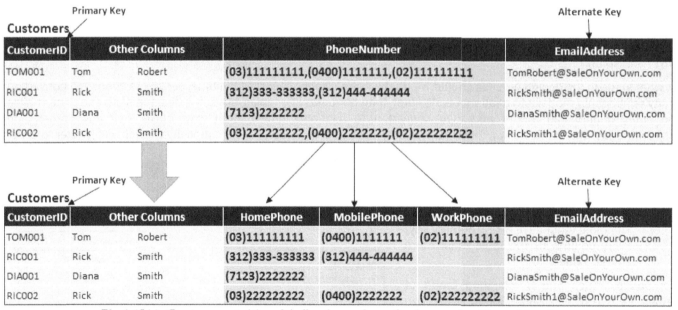

Primary Key | | | Alternate Key

Customers

CustomerID	Other Columns		PhoneNumber	EmailAddress
TOM001	Tom	Robert	(03)111111111,(0400)1111111,(02)111111111	TomRobert@SaleOnYourOwn.com
RIC001	Rick	Smith	(312)333-333333,(312)444-444444	RickSmith@SaleOnYourOwn.com
DIA001	Diana	Smith	(7123)2222222	DianaSmith@SaleOnYourOwn.com
RIC002	Rick	Smith	(03)222222222,(0400)2222222,(02)222222222	RickSmith1@SaleOnYourOwn.com

Primary Key | | | Alternate Key

Customers

CustomerID	Other Columns		HomePhone	MobilePhone	WorkPhone	EmailAddress
TOM001	Tom	Robert	(03)111111111	(0400)1111111	(02)111111111	TomRobert@SaleOnYourOwn.com
RIC001	Rick	Smith	(312)333-333333	(312)444-444444		RickSmith@SaleOnYourOwn.com
DIA001	Diana	Smith	(7123)2222222			DianaSmith@SaleOnYourOwn.com
RIC002	Rick	Smith	(03)222222222	(0400)2222222	(02)222222222	RickSmith1@SaleOnYourOwn.com

Fig 1.12(c): Customers table with fixed number of columns for PhoneNumbers

If the number of different phone number columns varies greatly between customers and you do not know the limit, the limit is liable to change, or the limit is quite big, then we recommend you create a new table (let's call it *CustomerPhoneNumbers*) and use *CustomerID* from the *Customers* table as a foreign key for the new table. *CustomerID* will be the first column of this new table, and *PhoneNumber* will be the other column. These two columns combine to form a composite primary key so that, any time a phone number is added to *CustomerPhoneNumbers*, it will be linked to that customer by the *CustomerID*. In this scenario, we must be sure to remove *PhoneNumber* column from *Customers* table.

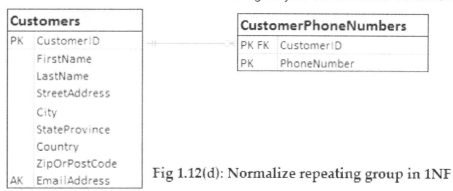

Fig 1.12(d): Normalize repeating group in 1NF

The entity model and relational model of the *Customers* and *CustomerPhoneNumbers* tables can be represented by Fig 1.12(d) and Fig 1.12(e).

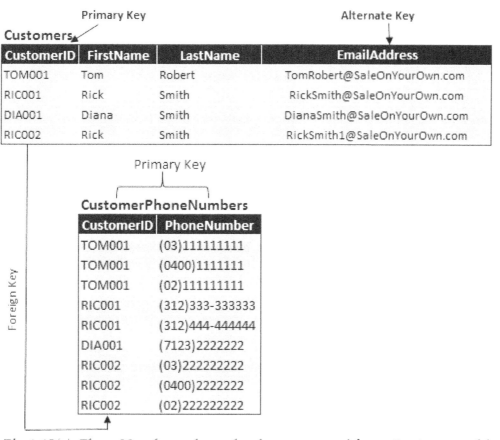

Fig 1.12(e): PhoneNumber column has been removed from **Customers** table and new table **CustomerPhoneNumbers** has been created to satisfy 1NF

Second Normal Form (2NF)

A table is in Second Normal Form (2NF) if it satisfies both of the conditions below:

1. The table must be in 1NF
2. Every non-key column must depend on the whole primary key (and alternate keys if any), not the part of the keys

To demonstrate, let's take a second look at the *SalesOrders* table's data in Fig 1.11(a).

SalesOrderID	ProductID	OrderDate	CustomerID	BillingAddress	ShippingAddress	ProductUnitPrice	ProductQuantity	ProductTotalAmount	OrderTotalAmount
20160001	1	15-Oct-16	TOM001	5001 Sydney Rd, Melbourne, Victoria, Australia	5001 Sydney Rd, Melbourne, Victoria, Australia	1500.00	1		1740.00
20160001	3	15-Oct-16	TOM001	5001 Sydney Rd, Melbourne, Victoria, Australia	5001 Sydney Rd, Melbourne, Victoria, Australia	120.00	2		1740.00
20160002	1	19-Oct-16	RIC001	7007 Friars Rd, San Diego, California, USA	7007 Friars Rd, San Diego, California, USA	1500.00	1		1610.45
20160002	4	19-Oct-16	RIC001	7007 Friars Rd, San Diego, California, USA	7007 Friars Rd, San Diego, California, USA	110.45	1		1610.45
20160003	2	26-Oct-16	RIC001	7007 Friars Rd, San Diego, California, USA	7007 Friars Rd, San Diego, California, USA	1550.00	1		1550.00

Fig 1.11(a): SalesOrders table with key identified

Is the table in 1NF? The *BillingAddress* and *ShippingAddress* columns store non-atomic values, so it violates 1NF. You can easily fix this by splitting each of these columns into four distinct columns (*StreetAddress*, *City*, *StateProvince* and *Country*), and the table will satisfy 1NF.

Do all of the non-key columns depend only on the whole primary key or, do all of them depend on an alternate key? The table has one composite primary key (a combination of the *SalesOrderID* and *ProductID* columns). Notice that certain values (such as *OrderDate*, *CustomerID*, *BillingAddress*) do not change even if the *ProductID* changes. This means that these columns only depend on *SalesOrderID*, not the combination of *SalesOrderID* and *ProductID*. Since *SalesOrderID* and *ProductID* form a composite key together, this setup violates 2NF.

The columns that violate 2NF are: *OrderDate*, *CustomerID*, *BillingAddress* (*StreetAddress*, *City*, *StateProvince* and *Country*), *ShippingAddress* (*StreetAddress*, *City*, *StateProvince* and *Country*) and *OrderTotalAmount*. All of these columns need to be fixed. All other columns depend on both *SalesOrderID* and *ProductID* columns and do not need to be fixed.

Here's the solution: move all columns that depend on the partial primary key (or partial alternate keys) into a new table and add the column(s) they depend on as the primary key(s) of this new table. This new table becomes a parent table, and the existing table becomes its child table in a one-to-many relationship. Specifically, you need to move *OrderDate*, *CustomerID*, *BillingAddress* (*StreetAddress*, *City*, *StateProvince* and *Country*), *ShippingAddress* (*StreetAddress*, *City*, *StateProvince* and *Country*) and *OrderTotalAmount* from the *SalesOrders* table into a new table and then add *SalesOrderID* to the new table as its primary key.

After confirming 2NF, the new *SalesOrders* table will look like Fig 1.12(f) below:

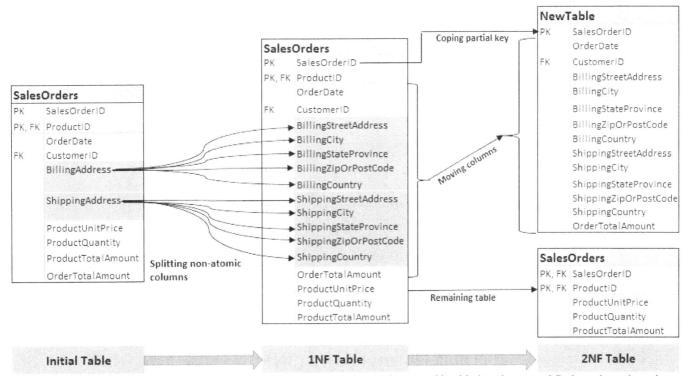

Fig 1.12(f): Confirm 1NF by splitting non-atomic columns then confirm 2NF by creating new table with the columns partially depend on primary key

Since the *SalesOrders* table has now been divided into two tables, we need to check if the names of the tables are still relevant. Notice that *NewTable* stores the summarized information about each order and the *SalesOrders* table stores item-wise detailed information about each order. Therefore, we can rename the *NewTable* as *SalesOrderSummary*, or

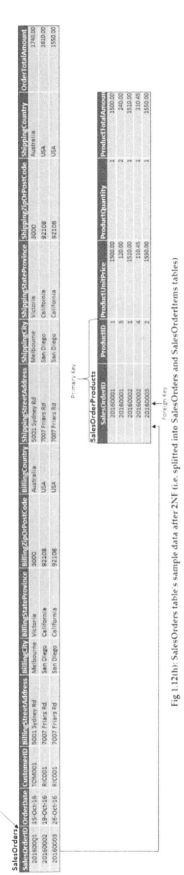

Fig 1.12(h): SalesOrders table's sample data after 2NF (i.e. splitted into SalesOrders and SalesOrderItems tables)

simply *SalesOrders*, and the old *SalesOrders* as *SalesOrderProducts*; and the relationship between *SalesOrder* and *SalesOrderProducts* tables will be one-to-many via *SalesOrderID* as in Fig 1.12(g).

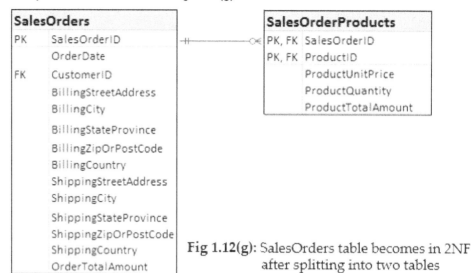

Fig 1.12(g): SalesOrders table becomes in 2NF after splitting into two tables

And here is the sample data of Fig 1.11(a) will be transformed into Fig 1.12(h) after 2NF.

Third Normal Form (3NF)

A table is in Third Normal Form (3NF) if it satisfies both of the conditions below:

1. The table must be in 2NF
2. Any non-key columns (or combination of columns) must not depend on one or more other non-key columns

Our current *SalesOrderProducts* table is in 2NF, so let's see how we can make it satisfy 3NF. As you can see in Fig 1.12(h), *ProductTotalAmount* is a calculated attribute and can be computed multiplying *ProductUnitPrice* by *ProductQuantity*

$$i.e.\ f(ProductUnitPrice \times ProductQuantity) = ProductTotalAmount$$

For each combination of *ProductUnitPrice* and *ProductQuantity*, only one *ProductTotalAmount* can be computed. Therefore, a non-key attribute, *ProductTotalAmount*, depends on both of the non-key attributes *ProductUnitPrice* and *ProductQuantity*, which is a violation of 3NF.

The violation of this type of 3NF is very easy to fix—just remove the calculated attribute as you see in Fig 1.12(i):

Fig 1.12(i): Confirm 3NF by removing calculated column

There could be natural dependencies between non-key columns. To check for any natural functional dependencies between the non-key columns of the *Customers* table, let's add some more sample data into it in Fig 1.12(j):

CustomerID	FirstName	LastName	DateOfBirth	StreetAddress	City	StateProvince	Country	ZipOrPostCode	EmailAddress
TOM001	Tom	Robert	11-Feb-2000	5001 Sydney Rd	Melbourne	Victoria	Australia	3000	TomRobert@SaleOnYourOwn.com
RIC001	Rick	Smith	02-Jun-1992	7007 Friars Rd	San Diego	California	USA	92108	RickSmith@SaleOnYourOwn.com
DIA001	Diana	Smith	25-May-1996	125 St George's Pl	Liverpool	England	UK	L1 1LY	DianaSmith@SaleOnYourOwn.com
RIC002	Rick	Smith	26-Sep-2001	6120 Adam Rd	Melbourne	Victoria	Australia	3000	RickSmith1@SaleOnYourOwn.com
HEN001	Henry	Tobias	02-Jun-1992	67 Gouda St	Billings	Montana	USA	59101	HenryTobias@SaleOnYourOwn.com
BRI001	Brian	Hunt	15-Mar-1986	240 Garfield St	Melbourne	Florida	USA	32935	BrianHunt@SaleOnYourOwn.com
TOM002	Tom	Phillips	27-Sep-1989	1052 North Park St	Victoria	British Columbia	Canada	V8T 1C6	TomPhillips@SaleOnYourOwn.com
BEN001	Ben	Cook	11-Feb-2000	5001 Sydney Rd	Melbourne	Florida	USA	32935	BenCook@SaleOnYourOwn.com
PAT001	Patel	Dev	15-Mar-1986	240 Garfield St	Melbourne	Victoria	Australia	3000	PatelDev@SaleOnYourOwn.com
AKI001	Akidul	Islam	27-Sep-1989	H#12, R#10, Uttara	Dhaka		Bangladesh	1230	AkidulIslam@SaleOnYourOwn.com
LIS001	Lisa	Klein	13-Aug-1997	67 Gouda St	Tel Aviv	Gush Dan	Israel	59101	LisaKlein@SaleOnYourOwn.com
MAR001	Mark	Jobs	13-Aug-1997	43 Anderson Ave	Liverpool	New South Wales	Australia	2170	MarkJobs@SaleOnYourOwn.com

Fig 1.12(j): Customers table after adding more data to check non-key columns functional dependencies

Notice that for a single value of *FirstName* Tom, two values can be computed for every column you see above:

- *LastName* (Robert and Phillips)
- *DateOfBirth* (11-Feb-2000 and 27-Sep-1989)
- *StreetAddress* (5001 Sydney Rd and 1052 North Park St)
- *City* (Melbourne and Victoria)
- *StateProvince* (Victoria and British Columbia)
- *Country* (Australia and Canada)
- *ZipOrPostCode* (3000 and V8T 1C6)

Since more than one value can be computed by a single value of *FirstName*, none of the non-key attributes depend on *FirstName* attributes. Similarly, we can work out that none of other single non-key attributes depend on another single non-key attribute.

Now we need to check for multi-column dependencies. *StreetAddress* can be duplicated within *City*, *StateProvince* and *Country*, but can't be duplicated within *ZipOrPostCode*. So, any values of the combination of *StreetAddress* and *ZipOrPostCode* can compute either one value or no value for the *City*, *StateProvince* and *Country* attributes. Therefore, the attributes *City*, *StateProvince* and *Country* depend on the combination of *StreetAddress* and *ZipOrPostCode*, which is a violation of 3NF. The fix for this violation of 3NF is similar to the 2NF. You must:

- Move the dependent attributes into a new table
- Copy the determinant (attributes they depend on) attributes to the new table and make them primary keys
- Make the determinant attributes in the existing table as foreign keys and use them to create one-to-many (primary key – foreign key) relationships between new table and the existing table

So, you need to move the *City*, *StateProvince* and *Country* attributes from the *Customers* table into a new table (let's call it Addresses), and then add *StreetAddress* and *ZipOrPostCode* to the new table as its primary key. After confirming 3NF, the Customers table will look like Fig 1.12(k):

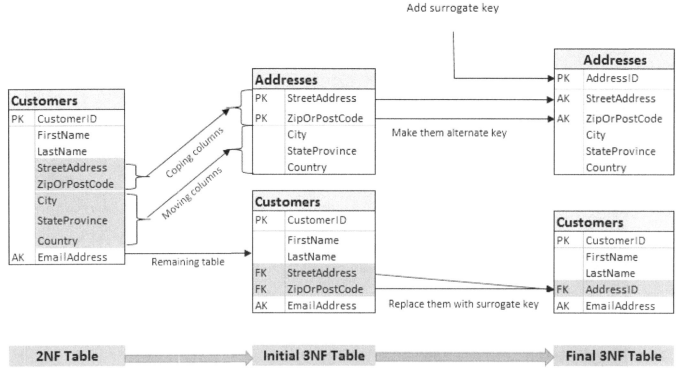

Fig 1.12(k): Confirm 3NF by creating new table with the dependent and determinant columns

Here, the StreetAddress is not a good candidate for primary key because it can be changed (e.g. *5001 Sydney Rd* can be subdivided into two new addresses such as *5001/A Sydney Rd* and *5001/B Sydney Rd*). Therefore, an artificial surrogate key (e.g. an auto-number) will be a better primary key option, and that is why the *AddressID* surrogate key has been added to serve as the primary key of the *Addresses* table, and the combination of *StreetAddress* and *ZipOrPostCode* has also been made as alternate key. The foreign key (*StreetAddress, ZipOrPostCode*) in the *Customers* table has been replaced by *AddressID*. The relationship between the *Addresses* and *Customers* tables will be one-to-many through their *AddressID* like you see in Fig 1.12(l).

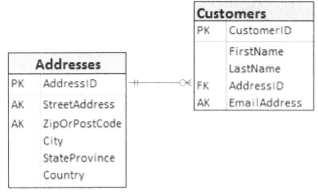

Fig 1.12(l): Customers table becomes in 3NF after
splitting into two tables

Sample data of Fig 1.12(j) will be transformed into Fig 1.12(m) after 3NF:

Primary Key

AddressID	StreetAddress	ZipOrPostCode	City	StateProvince	Country
1	5001 Sydney Rd	3000	Melbourne	Victoria	Australia
2	7007 Friars Rd	92108	San Diego	California	USA
3	125 St George's Pl	L1 1LY	Liverpool	England	UK
4	6120 Adam Rd	3000	Melbourne	Victoria	Australia
5	67 Gouda St	59101	Billings	Montana	USA
6	240 Garfield St	32935	Melbourne	Florida	USA
7	1052 North Park St	V8T 1C6	Victoria	British Columbia	Canada
8	H#12, R#10, Uttara	1230	Dhaka		Bangladesh
9	43 Anderson Ave	2170	Liverpool	New South Wales	Australia

Primary Key   Foreign Key

CustomerID	FirstName	LastName	DateOfBirth	AddressID	EmailAddress
TOM001	Tom	Robert	36567	1	TomRobert@SaleOnYourOwn.com
RIC001	Rick	Smith	33757	2	RickSmith@SaleOnYourOwn.com
DIA001	Diana	Smith	35210	3	DianaSmith@SaleOnYourOwn.com
RIC002	Rick	Smith	37160	4	RickSmith1@SaleOnYourOwn.com
HEN001	Henry	Tobias	33757	5	HenryTobias@SaleOnYourOwn.com
BRI001	Brian	Hunt	31486	6	BrianHunt@SaleOnYourOwn.com
TOM002	Tom	Phillips	32778	7	TomPhillips@SaleOnYourOwn.com
BEN001	Ben	Cook	36567	1	BenCook@SaleOnYourOwn.com
PAT001	Patel	Dev	31486	6	PatelDev@SaleOnYourOwn.com
AKI001	Akidul	Islam	32778	8	AkidulIslam@SaleOnYourOwn.com
LIS001	Lisa	Klein	35655	5	LisaKlein@SaleOnYourOwn.com
MAR001	Mark	Jobs	35655	9	MarkJobs@SaleOnYourOwn.com

Fig 1.12(m): Customers table's sample data after 3NF (i.e. splitted into Customers and Addresses tables)

You might already have noticed that the *SalesOrders* table in Fig 1.12(g) has similar dependencies as the *Customers* table on two groups of attributes below:

(BillingStreetAddress, BillingCity, BillingSateProvince, BillingCountry and BillingZipOrPostCode)
and
(ShippingStreetAddress, ShippingCity, ShippingSateProvince, ShippingCountry and ShippingZipOrPostCode)

One group of attributes represents the customer's billing address and the other represents the customer's shipping address. Each of these addresses can be represented by a row in the *Addresses* table. So, to confirm 3NF of the *SalesOrders* table, you do not need a new table. You can use the existing *Addresses* table as a parent table and (*BillingStreetAddress, BillingCity,*

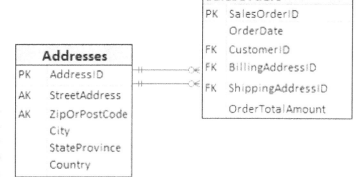

Fig 1.12(n): SalesOrders table becomes in 3NF after splitting into two tables

BillingSateProvince, BillingCountry and *BillingZipOrPostCode*) group of attributes with *BillingAddressID* (as a foreign key from *Addresses* table), and (*ShippingStreetAddress, ShippingCity, ShippingSateProvince, ShippingCountry* and *ShippingZipOrPostCode*) group of attributes with *ShippingAddressID* (as a foreign key from *Addresses* table), like Fig 1.12(n).

Now you have seen how a database model can evolve from one huge table containing duplicate information to a highly organized model that is normalized to satisfy third normal form. There are higher normal forms that exist, but these are rarely used and the discussion about them is beyond the scope of this book. If you normalize all the tables in your database for 3NF, it should be good enough for most of the business applications. Therefore, let's put all of the 3NF tables of our *Sales Order processing system* together, and see how it looks. The final version of our ER diagram is shown below in Fig 1.12(o).

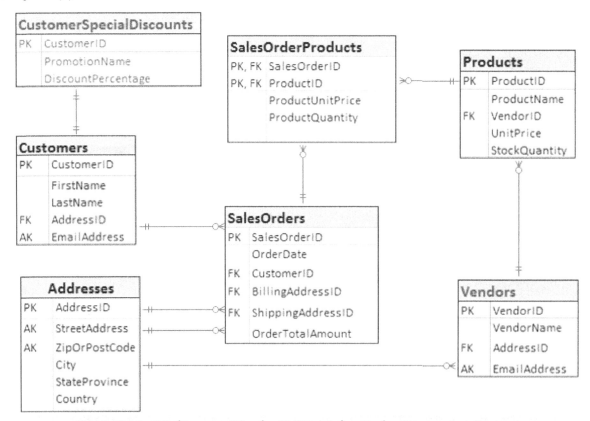

Fig 1.12(o): ER diagram (Final – 3NF) – Sales Order Processing System

The data modelling process

You have already learned the basic concepts of data modelling and we have given you quite a bit of information so far, so let's briefly summarize the steps of the process. Note that this process somewhat depends on the designer, but most will follow these common steps:

1. **Identify the entity class**
   First, you should review the business case/requirements and highlight the subjects (i.e. objects, persons, activities or abstractions) for which you need to store the data. Each of these subjects will become an entity class.

2. **Identify the attributes**
   Attributes are the details about the entity class. In most cases, the attributes for all entity classes will be readily available in the business case or a requirement specification document, but sometimes you may not have all attributes in the business case, and you'll need to ask the business user to get more details.

3. **Identify the candidate keys**

   Next, you'll group all identified attributes by their entity class, and for each entity class you should follow the steps below:

   i)   Create an entity diagram with the identified attributes

   ii) Review the entity diagram with the business user to find any more missing attributes, then add these attributes (if any) to the entity diagram

   iii) Identify all candidate keys. If an attribute or combination of multiple attributes stores unique values within a table, the attribute or combination of attributes are eligible to become candidate keys.

       (a) If the value of a candidate key is likely to be changed, mark the candidate key as an alternate key (AK).
       (b) If the value of a candidate key is not likely to be changed, it will eligible to become a primary key.
       (c) If you found only one eligible primary key, mark it as the primary key (PK).
       (d) If you found more than one eligible primary key, you should choose one of them as primary key (PK) and the others as an alternate key (AK).

   iv) If no primary key was found during the process so far, please create and add a surrogate key (usually an auto-incremental integer number) as the primary key (PK).

   v)   If any attribute or combination of attributes represents the primary key (or an alternate key) of another entity class, mark them as foreign keys (FK).

4. **Identify relationships and put them together**

   Identify any one-to-many, one-to-one, or many-to-many relationships between entity classes and connect them together to create a logical data model diagram (i.e. your ER diagram).

5. **Normalize the data model**

   At this point, some designers decide to convert each entity class into a table and then normalize the tables, while other designers decide to normalize the data model before converting each entity class into the table. In this book we will address both approaches, but please note that if you want to convert an entity class to a table you need to choose a data type for each attribute that is RDBMS dependent. We'll cover this concept in more detail later on.

Regardless of the route you take, normalizing the data model is the final step in making it ready to implement.

Lesson summary

From the basic structures and concepts to 3NF design steps, our goal in this lesson was to convey the fundamentals that will empower you to design an optimized database that ensures the data integrity of your vital business information. That's why we started this lesson at the very beginning comparing a file cabinet to a database, before covering various terminologies, rules and processes for transforming a business case into a relational data model. You learned that a database is a vast collection of data (business facts) organized in such a way that it is optimized for addition, modification, deletion and retrieval, a process called data modelling. The process begins with identifying various entity classes (subjects) and their attributes (characteristics) which implemented as a table with columns and rows.

Here are some key points to remember about tables, columns, and rows:

- Each table should have at least a column (or set of columns) that uniquely identify each row which is called primary key. If a table has more than one columns (or set of columns) uniquely identify each row, one of them becomes primary key and others become candidate/alternate keys. If none of the columns uniquely identify each row, an artificial key must be created for the primary key which is called surrogate key.

- When you define a primary key, RDBMS refuse to enter duplicate rows in the table which ensure table-level data integrity. When two tables are related to each other, you have added the primary key of the parent table as a column of child table which is called a foreign key and establish a one-to-many relationship. When you define one-to-many relationships, RDBMS refuse to insert/update/delete data from any table which is not compatible with the related tables.

- You have also learned that after you identified all tables and relationships between tables for your business case, your data model may still have some hidden problems such as some tables may have non-atomic columns, some non-key columns may depend on other non-key columns within a table. These problems can cause data redundancy and data integrity.

A note about Normal Forms (1NF, 2NF, 3NF and so on): 3NF is generally sufficient for most applications, and the normal forms higher than that are rarely used. If a table has a primary key and all other columns store atomic values, the table will become 1NF. Then if none of the non-key columns of the table depends on partial primary key, the table will become 2NF. Then if none of the non-key columns of the table depends on another non-key column(s), the table will become 3NF.

Lesson 2
The E-commerce Site Case Study

Lesson Objective
In this lesson, you will learn the step by step processes of building logical data model from a business case. You will see how you can create a logical data model for an e-commerce website business case.

The Business case: SaleOnYourOwn.com
Let's assume that you are responsible for designing the SaleOnYourOwn.com's (our fictional company) database. You will be the one providing SQL to the application developers for every activity (from data manipulations to reporting), but first you must design the logical model that the database will be built upon. First, let's examine SaleOnYourOwn.com's business practice and consider how these need to be implemented into the database. As you're reading about the different functions company needs to have, consider how each aspect might be organized into a data model. If you're unsure, don't worry—we'll show you an ideal model (and what that ER diagram would look like) in the next section.

Vendors

We already know that SaleOnYourOwn.com sells products supplied by third-party vendors to customers. These vendors will need to be divided into categories.

SaleOnYourOwn.com divides its vendors into three categories: regular, gold, and diamond:

- All new vendors start in the regular category. SaleOnYourOwn.com expects them to meet a monthly sales target ($30K) and also requires them to pay 20% commission on gross sales.

- If a regular vendor meets its monthly sales target continuously for 3 months, it will be promoted to the higher gold category with a monthly sales target of $50K and lower commission rate, 15%.

- If a gold vendor meets its monthly sales target continuously for 3 months, it will be promoted to the highest diamond category with a monthly sales target of$80K and commission rate of 10%.

- Each month, vendors will be paid the remainder of their total sales amount for the previous month minus the total commission it needs to pay to the company.

- Any new vendor should be able to register by providing its' details via the website [name, mailing address, phone number, fax number (optional), email address and contact person's name].

- An employee (who will become the vendor's relationship manager) will then review the details and create a login for the vendor if he/she finds the vendor suitable.

- The system must enforce vendor to reset its password at first login and system should track any failed login attempt and lock the vendor if it has 5 invalid password attempts.

Products

- *Vendors* can log in to the website and list their products under related subcategories. The system will need to allow these business users to add, remove, discontinue, and re-continue any product.

- SaleOnYourOwn.com will offer products in various categories and each category will be divided into relevant subcategories.

- Anyone (including customers) can search for products on the website or navigate via a category browser on the website's menu. When someone navigates via category or subcategory, it should display a brief description of our product offerings.

- For each product, the vendor must provide its name, sales price, stock quantity and the maximum estimated number of days it will take to deliver the product to a customer.

- The product should include a brief description and there must be an option to offer a fixed discount or discount as a percent of standard sales price.

- The system should allow an employee or vendor to deactivate/reactivate any products at any time.

- Each sales invoice should include the relevant data automatically (a unique order ID, customer ID, name, billing address, shipping addresses, order date, due date, total, discount & net values, and the list of products along with their unit prices, discount amounts and quantities).

- The sales order due date (expected delivery date) will be calculated by adding a maximum number of days need to be delivered for all products within an order to the order date. For example, if a customer placed an order that includes three products: two of them can be delivered within three days and another one can be delivered within five days, the order's due date will be the order date plus five days.

- The system should send a notification email to vendors whose products have been ordered by customers within the last hour. Vendors should then update the ship date in the corresponding sales order as soon as products have been shipped and the postal service should update the delivery date in the corresponding sales order as soon as products have been delivered.

- Vendors, employees, and customers should be all able to track relevant information about the status of sales orders.

- When all products under a sales order have been delivered, the system should update the order's delivery date.

- Each vendor will receive the total sales amount for its products minus the total commission it pays to SaleOnYourOwn.com, and each relationship manager will receive 25% of the commission received from his/her vendors, and the supervisor overseeing each relationship manager takes 20% of the commission received.

Customers

- If a new customer wants to buy one or more products, he/she needs to sign up. The system must have functionality so the customer can add his/her relevant info [name, mailing address, phone number, email address, credit card details, login (User ID) and password, mobile/landline numbers, date of birth and gender].

- As soon as the customer saves his/her signup detail, the system should create a login for the customer with the current date as a joining date and sign him/her into the website. Any customer who has signed in to the website can start adding products to his/her shopping basket.

- When the customer proceeds to the checkout, the system must add his/her billing and shipping addresses, credit card details, etc. with an option to edit them. Once he/she confirms the order details, the total order amount will be charged to his/her credit card and an invoice will be generated and emailed to him/her.

- Customers should be able to provide one feedback comment for products he/she has purchased (but will allowed only one feedback per product).

Identifying entity classes

Now let's start categorizing all our business case subjects (i.e. objects, persons, activities or abstractions) into entity classes. A good way to determine whether a subject should be an entity class is whether or not you'll need to store data for that subject.

Vendors, Products, & Customers

We know that our business will need to store data for our customers, our vendors, and their products. The customers, vendors and products are three subjects here. Therefore, we know will that vendors, products and customers should each represent an entity class.

Product Categories & Product Subcategories

'SaleOnYourOwn.com will offer products in various categories and each category will be divided into relevant subcategories' - Based on this extract from our business case description, we can assume that product categories and product subcategories are two subjects for which our business need to store data. Therefore, these are two separate entity classes.

Employee Logins & Vendor Logins

'An employee…will then…create a login for the vendor if he/she finds the vendor suitable' - This extract from the business case describes employee and vendor logins as two separate subjects for which you'll need store data. Therefore, we'll need to create an entity class for each.

Vendor Categories

'SaleOnYourOwn.com divides its vendors into three categories: regular, gold, and diamond' - We can gather from this extract from the business case that we'll need to store data for vendor categories. Therefore, we'll need to create a vendor category entity class.

Vendor Payments & Employee Payments

Recall that, 'Each vendor will receive the total sales amount for its products minus the total commission it pays to SaleOnYourOwn.com, and each relationship manager will receive 25% of the commission received from his/her vendors' – Based on this information, we know that we'll need to store data for vendor payments and relationship manager's commission payments, so these must be two more entity classes. Note that the relationship managers are SaleOnYourOwn.com employees, and so we'll call their payment entity class employee payments.

Customer Logins

'As soon as the customer saves his/her signup detail, the system should create a login for the customer' - Based on this detail, we'll need to create an entity class for customer logins.

Sales Orders

'Once he/she confirms the order details, the total order amount will be charged to his/her credit card and an invoice will be generated and emailed to him/her' - Here, we can assume that we'll need to store data for all our sales orders, so this will be yet another entity class.

Customer Feedback

'Customers should be able to provide…feedback…for products' - This feedback will be stored as soon as the customer submits it, so we'll need to create a CustomerFeedbacks an entity class for it.

So, if you've been keeping track you'll know that we will need to create the follow entity classes:

- *ProductCategories*
- *ProductSubcategories*
- *Products*
- *VendorCategories*
- *Vendors*
- *VendorPayments*
- *VendorLogins*
- *Customers*
- *CustomerLogins*
- *SalesOrders*
- *CustomerFeedbacks*
- *Employees*
- *EmployeeLogins*
- *EmployeePayments*

You can certainly use whatever naming system is logical for your own purposes, but we strongly suggest you stick to the names on this list when you're following along with our examples.

Here, we don't need to create separate entity classes for *VendorLogins, CustomerLogins* and *EmployeeLogins* because, for our purposes, the data for any login can be stored in the same table. That's why we have created only one entity class for all logins. The list of entity classes as per the entity class diagram will look like below:

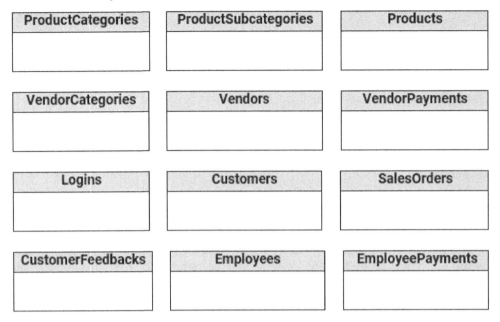

Fig 2.1 Our Current SaleOnYourOwn.Com Entity Class diagram

Identifying Attributes

Now that we know the entity classes for our business case, it's time to find out attributes for each of them. In most cases, the attributes for all the entity classes will be readily available in the business case or a specification document, but you may find some attributes are missing in the business case. In this scenario, you need to reach out to the business user and identify those missing attributes.

This next exercise will help you to understand how to identify attributes and group them under entity classes. In order to create an efficient and fully-functional data model for our business case, we will show you exactly which attributes to create and explain why each they are needed. As we review our business case, when you find an attribute in a given statement, first write down the statement, and then write the attribute in the following format:

Entity Class → Attribute.

Each product, category and subcategory of products must have a name to identify it. Therefore, the *ProductName, ProductCategoryName* and *ProductSubCategoryName* should be the attributes of *Product, ProductCategories* and *ProductSubCategories* entity classes respectively:

- Products → ProductName
- Product*Categories* → Product*CategoryName*
- Product*Subcategories* → Product*SubcategoryName*

Each product category is divided into subcategories, and each subcategory is divided into products—i.e. a group of products is linked to a subcategory and a group of subcategories is linked to a category. Therefore, each product should have a subcategory identifier (which is the primary key of the *ProductSubcategories* entity class) and each subcategory should have a category identifier (which is the primary key of the *ProductCategories* entity class) as attributes:

- Products → *Primary key of ProductSubcategories*
- Product*Subcategories* → *Primary key of ProductCategories*

If management wants to discontinue or resume any product category or subcategory, the system should allow it. Specifically, we need to add an activation flag (let's call it *IsActive*) so that any category or subcategory can be discontinued or resumed by changing the activation flag to *FALSE* or *TRUE*:

- Product*Categories* → *IsActive*
- Product*Subcategories* → *IsActive*

'Any new vendor should be able to register by providing its' details via the website [name, mailing address, phone number, fax number (optional), email address and contact person's name]'. Therefore, we will need to designate each of these types of information as an attribute of the *Vendors* entity class:

- *Vendors* → *VendorName*
- *Vendors* → Vendor*MailingAddress*
- *Vendors* → Vendor*PhoneNumber*
- *Vendors* → VendorFaxNumber
- *Vendors* → VendorEmail
- *Vendors* → ContactPersonName

Since SaleOnYourOwn.com will designate an employee to become that vendor's relationship manager, (who will supervise the vendor on a day-to-day basis), we need to create an attribute for relationship managers. The relationship manager's identifier (which is the primary key of the *Employees* entity class) will be an attribute of the *Vendors* entity class:

- Vendors → RelationshipManagerID

The *Login* entity class will be used to store logins for vendors, customers and employees. So, the *email address* can be used as a unique identifier for this. Therefore, *email* will be an attribute of *Login* entity class:

- Logins → Email

'The system must enforce vendor to reset its password at first login and system should track any failed login attempt and lock the vendor if it has 5 invalid password attempts'. So, in order to create attributes built around the vendor login event, we should consider the *'password'*, *'resetting the password at next login attempt'* , *'the number of failed login attempts'* and a lock flag *'IsLocked'* as attributes of the *Logins* entity class. So our *Logins* attributes are:

- Logins → ChangePasswordInNextLogin
- Logins → NoOfFailedAttempt
- Logins → IsLocked
- Logins → Password

As you know, SaleOnYourOwn.com divides their vendors into three categories. The vendor's category identifier (which is the primary key of *VendorCategories* entity class) should be considered an attribute of *Vendors* entity class so that we can store data pertaining to each vendor's category status:

- Vendors → Primary key of VendorCategories

We also need to be able to set the category details. Recall that regular category vendors should meet a monthly sales target of $30K and must pay 20% commission on gross sales; gold category vendors must maintain a monthly sales target of $50K and must pay a commission rate of15%; and diamond category vendors are required to meet a monthly sales target of $80K and pay 10% commission.

Vendors are required to meet their sales targets, and if they fail to do so for a certain period of time, they will be forced to pay a higher commission (temporarily). On the other hand, a lower category vendor can be promoted if it meets the higher category sales target for three months.

What does all this mean for our database? If you carefully analyse these facts, we can conclude that *each vendor within a specific category has a monthly sales target and also has to pay a specific percentage of commission on their sales. It also will be promoted to a higher category if it meets its target continuously for a specific number of months.* Each vendor category should also have a name. Therefore, *name, monthly target, number of months for promotion* and *commission rate percentage* describe different characteristics of each vendors category. We'll create these attributes in the *VendorCategories* entity class like so:

- VendorCategories → VendorCategoryName
- VendorCategories → VendorMonthlyTarget
- VendorCategories → VendorNoOfMonthsForPromotion
- VendorCategories → VendorCommissionRatePercentage

Now that we have designated some vendor attributes, let's create attributes for all the product details the vendor must supply for each. The vendor must provide its name, sales price, stock quantity and maximum number of days they require to deliver the product to customers. They can offer a fixed discount or discount as a percent of standard sales price. And of course they should also provide a brief product description. The system should allow an employee or vendor to deactivate/reactivate a product at any time.

So, the *name, standard sales price, stock quantity, days to deliver, description, sales discount amount, sales discount percentage, activation flag (IsActive) and identifier of the vendor who is selling the product* (which is the primary key of *Vendors* entity class) are all various pieces of information that describe the characteristics of each product. We will designate them as attributes of *Products* entity class like so:

- *Products* → StandardSalesPrice
- *Products* → *StockQuantity*
- *Products* → DaysToDeliver
- *Products* → *Product*Description
- *Products* → SalesDiscountAmount
- *Products* → Sales*DiscountPercentage*
- *Products* → IsActive
- *Products* → Primary key of *Vendors*

With regard to vendor payments, vendors will receive payment on the first day of every month for the previous month's sales. We know that their payment will be a net value after SaleOnYourOwn.com has taken its commission. So, the company needs to keep track of the *payment date, total sales amount, total commission amount* and *the identifier of the vendor who has received the payment* (which is the primary key of *Vendors* entity class). These will be attributes of the *VendorPayments* entity class:

- VendorPayments → VendorPaymentDate
- VendorPayments → TotalSalesAmount
- VendorPayments → TotalCommissionAmount
- VendorPayments → Primary key of *Vendors*

Each relationship manager will receive 25% of the commission received from his/her vendors, and the supervisor overseeing each relationship manager takes 20% of the commission received. The *commission rate percentage* is the rate each employee receives, and the *manager ID* is the identifier of the employee who is supervising him/her. These are the attributes of *Employees* entity class. The *payment date, payment amount* and *the identifier of employee who receives payment* (which is the primary key of the *Employees* entity class) describe the employee payment event. These are attributes of *EmployeePayment* entity class. So we have:

- Employees → EmployeeCommissionRatePercentage
- Employees → ManagerID
- EmployeePayments → EmployeePaymentDate
- EmployeePayments → EmployeePaymentAmount
- EmployeePayments → Primary key of Employees

When someone navigates via category or subcategory, it should display a brief description of our product offerings. Therefore, both *ProductCategories* and *ProductSubcategories* should have a description attribute:

- *Product*Categories → *Product*CategoryDescription
- *Product*Subcategories → *Product*SubcategoryDescription

Customers must sign up in order to buy products from our company. During the signup process, we know that the customer's various details must be stored in the database. We can store all this information as attributes of the Customers entity class: *name, mailing address, phone number, email address, credit card number, cardholder's name, card type, card expiry month and expiry year, mobile number, date of birth, gender* and *joining date* describe the details about each customer. These attributes can be named as follows:

- *Customers → CustomerName*
- *Customers → CustomerMailingAddress*
- *Customers → CustomerPhoneNumber*
- *Customers → CustomerEmail*
- *Customers → CreditCardNumber*
- *Customers → CardHolderName*
- *Customers → CreditCardType*
- *Customers → CreditCardExpiryMonth*
- *Customers → CreditCardExpiryYear*
- *Customers → CustomerMobileNumber*
- *Customers → CustomerDateOfBirth*
- *Customers → CustomerGender*
- *Customers → CustomerJoinDate*

In the above statement, one additional attribute *UserID* of *Logins* entity class has also been mentioned:

- Logins → UserID

Any customer who has signed in to the website can start adding products into his/her shopping basket. When he/she proceeds to the checkout his/her billing and shipping addresses and credit card details should automatically be added from his/her account with an option to edit the details. Once he/she confirms the order details, the total order amount will be charged to his/her credit card and an invoice will be generated and emailed to him/her. All of this customer information will be added as attributes to the *SalesOrders* entity class as you'll see below.

There are quite a few more attributes we need to create for sales orders. Each invoice should include a unique order ID, customer ID, name, billing address, shipping address, order date, due date, total, discount & net values of the order and the list of products along with their unit price, discount amount and quantity. The due date (expected delivery date) will be calculated by adding the maximum number of days needed for all the products within an order to be delivered to the order date. For example, if a customer placed an order that includes three products: two of them can be delivered within 3 days and another one can be delivered within 5 days, the order's due date will be the order date plus 5 days. Every hour, the system should send a notification email to vendors if their products have been ordered by customers within last hour (so that the vendor can respond and begin the process of shipping the product). Vendors should update the ship date in the corresponding sales order as soon as products have been shipped and the postal service should update the delivery date in the corresponding sales order as soon as products have been delivered. When all products under a sales order have been delivered, system should update the order's delivery date.

All of the sales order details, in combination with the ordering customer's details, are attributes of *SalesOrders* entity class:

- *SalesOrders* → *SalesOrderID*
- *SalesOrders* → *CustomerID*
- *SalesOrders* → Order*BillingAddress*
- *SalesOrders* → Order*ShippingAddress*
- *SalesOrders* → CreditCardNumber
- *SalesOrders* → CardHolderName
- *SalesOrders* → CreditCardType
- *SalesOrders* → CreditCardExpiryMonth
- *SalesOrders* → CreditCardExpiryYear
- *SalesOrders* → *OrderDate*
- *SalesOrders* → OrderDueDate
- *SalesOrders* → OrderTotal
- *SalesOrders* → OrderDiscountTotal
- *SalesOrders* → OrderDeliveryDate
- *SalesOrders* → Primary key of *Products*
- *SalesOrders* → *ProductQuantity*
- *SalesOrders* → *ProductUnitPrice*
- *SalesOrders* → *ProductUnitPrice*Discount
- *SalesOrders* → *ProductShipDate*
- *SalesOrders* → *ProductDeliveryDate*

Although the customer's addresses (billing & shipping) and credit card details are the attributes of the *Customers* entity class, the customer may decide to use different billing address, shipping address and credit card details for some of their orders—and that is why these are attributes of *SalesOrders* entity class as well.

Any customer may provide one feedback comment for each product he/she has purchased. Here a customer is providing a feedback for a product with a *rating* and a *feedback statement* on a *date* are attributes of the *CustomerFeedbacks* entity class. To store this data, we need to create following attributes:

- CustomerFeedbacks → Primary key of *Customers*
- CustomerFeedbacks → Primary key of *Products*
- CustomerFeedbacks → CustomerFeedbackRating
- CustomerFeedbacks → CustomerFeedback
- CustomerFeedbacks → FeedbackDate

Identifying keys and relationships

We have our entity classes and attributes. Now let's identify candidate keys and foreign keys of each entity classes based on the five steps mentioned in *Lesson 1*.

ProductCategories

Step 1: Our initial set of attributes is:

> ProductCategories → ProductCategoryName
> ProductCategories → ProductCategoryDescription
> ProductCategories → IsActive

Step 2: Business users do not need any additional information about product categories.

Step 3: *ProductCategoryName* will store unique values, but it can be changed (sometimes a business may decide to change product category names to suit market expectations). Therefore, *ProductCategoryName* is not eligible to become a primary key. We will mark it as an alternate key (*AK*) instead:

> ProductCategories → ProductCategoryName (AK)

Step 4: There is no eligible primary key identified so far. Therefore, add a surrogate key, call it *ProductCategoryID,* and mark it as primary key (*PK*):

> ProductCategories → ProductCategoryID (PK)

Step 5: So far, we don't have an attribute that can represent another entity's primary key—i.e. there is no foreign key for this entity class. Therefore, the entity diagram for the *ProductCategories* entity class will be like Fig 2.2.

ProductCategories	
PK	ProductCategoryID
AK	ProductCategoryName
	ProductCategoryDescription
	IsActive

Fig 2.2: Entity diagram for ProductCategories

ProductSubcategories

Step 1: Our initial set of attributes is:

> ProductSubcategories → ProductSubcategoryName
> ProductSubcategories → ProductSubcategoryDescription
> ProductSubcubcategories → ProductCategoryID (primary key of ProductCategories)
> ProductSubcategories → IsActive

Step 2: Business users do not need any additional information about product subcategories.

Step 3: *ProductSubcategoryName* will store unique values, but it can be changed (if the business decides to change product subcategory names). Therefore, it is not eligible to become a primary key and mark it as an alternate key (*AK*):

> ProductSubcategories → ProductSubcategoryName (AK)

Step 4: As was the case before, we don't have an eligible primary key identified for *ProductSubcategories*. Therefore, add a surrogate key named *ProductSubcategoryID* and mark it as the primary key (*PK*):

> ProductSubcategories → ProductSubcategoryID (PK)

Step 5: *ProductCategoryID* represents the primary key of the *ProductCategories* entity class, so we'll mark it as a foreign key (*FK*). Our entity diagram for the *ProductSubcategories* entity class will be like Fig 2.3.

ProductSubcategories	
PK	ProductSubcategoryID
AK	ProductSubcategoryName
	ProductSubcategoryDescription
FK	ProductCategoryID
	IsActive

Fig 2.3: Entity diagram for ProductSubcategories

This foreign key *ProductCategoryID* will be used to join this entity class with the *ProductCategories* entity class. Since one product category can have multiple subcategories, the relationship between these entity classes will be one-to-many. Therefore, the ER diagram between the *ProductCategories* and *ProductSubcategories* entity classes will be like Fig 2.4:

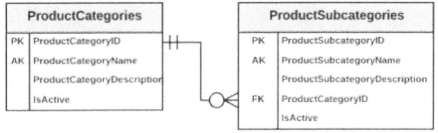

Fig 2.4: Entity relationship diagram between
ProductCategories and ProductSubcategories

VendorCategories

Step 1: Our initial set of attributes is:

> VendorCategories → VendorCategoryName
> VendorCategories → VendorMonthlyTarget
> VendorCategories → VendorNoOfMonthsForPromotion
> VendorCategories → VendorCommissionRatePercentage

Step 2: Business users would like to add a detail description or notes for most of the vendor categories. Therefore, add this attribute:

> VendorCategories → VendorCategoryDescription

Step 3: *VendorCategoryName* will store unique values, but it can be changed (when more categories have been added, the business user may decide to rearrange the names). Therefore, it is not eligible to become a primary key and we will mark it as an alternate key (*AK*):

> VendorCategories → VendorCategoryName (*AK*)

Step 4: There is no eligible primary key identified so far. Therefore, add a surrogate key, *VendorCategoryID,* and mark it as a primary key (*PK*):

> VendorCategories → VendorCategoryID (PK)

Step 5: There are no attributes here that represent another entity's primary key—i.e. there is no foreign key for this entity class. Therefore, the entity diagram for our *VendorCategories* entity class will simply look like Fig 2.5.

VendorCategories	
PK	VendorCategoryID
AK	VendorCategoryName
	VendorCategoryDescription
	VendorMonthlyTarget
	VendorNoOfMonthsForPromotion
	VendorCommissionRatePercentage

Fig 2.5: Entity diagram for VendorCategories

Vendors

Step 1: Our initial set of attributes is:

> Vendors → VendorName
> Vendors → VendorMailingAddress
> Vendors → VendorPhoneNumber
> Vendors → VendorFaxNumber
> Vendors → VendorEmail
> Vendors → ContactPersonName
> Vendors → RelationshipManagerID
> Vendors → VendorCategoryID (primary key of VendorCategories)

Step 2: Business users would like to temporarily blacklist a vendor if they are in non-compliance with the company policies. On the other hand, a blacklisted vendor who becomes compliant should be reinstated. That means we need an activation flag so that business user can turn the flag 'on' or 'off' whenever needed. Therefore, add this attribute:

> Vendors → IsActive

Step 3: *VendorName* will store unique values, but it can be changed (if, for example, a vendor merges with another company). *VendorEmail* will also store unique values, but it can be changed as well. Therefore, none of these attributes are eligible to become a primary key. We'll mark them as alternate keys (*AK*):

> Vendors → VendorName (AK)
> Vendors → VendorEmail (AK)

Step 4: There is no eligible primary key identified so far, so we'll create a surrogate key *VendorID* and mark it as the primary key (*PK*):

Vendors → VendorID (PK)

Step 5: *VendorCategoryID* represents the primary key of the *VendorCategories* entity class. So, mark it as foreign key (*FK*). Similarly, *RelationshipManagerID* will represent the primary key of the *Employees* entity class (we will see this later). So, mark it as foreign key (*FK*) as well. Therefore, the entity diagram for *Vendors* entity class will be like Fig 2.6.

The foreign key *VendorCategoryID* will be used to join this entity class with *VendorCategories* entity class. Since one vendor can only belong to one category, but multiple vendors can belong to the same category, the relationship between these entity classes will be one-to-many. Therefore, the ER diagram between the *VendorCategories* and *Vendors* entity classes will be like Fig 2.7.

Similarly, the foreign key *RelationshipManagerID* will be used to join this entity class with *Employees* entity class. Since one employee (relationship manager) can be assigned to support multiple vendors, but one vendor will primarily be supported by one relationship manager, the relationship between entity classes *Employees* and *Vendors* will be one-to-many. Since the entity diagram for **Employees** has not yet been done, the ER diagram between entity classes *Employees* and *Vendors* will be shown later.

	Vendors
PK	VendorID
AK	VendorName
	VendorMailingAddress
	VendorPhoneNumber
	VendorFaxNumber
AK	VendorEmail
	ContactPersonName
FK	RelationshipManagerID
FK	VendorCategoryID
	IsActive

Fig 2.6: Entity diagram for Vendors

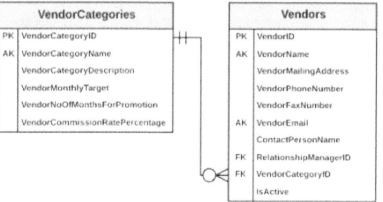

Fig 2.7: ERD between VendorCategories and Vendors

Employees

Step 1: Our initial set of attributes is:

Employees → EmployeeCommissionRatePercentage
Employees → ManagerID

Step 2: Some of the basic attributes that company would like to store about their employees are their name, address, phone number, mobile number, email address, date of birth and gender. The company also keeps their previous employee's details in their database for a certain period. So, we need another attribute to differentiate the previous employee with the current employee. Let's call it as *IsActive*. Therefore, add this attribute:

Employees → EmployeeName
Employees → EmployeeMailingAddress
Employees → EmployeePhoneNumber
Employees → EmployeeMobileNumber
Employees → EmployeeEmail
Employees → EmployeeDateOfBirth
Employees → EmployeeGender
Employees → IsActive

Step 3: *EmployeeEmail* will store unique values, but emails can be changed. Therefore, it is not eligible to become a primary key and we'll mark it as an alternate key (*AK*):

Employees → EmployeeEmail (AK)

Step 4: There are no eligible primary keys identified so far. As you may have guessed, we'll create a surrogate key and mark it as primary key (*PK*). This time, we'll call it *EmployeeID*:

Employees → EmployeeID (PK)

Step 5: There are no attributes here that represent another entity's primary key (i.e. there is no foreign key for this entity class). But the *ManagerID* refers to another *EmployeeID*, so the *ManagerID* is treated as a foreign key within the same table. Almost all mainstream RDBMSs support primary key – foreign key relationships within the same table. One manager can manage many employees, but one employee can have only one manager. So, the manager–employee relationship will be one-to-many. Therefore, the entity diagram for the *Employees* entity class with a self-relationship between employees and their managers will look like Fig 2.8.

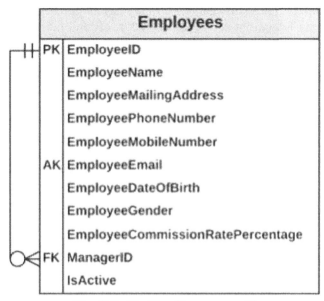

Fig 2.8: Entity diagram with self-relationship for Employees

If you add the *Employees* entity class to the ER diagram in Fig 2.7, the ER diagram between the *VendorCategories, Vendors* and *Employees* entity classes will be like Fig 2.9:

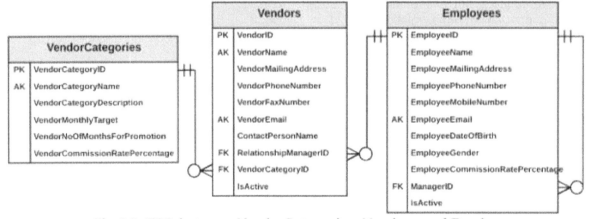

Fig 2.9: ERD between VendorCategories, Vendors and Employees

Products

Step 1: Our initial set of attributes is:

Products → ProductName
Products → ProductSubcategoryID (primary key of ProductSubcategories)
Products → StandardSalesPrice
Products → StockQuantity
Products → DaysToDeliver
Products → ProductDescription
Products → SalesDiscountAmount
Products → SalesDiscountPercentage
Products → VendorID (primary key of Vendors)
Products → IsActive

Step 2: Vendors also need to know how many outstanding ordered quantities have not yet been shipped for each product. This is a very useful attribute for products. It helps vendors to decide what quantity to produce to keep up with sales. Therefore, add this attribute:

Products → OrderedQuantity

Step 3: None of the attributes seem to be unique here, so no candidate key (primary key or alternate key) can be identified.

Step 4: There is no eligible primary key among the attributes listed above. We'll create a surrogate key named *ProductID* and mark it as the primary key (*PK*) for this table/entity class:

Products → ProductID (PK)

Step 5: *ProductSubcategoryID* represents the primary key of the *ProductSubcategories* entity class and *VendorID* represents the primary key of the *Vendors* entity class. So, mark them as foreign keys (*FK*). Based on what we know, we can create the following entity diagram for *Products* entity class (Fig 2.10).

This *ProductSubcategoryID* and *VendorID* foreign keys will be used to join this entity class with the *ProductSubcategories* and *Vendors* entity classes, respectively. Since one product subcategory can have multiple products, but one product can only belong to one subcategory (in our system), the relationship between the *ProductSubcategories* and *Products* entity classes will be one-to-many. Similarly, one vendor can supply multiple products, but one product will be supplied by only one vendor. So, the relationship between the *Vendors* and *Products* entity classes will be one-to-many. Therefore, the ER diagram between the *ProductCategories, ProductSubcategories, Products* and *Vendors* entity classes will be like you see here in Fig 2.11.

Products	
PK	ProductID
	ProductName
	ProductDescription
FK	ProductSubcategoryID
	StandardSalesPrice
	StockQuantity
	OrderedQuantity
	DaysToDeliver
	SalesDiscountAmount
	SalesDiscountPercentage
FK	VendorID
	IsActive

Fig 2.10: Entity diagram for Products

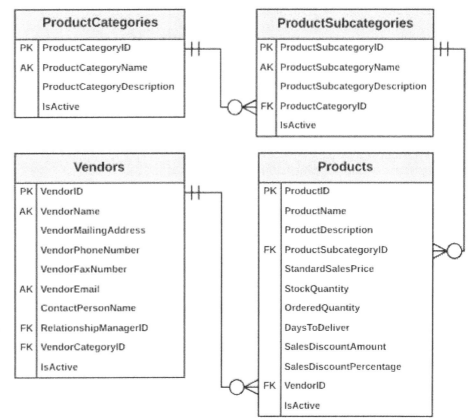

Fig 2.11: ERD between ProductCategories, ProductSubcategories, Products and Vendors

EmployeePayments

Step 1: Our initial set of attributes is:

> EmployeePayments → EmployeePaymentDate
> EmployeePayments → EmployeePaymentAmount
> EmployeePayments → EmployeeID (primary key of Employees)

Step 2: Business users do not need any additional information about *EmployeePayments*.

Step 3: None of the attributes seems to be unique. Therefore, there is no candidate key (primary key or alternate key) can be identified.

Step 4: There is no eligible primary key identified so far. Therefore, add an *EmployeePaymentID* surrogate key and mark it as a primary key (*PK*):

> EmployeePayments → EmployeePaymentID (PK)

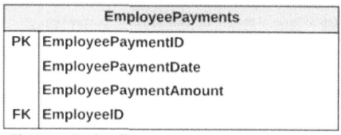

Fig 2.12: Entity diagram for EmployeePayments

Step 5: *EmployeeID* represents the primary key of *Employees* entity class, so mark it as a foreign key (*FK*). Therefore, the entity diagram for the *EmployeePayments* entity class will be like Fig 2.12.

This *EmployeeID* foreign key will be used to join this entity class with the *Employees* entity class. Since one employee can receive multiple payments (one payment for every month) but one specific payment should be received by only one employee, the relationship between *Employees* and *EmployeePayments* will be one-to-many. Let's add *EmployeePayments* to our ER diagram from Fig 2.9. The updated ER diagram between *VendorCategories*, *Vendors*, *Employees* and *EmployeePayments* will be like you see here in Fig 2.13:

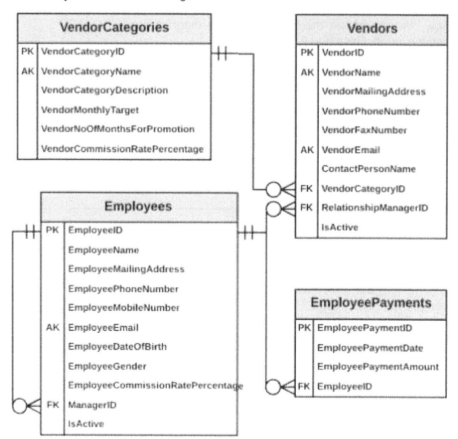

Fig 2.13: ERD between VendorCategories, Vendors, Employees and EmployeePayments

VendorPayments

Step 1: Our initial set of attributes is:

>VendorPayments → VendorPaymentDate
>VendorPayments → TotalSalesAmount
>VendorPayments → TotalCommissionAmount
>VendorPayments → VendorID (primary key of Vendors)

Step 2: Business users do not need any additional information about *VendorPayments*.

Step 3: None of the attributes seems to be unique, so no candidate key (primary key or alternate key) can be identified.

Step 4: We don't have an eligible primary key so far, so add a *VendorPaymentID* surrogate key and mark it as a primary key (*PK*):

>VendorPayments → VendorPaymentID (PK)

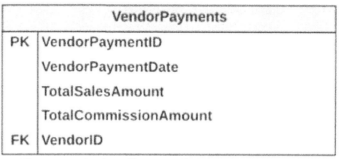

Fig 2.14: Entity diagram for VendorPayments

Step 5: *VendorID* represents the primary key of the *Vendors* entity class, so mark it as a foreign key (*FK*). Here's what our *VendorPayments* ER diagram will look like (Fig 2.14).

The *VendorID* foreign key will be join this entity class with *Vendors*. Since one vendor can receive multiple payments (one payment for every month) but one specific payment should be received by only one vendor, the relationship between *Vendors* and *VendorPayments* will be one-to-many. Let's add *VendorPayments* to our ER diagram for vendor-employee relationships (from Fig 2.13). Our updated ER diagram can be seen below in Fig 2.15.

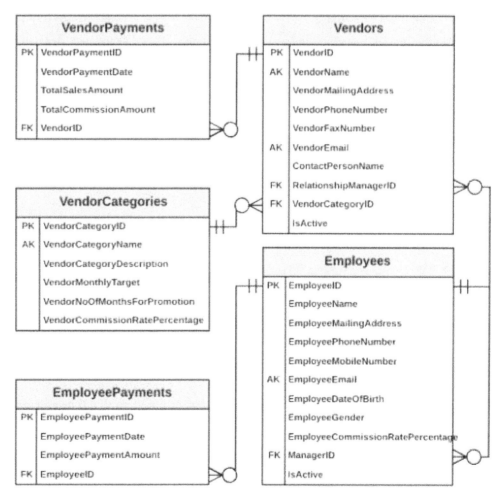

Fig 2.15: ERD between VendorCategories, Vendors, Employees, EmployeePayments and VendorPayments

Customers

Step 1: Our initial set of attributes is:

Customers → CustomerName
Customers → CustomerMailinglAddress
Customers → CustomerPhoneNumber
Customers → CustomerEmail
Customers → CreditCardNumber
Customers → CardHolderName
Customers → CreditCardType
Customers → CreditCardExpiryMonth
Customers → CreditCardExpiryYear
Customers → CustomerMobileNumber
Customers → CustomerDateOfBirth
Customers → CustomerGender
Customers → CustomerJoinDate

Step 2: Business users would like to add an additional attribute so that they can activate and de-activate a customer if needed. Therefore, add this attribute:

Customers → IsActive

Step 3: *CustomerEmail* will store unique values, but it can be changed. Therefore, it is not eligible to become a primary key. Mark it as an alternate key (*AK*):

Customers → CustomerEmail (AK)

Step 4: There is no eligible primary key identified here. We'll create a surrogate key named *CustomerID* and mark it as a primary key (*PK*):

Customers → CustomerID (PK)

Customers	
PK	CustomerID
	CustomerName
	CustomerMailingAddress
	CustomerPhoneNumber
AK	CustomerEmail
	CreditCardNumber
	CardHolderName
	CreditCardType
	CreditCardExpiryMonth
	CreditCardExpiryYear
	CustomerMobileNumber
	CustomerDateOfBirth
	CustomerGender
	CustomerJoinDate
	IsActive

Fig 2.16: Entity diagram for Customers

Step 5: There are no attributes here that represent another entity's primary key, so we don't need to designate a foreign key for this entity class. Therefore, the entity diagram for the *Customers* entity class can be seen in Fig 2.16.

Logins

Step 1: Our initial set of attributes is:

Logins → ChangePasswordInNextLogin
Logins → NoOfFailedAttempt
Logins → IsLocked
Logins → Password
Logins → Email

Step 2: Business users would like to add an additional attribute so that they can activate and de-activate a login for a customer, vendor or employee if needed. Therefore, add this attribute:

Logins → IsActive

Step 3: Since any customer, vendor or employee will have only one login, *Email* will store unique values, but it can be changed. Therefore, it is not eligible to become a primary key. Mark it as an alternate key (*AK*):

Logins → Email (AK)

Step 4: There is no eligible primary key identified so far. Therefore, add a *UserID* surrogate key and mark it as primary key (*PK*):

Logins → UserID (PK)

Step 5: None of our attributes represent another entity's primary key, so there is no foreign key for this entity class. Therefore, this is what the entity diagram for the *Logins* entity class will look like (Fig 2.17).

Logins	
PK	UserID
AK	Email
	Password
	ChangePasswordInNextLogin
	NoOfFailedAttempt
	IsLocked
	IsActive

Fig 2.17: Entity diagram for Logins

CustomerFeedbacks

Step 1: Our initial set of attributes is:

CustomerFeedbacks → CustomerID (primary key of Customers)
CustomerFeedbacks → ProductID (primary key of Products)
CustomerFeedbacks → CustomerFeedbackRating
CustomerFeedbacks → CustomerFeedback
CustomerFeedbacks → FeedbackDate

Step 2: Business users do not need any additional attributes that we need to store for this entity class.

Step 3: Together, *CustomerID* and *ProductID* will store unique values, and the values of *CustomerID* and *ProductID* are unlikely to change. Therefore, *CustomerID* and *ProductID* are eligible to become a composite primary key.

Step 4: There is only one eligible composite primary key identified so far. Therefore, mark both attributes as primary keys (*PK*):

CustomerFeedbacks → CustomerID (PK)
CustomerFeedbacks → ProductID (PK)

Step 5: *CustomerID* and *ProductID* represent the primary keys of the *Customers* and *Products* entity classes, respectively. So, mark them as foreign keys (*FK*).

CustomerFeedbacks	
PK, FK	CustomerID
PK, FK	ProductID
	CustomerFeedbackRating
	CustomerFeedback
	FeedbackDate

Fig 2.18: Entity diagram for CustomerFeedbacks

Therefore, the entity diagram for the *CustomerFeedbacks* entity class will be like you see here in Fig 2.18.

The *CustomerID* foreign key will be used to join this entity class with the *Customers* entity class. Since one customer can provide multiple feedback comments but one specific comment will always be provided by only one customer, the relationship between *Customers* and *CustomerFeedbacks* will be one-to-many. The foreign key *ProductID* will be used to join this entity class with *Products*.

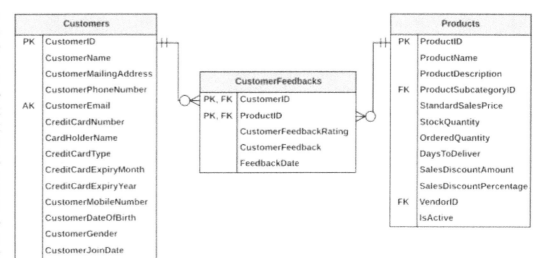

Fig 2.19: ERD between Customers, Products and CustomerFeedbacks

Multiple feedback instances can be associated with one product (e.g. if more than one customer has provided feedback), but each feedback instance will always have only one associated product, so the relationship between the *Products* and *CustomerFeedbacks* entity classes will be one-to-many. Fig 2.19 shows our updated ER diagram for the *Customers, Products* and *CustomerFeedbacks* entity classes:

SalesOrders

Step 1: Our initial set of attributes is:

SalesOrders → SalesOrderID
SalesOrders → CustomerID
SalesOrders → OrderBillingAddress
SalesOrders → OrderShippingAddress
SalesOrders → CreditCardNumber
SalesOrders → CardHolderName
SalesOrders → CreditCardType
SalesOrders → CreditCardExpiryMonth
SalesOrders → CreditCardExpiryYear
SalesOrders → OrderDate
SalesOrders → OrderDueDate
SalesOrders → OrderTotal
SalesOrders → OrderDiscountTotal
SalesOrders → OrderDeliveryDate
SalesOrders → ProductID (primary key of Products)
SalesOrders → ProductQuantity
SalesOrders → ProductUnitPrice
SalesOrders → ProductUnitPriceDiscount
SalesOrders → ProductShipDate
SalesOrders → ProductDeliveryDate

Step 2: Business users do not need any additional attributes to be stored for this entity class.

Step 3: Together, *SalesOrderID* and *ProductID* will store unique values and the values of *SalesOrderID* and *ProductID* are unlikely to change. Therefore, *SalesOrderID* and *ProductID* are eligible to become a composite primary key.

Step 4: We have just one eligible composite primary key identified, so mark both attributes as primary keys (*PK*):

SalesOrders → SalesOrderID (PK)
SalesOrders → ProductID (PK)

	SalesOrders
PK	SalesOrderID
PK, FK	ProductID
FK	CustomerID
	OrderBillingAddress
	OrderShippingAddress
	CreditCardNumber
	CardHolderName
	CreditCardType
	CreditCardExpiryMonth
	CreditCardExpiryYear
	OrderDate
	OrderDueDate
	OrderTotal
	OrderDiscountTotal
	OrderDeliveryDate
	ProductQuantity
	ProductUnitPrice
	ProductUnitPriceDiscount
	ProductShipDate
	ProductDeliveryDate

Fig 2.20: Entity diagram for SalesOrders

Step 5: We can mark *CustomerID* and *ProductID* as foreign keys since they represent the primary key of the *Customers* and *Products* entity classes, respectively. . Therefore, we have the following *SalesOrders* liker diagram that you see in Fig 2.20.

The *CustomerID* foreign key joins *SalesOrders* with the *Customers* entity class. Since one customer can place multiple orders but one specific order will always be placed by only one customer, the relationship between *Customers* and *SalesOrders* will be one-to-many. The *ProductID* foreign key joins *SalesOrders* with the *Products* entity class. Since one product can be included in multiple orders, but one specific order can only include a product once (meaning the product *type* can only be included once, although the *quantity* can be higher than one), the relationship between these entity classes will be one-to-many. Now that we've added keys for *SalesOrders,* our new ER diagram between *Customers, Products* and *SalesOrders* can be seen in Fig 2.21:

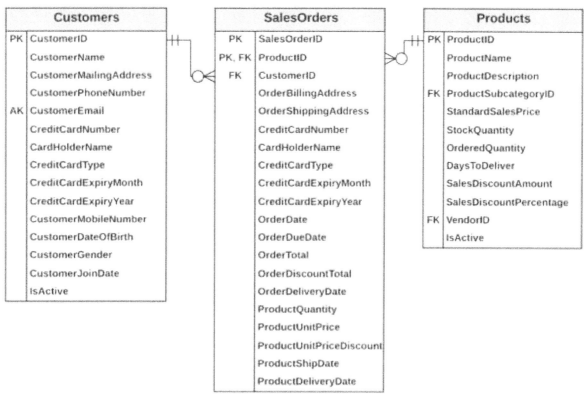

Fig 2.21: ERD between Customers, Products and SalesOrders

Completing Our Initial Entity Relationship Diagram

Congratulations! By now, you've identified all of the entity classes and their attributes, keys and relationships. At this stage in the data modelling process, there may still be some lingering one-to-one relationships between entity classes that haven't yet been identified. Next, we'll check for missing relationships, and once we've added them, our initial ER diagram will be complete.

Notice that we have not yet identified the relationships between the *Logins, Customers, Employees* and *Vendors* entity classes. We have already identified that the email address is an alternate key for all of these entity classes. Fig 2.22 represents a sample data distribution between *Customers, Employees, Vendors* and *Logins* tables:

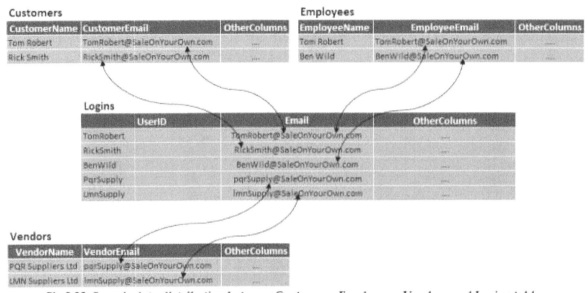

Fig 2.22: Sample data distribution between Customers, Employees, Vendors and Logins tables

If we carefully review the data in Fig 2.22 above, we can conclude the following:

- Each customer must have a login. However, each login can be associated with either one or zero customers. Therefore, we have a one-to-one relationship between *Logins* and *Customers* where *Logins* refer to the parent entity class.

- As in the case of customer logins, each employee must have a login, but each login is associated with either one or zero employees. Therefore, we have a one-to-one relationship between *Logins* and *Employees* where *Logins* refer to the parent entity class

- As for vendors, each vendor must have a login, and each login is associated with one or zero vendors. Therefore, we have a one-to-one relationship between *Logins* and *Vendors* where *Logins* refer to the parent entity class

Knowing these relationships, we can put together an ER diagram for *Customers, Employees, Vendors* and *Logins* that will look like Fig 2.23:

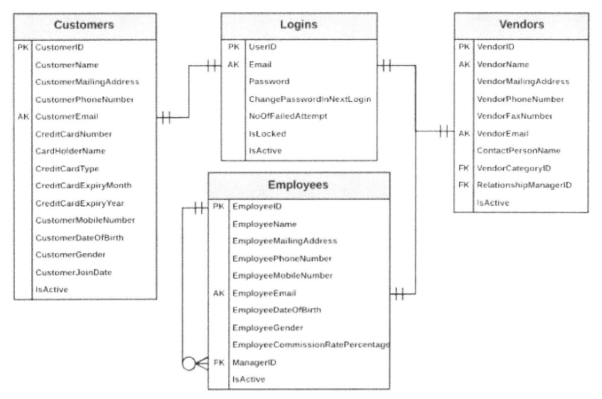

Fig 2.23: ERD between Customers, Vendors, Employees and Logins

Now let's put everything together. If we combine all our ER diagrams, our initial ER diagram for SaleOnYourOwn will look like Fig 2.24.

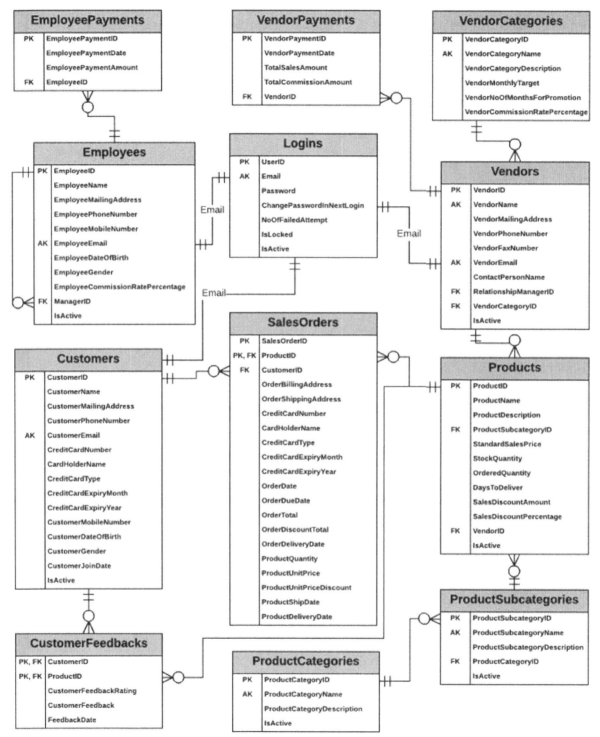

Fig 2.24: Entity relationship diagram before normalization

Normalization

It's time to refine our design. We need to check if each entity class (table) confirms the third normal form (3NF).Of course, we will start by checking for first normal form (1NF) and second normal form (2NF) before we arrive at third normal form. You can refer back to *Lesson 1's* discussion of 1NF, 2NF, and 3NF if you feel that you need a review, but we suggest you first read along as we check for each normal form below.

ProductCategories, ProductSubcategories, Products, VendorCategories, VendorPayments, EmployeePayments and Logins Tables

1NF: Each of these tables now has a primary key, and some of them have an alternate key too. None of the attributes of these tables stores either a repeating group of values or composite values (that means all attributes store atomic values). Therefore, all of these tables satisfy 1NF.

2NF: Each primary key and alternate key represents a single attribute. Since all keys are single attribute keys, the non-key attributes must depend on the whole key. Therefore, all of these tables satisfy 2NF.

3NF: For at least one single value of every non-key attribute, multiple values can be computed for all others non-key attributes within the same table. So, none of the non-key attributes functionally depend on other non-key attributes within the same table. Therefore, all of these tables satisfy 3NF.

CustomerFeedback Table

1NF: This table has a composite primary key (the combination of *CustomerID* and *ProductID*). None of the attributes of this table store either a repeating group of values or composite values (that means all attributes store atomic values). Therefore, this table satisfies 1NF.

2NF: The primary key is composite here. So, we need to check if any non-key attributes functionally depend on part of that primary key. To check the functional dependencies, let's assume that the sample data for the *CustomerFeedbacks* table in Fig 2.25 is a true representation of data distribution for the table. First, let's take a look at what the table would look like containing data from this entity class:

CustomerID	ProductID	CustomerFeedback Rating	CustomerFeedback	FeedbackDate
TOM001	1	5	Excellent service and product quality was very good	11-Feb-2000
TOM001	2	4	Excellent service but product quality was not very good	02-Jun-1992
DIA001	1	4	Service was not very good but product quality was excellent	25-May-1996
DIA001	3	3	Excellent service but product quality was not very good	26-Sep-2001
HEN001	1	5	Excellent service and product quality was very good	26-Sep-2001

Fig 2.25: Sample data for CustomerFeedbacks table

Fig 2.26 shows the non-key attribute's functional dependencies on the key attributes for the table.

Determinant	Non-key Attributes		
	CustomerFeedback Rating	CustomerFeedback	FeedbackDate
$f(CustomerID) = f(TOM001)$	5	Excellent service and product quality was very good	11-Feb-2000
	4	Excellent service but product quality was not very good	02-Jun-1992
$f(ProductID) = f(1)$	5	Excellent service and product quality was very good	11-Feb-2000 26-Sep-2001
	4	Service was not very good but product quality was excellent	25-May-1996
$f(CustomerID, ProductID) = f(TOM001,1)$	5	Excellent service and product quality was very good	11-Feb-2000
$f(CustomerID, ProductID) = f(TOM001,2)$	4	Excellent service but product quality was not very good	02-Jun-1992
$f(CustomerID, ProductID) = f(DIA001,1)$	4	Service was not very good but product quality was excellent	25-May-1996
$f(CustomerID, ProductID) = f(DIA001,3)$	3	Excellent service but product quality was not very good	26-Sep-2001
$f(CustomerID, ProductID) = f(HEN001,1)$	5	Excellent service and product quality was very good	26-Sep-2001

Fig 2.26: Non-key attribute's functional dependencies on the key attributes for CustomerFeedbacks table

Notice that the first two feedback instances have been provided by the same *CustomerID (TOM001),* but each with two different ratings (in the *CustomerFeedbackRating* column, the ratings were *5* and *4*). Also, each feedback instance includes a different comment *(see the CustomerFeedback* column*).* These feedback instances also have different dates as well. Therefore, none of the non-key attributes (*CustomerFeedbackRating, CustomerFeedback* or *FeedbackDate*) depend on *CustomerID.*

Similarly the first, third and fifth feedback instances were provided for the same *ProductID* (*1*), but two values for *CustomerFeedbackRating,* two values for *CustomerFeedback* and three values for *FeedbackDate* can be computed here. Therefore, none of the non-key attributes (*CustomerFeedbackRating, CustomerFeedback* or *FeedbackDate*) depend on *ProductID.* But for each combination of *CustomerID* and *ProductID,* only one value can be computed for each non-key attribute. So then, all non-key attributes depend on the whole primary key and there is no alternate key in this table. Therefore, the table satisfies 2NF.

3NF: Let's check the non-key attribute's functional dependencies.

Is $f(CustomerFeedbackRating) = CustomerFeedback$?

$$f(4) = Excellent\ service\ but\ product\ quality\ was\ not\ very\ good$$
$$f(4) = Service\ was\ not\ very\ good\ but\ product\ quality\ was\ excellent$$
$$Therefore, f(CustomerFeedbackRating) \neq CustomerFeedback$$

Since more than one instance of *CustomerFeedback* can be computed by the same *CustomerFeedbackRating, CustomerFeedback* does not depend on *CustomerFeedbackRating.*

Is $f(CustomerFeedbackRating) = FeedbackDate$?

$$f(4) = 02 - Jun - 1992$$
$$f(4) = 25 - May - 1996$$
$$Therefore, f(CustomerFeedbackRating) \neq FeedbackDate$$

Since multiple *FeedbackDate* instances can be computed by the same *CustomerFeedbackRating, FeedbackDate* does not depend on *CustomerFeedbackRating.*

Similarly, from the data in Fig 2.25, we can conclude below:

- Multiple *CustomerFeedbackRating* instances (e.g. the second and forth rows) can be computed by the same *CustomerFeedback* instance, Therefore, *CustomerFeedbackRating* does not depend on *CustomerFeedback.*
- Multiple *FeedbackDate* instances (e.g. second and forth rows) can be computed by the same *CustomerFeedback* instances, Therefore, *FeedbackDate* does not depend on *CustomerFeedback.*
- Multiple *CustomerFeedbackRating* instances (e.g. fourth and fifth rows) can be computed by the same *FeedbackDate* instance. Therefore, *CustomerFeedbackRating* does not depend on *FeedbackDate.*
- Multiple *CustomerFeedback* instances (e.g. fourth and fifth rows) can be computed by the same *FeedbackDate* instance. Therefore, *CustomerFeedback* does not depend on *FeedbackDate.*

So, none of the non-key attributes functionally depend on other non-key attributes for the table. This table satisfies 3NF.

Vendors Table

Fig 2.27 shows the steps we took to transform the *Vendors* table up to 3NF.

1NF: All attributes except *VendorMailingAddress* of the *Vendors* table store non-atomic values. When you split *VendorMailingAddress* into *StreetAddress, ZipOrPostalCode, City, StateProvince* and *Country* attributes, all attributes of the table become atomic. Hence it becomes 1NF.

2NF: The table has a single attribute primary key, *VendorID,* and two single attribute alternate keys, *VendorName* and *VendorEmail.* There are no multi-attributes (composite) keys. Hence, there is no need to check further for 2NF; the table becomes automatically 2NF.

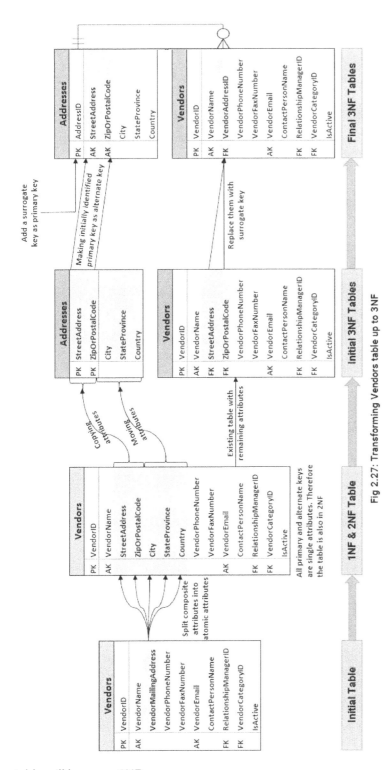

Fig 2.27: Transforming Vendors table up to 3NF

3NF: The non-key attributes *City, StateProvince* and *Country* functionally depend on the combination of the *StreetAddress* and *ZipOrPostalCode* attributes (please see *Lesson 1* for details about functional dependencies). This violates 3NF. How do we fix this?

1.   First, you need to move all dependent attributes (*City, StateProvince* and *Country*) into a new table (let's call it as *Addresses*), then copy the determinant attributes (*StreetAddress* and *ZipOrPostalCode*) into the new table.

2.   Next, make *StreetAddress* and *ZipOrPostalCode* as composite candidate key (primary key). You must also mark the determinant attributes (*StreetAddress* and *ZipOrPostalCode*) in the existing table as foreign keys.

3.   Since the values stored in *StreetAddress* attributes can change, please mark the candidate key attributes (*StreetAddress* and *ZipOrPostalCode*) as alternate keys (*AK*) and create a surrogate key (let's call it as *AddressID*)

4.   You'll also need to mark *AddressID* as the primary key.

5.   Replace the foreign key (*StreetAddress* and *ZipOrPostalCode*) of the *Vendors* table with *AddressID* (let's now call it *VendorAddressID*).

6.   Finally, create the one-to-many relationship between *Addresses* and *Vendors* by their *AddressIDs* (*AddressID* and *VendorAddressID*).

Therefore, the transformation of the *Vendors* table into distinct *Addresses* and *Vendors* tables satisfies 3NF.

Customers Table

Fig 2.28 shows the steps we'll follow to transform the *Customers* table up to 3NF.

1NF: Similar to the *Vendors* table, you need to split the *CustomerMailingAddress* attribute into *StreetAddress, ZipOrPostalCode, City, StateProvince* and *Country* attributes and *CustomerName* attribute into *CustomerFirstName* and *CustomerLastName* attributes. Once this is done, then the *Customers* table will become 1NF.

2NF: Since the *Customers* table does not have any multi-attributes as primary key and it has no alternate key, after our previous step to conform to 1NF, the *Customers* table will automatically become 2NF.

3NF: Similar to the *Vendors* table, there are non-key attribute dependencies that need to be resolved to satisfy 3NF guidelines.

1. First, you must move all address-related attributes (*StreetAddress, ZipOrPostalCode, City, StateProvince* and *Country*) into a new table (let's call it as *Addresses*)
2. Next, add a surrogate primary key (*AddressID*) in the *Addresses* table
3. Next, add the *AddressID* (as *CustomerAddressID*) back to the *Customers* table as a foreign key
4. Next, create a one-to-many relationship between the *Addresses* and *Customers* tables, and the non-key dependencies between address related attributes will be resolved.

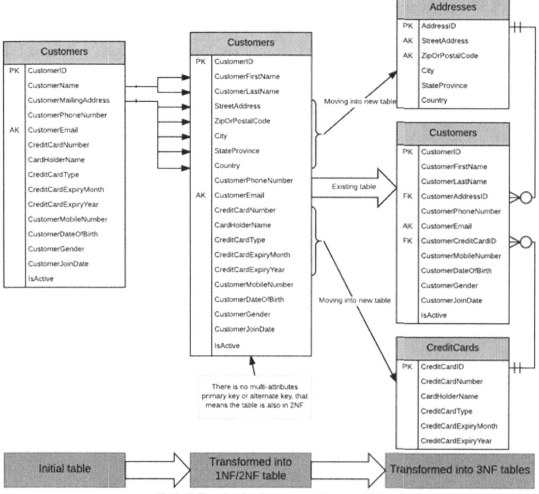

Fig 2.28: Transforming **Customers** table up to **3NF**

We still need to check if any other non-key attribute dependencies exist. For each credit card number, you will always have the same *cardholder name, card type* and *expiry date*. That means the attributes *CardHolderName, CreditCardType, CreditCardExpiryMonth* and *CreditCardExpiryYear* functionally depend on *CreditCardNumber*. To fix this:

1. Move all credit card related attributes (*CreditCardNumber, CardHolderName, CreditCardType, CreditCardExpiryMonth* and *CreditCardExpiryYear*) into a new table (let's call it as *CreditCards*)
2. Add a surrogate primary key (*CreditCardID*) in the *CreditCards* table.
3. Add the *CreditCardID* (as *CustomerCreditCardID*) back to the *Customers* table as a foreign key.
4. Create a one-to-many relationship between the *CreditCards* and *Customers* tables.
5. Having done all this, the non-key dependencies between the credit card-related attributes will be resolved.

No other non-key attributes depend on each other. Therefore, our transformation of the *Customers* table into *Addresses, CreditCards* and *Customers* tables now satisfies 3NF.

Employees Table

Similar to the *Customers* and *Vendors* tables, we can easily bring *Employees* table up to 3NF, as you can see in Fig 2.29:

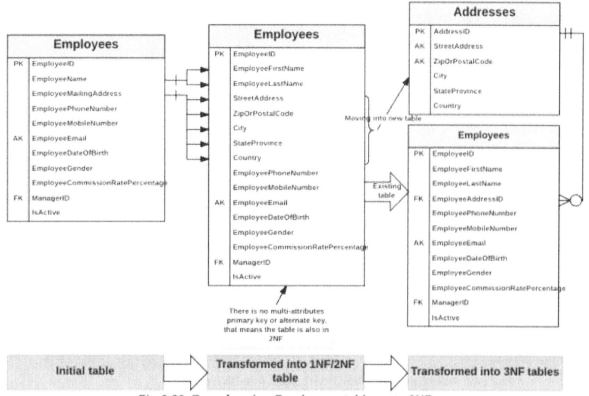

Fig 2.29: Transforming Employees table up to 3NF

SalesOrders Table

Similarly, we can easily transform the *SalesOrders* table to 3NF by following the steps we briefly outline in Fig 2.30:

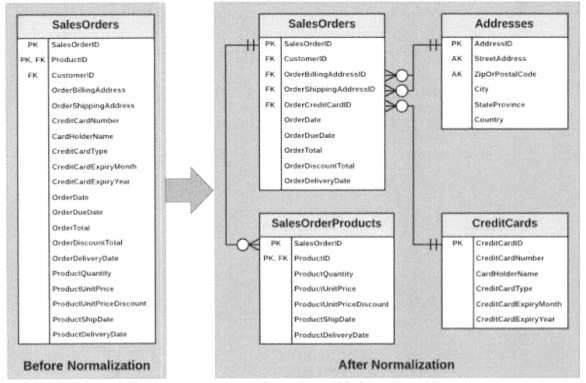

Fig 2.30: Transforming SalesOrders table into 3NF tables

Our Complete ER Diagram after Normalization

Well then, our data model has undergone quite a transformation in this lesson. If you put all the tables together including the new relationships we have found, our completed ER diagram will look like Fig 2.31:

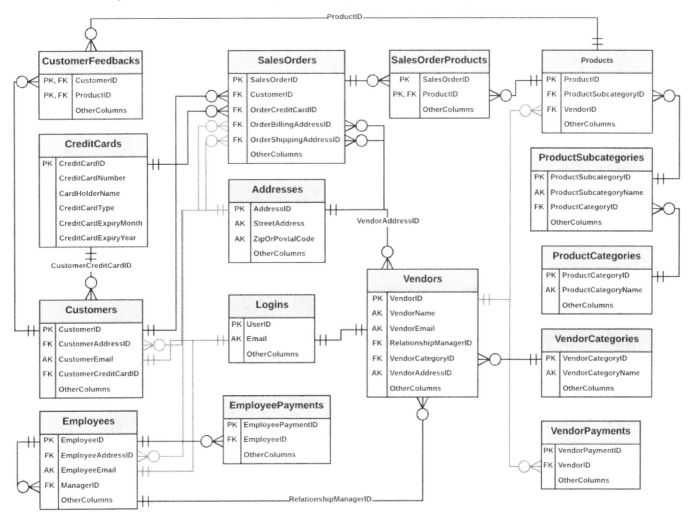

Fig 2.31: Entity relationship diagram after normalization (Only key columns included)

Lesson Summary

This lesson has started you on the path to becoming a confident data modeller by describing how our e-commerce business case can be analysed to identify its subjects (i.e. its objects, persons, activities or abstractions). We then identified the characteristics of each subject and verified any missing characteristics (in the real world, you would do this by interviewing your expert business users). Each subject became a table or entity class, and each characteristic of the subject became a column or attribute. After we identified primary keys, foreign keys and alternate keys for our tables, we made sure to outline all these tables' relationships. We then put all the tables and their relationships together to form our initial logical data model, and finally we normalized each table using the steps described in Fig 2.32:

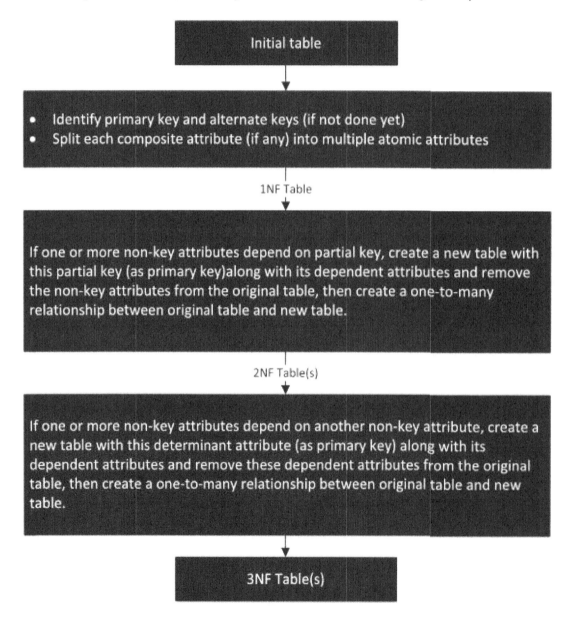

At this point, the logical data model is in its matured form and it is ready for us to implement using physical database design using SQL.

Lesson 3
Installing SQL Tools

Lesson objective
You've learned the fundamentals of converting a real-world business case into a logical data model, and the next step is the one you've been waiting for—it's time to start using SQL. Everything you've learned so far could be done with a good old-fashioned pen and paper, but in order to create a physical database from our logical data model, you're going to need a SQL software tool. In this lesson, we'll show you how to install MySQL and Microsoft SQL Server, which are two of the most popular SQL software tools. FYI, we call this type of software a relational database management system (or RDBMS, for short). So if you already have an RDBMS installed on your computer, feel free to skip this lesson.

Installing Microsoft SQL Server 2016
Microsoft SQL Server is one of the most widely used systems out there, with several different editions offered by Microsoft to appeal to a wide audience. While most of these editions are not free for commercial use, the express edition of SQL Server is free for commercial use and the developer edition is free for private or home use. We're going to show you how to install SQL Server 2016 and SQL Server Management Studio (SSMS) so that you can practice the examples and exercises in this book. Note that you'll need a Microsoft account to download these.

Use this link to download the setup for the current release of SQL Server Management Studio:
https://docs.microsoft.com/en-us/sql/ssms/download-sql-server-management-studio-ssms)

The SQL Server 2016 developer edition's setup discs can be found here (if you do not have a visual studio account, you need to create one to proceed with the download):
https://my.visualstudio.com/Downloads?q=SQL%20Server%202016%20Developer.

Once you downloaded both the SSMS and SQL Server setup files, please use the below steps to install.

Step 1: You'll need to mount the SQL Server 2016 Setup Disc using a program like WinCDEmu (it can be downloaded from http://wincdemu.sysprogs.org/download). If you're not familiar with the process of mounting a disc, it's fairly simple. In this case, the SQL Server file is a virtual copy of a compact disc, so you need to use an emulator to access it because you don't have a physical compact disc to insert into your computer. If you're running Windows 10 or later version of Windows, you can mount the setup without any external program (right-click the setup disc and then select mount).

Step 2: Run the *setup.exe* file located in the mounted disc drive.

1033_ENU_LP	30/10/2016 8:51 PM	File folder	
PCUSOURCE	30/10/2016 8:51 PM	File folder	
redist	30/10/2016 8:51 PM	File folder	
resources	30/10/2016 8:51 PM	File folder	
Tools	30/10/2016 8:51 PM	File folder	
x64	1/11/2016 5:05 AM	File folder	
autorun	10/02/2016 2:38 PM	Setup Information	1 KB
MediaInfo	30/10/2016 10:09 ...	XML Document	1 KB
setup	29/10/2016 11:19 ...	Application	107 KB
setup.exe	10/02/2016 2:34 PM	XML Configuratio...	1 KB
SqlSetupBootstrapper.dll	29/10/2016 11:20 ...	Application extens...	234 KB
sqmapi.dll	1/05/2016 2:12 AM	Application extens...	147 KB

Step 3: Once the setup launches, click the *Installation* tab on the left hand side.

Planning

Installation

Maintenance

Tools

Resources

Advanced

Options

Step 4: Click *New SQL Server stand-alone installation or add features to an existing installation*. This will launch the installation window for SQL Server 2016.

 New SQL Server stand-alone installation or add features to an existing installation

Launch a wizard to install SQL Server 2016 in a non-clustered environment or to add features to an existing SQL Server 2016 instance.

Step 5: Select the *Developer Edition* and click "*Next.*"

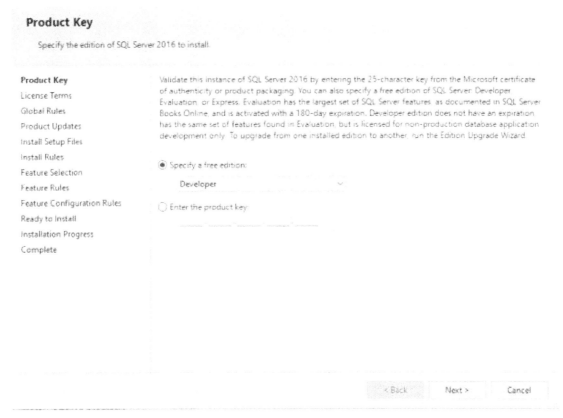

Step 6: Accept the terms of service and license terms to proceed with the installation.

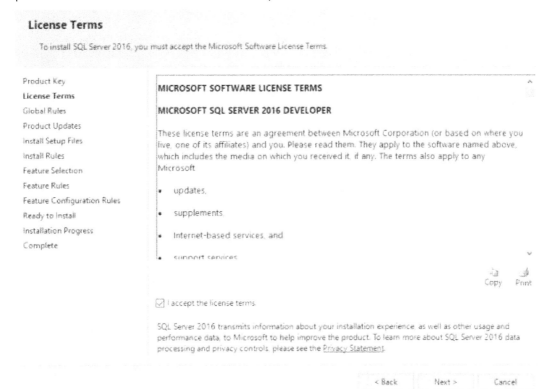

Step 7: Make sure all of the *Install Rules* passed (you can ignore the Windows Firewall warning) then click *Next* to proceed.

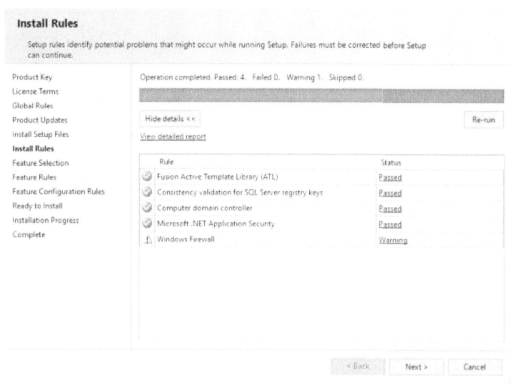

Step 8: On the *Feature Selection* tab, ensure that *Client Tools SDK* and *SQL Client Connectivity SDK* are checked. These are the only features you'll require for practising at home. Click *Next* to proceed.

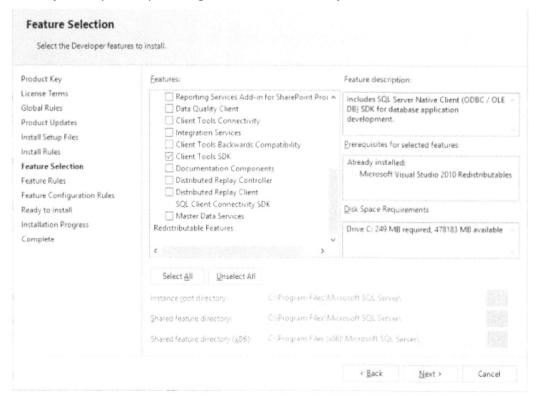

Step 9: Here you'll see the file path where the virtual disc is about to install the software. Ensure that everything is correct here and click *Install* to begin the installation.

Step 10: Once the installation is complete, it's time to install SQL *Server Management Studio*. No mounting is required for this installation. Simply run the *SSMS-Setup-ENU.exe* you have downloaded from the link provided.

SSMS-Setup-ENU   19/01/2017 7:38 PM   Application   915,733 KB

Step 11: Click *Install* to acknowledge Terms of Service and Privacy Policy and proceed with the SSMS installation. No further steps are required to finish the installation.

Step 12: Once installation is complete, simply run *Microsoft SQL Server Management Studio*. When the program opens, a pop-up window will come up asking you to connect to server. For the tutorials in the book, leaving everything default will work just fine. Now you can proceed with getting some hands-on experience with SQL databases! Next we'll show you how to install MySQL, so you're welcome to skip ahead to *Lesson 4* if you don't want to do that.

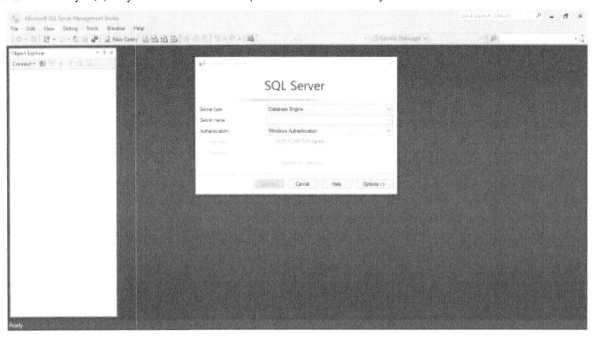

Installing MySQL

MySQL is an open source RDBMS actively developed by Oracle. While also not free for commercial use, MySQL has a free *Community Edition* which is available to anyone for private use. It is actively developed by Oracle and also has a very active open source developer community worldwide. You can find MySQL online at: https://dev.mysql.com/downloads/installer/. You'll want to download either the web version or the default version to proceed with the installation. You may be prompted to either sign in to or create a new Oracle account, but you can skip straight to the download if you like. As with MySQL, you will need to download additional software for our purposes. In this case, there are two. The first is Visual Studio, and a free *Community 2015 edition* can be found at https://www.visualstudio.com/downloads/. Second is Python 3.4.4, which can be found at https://www.python.org/downloads/release/python-344/.

Step 1: Installing Visual Studio and Python are requirements for MySQL so let's take care of them first because doing so will make the whole process easier for you. First, run the Visual Studio installer and use the default settings to install. Next, install Python 3.4.4, with the default settings as well. Both of these are fairly straightforward and easy to install and should not require much user input.

Step 2: After you've installed Visual Studio and Python, run the MySQL Installer and accept the license terms. Click *Next* to proceed.

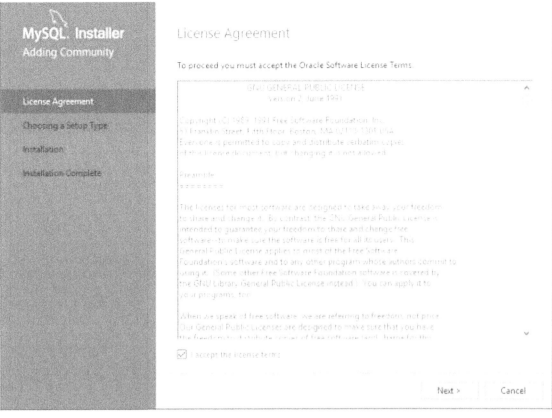

Step 3: Select the *Developer Default* setup type and click *Next* to continue with the setup.

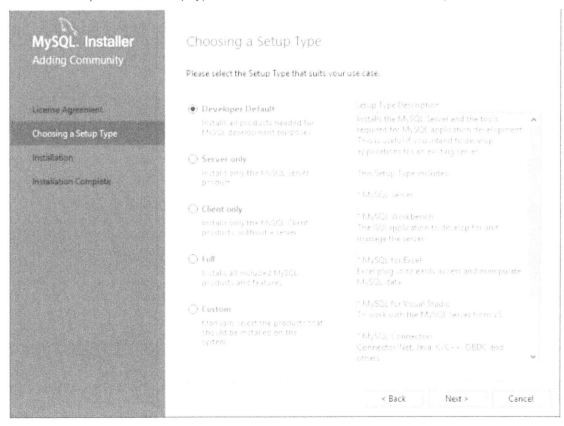

Step 4: Check the software requirements for installing MySQL. This is where previously installing Python and Visual Studio makes the process easier. To auto-install Visual Tools for Microsoft Office, simply click *Execute.* The setup should run on its own. Again, use default settings to complete the setup.

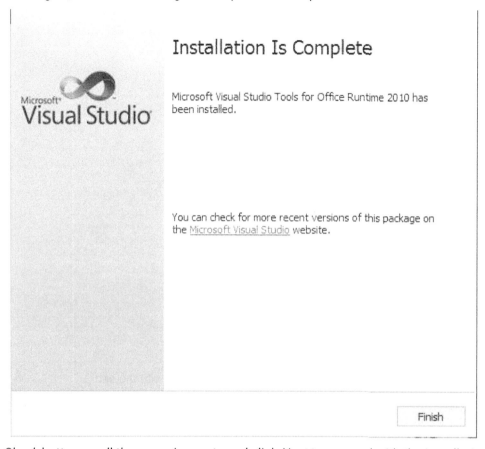

Step 5: Click the *Check* button on all three requirements and click *Next* to proceed with the installation.

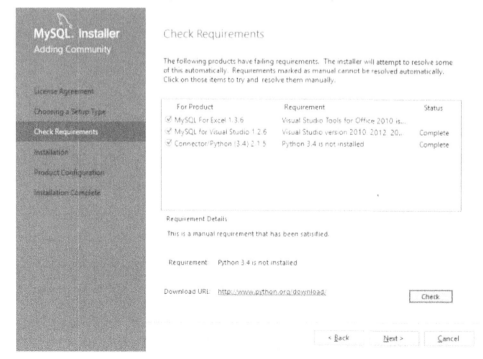

Step 6: On the *Installation* tab, click *Execute* to download and install all the required components of MySQL.

Step 7: When asked to configure your installation, leave all fields default for all sections. The only input required at this point is in *Accounts and Roles*, where you will be asked to input a root account password. Enter and confirm a password of your choosing (please do not forget the password, you will need it later!) and proceed with the remainder of the configuration until you have completed the setup.

Step 8: Now, launch MySQL Workbench and your RDBMS is ready to go.

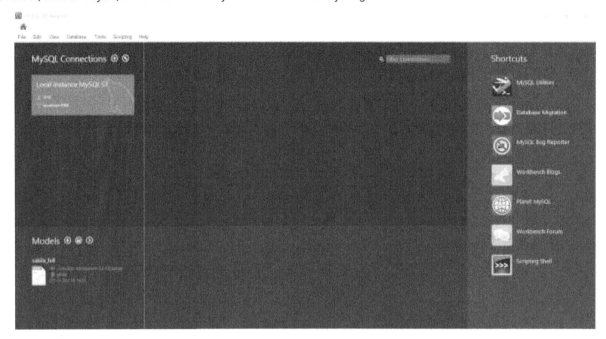

Lesson summary

Access to an RDBMS is essential for learning SQL. This lesson has shown you how to download and install the free versions of SQL Server and MySQL on your computer or laptop. Note that we'll be showing you how to write SQL statements in each of these RDBMSs side-by-side, and from time to time we will ask you to refer to your RDBMSs documentation in case of you are using other than these RDBMSs.

Get ready, because in the next lesson we'll get started using SQL.

Lesson 4
Converting a logical data model into a physical database

NEW SQL STATEMENTS AND KEYWORDS COVERED IN THIS LESSON:

CREATE DATABASE	DROP DATABASE
CREATE TABLE	DROP TABLE
ALTER TABLE...ADD COLUMN	ALTER TABLE ...DROP COLUMN

Lesson Objective

Now that you have your preferred RDBMS installed on your computer or laptop, it's time to start using SQL. In this lesson we will show you:

- How to execute SQL statements
- How to create a database
- How to remove a database
- Frequently used data types
- How to create a table in a database
- How to remove a table from a database
- How to add a column to a table
- How to remove a column from a table

We'll start by showing you how to connect to your preferred RDBMS and start a new query window. After that, you'll learn how to create a physical database for the logical data model we developed over the previous chapters. Finally, you'll learn how to add tables for entity classes, columns for attributes, and constraints for relationships.

As you are reading, you will see examples and business problems for both SQL Server and MySQL. For your convenience while you are testing the code out yourself, we have provided all of the code online at the following links:

Examples and business problems for SQL Server:
https://drive.google.com/open?id=1OurpVpKQQBPdcHiy75JZm_0AUCRPc2xA

Examples and business problems for MySQL:
https://drive.google.com/open?id=14nZSysDrVeRadqgWjIiGUc4TdkVh2zaU

How to execute SQL statements?

For every operation you perform against an RDBMS—whether it's creating a database or retrieving data from it—you need to execute a SQL statement. The common steps you need to follow to execute a SQL statement (or multiple SQL statements) are:

- Connect to the RDBMS (server)
- Start a new query window
- Write the SQL statement(s) in the query window
- Execute the SQL statement(s)

For those of you who are absolute beginners, the following section will show you how to execute SQL statements in both of the RDBMSs that you learned to install in the previous lesson, *Microsoft SQL Server* and *MySQL*. Let's start with *Microsoft SQL Server*.

How to execute SQL statement in SQL Server?

Simply run *Microsoft SQL Server Management Studio* to begin. When the program opens, a pop-up window will come up asking you to connect to a server as seen in Fig 4.1 below:

Fig 4.1 – Connecting to a SQL Server using Microsoft SQL Server Management Studio

For this tutorial you can leave the default selection and simply click the *Connect* button which will open up a Microsoft SQL Server Management Studio (SSMS) working environment as in Fig 4.2 below:

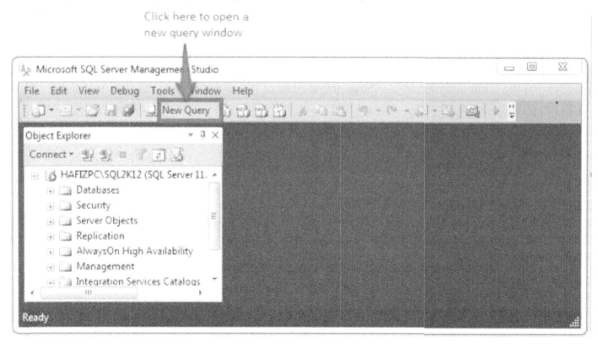

Fig 4.2 – Starting a new query window in Microsoft SQL Server Management Studio

In this working environment, you can click the *New Query* option from the toolbar to open the new query window. This query window is where you will be writing queries for execution in SQL, and you'll see it displayed in the top-right window in the SSMS working environment when you open it, as you can see in Fig 4.3 below:

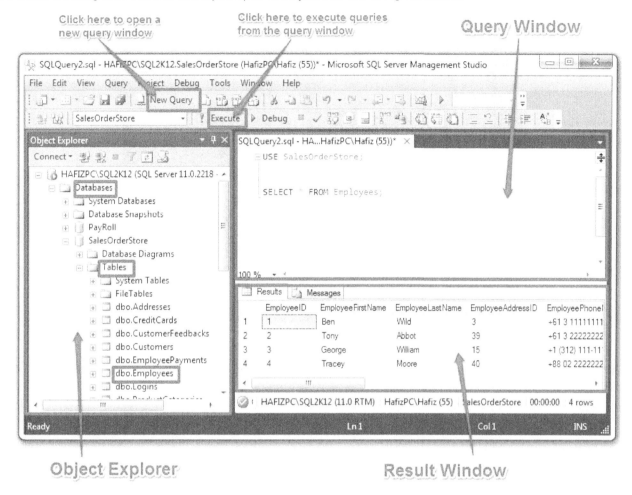

Fig 4.3 - Microsoft SQL Server Management Studio (SSMS) working environment

This working environment has three windows: The left window is the *Object Explorer* which lists all the objects that exist in this instance of SQL Server. You can expand the *Databases* folder to see all of the names of databases on the server, or you can expand a particular database (for example *SalesOrderStore* database) then expand *Tables* to see all of the table names within the database, and so on.

As we mentioned earlier, the top-right window is the *Query Window* where you can write your SQL statement (often called a query). After writing your SQL statement, you can click the *Execute* button from the toolbar that will execute the SQL statement and show the output in the *Result Window* which is located in the bottom-right.

How to execute SQL statement in MySQL

Simply run *MySQL Workbench* to begin. Doing so will open up connection window like the one you can see below (Fig 4.4):

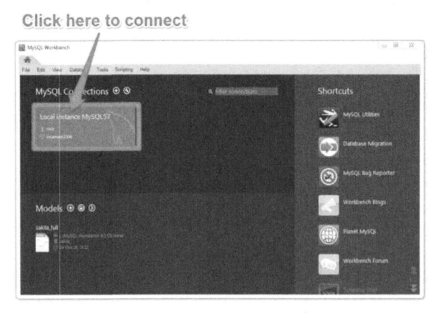

Fig 4.4 – MySQL connection window

For this book's tutorial, you can click *Local instance MySQL57* to connect to the default MySQL instance of your computer or laptop. This will open up a working environment that contains a few windows. At this moment we will focus on *Schema Navigator*, *Query Window* and *Result Window*. All of these windows have been marked in the below picture (Fig 4.5):

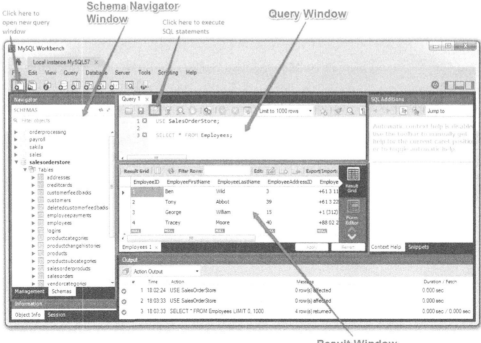

Fig 4.5 – MySQL Workbench working environment

Creating a database

Creating a database is the first step for converting your logical data model into a physical database. This database will contain all the tables which ultimately store all the facts (data) for the business. To create a database you need to write and execute a SQL statement. The basic syntax for this SQL statement is:

CREATE DATABASE database name;

Here, *database name* is the name of the database that you want to create. Note that the use of a semicolon (;) at the end of a statement is optional for most RDBMSs. If we use the same database name from our data model example (*SalesOrderStore*), the SQL statement for creating this database will look like:

CREATE DATABASE SalesOrderStore;

Notes

ANSI-standard's semicolon statement terminator is optional for some RDBMSs (e.g. SQL Server). If the RDBMS you are using (e.g. MySQL), the semicolon statement terminator is mandatory, you must use the semicolon after each SQL statement. If you are using an RDBMS where the semicolon statement terminator is optional, you do not have to use semicolon at end of each statement, but it is still recommended to use. The usage of semicolon statement terminator will make your code more portable across RDBMSs.

Now let's learn how to create a database by solving a business problem.

Business Problem 1

A team of developers are developing a payroll system and have requested you to create a database for them where they can store all payroll-related data. The database name should be *Payroll*. What SQL statement do you need to execute to create the database?

Solution SQL

CREATE DATABASE Payroll;

SQL Result – SQL Server

Fig 4.6 – Creating a Payroll Database in SQL Server

SQL Result - MySQL

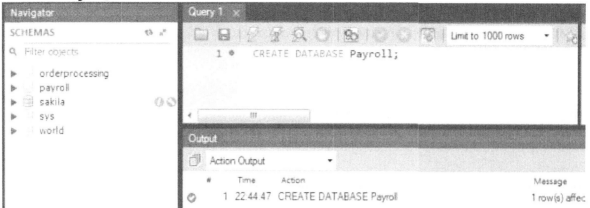

Fig 4.7 – Creating a Payroll Database in MySQL

Solution Review

Remember that the semicolon (;) is optional for most RDBMSs. If this is the case for your RDBMS, you can also write the SQL statement like you see below:

```
CREATE DATABASE Payroll
```

You will need to refresh the *Object Explorer* or *Schema Navigator* to see the newly created *Payroll* database.

Notes

The name of all databases in each instance of your RDBMS must be unique. If the user tries to create a database with a duplicate name, the RDBMS will return an error message.

The semicolon (;) can be used to indicate the end point for any SQL statement.

Frequently used data types

By now you should have your database created, so our next step will be to learn how to convert an entity class to a table, and then convert an attribute to a column within the table. But first, you need to define the column's data type, so in this section we'll discuss the different data types you need to understand.

Each column in a table should have a data type. Defining the data type allows the RDBMS to prevent an incorrect type of data from entering a column. That means the RDBMS will reject an attempt to add numeric data into a date column, date data into a numeric column and so on. Most of basic data types are supported by every RDBMS, but support for the more advanced data types vary between different RDBMSs. Below, we show you some of the frequently used data types, but for a comprehensive list of data types please refer to your RDBMSs manual.

(Please note that '*INT*' stands for integer in the data type names shown below)

Numeric data types

Exact numeric data:

Data Type	Value Range
BIGINT	-9,223,372,036,854,775,808 to 9,223,372,036,854,775,807
INT	-2,147,483,648 to 2,147,483,647
SMALLINT	-32,768 to 32,767
TINYINT	0 to 255

Numeric data with fixed precision and scale:

Data Type	Value Range
DECIMAL(p.s.)	- 10^38 +1 through 10^38 − 1
MONEY	Supported by SQL Server only

Boolean data types:

Data Type	Value Range
BIT	0 or 1 (i.e. false or true)

Date and Time data types

The date and time data types widely vary between RDBMSs. This topic mentions the two most widely used date and time datatypes for SQL Server and MySQL (*DATETIME* and *SMALLDATETIME*). Please refer to your RDBMS for further details.

Date and Time data types for SQL Server

Data Type	Value Range
DATETIME	0001-01-01 through 9999-12-31. That is January 1, 1 CE through December 31, 9999 CE
SMALLDATETIME	1900-01-01 through 2079-06-06. That is January 1, 1900, through June 6, 2079

Date and Time data types for MySQL

Data Type	Value Range
DATETIME	1000-01-01 through 9999-12-31. That is January 1, 1000, CE through December 31, 9999 CE

String data types

Data Type	Notes
CHAR(n)	This datatype is used to store a fixed-length non-Unicode string. *n* is a positive integer which represents the maximum number of characters for the string. Each character will take 1 byte of storage for most RDBMSs. If, for example, you want to store the maximum 10 characters in a column, you can specify this datatype as *CHAR(10)*.
VARCHAR(n)	This datatype is used to store a variable-length non-Unicode string. *n* is a positive integer which represents the maximum number of character for the string. Each character will take 1 byte of storage for most RDBMSs plus some additional bytes for the whole string. If you want to store the maximum 10 characters in a column, you can specify this datatype as *VARCHAR(10)*.
NCHAR(n)	This datatype is used to store the fixed-length Unicode string. *n* is a positive integer which represents the maximum number of characters for the string. Each character will take 2 bytes of storage for most RDBMSs. If you want to store the maximum 10 characters in a column, you can specify this datatype as *NCHAR(10)*.
NVARCHAR(n)	This datatype is used to store the variable-length Unicode string. *n* is a positive integer which represents the maximum number of character for the string. Each character will take 2 bytes of storage for most RDBMSs plus some additional bytes for the whole string. If you want to store the maximum 10 characters in a column, you can specify this datatype as *NVARCHAR(10)*.

When should you use CHAR, VARCHAR, NCHAR, or NVARCHAR

Unlike English, some languages do not support single-byte character sets, meaning you cannot store a single character within a byte. For these so-called double-byte character-sets, it usually takes 2 bytes to store each character. Some examples of double-byte character-sets are Chinese, Japanese, Korean, and Arabic. If you need to store a double-byte character-set in a column of a table, you must use either *NCHAR* or *NVARCHAR* instead of *CHAR* or *VARCHAR*, respectively. If you need to store a single-byte character-set in a column of a table, you can use any of the 4 datatypes listed above, but it is recommended to use either *CHAR* or *VARCHAR* instead of *NCHAR* or *NVARCHAR* in order for your database to save some storage and perform better.

So then, should you use *CHAR/NCHAR* or *VARCHAR/NVARCHAR* for other types of data?

The answer is again that it depends on the data you are storing. If the length of your data is fixed or minimally varied, then it is recommended to use *CHAR/NCHAR*, otherwise, use *VARCHAR/NVARCHAR* (you can see the difference in storage requirements for each command in the following table). Let's assume your company is operating within Australia. The zip code in Australia is always 4 digits, so you can use either *CHAR(4)* or *VARCHAR(4)* to store a zip code. *CHAR(4)* will take 4 bytes for each zip code but *VARCHAR(4)* will take 6 (4+2) bytes for each zip code. Therefore, *CHAR(4)* will be a better option here. But if your company operates globally you may need 10 digits i.e. *CHAR(10)* or *VARCHAR(10)*. The table below shows some example zip and postal codes and how many storage they require to store them:

Example Zip/Post Code	Storage Needed for CHAR(10)	Storage Needed for VARCHAR(10)
3000	10 bytes	(4+2) = 6 bytes
90402	10 bytes	(5+2) = 7 bytes
SW1W 9SJ	10 bytes	(8+2) = 10 bytes

In this scenario, if you use *VARCHAR(10)* you can save some storage and perform better. So, it is recommended to use *VARCHAR(10)* instead of *CHAR(10)* in this scenario.

Other datatypes

Each RDBMS supports a wide variety of datatypes, but many are not frequently used. In your database, you may only need to use *TEXT, IMAGE, XML, SQL_VARIANT* or a few other datatypes. The datatypes you will learn in this eBook will cover almost 95% of your requirements in most cases. For the full list of datatypes available in your RDBMS of choice, Please refer to your RDBMS manual.

Creating a table in a database

In your new database, each table will contain your business data. Each entity class of your ER diagram will be implemented as a table. The basic syntax of the SQL statement which creates a table is:

```
CREATE TABLE table name (
        1st Column Name   Datatype  1st Constraint 2nd Constraint ...,
        2nd Column Name  Datatype  1st Constraint 2nd Constraint ...,
        .........................................................................................
    );
```

Table Name: There are specific rules for naming objects such as tables, columns, etc. in SQL. The table name must be unique within a database schema. The maximum length of a table name varies between RDBMSs, but all mainstream RDBMSs support at least 30 characters. The name should be meaningful but as small as possible. Therefore, 30 characters should be more than enough. Please follow the below rules while naming a table:

The name can start with any character (A-Z or a-z), and can then be followed by any combination of characters, numbers (0-9) or underscores (_). The name cannot include special characters (space, @, $ etc.). The name is also not case sensitive. Here are a few examples of valid table names: *Employees, employees, EMPLOYEES2016* etc.

In case you wish to use multiple words in the name, we recommend using an underscore (_) instead of a simple space. For example, *Employee_Payments, EmployeePayments, ProductCategories, Product_Categories* etc.

You should not use a keyword as your table name. For example, *CREATE, TABLE, VIEW,* and *DATE* are all keywords and should not be used as a table name. You can find commonly used keywords for SQL Server in https://docs.microsoft.com/en-us/sql/t-sql/language-elements/reserved-keywords-transact-sql?view=sql-server-2016 and for MySQL in https://dev.mysql.com/doc/refman/5.5/en/keywords.html.

It is not recommended to use numbers at the start of the name, nor is it recommended to include special characters or keywords within the name. However, if you feel the need, you can work around this by enclosing the name with brackets []. Some examples of this are: *[Date], [2016Employee], [Employee Payments], [Lives@], [% Payments]* etc.

Column Name: The column name must be unique within a table. You can use the same column name in two different tables, but you cannot use the same name within a table. All of the naming rules specified above for table names also apply for column names.

Now let's learn a few different ways to create a table by converting our *Customers* entity class into a *Customers* table using SQL. Each attribute of the *Customers* entity class will be used as a column in our *Customers* table. First, you'll need to identify all the datatypes and constraints for each column. Before creating a table you should identify below constraints:

NOT NULL: If the *NOT NULL* constraint is active, it will not allow a column to store unknown/empty/missing values. If a user tries to store a *NULL* value in a column that has the *NOT NULL* constraint, the RDBMS will return an error, so setting the *NOT NULL* constraint is a good way to enforce users entering necessary data in a column if you know that column should always have a value. For example, each customer must have a first name and last name. So, the *CustomerFirstName* and *CustomerLastName* columns must be *NOT NULL*.

NULL: The *NULL* constraint allows a column to store unknown/empty/missing values. If you know a column may not always have a value (and you want to prevent errors), you should set a *NULL* constraint on it. If you do not set either *NULL* or *NOT NULL* constraints, your RDBMS will set the column to *NULL* by default. For example, some customers may not disclose their genders and data of births. So, *CustomerGender* and *CustomerDateOfBirth* must allow *NULL* values.

DEFAULT: The *DEFAULT* constraint allow a column to store a default value when a new row has been added to the table and no value has been supplied for the column. For new rows, if the column values of a table mostly (or always) store a particular value, you should specify that value as a *DEFAULT* value. For example, the joining date of all new customers should be the time when they submit their registration details and they should be made active as soon as they have registered. So, the *CustomerJoinDate* column should set the current date time as the default value and the *IsActive* column should set "1" as the default value when the system sees that a new customer has registered. If a column has a *DEFAULT* constraint, users only have to supply a specific value for the column if they want to store a value other than the default for the column.

PRIMARY KEY: The *PRIMARY KEY* constraint restricts user from storing duplicate rows in a table. If a table has a single column primary key, then that column will not be allowed to store duplicate values (i.e. the same value multiple times). If a table has a composite primary key, then the combination of the columns that participated in the primary key will not be allowed to store duplicate values. For example, *CustomerID* is the primary key of the *Customers* table, so two customers will not be allowed to have same *CustomerID*.

In case of a surrogate primary key, we usually use auto-increment numbers. If this is the case, you should specify your RDBMS keyword to enforce unique auto-increment numbers. This keyword varies between RDBMSs. *SQL Server* uses the *IDENTITY (1, 1)* function and MySQL uses *AUTO_INCREMENT* keyword. If you specify a column to use auto-increment numbers, you will not be allowed to enter any value into the column; instead, RDBMS will automatically assign a value. The first value RDBMS will assign is 1, then 2, 3, 4 and so on.

RDBMSs do not allow a *NULL* value in a column that is being used as a primary key. In the ER diagram, the columns marked as *PK* will be implemented by *PRIMARY KEY* constraints in the corresponding table.

UNIQUE KEY: The *UNIQUE KEY* constraint restricts the user from storing duplicate values in a way similar to *PRIMARY KEY*, but it will allow a single *NULL* value for each column that participates in the *UNIQUE KEY*. For example, *CustomerEmail* is the unique key for the *Customers* table, so two customers will not be allowed to have the same email, but one customer will be allowed to have a *NULL* (missing) value.

In the ER diagram, the columns marked as *AK* will be implemented by *UNIQUE KEY* constraints in the corresponding table. Next, let's learn how to create a table by solving some more business problems.

Business Problem 2

Recall from *Lesson 2* that you have already identified the datatypes and constraints for all the attributes of the *Customers* entity class. as you can see here:

Column Name	Datatype	Constraints
CustomerID	INT	Auto-Increment Number, PRIMARY KEY, NOT NULL
CustomerFirstName	VARCHAR(20)	NOT NULL
CustomerLastName	VARCHAR(20)	NOT NULL
CustomerAddressID	INT	NOT NULL
CustomerPhoneNumber	VARCHAR(25)	NOT NULL
CustomerMobileNumber	VARCHAR(25)	NULL
CustomerEmail	VARCHAR(50)	NOT NULL, UNIQUE KEY
CustomerCreditCardID	INT	NOT NULL
CustomerDateOfBirth	DATETIME	NULL
CustomerGender	VARCHAR(15)	NULL
CustomerJoinDate	DATETIME	NOT NULL, Default value is Current Date
IsActive	BOOLEAN	NOT NULL, Default value is 1

Now you need to create a *Customers* table for the *Customers* entity class in your *SalesOrderStore* database. What SQL statement do you need to execute to do this? Solve this problem on your own if you can, or follow along with the solution shown here:

Solution SQL – SQL Server

```
USE SalesOrderStore;
CREATE TABLE Customers (
            CustomerID INT NOT NULL IDENTITY(1,1) PRIMARY KEY,
            CustomerFirstName VARCHAR(20) NOT NULL,
            CustomerLastName VARCHAR(20) NOT NULL,
            CustomerAddressID INT NOT NULL,
            CustomerPhoneNumber VARCHAR(25) NOT NULL,
            CustomerMobileNumber VARCHAR(25) NULL,
            CustomerEmail VARCHAR(50) NOT NULL UNIQUE,
            CustomerCreditCardID INT NOT NULL,
            CustomerDateOfBirth DATETIME NULL,
            CustomerGender VARCHAR(15) null,
            CustomerJoinDate DATETIME NOT NULL DEFAULT GETDATE(),
            IsActive BIT NOT NULL DEFAULT 1
       );
```

Solution SQL – MySQL

```
USE SalesOrderStore;
CREATE TABLE Customers (
            CustomerID INT AUTO_INCREMENT NOT NULL PRIMARY KEY,
            CustomerFirstName VARCHAR(20) NOT NULL,
            CustomerLastName VARCHAR(20) NOT NULL,
            CustomerAddressID INT NOT NULL,
            CustomerPhoneNumber VARCHAR(25) NOT NULL,
            CustomerMobileNumber VARCHAR(25) NULL,
            CustomerEmail VARCHAR(50) NOT NULL UNIQUE,
            CustomerCreditCardID INT NOT NULL,
            CustomerDateOfBirth DATETIME NULL,
            CustomerGender VARCHAR(15) null,
            CustomerJoinDate DATETIME NOT NULL DEFAULT NOW(),
            IsActive BIT NOT NULL DEFAULT 1
        );
```

Solution Review

Before you create a table, you have to make sure you are in the context of the database where you want to create it. The *USE* statement sets a database context. Therefore, start with the *USE SalesOrderStore* statement to set the database context to the proper database, then type the *CREATE TABLE Customers ()* statement to create the *Customers* table within this database.

However, if your query execution tool is already in the context of the *SalesOrderStore* database, you do not have to execute *USE* statement. For example, notice that each column in the table follows the structure as shown in Fig 4.8. It starts with its name followed by a blank space, its datatype, another blank space, a list of constraints (each constraint must be separated by one or more blank space), and then a comma (if it is not the last column of the table). In this demonstration we show the comma after each column, but after last column there is no comma shown.

See Fig 4.8 below for a demonstration of this:

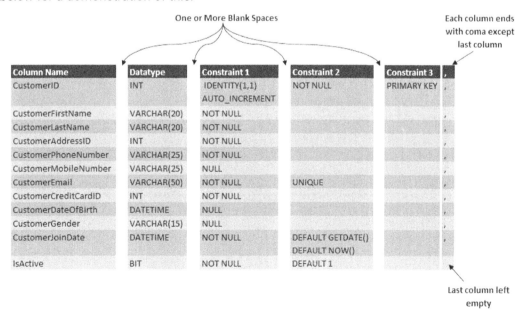

Fig 4.8 – Table with all constraints applied on single column

For the *UNIQUE KEY* constraint you just need to use the *UNIQUE* keyword, but for the default value, you need to use the *DEFAULT* keyword followed by the value you want to set as default. There is no common date function that returns current date and time for all RDBMSs, and that is why the *GETDATE()* function has been used for SQL Server and the *NOW()* function has been used for MySQL.

Notes

From this point onwards, we will only mention the SQL statement that needs to be executed to solve a business problem. Therefore, if your tool is not on the context of the correct database i.e. *SalesOrderStore*, please add the USE statement before any other statements.

Business Problem 3

You have already identified the datatypes and constraints for all the attributes of the *CustomerFeedbacks* entity class like below:

Column Name	Datatype	Constraints	Composite Keys
CustomerID	INT	NOT NULL	PRIMARY KEY
ProductID	INT	NOT NULL	
CustomerFeedbackRating	INT	NOT NULL	
CustomerFeedback	VARCHAR(300)	NULL	
FeedbackDate	DATETIME	NOT NULL, Default value is Current Date	

Now you need to create the *CustomerFeedbacks* table for the *CustomerFeedbacks* entity class in your *SalesOrderStore* database. What SQL statement do you need to execute? Solve this problem on your own if you can, or follow along with the solution shown here:

Solution SQL – SQL Server

```
CREATE TABLE CustomerFeedbacks (
        CustomerID INT NOT NULL,
        ProductID INT NOT NULL,
        CustomerFeedbackRating INT NOT NULL,
        CustomerFeedback VARCHAR(300) NULL,
        FeedbackDate DATETIME DEFAULT GETDATE(),
        PRIMARY KEY (CustomerID, ProductID)
    );
```

Solution SQL – MySQL

```
CREATE TABLE CustomerFeedbacks (
        CustomerID INT NOT NULL,
        ProductID INT NOT NULL,
        CustomerFeedbackRating INT NOT NULL,
        CustomerFeedback VARCHAR(300) NULL,
        FeedbackDate DATETIME DEFAULT NOW(),
        PRIMARY KEY (CustomerID, ProductID)
    );
```

Solution Review

Notice that the *CustomerFeedbacks* table has been created the same way as the *Customers* table, and the only difference is the primary key. The primary key of the *CustomerFeedbacks* table is not a single column. It is a combination of the *CustomerID* and *ProductID* columns. Since the primary key spans two columns, we cannot add it next to the column's datatype. In this scenario, you need to add a comma at the end of the last column (*FeedbackDate*) followed by the *PRIMARY KEY* constraint in this format: *PRIMARY KEY (1st column name, 2nd column name, ...)*.

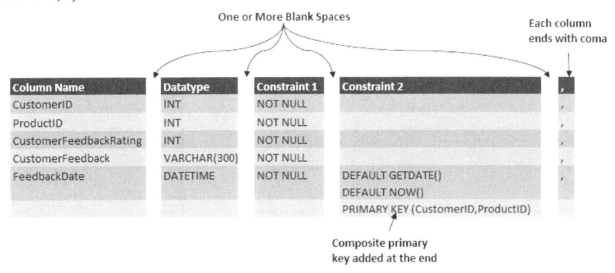

Fig 4.9 – Table with composite primary key constraint

Notes

If you want to add a composite *UNIQUE KEY* constraint, you should use the constraint definition like:

UNIQUE (1st column name, 2nd column name, ...).

Removing a table from a database

As businesses continue to grow, the requirements are bound to change. To adopt these changes, you may need to re-design your database. This re-design can lead to creating new tables, modifying existing tables or even removing existing tables. The modification of an existing table can entail adding new columns into a table or removing columns from a table, a skill that we will be discussed later. For now, let's focus on practicing how to remove a table from a database.

The syntax of the SQL statement which removes a table from a database is:

DROP TABLE table name;

Let's learn how to remove a table from a database by solving a business problem.

Business Problem 4

During the initial trial, business stakeholders changed their minds and now would like to allow any customer to provide multiple feedback comments for a given product—as long as they do not attempt to make more than one comment on the same day. They also would like to allow non-customers to provide feedback, and anyone (customers or non-customers) should be able to indicate whether existing particular feedback comment about a product is helpful or not.

Since these changes are significant and the database is still in trial, you have decided to remove the *CustomerFeedbacks* table and re-create it to accommodate the new requirements. You know how to re-create a table, but can you figure out how to remove a table?

What SQL statement do you need to execute to remove *CustomerFeedbacks* table? Solve this problem on your own if you can, or follow along with the solution shown here:

Solution SQL

```
DROP TABLE CustomerFeedbacks;
```

Notes

If a table's primary key or alternate key has been referenced by another table using the foreign key constraint, the parent table cannot be removed (dropped) before you have removed the foreign key constraint from the child table. For example, *CustomerID* is the primary key of *Customers* table, but it is a foreign key of the *CustomerFeedbacks* table. If you try to remove **Customers** table before removing *CustomerFeedbacks* table, your RDBMS will not allow that, it will return below error message instead:

SQL Server – 'Could not drop object *'Customers'* because it is referenced by a FOREIGN KEY constraint'

MySQL – 'Cannot delete or update a parent row: a foreign key constraint fails'

Adding a new column to a table

The syntax of the SQL statement for adding a column into a table is:

```
ALTER TABLE table name ADD column name datatype 1st constraint 2nd constraint .....;
```

Let's learn how to add a new column to a table by solving another business problem.

Business Problem 5

Business stakeholders would like to collect additional information (number of children) for each customer so that they can do some target marketing. The parameters are that the number of children should be an integer, and any customer may choose not to disclose the number of children they have. Based on this scenario, what SQL statement should you execute to add this new column, (*CustomerNoOfChildren*), into *Customers* table?

Solution SQL

```
ALTER TABLE Customers ADD CustomerNoOfChildren INT NULL;
```

Solution Review

Since customers are allowed to opt out of disclosing the number of children they have, the column's constraint should be *NULL*. Notice that we have replaced the table name with *Customers*, the column name with *CustomerNoOfChildren*, the datatype with *INT* and the 1st constraint with *NULL*. There are no more constraints, so the 2nd constraint has been replaced with nothing.

Removing a column from a table

The syntax of the SQL statement which removes a column from a table is:

```
ALTER TABLE table name DROP COLUMN column name;
```

Let's learn how to remove a column from a table by solving a business problem.

Business Problem 6

A year after adding data into the *CustomerNoOfChildren* column in the *Customers* table, business stakeholders have realized that very few customers chose to disclose the number of children they have. Therefore, they have decided to remove the column completely. What SQL statement do you need to execute to remove *CustomerNoOfChildren* column from *Customers* table?

Solution SQL

```
ALTER TABLE Customers DROP COLUMN CustomerNoOfChildren;
```

Solution Review

Notice that we have replaced the table name with the *Customers* and column name with *CustomerNoOfChildren*.

Removing a database

There will be occasions when you need to remove a database from your RDBMS server. To remove the database, you would use the following syntax:

```
DROP DATABASE database name;
```

Here, *database name* is generic, and in practice you would substitute the name of the database that you want to remove. If you want to remove the *SalesOrderStore* database, the SQL statement you need to execute would be:

```
DROP DATABASE SalesOrderStore;
```

Let's explore removing a database further by solving a business problem.

Business Problem 7

The *Payroll* database is using most of the RAM and CPUs in your database server, which is slowing down other application systems in your company. You have already migrated the *Payroll* database to a new server, which solves the slowness problem that was plaguing your other application systems. Now you should free-up the storage space in your existing database server by removing the *Payroll* database. What SQL statement do you need to execute?

Solution SQL

```
DROP DATABASE Payroll;
```

Notes

In the rare case that you receive an error message like *"Cannot drop database 'Payroll' because it is currently in use"* and the *DROP DATABASE* statement fails to execute, it is probably because the system thinks someone is using the *Payroll* database. In your situation, you are most likely the only one who is using the *Payroll* database. Check to be sure it is not open in the different window, and if so, close the opened window or close your RDBMS tool (e.g. SQL Server Management Studio or MySQL Workbench etc.). Then, reopen it and then re-execute your SQL statement and you should be able to execute the statement without a problem.

Practice Business Problems

The best way to learn is to do the process hands-on, so here's a list of business problems for you to solve. If you can't work out a solution for a problem on your own at first, please do not stress too much. Practice and repetition will help you master these skills.

IMPORTANT NOTE: As we mentioned at the beginning of this chapter, all of the solutions to the following practice business problems can be found at the following links as well as in the appendix A of this book::

Practice business problems for SQL Server:
https://drive.google.com/open?id=1CL9YBqCxmdxfJ_cdlW5ZAqNZopuosKAS

Practice business problems for MySQL:
https://drive.google.com/open?id=10-mo7FCjcYhZxBBcTB8MhGiKvuLzapwu

Practice Business Problem 1

The datatypes and constraints for all attributes of the *Addresses* entity class are as follows:

Column Name	Datatype	Constraints
AddressID	*INT*	*AUTO-INCREMENT NUMBER, PRIMARY KEY, NOT NULL*
StreetAddress	*VARCHAR(100)*	*NOT NULL*
City	*VARCHAR(25)*	*NOT NULL*
StateProvince	*VARCHAR(25)*	*NULL*
Country	*VARCHAR(25)*	*NOT NULL*
ZipOrPostalCode	*VARCHAR(20)*	*NULL*

What SQL statement do you need to execute to create the *Addresses* table for the *Addresses* entity class? Write the SQL statement that would accomplish this task, then execute the statement and verify the results.

Practice Business Problem 2

The datatypes and constraints for all attributes of the *CreditCards* entity class are as follows:

Column Name	Datatype	Constraints
CreditCardID	INT	Auto-Increment Number, PRIMARY KEY, NOT NULL
CreditCardNumber	VARCHAR(20)	NOT NULL
CardHolderName	VARCHAR(50)	NOT NULL
CreditCardType	VARCHAR(25)	NOT NULL
CreditCardExpiryMonth	INT	NOT NULL
CreditCardExpiryYear	INT(20)	NOT NULL

What SQL statement do you need to execute to create the *CreditCards* table for the *CreditCards* entity class?

Practice Business Problem 3

The datatypes and constraints for all attributes of the *Logins* entity class are as follows:

Column Name	Datatype	Constraints
UserID	VARCHAR(50)	PRIMARY KEY, NOT NULL
Email	VARCHAR(50)	NOT NULL
Password	NVARCHAR(50)	NOT NULL
NoOfFailedAttempt	INT	NOT NULL, Default value is 3
ChangePasswordInNextLogin	BIT	NOT NULL, Default value is 1
IsLocked	BIT	NOT NULL, Default value is 0
IsActive	BIT	NOT NULL, Default value is 1

What SQL statement do you need to execute to create the *Logins* table for the *Logins* entity class?

Practice Business Problem 4

The datatypes and constraints for all attributes of *SalesOrderProducts* entity class are like below:

Column Name	Datatype	Constraints	Composite Key
SalesOrderID	INT	NOT NULL	PRIMARY KEY
ProductID	INT	NOT NULL	
ProductQuantity	INT	NOT NULL	
ProductUnitPrice	DECIMAL(18,4)	NOT NULL	
ProductUnitPriceDiscount	DECIMAL(18,4)	NOT NULL, Default value is 0	
ProductShipDate	DATETIME	NULL	
ProductDeliveryDate	DATETIME	NULL	

What SQL statement do you need to execute to create *SalesOrderProducts* table for *SalesOrderProducts* entity class?

Practice Business Problem 5

Assume that you have created an *Addresses* table with wrong attributes and want to re-create the table. But before re-create the table you need to remove the old table first. What SQL statement do you need to execute to remove the old *Addresses* table?

Practice Business Problem 6

Business stakeholders would like to add an additional feature to the customer login screen so that they can pass additional alerts or notes to the customers. To facilitate this request, you want to add a new column, (*AdditionalNotes*), into the *Logins* table. What SQL statement do you need to execute to achieve this?

Practice Business Problem 7

A year after the business stakeholders introduced additional notes in the login screen, they realized that this feature has never been used. So, they decided to remove the feature and now it's up to you need to make it happen. You need to remove the *AdditionalNotes* column from the *Logins* table. What SQL statement do you need to execute?

Lesson summary

In this lesson, you have learned all the SQL statements that are needed to design your own database from a logical data model. You have seen that:

- The *CREATE DATABASE* statement allows you to create a database.
- The *DROP DATABASE* statement allows you to remove a database.
- The *CREATE TABLE* statement allows you to create a table within a database.
- With the *PRIMARY KEY* keyword, you can enforce the primary key constraint on a column by adding the keyword in the column definition, but for the composite primary key, you have to use the keyword in a separate constraint definition. The *UNIQUE* keyword can also be used in a similar way to enforce the unique key constraint.
- With the *DEFAULT* keyword, you can set a default value for a column by adding the keyword in the column definition. You have also learned that, when a user does not supply a value for the column, RDBMS will add the default value into the column.
- The *ALTER TABLE … ADD* statement allows you to add a new column to a table.
- The *ALTER TABLE … DROP COLUMN* statement allows you to remove a column from a table.

Lesson 5
Manipulating data

Lesson Objective

This lesson will start showing you how to add data into a table similar to the ones you created in *Lesson 4*. You will then apply *FOREIGN KEY* constraints and check the impact of that, then modify data in a table, and finally remove data from a table.

Code Samples

As in *Lesson 4*, you will be asked to solve business problems in this lesson that require you to write SQL code and execute it in your database, and we have provided that code for you at the links below.

SQL Server:

https://drive.google.com/open?id=1oX55o2LB1l-mQMgcuCGJyuGBdYcw7m1T

MySQL:

https://drive.google.com/open?id=1a9dA-Wu2nI0c1Bh3QsJBK9Evl-G4u8T-

Before you start, you will need to create the business case tables we will be working with in SQL. We have provided the code for the tables here:

SQL Server tables:

https://drive.google.com/open?id=17rm8ai2vsFg1sMu_zpgK08qnyYyOVMJ3

MySQL tables:

https://drive.google.com/open?id=1ddmvGEltAu6QwCSFxt_URBAOjDRCKxP3

Adding a row of data into a table

Every business operation generates data that needs to be stored. Here are some examples of these kinds of business operations:

- When a customer places a purchase order and it needs to be added into the *SalesOrders* and *SalesOrderProducts* table
- When a vendor enlist a new product for sale it needs to be added to *Products* table
- When a new customer fill-up his/her registration form via website it needs to be added to *Customers* table
- When company wanted to organize their products into a new category it needs to be added to *ProductCategories* table and so on.

Whether you are collecting data through an application (e.g. website, corporate portal etc.) or directly adding into a table, you have to execute a SQL statement to add each row of data into a table. The basic syntax to add a new row to a table is:

INSERT INTO table name (first column name, second column name, ..., last column name)
VALUES (first column value, second column value, ..., last column value);

Let's learn how to add a new row of data into a table by solving some business problems. Follow along and examine the syntax of the solutions closely.

Business Problem 1

The datatypes and constraints for the columns in the *VendorCategories* table are as follows. Note that we have one column that will allow *NULL* values, while all the others will not:

Column Name	Datatype	Constraints
VendorCategoryID	INT	NOT NULL, PRIMARY KEY
VendorCategoryName	VARCHAR(20)	NOT NULL
VendorCategoryDescription	VARCHAR(500)	NULL
VendorMonthlyTarget	DECIMAL(18,4)	NOT NULL
VendorNoOfMonthsForPromotion	INT	NOT NULL, Default value is 3
VendorCommissionRatePercentage	DECIMAL(4,2)	

In the table below, we have listed the attribute values for the vendor category that we need to add:

Column Name	Column Value
VendorCategoryID	1
VendorCategoryName	Regular
VendorCategoryDescription	Basic category. All new vendors are in this category
VendorMonthlyTarget	30000
VendorNoOfMonthsForPromotion	3
VendorCommissionRatePercentage	20

You need to add the category to the *VendorCategories* table before you can enter the data. What SQL statement do you need to execute to add the category?

Solution SQL – Option 1

INSERT INTO VendorCategories (VendorCategoryID, VendorCategoryName, VendorCategoryDescription, VendorMonthlyTarget, VendorNoOfMonthsForPromotion,VendorCommissionRatePercentage)
VALUES (1, 'Regular', 'Basic category. All new vendors are in this category', 30000, 3, 20);

Solution SQL – Option 2

INSERT INTO VendorCategories
VALUES (1, 'Regular', 'Basic category. All new vendors are in this category', 30000, 3, 20);

Solution Review

You will see that we have mentioned two solutions here. There is often more than one way to solve a problem with SQL. If you're thinking that you will need to execute an *INSERT* statement to add a row to *VendorCategories* table, then you're correct:

In option 1, the *INSERT* statement follows this pattern:

INSERT INTO → Table Name → (Column list separated by commas) → VALUES (Value list separated by commas).

One of SQLs syntax rules is that non-numeric values must be enclosed in quotation marks. Numeric values can be entered as it is, but the non-numeric values must be entered within a single quotation ("). In our example above, the datatypes of the *VendorCategoryName* and *VendorCategoryDescription* columns are variable length character datatypes and their values have been enclosed within quotes (e.g. *'Regular'* and *'Basic category. All new vendors are in this category'*). Meanwhile, the other columns contain numeric data, and that is why their values have been used without quotes (like *1*, *30000, 3* and *20)*.

You can reorder the column list, but the order of value list must be the same as the order of column list. For example, you can re-write the SQL statement like you see below:

INSERT INTO VendorCategories (VendorCategoryID, VendorCategoryName, VendorMonthlyTarget, VendorCategoryDescription, VendorNoOfMonthsForPromotion, VendorCommissionRatePercentage)
VALUES (1, 'Regular', 30000, 'Basic category. All new vendors are in this category', 3, 20);

Notice that we have moved the *VendorMonthlyTarget* column between *VendorCategoryName* and *VendorCategoryDescription*, and at the same time we moved the value of *VendorMonthlyTarget (i.e. 30000)* between the values of *VendorCategoryName* and *VendorCategoryDescription* (i.e. *'Regular'* and *'Basic category. All new vendors are in this category'*). If you re-arrange only the column list or only the value list, the *INSERT* statement will add wrong values in the columns.

In option 2, the pattern of the *INSERT* statement we have used is:

INSERT INTO → Table Name → VALUES (Value list separated by commas).

Here, the column list has been removed from the earlier *INSERT* statement. If you use this *INSERT* statement, the value list must be in the same order as when the table has initially created—you cannot rearrange the value list. You must supply all of the column values as well.

In the next business problem, you will see that you do not have to supply all the column values in order to add a row to a table. You cannot use this pattern of the *INSERT* statement if you choose not to supply all values when you add the row. Due to this complication, Option 1 is the recommended format you should always use.

Notes

You have just added a row to *VendorCategories* table, but how do you confirm whether the row has been successfully added to the table or not? You will learn how to retrieve data from a table in Section B, but for now please note that the *SELECT * FROM table name* statement will retrieve all data from a table. Therefore, if you execute the statement *SELECT * FROM VendorCategories*, you can see the result will look like the our example below:

VendorCategoryID	VendorCategoryName	VendorCategoryDescription	VendorMonthlyTarget	VendorNoOfMonthsForPromotion	VendorCommissionRatePercentage
1	Regular	Basic category. All new vendors are ...	30000.0000	3	20.00

Business Problem 2

The attribute values for a vendor category have been identified as follows:

Column Name	Column Value
VendorCategoryID	2
VendorCategoryName	Gold
VendorMonthlyTarget	50000
VendorCommissionRatePercentage	15

You need to add the category to *VendorCategories* table. What SQL statement do you need to execute?

Solution SQL

```
INSERT INTO VendorCategories (VendorCategoryID, VendorCategoryName,
                    VendorMonthlyTarget, VendorCommissionRatePercentage)
VALUES (2, 'Gold', 50000, 15);
```

Solution Review

Recall that we added a row to the VendorCategories table in Business Problem 1 in two different ways, and in each example we had values to insert into all the columns that we added. In this business problem, our solution must be different because we do not know the values for the *VendorCategoryDescription* and *VendorNoOfMonthsForPromotion* columns.

Without known values for all the fields you want to add, you cannot use the INSERT statement pattern mentioned in Option 2 of Business Problem 1. Instead, we used a variation of Option 1's pattern here (as you see in the Solution SQL above) because it allowed us to leave some of the values as *NULL*. You'll see we excluded *VendorCategoryDescription* and *VendorNoOfMonthsForPromotion* from the column list. Now the question is, what values will be added to the row for these columns after executing the above *INSERT* statement?

Based on the table definition from *Business Problem 1* we can determine that:

The *VendorCategoryDescription* column accepts *NULL* values. Therefore, the value of this column will be *NULL*.

The *VendorNoOfMonthsForPromotion* column has a default value of *3*. Therefore, the value of this column will be *3*.

If you execute the *SELECT * FROM VendorCategories* statement, your table and columns should look like this:

	VendorCategoryID	VendorCategoryName	VendorCategoryDescription	VendorMonthlyTarget	VendorNoOfMonthsForPromotion	VendorCommissionRatePercentage
1	1	Regular	Basic category. All new vendors are in this category	30000.0000	3	20.00
2	2	Gold	NULL	50000.0000	3	15.00

As you can see, this *INSERT* statement successfully added a second row and the values in the *VendorCategoryDescription* and *VendorNoOfMonthsForPromotion* columns are *NULL* (unknown) and 3, respectively.

Notes

If a column neither accepts *NULL* nor has a default value, you must add the column to the column list and add a corresponding value for it, otherwise the *INSERT* statement will fail to execute.

Adding multiple rows of data into one or more tables

Some business operations generate multiple rows of data, sometimes this data is expanded to multiple tables. One of the ways you can add these rows is by writing *INSERT* statements for each row, one after another, and then execute the whole list of *INSERT* statement as a batch. Another way you can accomplish this is to create the list of *INSERT* statements inside a stored procedure and then execute the stored procedure. You will see the stored procedure method later in this book. In this topic, you will see the batch approach. Let's see an example. Here, let's assume you want to add the two addresses seen in the table below into the *Addresses* table:

Column Name	Address 1	Address 2
StreetAddress	475 Flinders Lane	9600 Firdale Avenue
City	Melbourne	Edmonds
StateProvince	Victoria	Washington
Country	Australia	United States
ZipOrPostalCode	3000	98020

You can write two *INSERT* statements sequentially, and then execute both statements as a single batch:

```
INSERT INTO Addresses (StreetAddress, City, StateProvince, Country, ZipOrPostalCode)
VALUES ('475 Flinders Lane', 'Melbourne', 'Victoria', 'Australia', '3000');
INSERT INTO Addresses (StreetAddress, City, StateProvince, Country, ZipOrPostalCode)
VALUES ('9600 Firdale Avenue', 'Edmonds', 'Washington', 'United States', '98020');
```

After executing the above batch of *INSERT* statements, you can (and should) verify if both rows of data have been added correctly into the *Addresses* table or not by executing the following statement:

```
SELECT * FROM Addresses;
```

Please note that both of the zip codes are numeric but they have been enclosed by single quotes in our example (''). This is because the datatype of the *ZipOrPostalCode* column is a string, i.e. *VARCHAR(20)*. If you want to add 3 addresses, you just need to add one more *INSERT* statement to the batch. Note that you can add as many *INSERT* statements as you want into a single batch. You can also execute multiple *INSERT* statements even if they add data to different tables in the same batch.

If the tables do not have any dependencies, writing a batch of *INSERT* statements is as simple as the process shown above. But if they do have dependencies, for example if there are parent-child relationships and the primary key of the parent table is *AUTO INCREMENT NUMBER*, then you need to write the batch of statements slightly differently. The most common way is to follow these 3 steps:

Write an *INSERT* statement to add a row to the parent table.

Place the newly added primary key number (i.e. *AUTO INCREMENT NUMBER*) into a temporary container—something we will explain below.

Write another *INSERT* statement to add each row to the child table, and use the value of the temporary container as a *FOREIGN KEY* value.

Variable: The temporary container mentioned above is called a variable. You need to provide each variable with a name, and that name must start with an '@' symbol. For example, to store an address ID, you might define the variable name as *@AddressID*. For some RDBMSs (e.g. SQL Server) assigning a value to a variable is a two-step process, whereas for other RDBMSs (e.g. MySQL) it is a one-step process.

Step 1: Declaring (defining) a variable

Before you assign a value to a variable, for some RDBMSs (e.g. SQL Server), you must declare the variable. For other RDBMSs (e.g. MySQL) you have to skip this step. The syntax to declare a variable is:

```
DECLARE variable name DATATYPE;
```

If you want to declare the *@AddressID* variable with an integer data type, the SQL statement will be like below:

```
DECLARE @AddressID INT;
```

Step 2: Assigning a value to a variable

The syntax to assign a value to a variable is:

```
SET @AddressID = value to be assigned;
```

If you want to assign a value *20* to the *@AddressID* variable, the SQL statement will be like below:

```
SET @AddressID = 20;
```

Each RDBMS provides one or more functions to return the last *AUTO INCREMENT NUMBER*, but it's important to know that they are incompatible with each other. To retrieve the last *AUTO INCREMENT NUMBER*, you would use the *SCOPE_IDENTITY()* function for SQL Server and you would use the *LAST_INSERT_ID()* function for MySQL. The *SQL Server* code for step two would look like this:

```
DECLARE @AddressID INT;
SET @AddressID = SCOPE_IDENTITY();
```

For MySQL, you do not need to *DECLARE* the variable, you just need to assign the value to the variable like:

```
SET @AddressID = LAST_INSERT_ID();
```

Notes

For SQL server, you can also use the *SELECT* keyword instead of *SET* to assign a value to a variable. Therefore the above statement can also be written as:

```
SELECT @AddressID = SCOPE_IDENTITY();
```

Now let's learn how to add multiple rows of data into one or more tables by solving some business problems.

Business Problem 3

For this problem, let's assume that your e-commerce website uses the *SalesOrders* and *SalesOrderProducts* tables to store customer order's data. The column's datatypes and constraints of these tables are:

SalesOrders

Column Name	Datatype	Constraints
SalesOrderID	INT	**AUTO-INCREMENT NUMBER, PRIMARY KEY, NOT NULL**
OrderDate	DATETIME	**NOT NULL**
OrderDueDate	DATETIME	**NOT NULL**
OrderShipDate	DATETIME	**NULL**
OrderDeliveryDate	DATETIME	**NULL**
CustomerID	INT	**NOT NULL**
OrderTotal	DECIMAL(18,4)	**NOT NULL**
OrderDiscountTotal	DECIMAL(18,4)	**NOT NULL**, Default value 0
OrderBillingAddressID	INT	**NOT NULL**
OrderShippingAddressID	INT	**NOT NULL**
OrderCreditCardID	INT	**NOT NULL**

SalesOrderProducts

Column Name	Datatype	Constraints	Composite Key
SalesOrderID	INT	**NOT NULL**	PRIMARY KEY
ProductID	INT	**NOT NULL**	
ProductQuantity	INT	**NOT NULL**	
ProductUnitPrice	DECIMAL(18,4)	**NOT NULL**	
ProductUnitPriceDiscount	DECIMAL(18,4)	**NOT NULL**, Default value is 0	
ProductShipDate	DATETIME	**NULL**	
ProductDeliveryDate	DATETIME	**NULL**	

Ricky Brown, one of your regular customers, is purchasing 5 different products via your website. His order details are shown here:

Order Summary			
CustomerID	1	OrderBillingAddressID	1
OrderDate	1st January 2015	OrderShippingAddressID	1
OrderDueDate	7th January 2015	OrderCreditCardID	1
OrderTotal	$1440.00	OrderDiscountTotal	$60.00

Order Details			
ProductID	Quantity	UnitPrice	UnitPriceDiscount
1	2	$310.00	$20.00
37	1	$300.00	$20.00
2	3	$100.00	$0.00
33	5	$20.00	$0.00
53	1	$120.00	$0.00

When a customer confirms his order, the website has to record the order details into *SalesOrders* and *SalesOrderProducts* tables. Considering the data shown above, what SQL statements does the website need to execute to record *Ricky Brown's* order details?

Solution SQL – *SQL Server*

```
/* Adding sales order summary into SalesOrders table */
INSERT INTO SalesOrders (OrderDate, OrderDueDate, CustomerID, OrderTotal,  OrderDiscountTotal,
                OrderBillingAddressID, OrderShippingAddressID, OrderCreditCardID)
VALUES ('2015-01-01', '2015-01-07', 1,1440.00, 60.00, 1, 1, 1);


/* Assigning previously added identity number into @SalesOrderID variable */
DECLARE @SalesOrderID INT;
SELECT @SalesOrderID = SCOPE_IDENTITY();


/* Adding products details of the sales order into SalesOrderProducts table */
INSERT INTO SalesOrderProducts (SalesOrderID, ProductID, ProductQuantity, ProductUnitPrice, ProductUnitPriceDiscount)
VALUES (@SalesOrderID, 1, 2, 310.00, 20.00);
INSERT INTO SalesOrderProducts (SalesOrderID, ProductID, ProductQuantity, ProductUnitPrice, ProductUnitPriceDiscount)
VALUES (@SalesOrderID, 37, 1, 300.00, 20.00);
INSERT INTO SalesOrderProducts (SalesOrderID, ProductID, ProductQuantity, ProductUnitPrice, ProductUnitPriceDiscount)
VALUES (@SalesOrderID, 2, 3, 100.00, 0.00);
INSERT INTO SalesOrderProducts (SalesOrderID, ProductID, ProductQuantity, ProductUnitPrice, ProductUnitPriceDiscount)
VALUES (@SalesOrderID, 33, 5, 20.00, 0.00);
INSERT INTO SalesOrderProducts (SalesOrderID, ProductID, ProductQuantity, ProductUnitPrice, ProductUnitPriceDiscount)
VALUES (@SalesOrderID, 53, 1, 120.00, 0.00);
```

Solution SQL – MySQL

```
/* Adding sales order summary into SalesOrders table */
INSERT INTO SalesOrders (OrderDate, OrderDueDate, CustomerID, OrderTotal,  OrderDiscountTotal,
                OrderBillingAddressID, OrderShippingAddressID, OrderCreditCardID)
VALUES ('2015-01-01', '2015-01-07', 1,1440.00, 60.00, 1, 1, 1);


/* Assigning previously added identity number into @SalesOrderID variable */
SET @SalesOrderID = LAST_INSERT_ID();


/* Adding products details of the sales order into SalesOrderProducts table */
INSERT INTO SalesOrderProducts (SalesOrderID, ProductID, ProductQuantity, ProductUnitPrice, ProductUnitPriceDiscount)
VALUES (@SalesOrderID, 1, 2, 310.00, 20.00);
INSERT INTO SalesOrderProducts (SalesOrderID, ProductID, ProductQuantity, ProductUnitPrice, ProductUnitPriceDiscount)
VALUES (@SalesOrderID, 37, 1, 300.00, 20.00);
INSERT INTO SalesOrderProducts (SalesOrderID, ProductID, ProductQuantity, ProductUnitPrice, ProductUnitPriceDiscount)
VALUES (@SalesOrderID, 2, 3, 100.00, 0.00);
INSERT INTO SalesOrderProducts (SalesOrderID, ProductID, ProductQuantity, ProductUnitPrice, ProductUnitPriceDiscount)
VALUES (@SalesOrderID, 33, 5, 20.00, 0.00);
INSERT INTO SalesOrderProducts (SalesOrderID, ProductID, ProductQuantity, ProductUnitPrice, ProductUnitPriceDiscount)
VALUES (@SalesOrderID, 53, 1, 120.00, 0.00);
```

Solution Review

When Ricky Brown confirms his order, he will receive a unique receipt number which is the auto-generated *SalesOrderID*. Here we have two sets of data: *Order Summary* data is stored in the *SalesOrders* table and *Order Details* data is stored in the *SalesOrderProducts* table. *Order Summary* contains 1 row per order and *Order Details* contains multiple rows (in this case 5 rows) per order, but 1 row per product within an order. Here, *SalesOrders* is the parent table and has an auto-generated number as its primary key. The *SalesOrders* table's primary key is a foreign key for the *SalesOrderProducts* table. Therefore, we have followed the 3-step process to add Ricky Brown's order information into the system:

Start with an *INSERT* statement in the first paragraph, which adds a new row to the *SalesOrders* table. The RDBMS generates a new number for the *SalesOrderID* column for the row.

The statement(s) in the second paragraph assign the newly generated *SalesOrderID* into the *@SalesOrderID* variable.

Each of the 5 *INSERT* statements in the third paragraph adds a single product's details for the order into the *SalesOrderProducts* table where the *SalesOrderID* has been taken from the *@SalesOrderID* variable.

After you execute the whole batch together, you can verify whether the data have been added by executing these *SELECT* statements:

```
SELECT * FROM SalesOrders;
SELECT * FROM SalesOrderProducts;
```

The results of these *SELECT* statements are:

	SalesOrderID	OrderDate	OrderDueDate	OrderShipDate	OrderDeliveryDate	CustomerID	OrderTotal	OrderDiscountTotal	OrderBillingAddressID	OrderShippingAddressID	OrderCreditCardID
1	1	2015-01-01...	2015-01-07 ...	NULL	NULL	1	1440.0000	60.0000	1	1	1

	SalesOrderID	ProductID	ProductQuantity	ProductUnitPrice	ProductUnitPriceDiscount	ProductShipDate	ProductDeliveryDate
1	1	1	2	310.0000	20.0000	NULL	NULL
2	1	2	3	100.0000	0.0000	NULL	NULL
3	1	33	5	20.0000	0.0000	NULL	NULL
4	1	37	1	300.0000	20.0000	NULL	NULL
5	1	53	1	120.0000	0.0000	NULL	NULL

Notice that one row has been added to the *SalesOrders* table and five rows have been added into the *SalesOrderProducts* table. Since this is the first order we have added to the *SalesOrders* table, *SalesOrderID* becomes 1. If you add one more order, *SalesOrderID* will become 2, the next one will be 3 and so on.

Notice that the date values also enclosed with single quote ("). Something else you should keep in mind is that the default date format for almost every mainstream RDBMS is *YYYY-MM-DD hh:mi:ss*. That is why we have mentioned '*The first of January, 2015*' as '*2015-01-01*' within the *INSERT* statement.

Notes

When you write a long batch of SQL statements, it is recommended to add comments in each section within the batch so that your code becomes self-explanatory. There are various ways you can add a comment to your code. The most common way is to place /* at the beginning of your comment, and */ at the end of your comment, like so:

```
/* Adding sales order summary into SalesOrders table */
```

Comment can also span multiple lines, like so:

```
/* Adding sales order summary
   into SalesOrders table */
```

If you want to add a single line comment, you can also place - - at beginning of your comment, like so:

```
-- Adding sales order summary into SalesOrders table
```

RDBMS's query processor skips all comments from execution, so nothing inside the comment will affect your code.

Modifying all rows of data in a table

There are many reasons why you might find the need to modify data in a table. Sometimes a mistake can happen while adding data to a table or the need arises to change certain attributes over the time. Some customers may not willing to disclose their gender initially but change their minds later, wrong products may be added to the shopping basket by mistake, or the vendor or postal service would like to update the tracking dates (ship & delivery dates) after an order has been shipped or delivered. In short, there is always some need to modify data in a table. Of course, it can be tedious to modify large tables one part at a time, so fortunately there's a simple syntax for modifying one or more columns of data for all rows in a table is:

```
UPDATE table name
SET first column name = first column value, second column name = second column value, ............
```

Earlier in this lesson, we added two rows of data to the *VendorCategories* table. If for whatever reason you want to change the *VendorCategoryName* for both of them to *Common Category*, the *UPDATE* statement will look like:

```
UPDATE VendorCategories SET VendorCategoryName = 'Common Category';
```

Here we have changed values of one column for all the rows in the table. If, on the other hand, you want to change *VendorMonthlyTarget* to *20000* and *VendorCommissionRatePercentage* to *12.50%* for all categories, the *UPDATE* statement will look like you see below:

```
UPDATE VendorCategories  SET VendorMonthlyTarget = 20000, VendorCommissionRatePercentage = 12.50;
```

Here we have changed values of two columns at the same time for all the rows of the table. Notice that we have separated the columns by a comma (,). In a similar way, you can add more columns to the *SET* list. You do not have to use the fixed value. Instead, you can use an expression or another column in the value list like:

```
UPDATE VendorCategories
SET VendorMonthlyTarget = VendorMonthlyTarget * 1.2, VendorCategoryDescription = VendorCategoryName;
```

Here we have used the expression *VendorMonthlyTarget * 1.2* to increase the values of the *VendorMonthlyTarget* column by 20% for all categories, and the column name *VendorCategoryName* has been used as a value to replace all values of the *VendorCategoryDescription* column.

Notes

Modifying every row of data rarely happens in real life, but if you do it by mistake it could lead to serious consequences. Some RDBMSs (e.g. MySQL) disable this feature by default, so you have to enable it manually before use. Therefore, it is not recommended unless you have no better alternative. If you are using MySQL, please execute the SQL statement below (then execute the above UPDATE statements) which will allow you to update every row of a table:

```
SET SQL_SAFE_UPDATES = 0;
```

Modifying a subset of rows in a table

If you want to modify data from a subset of rows in a table, you need to add what is called a *'WHERE'* clause in your *UPDATE* statement. Here is the basic syntax to modify the data in one or more columns for a subset rows in a table:

```
UPDATE table name
SET first column name = first column value, second column name = second value, ............
WHERE search conditions;
```

Here, only the rows that satisfy the search conditions will be modified (i.e. search conditions evaluates to TRUE). Before we proceed with an example, let's check the data in the *VendorCategories* table. If you execute the *SELECT * FROM VendorCategories* statement it should show results similar to what you can see below:

	VendorCategoryID	VendorCategoryName	VendorCategoryDescription	VendorMonthlyTarget	VendorNoOfMonthsForPromotion	VendorCommissionRatePercentage
1	1	Common Category	Common Category	24000.0000	3	12.50
2	2	Common Category	Common Category	24000.0000	3	12.50

Since we have modified all rows for the columns *VendorCategoryName*, *VendorCategoryDescription*, *VendorMonthlyTarget, VendorCommissionRatePercentage,* each of these columns become same values for all rows. If you want to modify the first category's data back to same as Business Problem 1 and the second category's data back to same as Business Problem 2, you can add a *WHERE* clause to the *UPDATE* statements like below:

```
UPDATE    VendorCategories
SET VendorCategoryName = 'Regular', VendorMonthlyTarget = 30000, VendorCommissionRatePercentage = 20,
        VendorCategoryDescription = 'Basic category. All new vendors are in this category'
WHERE VendorCategoryID = 1;

UPDATE VendorCategories
SET VendorCategoryName = 'Gold', VendorMonthlyTarget = 50000, VendorCommissionRatePercentage = 15
WHERE VendorCategoryID = 2;
```

The first *UPDATE* statement's *WHERE* clause will satisfy only the first row. It replaces the first row's values for the *VendorCategoryName* column to *Regular*, the *VendorMonthlyTarget* to *30000*, and the *VendorCommissionRatePercentage* to *20* and *VendorCategoryDescription* to the *Basic category. All new vendors are in this category.* The second *UPDATE* statement's *WHERE* clause condition will satisfy only the second row. It replaces the second row's values for the *VendorCategoryName* column to *Gold*, *VendorMonthlyTarget* to *50000* and *VendorCommissionRatePercentage* to *15*.

Notes

You can execute each UPDATE statement separately or within the same batch.

Let's learn how to modify data from a subset of rows in a table by solving some business problems.

Business Problem 4

For this problem, let's assume that all the products for *SalesOrderID 1* have been delivered by the postal service. However, they arrived on the 6th *of January, 2015*, which is a day earlier than anticipated. Until the delivery system updates the delivery date, it will remain flagged as *not yet delivered* (i.e. *NULL*). Therefore we need to execute a SQL statement to update the delivery date when a sales order is delivered. What SQL statements does the delivery application need to execute to update the delivery date for *SalesOrderID* to 6th *January 2015* for the *SalesOrders* and *SalesOrderProducts* tables?

Solution SQL

```
/* Modify OrderDeliveryDate to 6 Jan 2015 for SalesOrderID 1 */
UPDATE SalesOrders SET OrderDeliveryDate = '2015-01-06'
WHERE SalesOrderID = 1;
/* Modify ProductDeliveryDate to 6 Jan 2015 for SalesOrderID 1 */
UPDATE SalesOrderProducts SET ProductDeliveryDate = '2015-01-06'
WHERE SalesOrderID = 1;
```

Solution Review

The *WHERE* clause condition *SalesOrderID = 1* confirms that the *SET* clause will only apply to the rows for *SalesOrderID 1*. The first *UPDATE* statement will modify the *OrderDeliveryDate* column's value to 6th *January 2015* for the *SalesOrderID 1* in the *SalesOrders* table and the second *UPDATE* statement will modify the *ProductDeliveryDate* column's values to 6th *January 2015* for all products of *SalesOrderID 1* in the *SalesOrderProducts* table.

Removing all data from a table

Every business is continuously growing, and the constant accumulation of data from different operations of the business could eventually lead your operational database to grow to the petabyte range. When a table becomes very big, the query processor has to travel a long way to find a given subset of rows that you may be requesting. The update and insert operations are just as demanding when the database is large, and the result is the same—the query will perform poorly. Therefore, you may need to archive old data into separate storage so that you can remove the data from your operational database tables and keep your table sizes minimal.

There could be a lot of other reasons you do not want some or all data from a table. Every RDBMS allow users/applications to execute a *DELETE* statement to remove data from a table. The basic syntax to delete *all* data from a table is:

```
DELETE FROM table name;
```

We know the *VendorCategories* table has two rows of data. Now if you want to remove all data from *VendorCategories* table, you need to execute a *DELETE* statement, as shown below:

```
DELETE FROM VendorCategories;
```

Notes

Removing all data from a table is rarely used in real life, and if you do it by mistake it could have serious consequences. Some RDBMS even disable this feature by default. In these cases, you will need to enable it before use. We don't recommend using this statement unless you do not have a better alternative.

If you are using MySQL and this feature is not enabled, please execute the SQL statement below:

```
SET SQL_SAFE_UPDATES = 0;
```
For some RDBMS, the *FROM* keyword is optional here. Please check your RDBMS's documentation for details.

You can also remove all data from a table using a *TRUNCATE* statement such as:

```
TRUNCATE TABLE VendorCategories;
```

Removing a subset of rows from a table

If you want to remove a subset of rows from a table, you need to add a *WHERE* clause in your *DELETE* statement. The basic syntax to remove a subset rows from a table is:

```
DELETE FROM table name
WHERE search conditions;
```

Here, only the rows that satisfy the search conditions (i.e. search conditions evaluates to *TRUE*) will be removed. Please execute the *INSERT* statements from Business Problems 1 & 2 to add two rows of data into the *VendorCategories* table. Now, if you want to remove the vendor category "*Gold*," you need to execute a *DELETE* statement as below:

```
DELETE FROM VendorCategories WHERE VendorCategoryName = 'Gold';
```

Notice that the Gold category has only been deleted from the *VendorCategories* table. You can verify this by executing a *SELECT* statement before and after the *DELETE* statement in a batch like below:

```
SELECT * FROM VendorCategories;
DELETE FROM VendorCategories WHERE VendorCategoryName = 'Gold';
SELECT * FROM VendorCategories;
```

This will show the *VendorCategories* table before and after the deletion so that you can verify that it has been removed.

Notes

Some RDBMSs do not support the use of a non-key column in the *WHERE* clause of a *DELETE* statement. In that case, you need to use the key column like in the statement below:

```
DELETE FROM VendorCategories WHERE VendorCategoryID = 2;
```

Now let's practice deleting a subset of rows from a table by solving some business problems.

Business Problem 5

Assume that you have archived all the data for *SalesOrderID 1* from both *SalesOrders* and *SalesOrderProducts* tables. There is no need to keep this sales information in your database, so now you need to remove it from these tables. What SQL statements do you need to execute to do this?

Solution SQL

```
/* Removing order summaries from SalesOrders table for SalesOrderID 1 */
DELETE FROM SalesOrders WHERE SalesOrderID = 1;
/* Removing order details from SalesOrderProducts table for SalesOrderID 1 */
DELETE FROM SalesOrderProducts WHERE SalesOrderID = 1;
```

Solution Review

The *WHERE* clause condition, *SalesOrderID = 1*, confirms that the *DELETE* operation will only apply to the rows for *SalesOrderID 1*. If you want to verify your *DELETE* operations, you can use a *SELECT* statement before and after each *DELETE* statement and execute all statements within a batch.

Verifying the data-integrity of data manipulations

At this point, you have created a database, created tables within the database, added some data into those tables, modified some data in the tables, and removed some data from the tables. Now it's time to verify whether or not your database is protecting the business from users adding incorrect data to the database.

First, let's start with datatypes. Let's review all the *INSERT* and *UPDATE* statements we have executed. So far, we have inserted or updated integer values to the integer columns, updated string values to characters columns, and updated date-time values to date time columns. We have also inserted integer values into decimal columns, but notice that RDBMSs convert the integer to decimal and insert those integer values as decimal values. Both integer and decimal are numeric data. Therefore, RDBMS can convert them as needed, and they are called compatible datatypes. You have added numeric data to numeric columns, string data to string columns and date data to date columns, but you are probably still not sure your database table is allowing non-compatible data into columns (e.g. string data into numeric columns, numeric data into date columns etc.).

Let's try to add some non-compatible types of data into columns. If you execute the below *INSERT* statement, RDBMS will return an error like *"Conversion failed when converting the varchar value 'Cat3' to data type int"* or *"Incorrect integer value: 'Cat3' for column VendorCategoryID"*:

```
INSERT INTO VendorCategories
        (VendorCategoryID, VendorCategoryName, VendorMonthlyTarget, VendorCommissionRatePercentage)
    VALUES ('Cat3', 80000, 'Diamond', 10);
```

Here, *VendorCategoryID* is an integer column, but we were trying to add the string value *'Cat3'* and that is why RDBMS returned an error. As soon as any error occurs, the query processor will not proceed further and the row will not be added. If, however, you change the value of the *VendorCategoryID* column to an integer value such as '3' as in the *VALUE* list below, and then re-execute the statement, RDBMS will again return a similar data conversion error. In this case, however, the error will be for the *VendorCategoryName* column where we tried to add a numeric value to the string column:

```
INSERT INTO VendorCategories
        (VendorCategoryID, VendorCategoryName, VendorMonthlyTarget, VendorCommissionRatePercentage)
    VALUES ( 3, 80000, 'Diamond', 20);
```

If you change the value of the *VendorCategoryName* column to a string value (e.g. 'Diamond') like in the statement below, and then re-execute the statement, RDBMS will return another data conversion error, this time because we tried to add a string value to the *VendorMonthlyTarget* decimal column:

```
INSERT INTO VendorCategories
            (VendorCategoryID, VendorCategoryName, VendorMonthlyTarget, VendorCommissionRatePercentage)
VALUES (3, 'Diamond', 'Diamond', 20);
```

If you change the value of the *VendorMonthlyTarget* column to a decimal value (e.g. 80000.00) like below, and then re-execute the statement, the RDBMS will add the row to *VendorCategories* table:

```
INSERT INTO VendorCategories
            (VendorCategoryID, VendorCategoryName, VendorMonthlyTarget, VendorCommissionRatePercentage)
VALUES (3, 'Diamond', 80000.00, 20);
```

Therefore, we can conclude that the RDBMS prevents adding the wrong type of data into a table column, which is good. Now let's move on to the value itself—the column level constraints. We have already verified that you can skip adding a value to columns that have *NULL* constraints, and RDBMS adds the default value if to the column has default constraints (please see Business Problems 2 & 3 for details).

Now we need to test whether our database is preventing empty values from being entered into columns that have *NOT NULL* constraints. Let's see what happens when we execute the below *INSERT* statement without adding a value to the *NOT NULL* column:

```
INSERT INTO VendorCategories
            (VendorCategoryID, VendorCategoryName, VendorMonthlyTarget)
VALUES (4, 'Super Gold', 80000);
```

Notice that the RDBMS has returned an error. This is because the *INSERT* statement did not include the *VendorCommissionRatePercentage* column. This is as it should be, because this column does not allow *NULL* values. Therefore, the RDBMS is preventing the entry of empty values to the column. Let's try adding a duplicate value in the key column *VendorCategoryID*:

```
INSERT INTO VendorCategories
(VendorCategoryID, VendorCategoryName,VendorMonthlyTarget,VendorCommissionRatePercentage)
VALUES (1, 'Gold', 80000, 10);
```

This will also fail to execute because the *VendorCategoryID* is the primary key to the table and the value '1' is already in the table. This is what we want to happen. We can conclude that our database ensures the row and column level data integrities within each table. Now we need the check the data integrities between multiple rows and tables. If you look at Business Problem 3, you may notice that we have added *CustomerID 1* into the *SalesOrders* table, but *CustomerID 1* has not yet been added to *Customers* table. This means that, although customer *Ricky Brown* was able to place an order to purchase some products, he has not yet been registered as a customer. This is a serious data integrity issue.

To solve this issue, you need to create the *FOREIGN KEY* constraints that you learned in *Lesson 4*. Note that we have postponed teaching you how to implement relationships between tables so that we can show you the impact of failing to implement relationship constraints (*FOREIGN KEY*). We will show you this later in this lesson.

For now, follow along with the statements below to see how to check the data integrities between multiple rows. Let's add another sales order:

```
/* Adding sales order summary into SalesOrders table */
INSERT INTO SalesOrders
                ( OrderDate, OrderDueDate, CustomerID, OrderTotal, OrderDiscountTotal,
                     OrderBillingAddressID, OrderShippingAddressID, OrderCreditCardID )
VALUES ('2016-01-15', '2016-01-20', 1,810, 40, 1, 1, 1);


/* Assigning previously added identity number into @SalesOrderID variable */
DECLARE @SalesOrderID INT;
SELECT @SalesOrderID = SCOPE_IDENTITY();


/* Adding products details of the sales order into SalesOrderProducts table */
INSERT INTO SalesOrderProducts(SalesOrderID, ProductID, ProductQuantity, ProductUnitPrice, ProductUnitPriceDiscount)
VALUES ( @SalesOrderID, 1, 1, 310, 20);
INSERT INTO SalesOrderProducts(SalesOrderID, ProductID, ProductQuantity, ProductUnitPrice, ProductUnitPriceDiscount)
VALUES ( @SalesOrderID, 'ID37', 1, 300, 20);
INSERT INTO SalesOrderProducts(SalesOrderID, ProductID, ProductQuantity, ProductUnitPrice, ProductUnitPriceDiscount)
VALUES ( @SalesOrderID, 2, 2, 100, 0);
```

Notes

For MySQL, please replace these two lines of code:

```
DECLARE @SalesOrderID INT;
SELECT @SalesOrderID = SCOPE_IDENTITY();
with:

SET @SalesOrderID = LAST_INSERT_ID ();
```

Notice that this order has 3 products (look for the three *ProductID* entries shown above), but in the middle *INSERT* statement for the *SalesOrderProducts* table, we have intentionally tried to add a string value (*'ID37'*) to the *ProductID* column. When you execute the batch of statements, you can see it has successfully added a row to the *SalesOrders* table and also successfully added the first product, but failed to add second and third products of the order due to the error in the second product's *INSERT* statement. Now the order summary does not match with the order details. The summary will show an order value of $810, but the details will show a value of $310. If you were to let this error go, the customer would be charged the full $810 but would receive just one product out of three. Needless to say, you'd end up with an upset customer on your hands.

So then, how do you solve this problem? Well, you can either successfully execute all of the statements within a batch, or undo everything that has already been done—in other words you should add everything or do nothing for the batch. The next topic will show you how transaction processing will help you to solve problems like these by executing the whole batch as a single unit.

Managing transactions

Transaction processing is a system that ensures that all tasks within a single business operation will be completed successfully. When you use multiple data manipulation statements (*INSERT*, *UPDATE* or *DELETE*) within a transaction, the database engine will save the changes if all of the statements have been done successfully. If any of the statements fail to execute, the database engine undoes everything that have already been done. The syntax varies between RDBMSs.

We will show you the syntax for *SQL Server* here, so please refer to your RDBMS documentation for the syntax if you're using a different RDBMS:

```
BEGIN TRANSACTION
      List of statements;
COMMIT TRANSACTION
```

If you want to execute the previous batch of statements within a single transaction, you can start the batch with *BEGIN TRANSACTION* (or simply *BEGIN TRAN*) and end the batch with *COMMIT TRANSACTION* (or *COMMIT TRAN* or simply *COMMIT*) as shown below:

```
BEGIN TRANSACTION

      /* Adding sales order summary into SalesOrders table */
      INSERT INTO SalesOrders (OrderDate, OrderDueDate, CustomerID, OrderTotal, OrderDiscountTotal,
                        OrderBillingAddressID, OrderShippingAddressID, OrderCreditCardID )
      VALUES ( '2016-01-15', '2016-01-20', 1,810, 40, 1, 1, 1);

      /* Assigning previously added identity number into @SalesOrderID variable */
      DECLARE @SalesOrderID INT;
      SELECT @SalesOrderID = SCOPE_IDENTITY();

      /* Adding products details of the sales order into SalesOrderProducts table */
      INSERT INTO SalesOrderProducts (SalesOrderID, ProductID, ProductQuantity, ProductUnitPrice, ProductUnitPriceDiscount)
      VALUES (@SalesOrderID, 1, 1, 310, 20);
      INSERT INTO SalesOrderProducts (SalesOrderID, ProductID, ProductQuantity, ProductUnitPrice, ProductUnitPriceDiscount)
      VALUES ( @SalesOrderID, 'ID37', 1, 300, 20);
      INSERT INTO SalesOrderProducts (SalesOrderID, ProductID, ProductQuantity, ProductUnitPrice, ProductUnitPriceDiscount)
      VALUES ( @SalesOrderID, 2, 2, 100, 0);

COMMIT TRANSACTION
```

After executing the above batch of statements, you should verify that no data have been added to either the *SalesOrders* or *SalesOrderProducts* tables. If you correct the error—i.e. replace the value of *ProductID 'ID37'* with simply *37* and execute it again, you will see data have been added to both tables correctly:

```
BEGIN TRANSACTION

      /* Adding sales order summary into SalesOrders table */
      INSERT INTO SalesOrders (OrderDate, OrderDueDate, CustomerID, OrderTotal, OrderDiscountTotal,
                        OrderBillingAddressID, OrderShippingAddressID, OrderCreditCardID )
      VALUES ( '2016-01-15', '2016-01-20', 1,810, 40, 1, 1, 1);

      /* Assigning previously added identity number into @SalesOrderID variable */
      DECLARE @SalesOrderID INT;
      SELECT @SalesOrderID = SCOPE_IDENTITY();

      /* Adding products details of the sales order into SalesOrderProducts table */
      INSERT INTO SalesOrderProducts (SalesOrderID, ProductID, ProductQuantity, ProductUnitPrice, ProductUnitPriceDiscount)
      VALUES (@SalesOrderID, 1, 1, 310, 20);
      INSERT INTO SalesOrderProducts (SalesOrderID, ProductID, ProductQuantity, ProductUnitPrice, ProductUnitPriceDiscount)
      VALUES ( @SalesOrderID, 37, 1, 300, 20);
      INSERT INTO SalesOrderProducts (SalesOrderID, ProductID, ProductQuantity, ProductUnitPrice, ProductUnitPriceDiscount)
      VALUES ( @SalesOrderID, 2, 2, 100, 0);

COMMIT TRANSACTION
```

Note that, in this example, if you replace the *COMMIT* with *ROLLBACK*, RDBMS will undo everything even if there is no error.

Adding a constraint to a table

Foreign key constraint: As you can see from the previous examples, we have sold products to a customer who does not even exist in our database. Specifically, we added a row in the *SalesOrders* (child) table for *CustomerID 1* and that row does not exist in the *Customers* (parent) table. To solve this problem, you would add a *FOREIGN KEY* constraint on the *CustomerID* column (*FOREIGN KEY*) of the *SalesOrders* (child) table, then add a reference to the primary key column (*CustomerID*) of the *Customers* (parent) table.

The basic syntax to add a *FOREIGN KEY* constraint is:

```
ALTER TABLE table name
ADD CONSTRAINT constraint name FOREIGN KEY (column list)
REFERENCES parent table name (column list from parent table);
```

Here, the constraint name must be unique within a database, and in case of a composite *FOREIGN KEY*, the columns must be separated by a comma (,). The constraint name can be any unique name, but the most common practice is to use the *FOREIGN KEY* constraint name in the format of: *FK_ChildTableName_ParentTableName*.

Therefore, the SQL statement to add the *FOREIGN KEY* constraint on the *CustomerID* column of the *SalesOrders* table will be as shown below:

```
ALTER TABLE SalesOrders
ADD CONSTRAINT FK_SalesOrders_Customers FOREIGN KEY(CustomerID) REFERENCES Customers (CustomerID);
```

Notes

Before you create the *FOREIGN KEY* constraint, please ensure that the table is empty. To do so, execute a *TRUNCATE TABLE SalesOrders* statement to remove all data from *SalesOrders* table.

After you create the *FOREIGN KEY* constraint, try to add a row into the *SalesOrders* table for a customer who does not exist in *Customers* table. Upon doing so, you will see that the RDBMS will return an error and will not add it.

Primary key constraint: In *Lesson 4*, you learned that how to enforce the *PRIMARY KEY*, *ALTERNATE KEY*, and *DEFAULT* constraints using the *PRIMARY KEY*, *UNIQUE* or *DEFAULT* keywords during the table creation. Sometimes you may need to add these constraints *after* the creation of the table because of a design change or other reasons. The basic syntax to add a *PRIMARY KEY* constraint is:

```
ALTER TABLE  table name ADD CONSTRAINT constraint name PRIMARY KEY (column list);
```

Here the constraint name must be unique within a database, and in the case of the composite primary key, the columns must be separated by a comma (,).The constraint name can be any unique name, but the most common practice is to use the primary key constraint name in the format of *PK_TableName*.

Let's create the *ProductCategories* table using the SQL statement below:

```
CREATE TABLE ProductCategories (
                ProductCategoryID INT NOT NULL,
                ProductCategoryName VARCHAR(50) NOT NULL,
                ProductCategoryDescription VARCHAR(500) NULL,
                IsActive BIT NOT NULL
        );
```

Now you will see how to create a primary key constraint in the *ProductCategoryID* column, the unique key constraint on the *ProductCategoryName* column, and the default value constraint on the *IsActive* column.

The SQL statement to add primary key constraint on *ProductCategoryID* will be like below:

```
ALTER TABLE  ProductCategories  ADD CONSTRAINT PK_ProductCategories PRIMARY KEY(ProductCategoryID);
```

Unique key constraint: The basic syntax to add a unique key constraint is:

```
ALTER TABLE  table name ADD CONSTRAINT constraint name UNIQUE (column list);
```

Here, the constraint name must be unique within a database. Remember that, as with primary keys, if you are using a composite unique key, the columns must be separated by a comma (,). The SQL statement to add a unique key constraint on the *ProductCategoryName* column of the *ProductCategories* table with a name *UK_ProductCategories_ProductCategoryName* is as follows:

```
ALTER TABLE ProductCategories
ADD CONSTRAINT UK_ProductCategories_ProductCategoryName UNIQUE(ProductCategoryName);
```

Default value constraint: The way to create a default value constraint on a column varies widely between RDBMSs. Here, we will show you the basic syntax to add a default value constraint on a column for *SQL Server*:

```
ALTER TABLE table name ADD CONSTRAINT constraint name DEFAULT (value) FOR column name;
```

Again, the constraint name must be unique within a database. Therefore, the SQL statement (for *SQL Server*) to add a default value constraint of '1' to the *IsActive* column of the *ProductCategories* table with a name *DK_ProductCategories_IsActive* will be as follows:

```
ALTER TABLE ProductCategories ADD CONSTRAINT DK_ProductCategories_IsActive DEFAULT(1) FOR IsActive;
```

The basic syntax to add a default value constraint on a column for MySQL is:

```
ALTER TABLE table name ALTER column name SET DEFAULT value;
```

Therefore, the SQL statement (for MySQL) to add a default value constraint of '1' to the *IsActive* column of the *ProductCategories* table is:

```
ALTER TABLE ProductCategories ALTER IsActive SET DEFAULT 1;
```

Removing a constraint from a table

The statement for removing a constraint from a table varies widely between RDBMSs. Sometimes the syntax may even differ between constraint types in the same RDBMS, so be sure to consult your RDBMS documentation.

Removing a constraint from a table in *SQL Server*

The syntax for *SQL Server* to remove any type of constraints is:

```
ALTER TABLE table name DROP CONSTRAINT constraint name;
```

Therefore, if you want to remove the primary key constraint from the *ProductCategory* table that you have created in an earlier topic, the SQL statement will look like this:

```
ALTER TABLE ProductCategories DROP CONSTRAINT PK_ProductCategories;
```

Similarly, you can also remove the *FOREIGN KEY*, *unique key* and *default value* constraints you created earlier by executing the statements below:

```
ALTER TABLE SalesOrders DROP CONSTRAINT FK_SalesOrders_Customers;
ALTER TABLE ProductCategories DROP CONSTRAINT UK_ProductCategories_ProductCategoryName;
ALTER TABLE ProductCategories DROP CONSTRAINT DK_ProductCategories_IsActive;
```

Removing a constraint from a table in MySQL

In MySQL, the syntax of removing constraints differ between constraint types. The syntax to remove a primary key constraint is:

```
ALTER TABLE table name DROP PRIMARY KEY;
```

If you want to remove the primary key constraint from the *ProductCategory* table that you created earlier, the SQL statement would be:

```
ALTER TABLE ProductCategories DROP PRIMARY KEY;
```

The syntax to remove a *FOREIGN KEY* constraint is:

```
ALTER TABLE table name DROP FOREIGN KEY constraint name;
```

So if you want to remove the *FOREIGN KEY* constraint from the *SalesOrders* table that you created earlier, the SQL statement would be:

```
ALTER TABLE SalesOrders DROP FOREIGN KEY FK_SalesOrders_Customers;
```

The syntax to remove a *unique key* constraint is:

ALTER TABLE table name DROP INDEX constraint name/index name;

As such, to remove the *unique key* constraint from the *ProductCategories* table you created earlier, write the SQL statement you see below:

ALTER TABLE ProductCategories DROP INDEX UK_ProductCategories_ProductCategoryName;

The syntax to remove a *default value* constraint is:

ALTER TABLE table name ALTER column name DROP DEFAULT;

Therefore, if you want to remove the default value constraint from the *ProductCategories* table that you created earlier, the SQL statement would be:

ALTER TABLE ProductCategories ALTER IsActive DROP DEFAULT;

Practice Business Problems

Here is another batch of business problems for you to solve so you can practice the skills you just learned. As with the *Lesson 4* Practice Business Problems, all of the solutions to these problems can be found online at the following links as well as in the appendix A of this book:

SQL Server:

https://drive.google.com/open?id=1u8OqcB564KSgRIcVOyZIwyoMscpJazlF

MySQL:

https://drive.google.com/open?id=17o0CMWzsJWVQU0gE5XjzLhv5r_IKoJpt

Practice Business Problem 1

A new employee named Tracey Moore has joined the marketing department at your company. The marketing department has forwarded her details (as shown below) and asked you to add them into the database and create a login for her:

Name	Tracey Moore	Street Address	8888 Flinders Street
Phone number	+61 3 222222222	City	Brisbane
Mobile number	+61 4222222222	State	Queensland
Date of birth	1st January 1980	Country	Australia
Email	TraceyMoore@Sale OnYourOwn.com	Post Code	4000
User ID	TraceyMoore	Temporary password	Welcome123 (user must change her password in the next login)

What SQL statement do you need to execute to perform the task?

Practice Business Problem 2

You have been asked to make some changes to Tracey Moore's employee account. She recently got married and her surname changed to William. Her email address will remain the same TraceyMoore@SaleOnYourOwn.com so there is no need to change it. What SQL do you need to execute to modify her surname?

Practice Business Problem 3

Tracey Moore is no longer working for your company and you have been asked to remove her from the database. What SQL statement do you need to execute to perform the task?

Lesson Summary

In this lesson, you learned techniques SQL statements needed to perform various data manipulations. We started showing you how to add data into tables, then showed you how to modify or remove data from tables, and finally, we showed you how to ensure data-integrities within tables.

You have seen that:

- The *INSERT* statement allows you to add one or more rows of data into a table.
- You can use a variable to get the value of parent table's surrogate key when adding multiple rows of data into two tables that are related by way of a parent-child (one-to-many) relationship.
- The *UPDATE* statement without *WHERE* clause will modify all rows of data in a table by a specified value for each specified columns, but usages of *WHERE* clause allow you to limit the changes within a subset of rows in the table.
- The *DELETE* statement without the *WHERE* clause will remove all data from a table, but usages of the *WHERE* clause allow you to remove a subset of rows from the table.
- You cannot add a non-compatible type of data into a column.
- The *BEGIN TRANSACTION* .... *COMMIT TRANSACTION* statement allows you to ensure all tasks within a single business operation will be done successfully or undone for every task that has been completed.
- The *ALTER TABLE* .... *ADD CONSTRAINT* statement with the keywords *PRIMARY KEY, FOREIGN KEY, UNIQUE* and *DEFAULT* allow you to add the primary key, foreign key, unique key and default value constraints in a table respectively.
- Statements for removing constraints from a table vary between RDBMSs, but you have learned how to remove constraints in MySQL and SQL Server.

Section B
Retrieving Business Insights from a Single Table

Section Overview

In our previous lessons you learned how to design a database from the ground up to store valuable business data. As valuable as this skill is, few business users are going to be concerned with how you store their data. What they want to know is what they (and you) can do with that data. Senior managers, analysts, customers and vendors alike need to be able to access their data to answer questions such as:

- *What's the status of my order?*
- *What are our ten bestselling products?*
- *What age group does most of our customer belong to?*

Answering these questions is where you come in. If you want to be the go-to SQL expert for your business, then you'll need to know how to retrieve data from multiple database tables, supply constant values, and so on. This section is just the beginning—we'll cover all that in later chapters.

For now, we're going to start by exploring one of SQL's fundamental commands: the *SELECT* statement. We will show you how to retrieve data from tables to answer business questions. In this section, we will focus on retrieving data from a single table. The basic syntax of the *SELECT* statement to retrieve data from a single table is:

```
SELECT column list, literals and/or expressions
FROM table
WHERE filter conditions
GROUP BY column list and/or expressions
HAVING filter conditions
ORDER BY column list and/or expressions;
```

The SELECT statement has six clauses. They are the:

1. SELECT clause,
2. FROM clause,
3. WHERE clause,
4. GROUP BY clause,
5. HAVING clause and
6. ORDER BY clause

Only the *SELECT* clause is mandatory for any SQL statement to function correctly. You may not include all of the other clauses, but whatever clauses you have included in your *SELECT* statement *must be added in the order you see above*, otherwise your RDBMS will return an error. In this section, you will learn how to apply the six clauses of the *SELECT* statement above to retrieve business insights from a single table. We'll explain these concepts to you in a similar fashion as in previous lessons—by asking you to solve day-to-day business problems for our fictitious company, *SaleOnYourOwn.com*. The answer to each question will be a variation of the standard *SELECT* statement and will work for most RDBMSs. Any differences for a particular RDBMS will be mentioned and, as always, we'll demonstrate the example code for SQL Server and MySQL.

Before you start, you will need to create the business case tables and add some data into the tables. We have provided the script for this here:

SQL Server:
https://drive.google.com/open?id=1jVYeoDirukhMRChg9wrst8tLUqopDbwc

MySQL:
https://drive.google.com/open?id=1kGkBG_k3guGXEnMBK3LafPIpFBWAdPMB

Lesson 6
Retrieving Static Data Without a Table

NEW SQL STATEMENTS AND KEYWORDS COVERED IN THIS LESSON:

SELECT   AS

Lesson Objective

Some business questions can be answered without storing any data into user tables. Examples of these types of questions are:

- *What is the day of the week today?*
- *What is the title of the sales report for this month?*
- *Is this year a leap year?*
- *What is the square root of 121?*

Each RDBMS provides you with the functionality to retrieve and manipulate date, string and numeric literals. In this lesson you will learn:

- How to use the *SELECT* clause to retrieve string, numeric or date literals
- How to use an *alias* to provide a meaningful name to an output column
- How to use built-in functions to retrieve useful system properties

Code Samples

As in previous lessons, you will be asked to solve business problems in this lesson that require you to write SQL codes and execute them in your database, and we have provided that code for you at the links below.

SQL Server:
https://drive.google.com/open?id=18efBbp0wk6o3vOgtlF9WrxW5tRHm-zGb

MySQL:
https://drive.google.com/open?id=1pfKiFyxGh9I8zcYyVPhr5Usz9l_kRZAP

Retrieving String Literals

Sometimes you will find that simply retrieving the data from a table may not satisfy the business user's exact need. You may need to add one or more static string values with it. This type of static string value is called a string literal. String literals are usually enclosed with a series of single quotes ('), as in the example *'Sales Report'*. The syntax for retrieving one or more string literals is:

```
SELECT string literal1, string literal2, string literal3, ..................;
```

Next, let's learn the usage of the string literal by solving a business problem.

Business Problem 1

Show me the monthly sales report entitled *Monthly Sales Report*.

Solution SQL

```
SELECT 'Monthly Sales Report';
```

SQL Result

Monthly Sales Report

Solution Review

As you can see, the statement above uses a very simple *SELECT* clause to retrieve the string literal entitled *Monthly Sales Report*. Notice that the string literal has been used within a single quote (*Monthly Sales Report'*) just after the *SELECT* keyword and followed by the semicolon (;). Also notice that there is no column name in the above results; however, some RDBMSs will show the meaningless column name in the result.

Providing a Resulting Column with a Meaningful Name

In the above *SELECT* statement, if you want to use the result from another application, the column needs to have a static name. To do this, you can use the *AS* keyword after a literal (or a column name or an expression), and then provide a meaningful column name. This is often called a column *alias*.

Let's explore this concept by solving a business problem.

Business Problem 2

Show me the monthly sales report entitled *Monthly Sales Report* with the column name *ReportTitle*.

Solution SQL

```
SELECT 'Monthly Sales Report' AS ReportTitle;
```

SQL Result

ReportTitle
Monthly Sales Report

Solution Review

In order to show a name for the column at the beginning of the result, you can see that the *AS* keyword has been used after the literal followed by the desired column alias (*ReportTitle*).

Manipulating String Literals

Every RDBMS has a list of built-in functions for the manipulation of string literals or strings stored in a database table. These functions are very important to work with string data types. If you have *First Name* and *Last Name* and want to generate *Full Name* from them, you need to use a type of function that we haven't discussed yet, the *CONCAT* function. Let's find out how to use the *CONCAT* string function by answering another business question.

Business Problem 3

We have a string literal containing a customer's first name, '*Ricky*', and another literal containing customer's last name, '*Ponting*'. Please show me the customer's full name.

Solution SQL

SELECT CONCAT('Ricky', ' ', 'Ponting') AS FullName;

SQL Result

FullName
Ricky Ponting

Solution Review

Essentially, the *CONCAT* function combines two or more string literals. It places the first string literal first, then the second string literal following after the 1st string literal, then the 3rd string literal and so on. Notice that we are treating '*Ricky*', ' ', and '*Ponting*' as three string literals. We need to display a white space between '*Ricky*' and '*Ponting*' so that the first and last names will be easier to read, and to tell SQL to do so we must treat the space (' ') as a separate string literal. That is why we have used ' ' between the first name and last name strings. We have also used *FullName* to designate the column alias.

The table below shows the most frequently used string manipulation functions. You will learn their real business usages in the later lessons. As always, please refer to your RDBMS for a full list of string manipulation functions.

Function	Description	Example
CONCAT (String1, String2, String3,.....)	Return a combined string from two or more strings	CONCAT ('Good ', 'Morning') will return *Good Morning*
LEFT(String, N)	Return an N number of characters from the left part of the string	LEFT ('Good Morning', 4) will return *Good*
RIGHT(String, N)	Return an N number of characters from the right part of the string	RIGHT('Good Morning', 7) will return *Morning*
LEN(String)	Return the number of characters in the string. MySQL *uses LENGTH function instead of LEN.*	LEN('Good Morning') will return *12*
UPPER(String)	Convert all characters in a string to upper case.	UPPER('Good Morning') will return *GOOD MORNING*
LOWER(String)	Convert all characters in a string to lower case.	LOWER('Good Morning') will return *good morning*
LTRIM(String)	Remove all empty spaces from the beginning of a string	LTRIM(' Good Morning') will return *Good Morning*
RTRIM(String)	Remove all empty spaces from the ending of a string	RTRIM('Good Morning ') will return *Good Morning*
SUBSTRING(String expression, Start Position, Length)	Return a part of a string from a string expression	SUBSTRING('Good Morning', 6, 4) will return *Morn*
REPLACE(String, String to Search, String to Replace)	Return a string from a String Expression by replacing all occurrences of 'String to Search' with 'String to Replace'	REPLACE('ABCDEPQRSTCDEGHIJ', 'CDE' 'LM') will return *ABLMPQRSTLMGHIJ*

Retrieving Numeric Literals

The static numeric value is called a numeric literal. A numeric literal can be an integer, decimal number or exponential number. It can also include the positive (+) or negative (-) sign. The positive is optional for positive numeric literals, but the negative sign is *mandatory* for negative numeric literals.

Some examples of numeric literals are:

- A positive integer: 25 or +25
- A positive number with 2 decimal places: 25.56 or +25.56
- A positive exponential number: 2.34E3 or +2.34E3
- A negative integer: -25
- A negative number with two decimal places: -25.56
- A negative exponential number: -2.34E3

The syntax for retrieving one or more numeric literals is:

```
SELECT numeric literal1, numeric literal2, numeric literal3, ..................;
```

Let's learn the usages for numeric literal by solving a business problem.

Business Problem 4

Please show me the numeric values '*36*' and '*-57.78*' and an exponential value, '*4.678E4*'. Please also show the column names as *IntegerLiteral*, *DecimalLiteral* and *ExponentialLiteral*, respectively.

Solution SQL

```
SELECT 36 AS IntegerLiteral, -57.78 AS DecimalLiteral, 4.678E4 AS ExponentialLiteral;
```

SQL Result

IntegerLiteral	DecimalLiteral	ExponentialLiteral
36	-57.78	46780

Solution Review

We know that:

$$4.678E4 = 4.678 \times 10^4 = 46780$$

Notice that 46780 has been displayed as an *ExponentialLiteral* and we haven't used the + sign for positive numeric literals. The use of the + sign is optional. If you use the + sign it will show the same results, and the SQL statement will look like:

```
SELECT +36 AS IntegerLiteral, -57.78 AS DecimalLiteral, +4.678E4 AS ExponentialLiteral;
```

Manipulating Numeric Literals

Numeric literals are not very useful on their own, but they become useful when you use one or more of them along with mathematical functions and mathematical operators. To explain, if you ask '*Give me 25*', there is no real business value to this question, but if you ask '*What is the square root of 25?*', then there is a real business value to this question in various applications.

When you use a combination of numeric literals, variables, columns, mathematical operators or functions in a way which can evaluate to a single value, this combined form is called a *numeric expression*.

Some examples of numeric expressions are:

- 34 + 76 − 13
- 66 * 24 + SQRT(25)
- 48/12 + ROUND(5.6,0)

It is very important to understand the mathematical operators and their orders of execution in the database engine. The database engine evaluates the higher level of operators first, but in case of the same level of operators and parentheses, they will be evaluated in the order of left to right and innermost to outermost.

The table below shows the most frequently used mathematical operators in SQL and their order of execution:

Execution Order Level	Operator	Example
1	() Parenthesis	(3 * 5) − 2 = 15 − 2 = 13
		3 * (5 − 2) = 3 * 3 = 9
		((3 + 5) * (6 - 3)) = (8 * 3) = 24
2	* (multiply)	5 * 4 = 20
	/ (division)	22 / 5. MySQL evaluates it to 4.4 but SQL Server evaluates it to 4
	% (modulo)	22 % 5 = 2. Returns the reminder
	DIV	22 DIV 5 = 4. SQL Server doesn't support DIV function
3	+ (Add)	5 + 4 = 9
	- (Subtract)	5 − 4 = 1

Notes

Please use the '()' parenthesis carefully. As you can probably guess, adding a set of parentheses in wrong place will give you the wrong result. If you look at the 1st two examples in the table above, you'll notice that they both use exactly the same number of operators but they evaluate to two different results.

The table below shows the most frequently used mathematical functions. Please check your RDBMS for a full list of mathematical functions.

Function	Description	Example
ABS(Numeric Literal or Expression)	Returns the absolute (positive) value of the numeric literal or expression	ABS(-54.7) = 54.7 ABS(54.7) = 54.7
CEILING(Numeric Literal or Expression)	Returns the smallest integer greater than or equal to the numeric literal or expression	CEILING(-54.7) = -54 CEILING(54.7) = 55
FLOOR(Numeric Literal or Expression)	Return the largest integer less than or equal to the numeric literal or expression	FLOOR(-54.7) = -55 FLOOR(54.7) = 54
PI()	Returns the value of PI	PI() = 3.141593
POWER(X, Y)	Returns the value by raising the value of a numeric literal or expression X to the power of a numeric literal Y	POWER(5, 4) = 625 POWER(5.2, 3) = 140.6
ROUND(Numeric Literal or Expression, precision)	Returns the nearest precision by rounding up or down the numeric literal or expression	ROUND(6.52, 0) = 7 ROUND(6.49, 0) = 6
SQRT(Positive Numeric Literal or Expression)	Returns the square root of a positive numeric literal or expression	SQRT(25) = 5

Let's practice using numeric expressions in SQL by solving some business problems. Later you'll be using these methods to answer real-world business questions.

Business Problem 5

Please give me the smallest integer that is greater than 17.6, the largest integer that is less than 17.6, and the closest integer to 17.6.

Solution SQL

```
SELECT  CEILING(17.6) AS SmallestIntegerGreaterThan,
        FLOOR(17.6) AS LargestIntegerLessThan,
        ROUND(17.6,0) AS ClosestInteger;
```

SQL Result

SmallestIntegerGreaterThan	LargestIntegerLessThan	ClosestInteger
18	17	18

Solution Review

The smallest integer that is greater than 17.6 is 18, the largest integer that is less than 17.6 is 17, and the closest integer to 17.6 is 18.

As you can see, we used the *CEILING* function to show the smallest integer greater than 17.6. Next, we used the *FLOOR* function to show the largest integer less than 17.6. Finally, the *ROUND* function with 0 precision gave us the closest integer to 17.6.

Business Problem 6

The radius of a circle is 5cm. What is the *area* of the circle?

Solution SQL

```
SELECT PI() * POWER(5,2) AS Area;
```

SQL Result

Area
78.5398163397448

Solution Review

We know that the area of a circle (A) can be calculated with the following equation:

$$A = \pi r^2$$

Here, r = radius = 5cm. The function *PI()* will give you the value of π and the function *POWER(5,2)* will give you the value of 5^2. Please note that SQL Server supports another function, *SQUARE(5)*, which will give you the value of 5^2 as well. If you are using SQL Server, you can alternatively use the SQL statement below as well:

```
SELECT  PI() * SQUARE(5) AS Area;
```

Business Problem 7

Please solve the equation below:

$$f(x) = 24.25 \times \frac{(4 + 7 \times 8^4 - 45)^2}{58.1 - 23}$$

Solution SQL

SELECT 24.25 * (POWER((4+7*POWER(8,4)-45),2)/(58.1-23)) AS EquationResult;

SQL Result

EquationResult
566340552.82762075

Solution Review

The equation has three parts:

24.25,

$$(4 + 7 \times 8^4 - 45)^2$$

and 58.1 − 23.

Each part should evaluate before applying the result to other operators. Be sure that you apply parentheses to the last part (i.e. 58.1 − 23). If you apply the mathematical operators to the equation, it will look like:

$$f(x) = 24.25 * (4 + 7 * 8^4 - 45)^2/(58.1 - 23)$$

Now if you apply the mathematical functions, the equation will look like:

$$f(x) = 24.25 * (POWER((4 + 7 * POWER(8,4) - 45), 2)/(58.1 - 23))$$

The RDBMS evaluates the equation in the order shown below:

Step 1:	POWER(8 ,4) = 4096	
Step 2:	7 * 4096 = 28672	*7 multiplied by the result of step 1*
Step 3:	4 + 28672 = 28676	*4 plus the result of step 2*
Step 4:	28676 − 45 = 28631	*The result of step 3 minus 45*
Step 5:	POWER(28631, 2) = 819734161	*The square of the result of step 4*
Step 6:	(58.1 − 23) = 34.9	
Step 7:	24.25 * 819734161 = 19878553404.25	*24.25 multiplied by the result of step 5*
Step 8:	19878553404.25 / 34.9 = 566340552.82762075	*The result of step 7 divided by the result of step 6*

Retrieving Date Literals

A static date value is called a date literal. There are three types of date literals available: *date literal, time literal* and *timestamp literal.* Date literals are usually enclosed within single quotes (' '). The syntax for retrieving a date literal is:

SELECT date literal1, date literal2, date literal3, ...;

A date literal usually written in the 'year-month-day' format where 'year' represents a four-digit integer, 'month' represents a two-digit integer with a value between 01 and 12, and 'day' represents a two-digit integer with a value between 01 and 31. Some examples of date literal retrievals are:

```
SELECT '2015-05-23';
SELECT '2016-12-07';
```

The time literal is usually written in the 'hour:minute:second' format where 'hour' represents a two-digit integer with a value between 01 and 24, 'minute' represents a two-digit integer with a value between 01 and 59, and 'second' represents real numbers with values between 01 and 59.999 (i.e. less than 60). Some examples of time literal retrievals are:

```
SELECT '15:35:59';
SELECT '16:59:23.145';
```

The timestamp literal is usually written in the 'year-month-day hour:minute:second' format. Some examples of timestamp literal retrievals are:

```
SELECT '2015-05-23 15:35:59';
SELECT '2016-12-07 16:59:23.145';
```

Manipulating Date Literals

As with string literals, date literals may not be interesting on their own, but they become quite handy when you use them with date functions. There is no real business value in asking, *'Give me the 7th of December 2016'* because the question lacks context. Likewise, asking, *'How many days have passed since the 7th December 2016?'* may seem trivial, but later we'll show you how this can be useful for retrieving data on specific dates and between date ranges.

Date functions allow you to answer these types of questions. The implementation of date functions varies widely between RDBMSs. The table below shows the most frequently used date functions for MySQL, and the full list can be found at: https://dev.mysql.com/doc/refman/5.7/en/date-and-time-functions.html.

Function	Description	Example
CURRENT_DATE()	Returns the current date of computer on which MySQL is running	
DAY(date)	Returns the day number for the date and time.	DAY('2015-05-23') = 23 DAY('2015-05-23 14:25:32') = 23
MONTH(date)	Returns the month number for the date and time.	MONTH('2015-05-23') = 5 MONTH('2015-05-23 14:25:32') = 5
YEAR(date)	Returns the year number for the date and time.	YEAR('2015-05-23') = 2015 YEAR('2015-05-23 14:25:32') = 2015
HOUR(date)	Returns the hour number for the date and time	HOUR('2015-05-23 14:25:32') = 14
MINUTE(date)	Returns the minute number for the date and time	MINUTE('2015-05-23 14:25:32') = 25
SECOND(date)	Returns the second number for the date	SECOND('2015-05-23 14:25:32') = 32
DATE_ADD(date, INTERVAL n unit)	Adds the **n unit** interval to the date and return the new date. Here **n** is a numeric value and the frequently used **units** are DAY, MONTH, YEAR, WEEK, HOUR, MINUTE and SECOND.	DATE_ADD('2015-05-23', INTERVAL 4 DAY) = 2015-05-27 DATE_ADD('2015-05-23', INTERVAL 4 MONTH) = 2015-09-23
DAYNAME(date)	Returns the day name of week for the date.	DAYNAME('2015-02-23') = Monday
MONTHNAME(date)	Returns the month name of the year for the date.	MONTHNAME('2015-02-23') = February

The table below shows the most frequently used date functions for SQL Server, but you can find the full list at this URL: https://msdn.microsoft.com/en-AU/library/ms186724.aspx.

Function	Description	Example
GETDATE()	Returns the current date and time of computer on which SQL Server is running	
DAY(date)	Returns the day number for the date and time.	DAY('2015-05-23') = 23 DAY('2015-05-23 14:25:32') = 23
MONTH(date)	Returns the month number for the date and time.	MONTH('2015-05-23') = 5 MONTH('2015-05-23 14:25:32') = 5
YEAR(date)	Returns the year number for the date and time.	YEAR('2015-05-23') = 2015 YEAR('2015-05-23 14:25:32') = 2015
DATEPART (datepart, date)	Returns the date part's numeric value for the date. The frequently used date parts in this function are: dd – day of month mm – month of year yyyy – year hh – hour mi – minute ss – second dy – day of year wk – week of year	DATEPART(dd, '2015-02-23 14:25:32') = 23 DATEPART(mm, '2015-02-23 14:25:32') = 2 DATEPART(yyyy, '2015-02-23 14:25:32') = 2015 DATEPART(hh, '2015-02-23 14:25:32') = 14 DATEPART(mi, '2015-02-23 14:25:32') = 25 DATEPART(ss, '2015-02-23 14:25:32') = 32 DATEPART(dy, '2015-02-23 14:25:32') = 54 DATEPART(wk, '2015-02-23 14:25:32') = 9
DATEADD (datepart, interval, date)	Adds the interval to the datepart of the date and return the new date. The frequently used dateparts in this function are: dd – day of month mm – month of year yy/yyyy – year	DATEADD(dd, 4, '2015-05-23') = 2015-05-27 DATEADD(mm, 4, '2015-05-23') = 2015-09-23
DATENAME (datepart, date)	Returns the datepart's string value for the date. The frequently used dateparts in this function are: dw – day of week mm – month of year	DATENAME(dw, '2015-02-23 14:25:32') = Monday DATENAME(mm, '2015-02-23 14:25:32') = February

Now let's see one of our date functions in action by solving a business problem.

Business Problem 8

On what day of the week was New Year's Day in 2016?

Solution SQL – SQL Server

```
SELECT DATENAME(dw,'2016-01-01') AS NewYearDay;
```

Solution SQL – MySQL

```
SELECT DAYNAME('2016-01-01') AS NewYearDay;
```

SQL Result

NewYearDay
Friday

Solution Review

In SQL Server we use the *DATENAME()* function to return the day name of the week for the new year day in 2016 which is *Friday*. The first parameter of the function *'dw'* represents the day of the week, and the second parameter represents the *1st of January, 2016*.

On the other hand, in MySQL we use the *DAYNAME()* function with the parameter value of the *1st of January, 2016*, which will return the day name of the week for New Year's Day 2016.

Practice Business Problems

Here are some more business problems for you to solve to practice the topics we've covered in this lesson. As always see *Appendix A* for the SQL code solutions to these problems, or you can visit the following links:

SQL Server:

https://drive.google.com/open?id=1NmJiaspCZVhiQHtu76MfeWllVLOGo4jC

MySQL:

https://drive.google.com/open?id=19wCYWaqArYM1P3BxrzpYnzm2TUeHK9H_

Practice Business Problem 1

Please tell me the following dates in the YYYY-MM-DD format:
- Today
- 3 days ago
- 3 weeks ago
- 3 months ago
- 3 years ago

Now, tell me what the date will be:
- 3 days from today?
- 3 weeks from today?
- 3 months from today?
- 3 years from today?

Practice Business Problem 2

Now please tell me the following dates, but format them in the DD-MM-YYYY format:
- Today
- 3 days ago
- 3 weeks ago
- 3 months ago
- 3 years ago

Now, tell me what the date will be:
- 3 days from today?
- 3 weeks from today?
- 3 months from today?
- 3 years from today?

Practice Business Problem 3

Please give me the following information:
- The number of the current day of the month
- The name of the current day of the week
- The number of the current month of the year
- The name of the current month
- The numerical value of the current year

Practice Business Problem 4

Show me the report title in the format of *Sales Report for the Month of [Current Month] [Current Year]*. For example, if today is the 24th of August, 2017, the report title should be:

Sales Report for the Month of August 2017

Lesson Summary

In this lesson, you have learned how to use the *SELECT* clause of the *SELECT* statement to retrieve system values and literals. You have also seen the usages of frequently used strings as well as the usages of numeric and date functions. You have also learned the *AS* keyword for giving a meaningful name to an output column.

Lesson 7
Retrieving All Rows from a Table

NEW SQL STATEMENTS AND KEYWORDS COVERED IN THIS LESSON:

SELECT	SELECT...FROM
SELECT...FROM...ORDER BY	CASE

Lesson Objective

In this lesson, you will learn how to use the *SELECT* and *FROM* clauses of the *SELECT* statement to retrieve all the rows from a table. You will also learn how the *ORDER BY* clause can provide you with a way to shorten your result, and predicates give you the power to populate an output column dynamically.

Code Samples

As in previous lessons, you will be asked to solve business problems in this lesson that require you to write SQL codes and execute them in your database, and we have provided that code for you at the links below:

https://drive.google.com/open?id=16AA9WpRllp7yljW_t8TaBk9vgqdFdRRW

Retrieving a Single Column

If you want to retrieve all rows within a single column from a table, you should use the *SELECT* statement as shown below:

```
SELECT column name
FROM table name;
```

The *SELECT* clause specifies which data (column) you want to retrieve, and the *FROM* clause specifies where you want to retrieve the data from (table). The *SELECT* statement is not case sensitive. So, you can rewrite the above *SELECT* statement like:

```
select column name
from  table name;
```

You can also use as many white spaces as you like. It would be perfectly fine to rewrite the above *SELECT* statement like so:

```
SELECT     column name      FROM table name;
```

Now let's see how to retrieve all the data from a table for a single column by solving a business problem.

Business Problem 1

Please give me the names of all the present and past vendors for our fictitious company, *SaleOnYourOwn.Com*. The company is currently storing its vendor names in the *VendorName* column of *Vendors* table.

Solution SQL

```
SELECT VendorName FROM Vendors;
```

SQL Result

VendorName
P & Q Traders Ltd
Asia Pacific Suppliers Ltd
UVWXYZ Suppliers Ltd
JKLMN Suppliers Ltd
Vision 2020 Electronics Ltd
PQRST Suppliers Ltd
A & B Traders Ltd
Things for Future Generations Ltd
ABCDE Suppliers Ltd
EFGHI Suppliers Ltd
Rahman Suppliers Ltd

Solution Review

SaleOnYourOwn.com has ten active vendors and one inactive vendor. The *Vendors* table contains all their details. The *SELECT* statement we show above has retrieved for you all eleven vendor names from the *Vendors* table.

You may have noticed that the *VendorName* column has been used just after the *SELECT* keyword and the *Vendors* table has been used just after the *FROM* keyword. When you execute the SQL, you may see the vendor names in different order. Unless you specify a short order in the *SELECT* statement, the order of the output may vary in different executions. Please do not worry about your result's order—as long as it gives you eleven vendor names it is OK.

In the next topic, you will see how to order the SQL result.

Ordering a Single Column Result

In the above SQL result, the vendor names are not in a particular order. If you want to show the vendor names in ascending or descending order, you need to use the *ORDER BY* clause. If you want to retrieve all the rows from a table but only a single column with ascending or descending order, you should use the *SELECT* statement shown below:

```
SELECT column name
FROM   table name
ORDER BY column name ASC/DESC;
```

If you want to show the result in descending order, the *DESC* keyword must be used in the *ORDER BY* clause. If you want to show the result in ascending order, you can use either the *ASC* keyword or do not use any keyword. Note that if you do not use an *ASC* or *DESC* keyword in the *ORDER BY* clause, the database engine will use the *ASC* keyword by default. Let's learn the usages of the *ORDER BY* clause by solving a business problem.

Business Problem 2

Please give me the names of all present and past vendors in descending order.

Solution SQL

```
SELECT VendorName FROM Vendors ORDER BY VendorName DESC;
```

SQL Result

VendorName
Vision 2020 Electronics Ltd
UVWXYZ Suppliers Ltd
Things for Future Generations Ltd
Rahman Suppliers Ltd
PQRST Suppliers Ltd
P & Q Traders Ltd
JKLMN Suppliers Ltd
EFGHI Suppliers Ltd
Asia Pacific Suppliers Ltd
ABCDE Suppliers Ltd
A & B Traders Ltd

Solution Review

You may have noticed that the same eleven vendor names have been shown in this result, but they are now in descending order. We added the *VendorName* column just after the *ORDER BY* keyword and followed by the *DESC* keyword. If you want to show the same result in ascending order, you can use either of the below SQL queries:

```
SELECT VendorName FROM Vendors ORDER BY VendorName ASC;
SELECT VendorName FROM Vendors ORDER BY VendorName;
```

Retrieving Multiple Columns

For retrieving multiple columns from a table in no particular order you should use the *SELECT* statement:

```
SELECT   column name1, column name2, column name3, …………
FROM    table name;
```

When listing two consecutive columns, they need to be separated by a comma (,). Let's explore the concept with a business problem.

Business Problem 3

Please give me all present and past vendors and include their IDs, names, phone numbers and email addresses.

SQL Solution

```
SELECT VendorID, VendorName, VendorPhoneNumber, VendorEmail
FROM Vendors;
```

SQL Result

VendorID	VendorName	VendorPhoneNumber	VendorEmail
1	P & Q Traders Ltd	+61 430 492550	pqTraders@SaleOnYourOwn.com
2	Asia Pacific Suppliers Ltd	+61 000 999999	acpacSupply@SaleOnYourOwn.com
3	UVWXYZ Suppliers Ltd	+44 7123 123456	uvwzyzSupply@SaleOnYourOwn.com
4	JKLMN Suppliers Ltd	+1 (312) 000-000000	ghijkSupply@SaleOnYourOwn.com
5	Vision 2020 Electronics Ltd	+1 (312) 806-9033	vision2010electronics@SaleOnYourOwn.com
6	PQRST Suppliers Ltd	+1 (312) 999-99999	pqrstSupply@SaleOnYourOwn.com
7	A & B Traders Ltd	+1 (704) 231-4370	abTraders@SaleOnYourOwn.com
8	Things for Future Generations Ltd	+86 10 123456789	FutureGen@SaleOnYourOwn.com
9	ABCDE Suppliers Ltd	+88 02 11111111	abcdeSupply@SaleOnYourOwn.com
10	EFGHI Suppliers Ltd	+91 000 999999	efghiSupply@SaleOnYourOwn.com
11	Rahman Suppliers Ltd	+88 02 33333333333	rahmanSupply@SaleOnYourOwn.com

Solution Review

You may have noticed in the SQL statement we have written above that the columns *VendorID*, *VendorName*, *VendorPhoneNumber* and *VendorEmail* have all been separated by commas. The results are similar to Business Problem 1, with the only difference being that it has some additional columns.

Ordering Results with Multiple Columns

If you want to sort multiple column results in ascending or descending order, you should use a *SELECT* statement like the one below:

```
SELECT  column name1, column name2, column name3, .........
FROM   table name
ORDER BY  order column name1 ASC/DESC, order column name2 ASC/DESC, ....;
```

Let's explore the topic by solving some more business problems.

Business Problem 4

Please give me all present and past vendors with their IDs, names, phone numbers and email addresses. Please show the results in ascending order by vendor name.

Solution SQL

```
SELECT VendorID, VendorName, VendorPhoneNumber, VendorEmail
FROM Vendors
ORDER BY VendorName;
```

SQL Result

VendorID	VendorName	VendorPhoneNumber	VendorEmail
7	A & B Traders Ltd	+1 (704) 231-4370	abTraders@SaleOnYourOwn.com
9	ABCDE Suppliers Ltd	+88 02 11111111	abcdeSupply@SaleOnYourOwn.com
2	Asia Pacific Suppliers Ltd	+61 000 999999	acpacSupply@SaleOnYourOwn.com
10	EFGHI Suppliers Ltd	+91 000 999999	efghiSupply@SaleOnYourOwn.com
4	JKLMN Suppliers Ltd	+1 (312) 000-000000	ghijkSupply@SaleOnYourOwn.com
1	P & Q Traders Ltd	+61 430 492550	pqTraders@SaleOnYourOwn.com
6	PQRST Suppliers Ltd	+1 (312) 999-99999	pqrstSupply@SaleOnYourOwn.com
11	Rahman Suppliers Ltd	+88 02 33333333333	rahmanSupply@SaleOnYourOwn.com
8	Things for Future Generations Ltd	+86 10 123456789	FutureGen@SaleOnYourOwn.com
3	UVWXYZ Suppliers Ltd	+44 7123 123456	uvwzyzSupply@SaleOnYourOwn.com
5	Vision 2020 Electronics Ltd	+1 (312) 806-9033	vision2010electronics@SaleOnYourOwn.com

Solution Review

In the above table, the result is similar to that of *Business Problem 3*, but the rows are now sorted by vendor name in ascending order. We didn't include the *ASC* keyword because we knew the database engine would add it by default. If you wanted to add the *ASC* keyword, the query would look like:

```
SELECT VendorID, VendorName, VendorPhoneNumber, VendorEmail
FROM Vendors
ORDER BY VendorName ASC;
```

Business Problem 5

Please give me a list of all our customers with their genders, first names, last names, phone numbers and email addresses. Show the results in descending order by gender, and then in ascending order by first name, and finally by last name.

Solution SQL

SELECT CustomerGender, CustomerFirstName, CustomerLastName, CustomerEmail
FROM Customers
ORDER BY CustomerGender DESC, CustomerFirstName ASC, CustomerLastName ASC;

SQL Result

CustomerGender	CustomerFirstName	CustomerLastName	CustomerEmail
Male	Adam	Green	AdamGreen@SaleOnYourOwn.com
Male	Adam	Wilson	AdamWilson@SaleOnYourOwn.com
Male	Akidul	Islam	AkidulIslam@SaleOnYourOwn.com
Male	Allen	Hall	AllenHall@SaleOnYourOwn.com
Male	Baldev	Singh	BaldevSingh@SaleOnYourOwn.com
Male	King	Smith	KingSmith@SaleOnYourOwn.com
Male	Louis	Hugo	LouisHugo@SaleOnYourOwn.com
Male	Michael	Jackson	MichaelJackson@SaleOnYourOwn.com
Male	Richard	Martin	RichardMartin@SaleOnYourOwn.com
Male	Rick	Strand	RickStrand@SaleOnYourOwn.com
Male	Ricky	Brown	RickBrown@SaleOnYourOwn.com
Male	Ricky	Ponting	RickyPonting@SaleOnYourOwn.com
Male	Robert	Smith	RobertSmith@SaleOnYourOwn.com
Male	Robinson	Clark	RobinsonClark@SaleOnYourOwn.com
Male	Ronald	White	RonaldWhite@SaleOnYourOwn.com
Male	Scott	Baker	ScottBaker@SaleOnYourOwn.com
Female	Adele	Renton	AdeleRenton@SaleOnYourOwn.com
Female	Ashley	Hawker	AshleyHawker@SaleOnYourOwn.com
Female	Bonnie	Horne	BonnieHorne@SaleOnYourOwn.com
Female	Caroline	Tran	CarolineTran@SaleOnYourOwn.com
Female	Chelsea	Hillman	ChelseaHillman@SaleOnYourOwn.com
Female	Crystal	Doslakoski	CrystalDoslakoski@SaleOnYourOwn.com
Female	Donna	Moore	DonnaMoore@SaleOnYourOwn.com
Female	Elle	Moloney	ElleMoloney@SaleOnYourOwn.com
Female	Emily	Maddicks	EmilyMaddicks@SaleOnYourOwn.com
Female	Emma	Stephens	EmmaStephens@SaleOnYourOwn.com
Female	Lauren	McIntosh	LaurenMcIntosh@SaleOnYourOwn.com
Female	Melanie	Bowell	KerrynWhite@SaleOnYourOwn.com
Female	Millie	Moloney	MillieMoloney@SaleOnYourOwn.com
Female	Rowena	Price	RowenaPrice@SaleOnYourOwn.com
Female	Sarah	Holian	SarahHolian@SaleOnYourOwn.com
Female	Sophie	Smith	SophieSmith@SaleOnYourOwn.com

Solution Review

When you use multiple columns with the *ORDER BY* clause (i.e. columns used after the *ORDER BY* keywords), the resulting rows will be sorted by the first column of the *ORDER BY* clause. If the first column has duplicate values, the rows with these duplicate values will be sorted by the second column of the *ORDER BY* clause. If the second column still has duplicate values, the rows with these duplicate values will be sorted by the third column of the *ORDER BY* clause, and so on. As per the above *ORDER BY* clause, the resulting rows should first order by the *CustomerGender* column in descending order, then the *CustomerFirstName* column in ascending order and then finally by the *CustomerLastName* column in ascending order.

To understand how a database engine does the sorting, compare the sorted data in the table above with the unsorted data in the table below:

RowNo	CustomerGender	CustomerFirstName	CustomerLastName	CustomerEmail
1	Male	Ricky	Brown	RickBrown@SaleOnYourOwn.com
2	Male	Adam	Wilson	AdamWilson@SaleOnYourOwn.com
3	Female	Crystal	Doslakoski	CrystalDoslakoski@SaleOnYourOwn.com
4	Female	Melanie	Bowell	KerrynWhite@SaleOnYourOwn.com
5	Female	Sophie	Smith	SophieSmith@SaleOnYourOwn.com
6	Male	Robert	Smith	RobertSmith@SaleOnYourOwn.com
7	Male	Michael	Jackson	MichaelJackson@SaleOnYourOwn.com
8	Male	Ronald	White	RonaldWhite@SaleOnYourOwn.com
9	Female	Adele	Renton	AdeleRenton@SaleOnYourOwn.com
10	Female	Emma	Stephens	EmmaStephens@SaleOnYourOwn.com
11	Female	Donna	Moore	DonnaMoore@SaleOnYourOwn.com
12	Female	Emily	Maddicks	EmilyMaddicks@SaleOnYourOwn.com
13	Female	Chelsea	Hillman	ChelseaHillman@SaleOnYourOwn.com
14	Female	Ashley	Hawker	AshleyHawker@SaleOnYourOwn.com
15	Male	Richard	Martin	RichardMartin@SaleOnYourOwn.com
16	Male	Robinson	Clark	RobinsonClark@SaleOnYourOwn.com
17	Female	Lauren	McIntosh	LaurenMcIntosh@SaleOnYourOwn.com
18	Male	Allen	Hall	AllenHall@SaleOnYourOwn.com
19	Male	King	Smith	KingSmith@SaleOnYourOwn.com
20	Male	Adam	Green	AdamGreen@SaleOnYourOwn.com
21	Male	Scott	Baker	ScottBaker@SaleOnYourOwn.com
22	Male	Ricky	Ponting	RickyPonting@SaleOnYourOwn.com
23	Male	Rick	Strand	RickStrand@SaleOnYourOwn.com
24	Female	Sarah	Holian	SarahHolian@SaleOnYourOwn.com
25	Female	Bonnie	Horne	BonnieHorne@SaleOnYourOwn.com
26	Female	Elle	Moloney	ElleMoloney@SaleOnYourOwn.com
27	Female	Millie	Moloney	MillieMoloney@SaleOnYourOwn.com
28	Female	Rowena	Price	RowenaPrice@SaleOnYourOwn.com
29	Male	Louis	Hugo	LouisHugo@SaleOnYourOwn.com
30	Male	Baldev	Singh	BaldevSingh@SaleOnYourOwn.com
31	Male	Akidul	Islam	AkidulIslam@SaleOnYourOwn.com
32	Female	Caroline	Tran	CarolineTran@SaleOnYourOwn.com

Notice that we have 16 male and 16 female customers. We have three columns in the *ORDER BY* clause. So, the database engine will follow the three steps below:

CustomerGender DESC: We will always have either a female or male value in the *CustomerGender* column. In descending order, 'M' should come before 'F', i.e. the males should come before the females. So, the database engine places 16 male customers in rows 1-15, then 16 female customers in rows 17-32, and the output will look like so:

RowNo	CustomerGender	CustomerFirstName	CustomerLastName	CustomerEmail
1	Male	Robert	Smith	RobertSmith@SaleOnYourOwn.com
2	Male	Michael	Jackson	MichaelJackson@SaleOnYourOwn.com
3	Male	Ronald	White	RonaldWhite@SaleOnYourOwn.com
4	Male	Allen	Hall	AllenHall@SaleOnYourOwn.com
5	Male	King	Smith	KingSmith@SaleOnYourOwn.com
6	Male	Adam	Green	AdamGreen@SaleOnYourOwn.com
7	Male	Scott	Baker	ScottBaker@SaleOnYourOwn.com
8	Male	Ricky	Ponting	RickyPonting@SaleOnYourOwn.com
9	Male	Rick	Strand	RickStrand@SaleOnYourOwn.com
10	Male	Ricky	Brown	RickBrown@SaleOnYourOwn.com
11	Male	Adam	Wilson	AdamWilson@SaleOnYourOwn.com
12	Male	Louis	Hugo	LouisHugo@SaleOnYourOwn.com
13	Male	Baldev	Singh	BaldevSingh@SaleOnYourOwn.com
14	Male	Akidul	Islam	AkidulIslam@SaleOnYourOwn.com
15	Male	Richard	Martin	RichardMartin@SaleOnYourOwn.com
16	Male	Robinson	Clark	RobinsonClark@SaleOnYourOwn.com
17	Female	Lauren	McIntosh	LaurenMcIntosh@SaleOnYourOwn.com
18	Female	Caroline	Tran	CarolineTran@SaleOnYourOwn.com
19	Female	Crystal	Doslakoski	CrystalDoslakoski@SaleOnYourOwn.com
20	Female	Melanie	Bowell	KerrynWhite@SaleOnYourOwn.com
21	Female	Sophie	Smith	SophieSmith@SaleOnYourOwn.com
22	Female	Sarah	Holian	SarahHolian@SaleOnYourOwn.com
23	Female	Bonnie	Horne	BonnieHorne@SaleOnYourOwn.com
24	Female	Elle	Moloney	ElleMoloney@SaleOnYourOwn.com
25	Female	Millie	Moloney	MillieMoloney@SaleOnYourOwn.com
26	Female	Rowena	Price	RowenaPrice@SaleOnYourOwn.com
27	Female	Adele	Renton	AdeleRenton@SaleOnYourOwn.com
28	Female	Emma	Stephens	EmmaStephens@SaleOnYourOwn.com
29	Female	Donna	Moore	DonnaMoore@SaleOnYourOwn.com
30	Female	Emily	Maddicks	EmilyMaddicks@SaleOnYourOwn.com
31	Female	Chelsea	Hillman	ChelseaHillman@SaleOnYourOwn.com
32	Female	Ashley	Hawker	AshleyHawker@SaleOnYourOwn.com

CustomerFirstName ASC: Next, the database engine will sort the first16 rows (i.e. for male customers) in ascending order based on the value of the *CustomerFirstName* column, then sort the second 16 rows (i.e. for female customers). In other words, it will sort them alphabetically by first name after it has sorted them by gender. The output will look like below:

RowNo	CustomerGender	CustomerFirstName	CustomerLastName	CustomerEmail
1	Male	Adam	Wilson	AdamWilson@SaleOnYourOwn.com
2	Male	Adam	Green	AdamGreen@SaleOnYourOwn.com
3	Male	Akidul	Islam	AkidulIslam@SaleOnYourOwn.com
4	Male	Allen	Hall	AllenHall@SaleOnYourOwn.com
5	Male	Baldev	Singh	BaldevSingh@SaleOnYourOwn.com
6	Male	King	Smith	KingSmith@SaleOnYourOwn.com
7	Male	Louis	Hugo	LouisHugo@SaleOnYourOwn.com
8	Male	Michael	Jackson	MichaelJackson@SaleOnYourOwn.com
9	Male	Richard	Martin	RichardMartin@SaleOnYourOwn.com
10	Male	Rick	Strand	RickStrand@SaleOnYourOwn.com
11	Male	Ricky	Ponting	RickyPonting@SaleOnYourOwn.com
12	Male	Ricky	Brown	RickBrown@SaleOnYourOwn.com
13	Male	Robert	Smith	RobertSmith@SaleOnYourOwn.com
14	Male	Robinson	Clark	RobinsonClark@SaleOnYourOwn.com
15	Male	Ronald	White	RonaldWhite@SaleOnYourOwn.com
16	Male	Scott	Baker	ScottBaker@SaleOnYourOwn.com
17	Female	Adele	Renton	AdeleRenton@SaleOnYourOwn.com
18	Female	Ashley	Hawker	AshleyHawker@SaleOnYourOwn.com
19	Female	Bonnie	Horne	BonnieHorne@SaleOnYourOwn.com
20	Female	Caroline	Tran	CarolineTran@SaleOnYourOwn.com
21	Female	Chelsea	Hillman	ChelseaHillman@SaleOnYourOwn.com
22	Female	Crystal	Doslakoski	CrystalDoslakoski@SaleOnYourOwn.com
23	Female	Donna	Moore	DonnaMoore@SaleOnYourOwn.com
24	Female	Elle	Moloney	ElleMoloney@SaleOnYourOwn.com
25	Female	Emily	Maddicks	EmilyMaddicks@SaleOnYourOwn.com
26	Female	Emma	Stephens	EmmaStephens@SaleOnYourOwn.com
27	Female	Lauren	McIntosh	LaurenMcIntosh@SaleOnYourOwn.com
28	Female	Melanie	Bowell	KerrynWhite@SaleOnYourOwn.com
29	Female	Millie	Moloney	MillieMoloney@SaleOnYourOwn.com
30	Female	Rowena	Price	RowenaPrice@SaleOnYourOwn.com
31	Female	Sarah	Holian	SarahHolian@SaleOnYourOwn.com
32	Female	Sophie	Smith	SophieSmith@SaleOnYourOwn.com

CustomerLastName ASC: As you can see above, rows 1 & 2 have same first name as each other (*Adam*), and rows 11 & 12 have same first name as each other as well (*Ricky*). Telling the database to sort by *CustomerLastName ASC* ensures that these customers with duplicate first names will be ordered properly. The final output will appear as shown below (which is same as the SQL results mentioned above):

RowNo	CustomerGender	CustomerFirstName	CustomerLastName	CustomerEmail
1	Male	Adam	Green	AdamGreen@SaleOnYourOwn.com
2	Male	Adam	Wilson	AdamWilson@SaleOnYourOwn.com
3	Male	Akidul	Islam	AkidulIslam@SaleOnYourOwn.com
4	Male	Allen	Hall	AllenHall@SaleOnYourOwn.com
5	Male	Baldev	Singh	BaldevSingh@SaleOnYourOwn.com
6	Male	King	Smith	KingSmith@SaleOnYourOwn.com
7	Male	Louis	Hugo	LouisHugo@SaleOnYourOwn.com
8	Male	Michael	Jackson	MichaelJackson@SaleOnYourOwn.com
9	Male	Richard	Martin	RichardMartin@SaleOnYourOwn.com
10	Male	Rick	Strand	RickStrand@SaleOnYourOwn.com
11	Male	Ricky	Brown	RickBrown@SaleOnYourOwn.com
12	Male	Ricky	Ponting	RickyPonting@SaleOnYourOwn.com
13	Male	Robert	Smith	RobertSmith@SaleOnYourOwn.com
14	Male	Robinson	Clark	RobinsonClark@SaleOnYourOwn.com
15	Male	Ronald	White	RonaldWhite@SaleOnYourOwn.com
16	Male	Scott	Baker	ScottBaker@SaleOnYourOwn.com
17	Female	Adele	Renton	AdeleRenton@SaleOnYourOwn.com
18	Female	Ashley	Hawker	AshleyHawker@SaleOnYourOwn.com
19	Female	Bonnie	Horne	BonnieHorne@SaleOnYourOwn.com
20	Female	Caroline	Tran	CarolineTran@SaleOnYourOwn.com
21	Female	Chelsea	Hillman	ChelseaHillman@SaleOnYourOwn.com
22	Female	Crystal	Doslakoski	CrystalDoslakoski@SaleOnYourOwn.com
23	Female	Donna	Moore	DonnaMoore@SaleOnYourOwn.com
24	Female	Elle	Moloney	ElleMoloney@SaleOnYourOwn.com
25	Female	Emily	Maddicks	EmilyMaddicks@SaleOnYourOwn.com
26	Female	Emma	Stephens	EmmaStephens@SaleOnYourOwn.com
27	Female	Lauren	McIntosh	LaurenMcIntosh@SaleOnYourOwn.com
28	Female	Melanie	Bowell	KerrynWhite@SaleOnYourOwn.com
29	Female	Millie	Moloney	MillieMoloney@SaleOnYourOwn.com
30	Female	Rowena	Price	RowenaPrice@SaleOnYourOwn.com
31	Female	Sarah	Holian	SarahHolian@SaleOnYourOwn.com
32	Female	Sophie	Smith	SophieSmith@SaleOnYourOwn.com

Notes

You can sort your result by column(s) that are not present in the result, meaning that the sorted column doesn't need to present in the *SELECT* list. This is handy if you want to use data for sorting purposes but not actually show that data in the result. For example, if you wanted exclude the *CustomerGender* column from our table example above, you would use the following SQL code:

```
SELECT CustomerFirstName, CustomerLastName, CustomerEmail
FROM Customers
ORDER BY CustomerGender DESC, CustomerFirstName ASC, CustomerLastName ASC;
```

Notice that the *CustomerGender* is being used in the *ORDER BY* clause but not in the *SELECT* clause.

Ordering Results by Column Position

If you want to sort multiple column results in ascending or descending order with the position of the column in the *SELECT* clause, you should use the *SELECT* statement like you see below:

```
SELECT  column name1, column name2, column name3, ......
FROM   table name
ORDER BY 1 ASC/DESC, 2 ASC/DESC, ....;
```

Let's explore this topic by solving some business problems.

Business Problem 6

As with *Business Problem 4* please give me a list of all present and past vendors including IDs, names, phone numbers and email addresses. However, this time use the column position in the *ORDER BY* clause and show the results in ascending order by vendor's name.

Solution SQL

```
SELECT VendorID, VendorName, VendorPhoneNumber, VendorEmail
FROM Vendors
ORDER BY 2;
```

SQL Result

VendorID	VendorName	VendorPhoneNumber	VendorEmail
7	A & B Traders Ltd	+1 (704) 231-4370	abTraders@SaleOnYourOwn.com
9	ABCDE Suppliers Ltd	+88 02 11111111	abcdeSupply@SaleOnYourOwn.com
2	Asia Pacific Suppliers Ltd	+61 000 999999	acpacSupply@SaleOnYourOwn.com
10	EFGHI Suppliers Ltd	+91 000 999999	efghiSupply@SaleOnYourOwn.com
4	JKLMN Suppliers Ltd	+1 (312) 000-000000	ghijkSupply@SaleOnYourOwn.com
1	P & Q Traders Ltd	+61 430 492550	pqTraders@SaleOnYourOwn.com
6	PQRST Suppliers Ltd	+1 (312) 999-99999	pqrstSupply@SaleOnYourOwn.com
11	Rahman Suppliers Ltd	+88 02 33333333333	rahmanSupply@SaleOnYourOwn.com
8	Things for Future Generations Ltd	+86 10 123456789	FutureGen@SaleOnYourOwn.com
3	UVWXYZ Suppliers Ltd	+44 7123 123456	uvwzyzSupply@SaleOnYourOwn.com
5	Vision 2020 Electronics Ltd	+1 (312) 806-9033	vision2010electronics@SaleOnYourOwn.com

Solution Review

In the table shown above, notice that the result is exactly same as in *Business Problem 4*. The positions of the columns in the above *SELECT* statement are as below:

So, the *ORDER BY 2* is the same as *ORDER BY VendorName*, because the position of *VendorName* is 2. Though you can get the same result by using column position or column name, you should always use column name instead of simply using its position in the *ORDER BY* clause in order to avoid a misleading result. For example, assume that you created a report to show the Vendor ID, Name, Phone & Email sorted by the respective vendor's name, and you are using the above SQL statement for the report. A few months later, the user of the report wants you to add a new column, *VendorCategoryID*, to the left of the *VendorID* column but also wants to keep the sorting order the same. To satisfy the user's requirement you have added the *VendorCategoryID* column to the left of the *VendorID* column, but you forgot to change the *ORDER BY* clause. The report will show the output in ascending order by the *VendorID* column instead of the *VendorName* column because the column position of *VendorName* has changed to '*3*'. Therefore, it's better to use the name rather than the numerical position, since the numerical position may change as your business changes.

Business Problem 7

As with *Business Problem 5*, please show the customer list with genders, first names, last names, phone numbers and email addresses, but this time use the column position in the *ORDER BY* clause.

Please show the results in descending order by gender, then in ascending order by first name, and then finally in ascending order by last name.

Solution SQL

```
SELECT CustomerGender, CustomerFirstName, CustomerLastName, CustomerEmail
FROM Customers
ORDER BY 1 DESC, 2 ASC, 3 ASC;
```

SQL Result

You should receive the same result as you did in *Business Problem 5*.

Retrieving All Columns

You can retrieve all of the columns from a table either by specifying all the columns in the *SELECT* clause or by using the wildcard character asterisk (*) as shown below:

```
SELECT *
FROM table name;
```

If you use wildcard (*), the order of the columns in the result set will usually be in the physical order of the underlying table's column. Business Problem 8 shows you how this would look in a real-world example.

Business Problem 8

Please give me all the details of our present and past vendors.

Solution SQL

```
SELECT * FROM Vendors;
```

SQL Result

VendorID	VendorName	VendorAddressID	VendorPhoneNumber	VendorFaxNumber	VendorEmail	VendorCategoryID	ContactPersonName	RelationshipManagerID	IsActive
1	P & Q Traders Ltd	4	+61 430 492550	+61 430 492550	pqTraders@SaleOnYourOwn.com	1	Rosie Jenkins	2	1
2	Asia Pacific Suppliers Ltd	7	+61 000 999999	+61 000 999999	acpacSupply@SaleOnYourOwn.cor	3	Melanie Bowell	2	1
3	UVWXYZ Suppliers Ltd	33	+44 7123 123456	+44 7123 123456	uvwzyzSupply@SaleOnYourOwn.co	1	Ben Cook	2	1
4	JKLMN Suppliers Ltd	10	+1 (312) 000-000000	+1 (312) 000-000000	ghijkSupply@SaleOnYourOwn.com	3	Emily Millar	3	1
5	Vision 2020 Electronics Ltd	14	+1 (312) 806-9033	+1 (312) 806-9033	vision2010electronics@SaleOnYou	2	Brooke Camden	3	1
6	PQRST Suppliers Ltd	22	+1 (312) 999-99999	+1 (312) 999-99999	pqrstSupply@SaleOnYourOwn.com	1	Tom Robert	3	1
7	A & B Traders Ltd	26	+1 (704) 231-4370	+1 (704) 231-4370	abTraders@SaleOnYourOwn.com	1	Elizabeth Kilduff	3	1
8	Things for Future Generations Ltd	36	+86 10 123456789	+86 10 123456789	FutureGen@SaleOnYourOwn.com	1	Melissa Hutch	4	1
9	ABCDE Suppliers Ltd	38	+88 02 11111111	+88 193 111111111	abcdeSupply@SaleOnYourOwn.cor	1	Sadman Rahman	4	1
10	EFGHI Suppliers Ltd	37	+91 000 999999	+91 000 9999999	efghiSupply@SaleOnYourOwn.com	2	Sabitri Chatterjee	4	1
11	Rahman Suppliers Ltd	38	+88 02 33333333333	+88 193 3333333333!	rahmanSupply@SaleOnYourOwn.c	2	Somjit Datta	4	0

Solution Review

As you can see, all rows and all columns from the Vendors table have been displayed in the result. Of course, you can get the same result by specifying all columns in the *SELECT* clause like you see below:

```
SELECT VendorID, VendorName, VendorAddressID, VendorPhoneNumber, VendorFaxNumber, VendorEmail,
    VendorCategoryID, ContactPersonName, RelationshipManagerID, IsActive
FROM Vendors;
```

The wildcard (*) is the quickest way to retrieve all columns. It is typically used for testing purposes. In a real production application, it is recommended that you use all of the column names instead of wildcard (*) just to be safe—if you use '*' and the underlying table schema changes, the application will break.

Retrieving a Simple Calculated Column

Often times, retrieving simple columns may not be enough. Perhaps you have an order quantity and unit price but want to show the order total. You need to create a calculated column to do this, which is essentially a multiplication equation of the order quantity and the unit price. Try solving *Business Problem 9* to see what we mean.

Business Problem 9

What is the minimum commission we can get from a vendor from each category if they meet their monthly sales target?

Solution SQL

```
SELECT   VendorCategoryID AS CategoryID, VendorCategoryName AS CategoryName,
        VendorMonthlyTarget AS SalesTarget, VendorCommissionRatePercentage AS CommissionRate,
        VendorMonthlyTarget * VendorCommissionRatePercentage/100 AS MinimumCommission
FROM VendorCategories;
```

SQL Result

CategoryID	CategoryName	SalesTarget	CommissionRate	MinimumCommission
1	Regular	30000.0000	20.00	6000.0000000000
2	Gold	50000.0000	15.00	7500.0000000000
3	Diamond	80000.0000	10.00	8000.0000000000

Solution Review

The *VendorCategories* table has *VendorMonthlyTarget* and *VendorCommissionRatePercentage* columns. Therefore, the minimum commission amount for a vendor who meets the monthly target can be calculated using the formula below:

$$Minimum\ Commission\ Amount = VendorMonthlyTarget \times \frac{VendorCommissionRatePercentage}{100}$$

In this example, we have used the *AS* keyword to provide each column a different column name (i.e. a column alias).

Retrieving a Complex Calculated Column

Sometimes you need to use conditional logic to show a calculated column. Assume that all the products at your company have a unit price, but some of them are offered at a fixed discount, others are discounted based on a percentage of the unit price, and the rest, of course, are offered at regular price. To calculate the discount amount column, you need to use conditional logic. In our example, the unit amount will be calculated based on one of three conditions:

1. Percentage of unit price
2. Fixed discount amount
3. $0 (no discount)

Almost all RDBMSs support the *CASE* expression which allows you to evaluate one or more conditions and return multiple results. These results can be literals, columns or value expressions (numeric/date/string), but the conditions will be either Boolean literals (true/false) or Boolean expressions. This Boolean expression often called as a predicate which can be evaluated to *TRUE*, *FALSE*, or *UNKNOWN*.

The basic syntax of the *CASE* expression is:

```
CASE WHEN predicate1 THEN literal1/column1/value expression1
     WHEN predicate1 THEN literal1/column1/value expression1

     ELSE literal1/column1/value expression1
END
```

It is essential to understand how database engines evaluate predicates. To give you enough confidence to use predicates, we are going to run through details next. The basic syntax of a simple predicate is:

```
column/literal/expression COMPARISON OPERATOR column/literal/expression
```

Both sides of the comparison operator must have compatible data types. The most frequently used simple predicates often compare a column with a literal. An example of this might be *CustomerGender = 'Male'*, where for each male customer the predicate evaluates to *TRUE*, and for each female or another type of customer the predicate evaluates to *FALSE*, and each customer whose gender is unknown the predicate evaluates to *UNKNOWN*. As you can see, this is an example of a boolean expression because a true or false or unknown result is possible. RDBMSs represent *UNKNOWN* as *NULL*.

Note: for the remainder of this book we will use *NULL* and *UNKNOWN* interchangeably.

The below table shows the commonly used comparison operators for a predicate:

Operator	Description	Examples
=	Equal to	Numeric: 2 = 2 evaluates to TRUE, 4 = 5 evaluates to FALSE
		Date: '2016-12-06' = '2016-12-06' evaluates to TRUE, '2016-12-06' = '2015-01-01' evaluates to FALSE
		String: 'Male' = 'Male' evaluates to TRUE, 'Male' = 'Female' evaluates to FALSE
<>	Not equal to	Numeric: 2 <> 2 evaluates to FALSE, 4 <> 5 evaluates to TRUE
		Date: '2016-12-06' <> '2016-12-06' evaluates to FALSE, '2016-12-06' <> '2015-01-01' evaluates to TRUE
		String: 'Male' <> 'Male' evaluates to FALSE, 'Male' <> 'Female' evaluates to TRUE
<	Less than	Numeric: 2 < 2 evaluates to FALSE, 4 < 5 evaluates to TRUE
		Date: '2016-12-06' < '2016-12-07' evaluates to TRUE, '2016-12-06' < '2015-01-01' evaluates to FALSE
		String: 'Male' < 'Male' evaluates to FALSE, 'Female' < 'Male' evaluates to TRUE
<=	Less than or equal to	Numeric: 2 <= 2 evaluates to TRUE, 4 <= 5 evaluates to TRUE, 7 <= 5 evaluates to FALSE
		Date: '2016-12-06' <= '2016-12-07' evaluates to TRUE, '2016-12-06' <= '2016-12-06' evaluates to TRUE , '2016-12-06' <= '2015-01-01' evaluates to FALSE
		String: 'Male' <= 'Male' evaluates to TRUE, 'Female' <= 'Male' evaluates to TRUE, 'Male' <= 'Female' evaluates to FALSE
>	Greater than	Numeric: 3 > 2 evaluates to TRUE, 4 > 5 evaluates to FALSE
		Date: '2016-12-06' > '2016-12-07' evaluates to FALSE, '2016-12-06' > '2015-01-01' evaluates to TRUE
		String: 'Male' > 'Female' evaluates to TRUE, 'Female' > 'Male' evaluates to FALSE
>=	Greater than or equal to	Numeric: 2 >= 2 evaluates to TRUE, 4 >= 5 evaluates to FALSE, 7 >= 5 evaluates to TRUE
		Date: '2016-12-06' >= '2016-12-07' evaluates to FALSE, '2016-12-06' >= '2016-12-06' evaluates to TRUE , '2016-12-06' >= '2015-01-01' evaluates to TRUE
		String: 'Male' >= 'Male' evaluates to TRUE, 'Female' >= 'Male' evaluates to FALSE, 'Male' >= 'Female' evaluates to TRUE

Predicates using numeric or date-valued expressions, literals or columns behave consistently—no matter the RDBMS's collation settings—but the behaviour of a predicate using string-valued expressions, literals or columns typically depends on the database's collation settings, as we're about to demonstrate. Most RDBMSs use an ASCII collating sequence. The case-sensitive ASCII collating sequence organizes characters from lowest value to highest value:

.........0123456789ABCDEFGHIJKLMNOPQRSTUVWXYZabcdefghijklmnopqrstuvwxyz..........

Meanwhile, the case-*insensitive* ASCII collating sequence organizes characters from lowest value to highest value:

..........01234356789{Aa}{Bb}{Cc}{Dd}{Ee}{Ff}{Gg}{Hh}{Ii}{Jj}{Kk}{Ll}{Mm}{Nn}{Oo}{Pp}{Qq}{Rr}{Ss}{Tt}{Uu}{Vv}{Ww}{Xx}{Yy}{Zz}.........

For the case-insensitive collation, the predicate *'Male' = 'male'* evaluates to *TRUE*, but for the case-sensitive collation, the same predicate evaluates to *FALSE* because it considers *'M'* and *'m'* as different characters. If a predicate uses strings with different lengths, the database engine adds a default padding character (typically a white space) to the right of the smaller string until it becomes the same length as the larger string, and then it does the comparison. In addition to the comparison operators *(=, <>, >, <, >=, <=)*, *BETWEEN, IN, LIKE* and *IS NULL* are the most commonly used operators in predicates.

The BETWEEN Operator for Predicates

The *BETWEEN* operator lets you check if a given value belongs to a specified range of values. The syntax of the *BETWEEN* operator used in a predicate is:

value to check BETWEEN minimum range value AND maximum range value

The range values, minimum and maximum, are both inclusive. Here are a few examples:

Predicate **200 BETWEEN 100 AND 400:** 200 is greater than 100 but less than 400. Therefore, it evaluates to *TRUE*

Predicate **95 BETWEEN 100 AND 400:** 95 is less than both 100 and 400. Therefore, it evaluates to *FALSE*

Predicate **405 BETWEEN 100 AND 400:** 405 is greater than both 100 and 400. Therefore, it evaluates to *FALSE*

The IN Operator for Predicates

The *IN* operator lets you check if a given value is a member of a specified list of values. The syntax of the *IN* operator used in a predicate is:

value to check IN (value1, value2, value3, ...)

Here are few examples:

Predicate **20 IN (10, 15, 8, 22, 20, 28, 30):** 20 is a member of the list. Therefore, it evaluates to *TRUE*

Predicate **14 IN (10, 15, 8, 22, 20, 28, 30):** 14 is not a member of the list. Therefore, it evaluates to *FALSE*

The LIKE Operator for Predicates

If you know an exact value and you want to match it with a column, a value expression, in a list or within a range of values, you now know how to do that. But what if you know only a part of a value and you want to find a list of values that match the pattern of that partial value? That's where the *LIKE* predicate becomes useful. The pattern can include regular characters and wildcard characters. The syntax of the *LIKE* operator used in a predicate will be one of the following:

character expression to match LIKE pattern
character expression to match LIKE pattern ESCAPE characters to escape

Some examples of wildcard characters you can use are '%', '_', and '[]'. Let's take a brief look at how each of them can be used:

The Percentage sign (%) wildcard

Within a pattern string, a percentage sign *(%)* wildcard character represents either zero, one or more arbitrary characters. If you use the percentage sign within a pattern string of a predicate, the database engine matches any number of any characters in the position of the percentage sign. Here are a few examples of the percentage sign:

1. Predicate **'Super' LIKE 'Super%':** If you remove the %, the values of both sides of the *LIKE* operator will become the same. Therefore, it evaluates to *TRUE*.

2. Predicate **'Superman' LIKE 'Super%':** If you replace the % with *man*, the values of both sides of the *LIKE* operator will become the same. Therefore, it evaluates to *TRUE*.

3. Predicate **'Superman action figure' LIKE 'Super%':** If you replace the % with *man action figure*, the values of both sides of the *LIKE* operator will become the same. Therefore, it evaluates to *TRUE*.

4. Predicate **'Spiderman' LIKE 'Super%':** If you replace the % with any character string, the values of both sides of the *LIKE* operator will never become the same. Therefore, it evaluates to *FALSE*.

The Underscore (_) wildcard

Within a pattern string, an underscore *(_)* wildcard character represents exactly one arbitrary character. If you use an underscore within a pattern string of a predicate, the database engine matches exactly one of any character in the position of the underscore. Here are a few examples of the underscore in action:

1. Predicate **'Michel' LIKE 'M_chel':** If you replace _ with *i*, the values of both sides of the *LIKE* operator will become same. Therefore, it evaluates to *TRUE*

2. Predicate **'Mechel' LIKE 'M_chel':** If you replace _ with *e*, the values of both sides of the *LIKE* operator will become same. Therefore, it evaluates to *TRUE*

3. Predicate **'Fisher' LIKE 'M_chel':** If you replace _ with any character, the values of both sides of the *LIKE* operator will never become same. Therefore, it evaluates to *FALSE*

Brackets ([]) wildcard

Within a pattern string, the brackets ([]) wildcard character represents a character from a set of characters specified within the brackets. If you use brackets within the pattern string of a predicate, the database engine matches exactly one of any character from a set of characters specified within the brackets in the position of brackets. Here are a few examples of brackets in use:

1. Predicate **'Michel' LIKE 'M[ia]chel':** If you replace *[ia]* with *i*, the values of both sides of the *LIKE* operator will become same. Therefore, it evaluates to *TRUE*

2. Predicate **'Mechel' LIKE 'M[ia]chel':** If you replace *[ia]* with either *'i'* or *'a'*, the values of both sides of the *LIKE* operator will not be same. Therefore, it evaluates to *FALSE*

Please note that not all RDBMSs support brackets wildcard. Please check your RDBMS before using it.

The IS NULL Operator for Predicates

Before we explain the *IS NULL* operator, we need to explain to you what the *NULL* value is and why we are using it. The *NULL* value in a database column means a missing or unknown value. It is not the same as an empty string or zero.

Let's assume that your e-commerce website has a customer registration page that has an optional mobile number field. Regardless of whether a customer provides his/her mobile number or skips the field, the database needs to store an input. When the customer provides a phone number, this data is stored into the mobile number column of a database table; if no number is provided, the column can either store a default value (e.g. an empty string '', blank space ' ', or 'NA') or a NULL value.

One thing to consider is, if you decide to store a NULL value for customers who do not have a mobile number, you will not be able to differentiate between those customers who do not have a mobile number and those who simply haven't provided one. So, your decision to implement NULL or not depends on your specific business needs.

With the knowledge you have gained so far, you can filter out a customer's details based on their phone number if the phone number column is stored as a value (meaning a full or partial phone number, an empty string, a blank space, or NA).However, you can't use the previous predicates to retrieve the details of customers whose mobile numbers are missing (i.e. NULL). You need to use IS NULL here. The basic syntax is:

```
column/expression IS NULL
```

If the *column or expression*'s value is missing (i.e. NULL), the predicate evaluates to *TRUE*; otherwise, it evaluates to *FALSE*.

As per the above discussion, you should have a very good understanding about the predicate, how different types of operators can be used in a predicate, and how the predicate can be used in a *CASE* expression to create a complex calculated column. If not, don't worry. You'll have plenty of opportunities to practice soon. Next, we will show you a *comparison operator (<>)* being used within a *CASE* expression to create a calculated column, but we'll save all other operator examples for later lessons when we explore the *WHERE* clause in greater detail.

For now, let's dive into solving a business problem:

Business Problem 10

Please give me a product list that includes the IDs, names, standard unit prices, unit discounts and net unit prices of each product.

Solution SQL

```
SELECT ProductID, ProductName, StandardSalesPrice AS StandardUnitPrice,
      CASE WHEN SalesDiscountPercentage <> 0 THEN StandardSalesPrice * SalesDiscountPercentage/100
          ELSE SalesDiscountAmount
      END AS UnitDiscount,
      StandardSalesPrice -
          (CASE WHEN SalesDiscountPercentage <> 0 THEN StandardSalesPrice * SalesDiscountPercentage/100
              ELSE SalesDiscountAmount
          END) AS NetUnitPrice
FROM Products;
```

SQL Result

ProductID	ProductName	StandardUnitPrice	UnitDiscount	NetUnitPrice
1	Ironman 3 Figures	310.0000	20.0000000000	290.0000000000
2	Magnetic Drawing Board	100.0000	20.0000000000	80.0000000000
3	Kids Batman Cape and Mask Dress Up Set	20.0000	0.0000000000	20.0000000000
4	My First Cash Register	60.0000	0.0000000000	60.0000000000
5	Vehicles Peg Puzzle	20.0000	0.0000000000	20.0000000000
6	Superman 3 Figures	320.0000	20.0000000000	300.0000000000
7	Build Your Own Aquarium	1000.0000	100.0000000000	900.0000000000
8	Giant Coloring Pages Disney Princess	30.0000	3.0000000000	27.0000000000
9	Kids Spiderman Cape and Mask Dress Up Set	20.0000	0.0000000000	20.0000000000
10	Electronic Toy Microwave	100.0000	0.0000000000	100.0000000000

Solution Review

The SQL solution above will display 66 rows, but to save space, we have shown only the first 10 rows. Notice that the *CASE* expression has been used to calculate the *UnitDiscount* column:

```
CASE WHEN SalesDiscountPercentage <> 0 THEN StandardSalesPrice * SalesDiscountPercentage/100
    ELSE SalesDiscountAmount
END AS UnitDiscount
```

This *CASE* expression will be executed for each rows of the *Products* table. The not equal to (<>) operator has been used in the predicate *SalesDiscountPercentage <> 0*. This predicate will evaluate to *TRUE* if the corresponding product is discounted based on the *percentage of unit price*, then the *UnitDiscount* will be calculated by the expression, *StandardSalesPrice * SalesDiscountPercentage/100*, otherwise *UnitDiscount* will return the value directly from *SalesDiscountAmount* column.

Meanwhile, the *NetUnitPrice* has been calculated by subtracting *UnitDiscount* from the *StandardSalesPrice*, which is:

```
StandardSalesPrice – UnitDiscount AS NetUnitPrice
```

i.e.

```
StandardSalesPrice -
    (CASE WHEN SalesDiscountPercentage <> 0 THEN StandardSalesPrice * SalesDiscountPercentage/100
        ELSE SalesDiscountAmount
    END) AS NetUnitPrice
```

Practice Business Problems

Here are some more practice business problems for you to solve for the topics we've covered in this lesson. As always, the solutions to this lesson's practice problems can be found in *Appendix A*. We have also provided them for you at the following Google Drive link:

https://drive.google.com/open?id=1KGYZ2G2q7vtKFg9e3R3eAWjrD6O3f1B1

Practice Business Problem 1

Please give me the names of all active and inactive product subcategories.

Practice Business Problem 2

Please give me the names of all active and inactive product subcategories in ascending order.

Practice Business Problem 3

What categories of vendors do we have? For each vendor, give me the category names with their monthly sales target and the percentage of commission on sales.

Practice Business Problem 4

Please give me a product list with the IDs, names, sales prices, quantities of each product in stock and the subcategory IDs they belong to. Please show the results in descending order by subcategory ID.

Practice Business Problem 5

Please give me a product list with the IDs, names, sales prices, quantities of each product in stock and the subcategory IDs they belong to. Please show the results in descending order by subcategory ID and in ascending order by quantity of stock.

Practice Business Problem 6

Please give me all the details stored for all our products.

Practice Business Problem 7

Please show me every sales order with its ID, customer ID, order date, delivery date, gross value, discount and net value.

Practice Business Problem 8

Please give me a list of all our products with their IDs, names, standard unit prices, unit discounts and net unit prices assuming we increase the standard price of each product by 10%.

Lesson Summary

In this lesson, you have learned various techniques to retrieve all of the rows from within a table. You have seen how to retrieve from a table the data for all its columns, only a few columns, or certain columns which meet a predicate. You have also seen how to organize your results by one or more columns. In summary:

- The *SELECT* clause allows you to specify output column list.
- The *FROM* clause allow you to specify the table from which you want to retrieve data.
- The *ORDER BY* clause allows you to specify the column list for which you want to sort your output.
- A calculated column allows you to combine multiple columns into one column.
- Predicate usages and calculated columns provide you with the power to solve various complex business problems. The *CASE* expression allows you to show different calculated values within a column based on different predicates.

Lesson 8

Retrieving subset of rows from a table

```
NEW SQL STATEMENTS AND KEYWORDS COVERED IN THIS LESSON:

SELECT...FROM...WHERE              SELECT...FROM...WHERE...ORDER BY
DISTINCT                          TOP N
LIMIT...OFFSET                    OFFSET...FETCH
GETDATE()                         EOMONTH()
AND                               OR
NOT                               INTERSECT
EXCEPT/MINUS                      UNION
```

Lesson Objective

Previously, you learned the techniques to retrieve all rows from a table. In this lesson, you will learn how to use the *WHERE* clause of the *SELECT* statement to retrieve a subset of rows from a table. You will also learn the techniques to combine multiple query results. Here are the SQL elements this lesson will introduce:

- *WHERE* clause
- *DISTINCT* keyword
- *TOP N* keyword
- *LIMIT-OFFSET* keyword
- *OFFSET-FETCH* keyword
- *AND, OR* and *NOT* operators
- *INTERSECT, EXCEPT/MINUS* and *UNION* operators
- Subqueries

Code Samples

As in previous lessons, you will be asked to solve business problems in this lesson that require you to write SQL codes and execute them in your database, and we have provided that code for you at the links below.

SQL Server:
https://drive.google.com/open?id=1jO58R3mmaT4Qwt43dnMTi2Y6CGFgwi4Z

MySQL:
https://drive.google.com/open?id=1p1tlicJfI1JFazdqPT14bWN_gVHsI8Ye

Retrieving Distinct Rows

In the previous lesson, you saw how to retrieve all rows from a table. Sometime the results may have duplicate rows. You can use the *DISTINCT* keyword just after the *SELECT* keyword, this will remove duplicates and only show the distinct rows in the result. If you use the *DISTINCT* keyword your *SELECT* statement will look like below:

```
SELECT DISTINCT  column name1, column name2, ..........
FROM  table name;
```

The business problems below will demonstrate how to retrieve distinct rows from a table.

Business Problem 1

What gender categories do our customers belong to?

Solution SQL

```
SELECT DISTINCT CustomerGender FROM Customers;
```

SQL Result

CustomerGender
Female
Male

Solution Review

As you may remember from the previous lesson, we currently have 32 customers: 16 females and 16 males. If you execute the above SQL statement without the *DISTINCT* keyword, it will return all 32 rows as you see below:

CustomerGender
Male
Male
Female
Female
Female
Male
Male
Male
Female
Female
Female
Female
Female
Female
Male
Male
Female
Male
Male
Male
Male
Male
Male
Female
Female
Female
Female
Female
Male
Male
Male
Female

As you can see, without the *DISTINCT* keyword your results can be quite redundant. The *DISTINCT* keyword is useful for removing all duplicate rows that it finds. In this case, it removed all but 2 distinct rows.

Business Problem 2

Please give me a list of IDs of all our relationship managers as well as the vendor categories they manage. Please show the results in ascending order by *RelationshipManagerID* and *VendorCategoryID*.

Solution SQL

SELECT DISTINCT RelationshipManagerID, VendorCategoryID
FROM Vendors
ORDER BY RelationshipManagerID, VendorCategoryID;

SQL Result

RelationshipManagerID	VendorCategoryID
2	1
2	3
3	1
3	2
3	3
4	1
4	2

Solution Review

If you execute the above SQL without the *DISTINCT* keyword, like so:

SELECT RelationshipManagerID, VendorCategoryID
FROM Vendors
ORDER BY RelationshipManagerID, VendorCategoryID;

...it will show a list of relationship manager IDs and the category of vendors like you see below:

RelationshipManagerID	VendorCategoryID
2	1
2	1
2	3
3	1
3	1
3	2
3	3
4	1
4	1
4	2
4	2

Notice the highlighted rows. We've highlighted these to show duplicates in the result. How did this happen? Because these particular relationship managers look after more than one vendor within the same category. That's where the *DISTINCT* keyword comes in handy—you can use it to remove duplicate rows. In this case, it would show seven distinct rows, thus creating a result that is much easier to read.

Retrieving the First 'N' Rows from an Unordered Result

In the real world, data tables can get very big. It is quite common; the transaction tables may even contain *billions* of rows. For sampling purposes, analysts often want only a few hundred rows from a table, and you therefore need to show the first N rows from the result. For our purposes, 'N' refers to the number that you would specify in the statement.

So, for example, '*Top 5*' refers to the top five rows, etc. Unfortunately, different RDBMSs have implemented this concept differently. *SQL Server* uses the *TOP N* keyword after the *SELECT* keyword to show first *N* rows:

```
SELECT TOP N column name1, column name2, .....
FROM     table name;
```

MySQL uses the *LIMIT* clause at the end of the *SELECT* statement to show *x* number of row starting from row *y+1*:

```
SELECT column name1, column name2, ..........
FROM table name
LIMIT x OFFSET y;
```

If you skip the *OFFSET y* part, it will show the first *x* rows. Let's review the concept by solving another business problem.

Business Problem 3

Please give me a list of five sample customers showing their IDs, genders, first names, last names and email addresses.

Solution SQL – SQL Server

```
SELECT TOP 5 CustomerID, CustomerGender, CustomerFirstName, CustomerLastName, CustomerEmail
FROM     Customers;
```

Solution SQL – MySQL

```
SELECT CustomerID, CustomerGender, CustomerFirstName, CustomerLastName, CustomerEmail
FROM Customers
LIMIT 5;
```

SQL Result

CustomerID	CustomerGender	CustomerFirstName	CustomerLastName	CustomerEmail
1	Male	Ricky	Brown	RickBrown@SaleOnYourOwn.com
2	Male	Adam	Wilson	AdamWilson@SaleOnYourOwn.com
3	Female	Crystal	Doslakoski	CrystalDoslakoski@SaleOnYourOwn.com
4	Female	Melanie	Bowell	KerrynWhite@SaleOnYourOwn.com
5	Female	Sophie	Smith	SophieSmith@SaleOnYourOwn.com

Solution Review

Notice that we used the *TOP 5* just after the *SELECT* keyword for the SQL Server users and *LIMIT 5* at the end of the *SELECT* statement for the MySQL users. Using *TOP 5* in SQL SERVER and *LIMIT 5* in MySQL allows you to retrieve only the first five rows from a table, as in this case with our *Customers* table. The key here is that the number '*5*' designates the number of rows to retrieve, whether you're using the *LIMIT* or the *TOP* keywords. Inputting '*6*' would show the first six rows, '*10*' would show the first ten, and so on.

Retrieving the First N Rows from an Ordered Result

As you can imagine, business users may need more than just the first few rows from an unordered result set for sampling purposes. They may need the first few rows from an ordered result set. Other times they will want a sample from the middle part of the ordered result. You may be called on to complete tasks such as:

- *Give me the 5 most recent orders.*
- *Give me the 10 more recent orders that are older than the 5 most recent orders.*
- *Give me a list of 2 percent of our total sales orders, starting with the most recent. .*

To complete tasks such as these, the database engine must order the rows by order date and then retrieve the specified number of rows. Unfortunately, different RDBMSs have implemented this concept differently.

SQL Server uses the *ORDER BY* clause along with an *OFFSET – FETCH* filtering option at end of the *SELECT* statement, as we demonstrate for you below, to show *x* number of rows starting from row *y+1*:

```
SELECT column name1, column name2, ………
FROM table name
ORDER BY ordered column1, ordered column2,.....
OFFSET y ROWS FETCH NEXT x ROWS ONLY;
```

Meanwhile, MySQL uses the *ORDER BY* clause along with a *LIMIT-OFFSET* filtering option at the end of the *SELECT* statement to show *x* number of rows starting from row *y+1*:

```
SELECT column name1, column name2, ………
FROM table name
ORDER BY ordered column1, ordered column2,.....
LIMIT x OFFSET y;
```

Follow along with us as we solve *Business Problem 4* to demonstrate this in action.

Business Problem 4

Please give me the five most recent sales orders. Please show each order including their IDs, order dates, due dates, customer IDs and the net values.

Solution SQL – SQL Server

```
SELECT SalesOrderID, OrderDate, OrderDueDate, CustomerID, OrderTotal - OrderDiscountTotal AS NetValue
FROM SalesOrders
ORDER BY OrderDate DESC
OFFSET 0 ROWS FETCH NEXT 5 ROWS ONLY;
```

Solution SQL – MySQL

```
SELECT SalesOrderID, OrderDate, OrderDueDate, CustomerID, OrderTotal - OrderDiscountTotal AS NetValue
FROM SalesOrders
ORDER BY OrderDate DESC
LIMIT 5 OFFSET 0;
```

SQL Result

SalesOrderID	OrderDate	OrderDueDate	CustomerID	NetValue
310	2019-01-21 00:00:00.000	2019-02-04 00:00:00.000	20	2195.0000
382	2019-01-20 00:00:00.000	2019-01-25 00:00:00.000	26	1540.0000
190	2019-01-16 00:00:00.000	2019-01-30 00:00:00.000	15	50000.0000
394	2019-01-16 00:00:00.000	2019-01-21 00:00:00.000	27	2730.0000
286	2019-01-12 00:00:00.000	2019-01-26 00:00:00.000	19	37495.0000

Solution Review

ORDER BY OrderDate DESC returns the most recent orders at the top of the result set. *OFFSET 0* starts showing the results from the 1st (0+1) row, then *LIMIT 5 (for MySQL)* and *FETCH NEXT 5 ROWS (for SQL Server)* limits the results to five rows only. If you are using SQL Server, you can achieve the same result by using the *TOP 5* keyword along with the *ORDER BY* clause:

```
SELECT TOP 5 SalesOrderID, OrderDate, OrderDueDate, CustomerID, OrderTotal - OrderDiscountTotal AS NetValue
FROM SalesOrders
ORDER BY OrderDate DESC;
```

Business Problem 5

Please give me ten recent sales orders that are older than the five most recent sales orders. Please show each order with their IDs, order dates, due dates, customer IDs and the net values.

Solution SQL – SQL Server

```
SELECT SalesOrderID, OrderDate, OrderDueDate, CustomerID, OrderTotal - OrderDiscountTotal AS NetValue
FROM SalesOrders
ORDER BY OrderDate DESC
OFFSET 5 ROWS FETCH NEXT 10 ROWS ONLY;
```

Solution SQL – MySQL

```
SELECT SalesOrderID, OrderDate, OrderDueDate, CustomerID, OrderTotal - OrderDiscountTotal AS NetValue
FROM SalesOrders
ORDER BY OrderDate DESC
LIMIT 10 OFFSET 5;
```

SQL Result

SalesOrderID	OrderDate	OrderDueDate	CustomerID	NetValue
166	2019-01-09 00:00:00.000	2019-01-23 00:00:00.000	14	52000.0000
262	2019-01-07 00:00:00.000	2019-01-21 00:00:00.000	18	37495.0000
142	2019-01-05 00:00:00.000	2019-01-19 00:00:00.000	13	52000.0000
238	2019-01-04 00:00:00.000	2019-01-18 00:00:00.000	17	36835.0000
334	2019-01-02 00:00:00.000	2019-01-07 00:00:00.000	22	22750.0000
118	2019-01-01 00:00:00.000	2019-01-15 00:00:00.000	12	52000.0000
214	2018-12-30 00:00:00.000	2019-01-04 00:00:00.000	16	3780.0000
94	2018-12-29 00:00:00.000	2019-01-12 00:00:00.000	11	46800.0000
370	2018-12-27 00:00:00.000	2018-12-31 00:00:00.000	25	1840.0000
28	2018-12-24 00:00:00.000	2018-12-29 00:00:00.000	4	1500.0000

Solution Review

The *ORDER BY OrderDate DESC* returns the most recent orders to the top of the result set. The usages of *OFFSET 5* starts showing the results from 6th (5+1) row, then *LIMIT 10 (for MySQL)* and *FETCH NEXT 10 ROWS (for SQL Server)* limits the results to ten rows only.

Business Problem 6

Please give me most recent 2% of all sales orders. Please show each order with their IDs, order dates, due dates, customer IDs and the net values.

Solution SQL – SQL Server

```
SELECT TOP 2 PERCENT SalesOrderID, OrderDate, OrderDueDate, CustomerID, OrderTotal - OrderDiscountTotal AS NetValue
FROM SalesOrders
ORDER BY OrderDate DESC;
```

SQL Result

SalesOrderID	OrderDate	OrderDueDate	CustomerID	NetValue
310	2019-01-21 00:00:00.000	2019-02-04 00:00:00.000	20	2195.0000
382	2019-01-20 00:00:00.000	2019-01-25 00:00:00.000	26	1540.0000
394	2019-01-16 00:00:00.000	2019-01-21 00:00:00.000	27	2730.0000
190	2019-01-16 00:00:00.000	2019-01-30 00:00:00.000	15	50000.0000
286	2019-01-12 00:00:00.000	2019-01-26 00:00:00.000	19	37495.0000
166	2019-01-09 00:00:00.000	2019-01-23 00:00:00.000	14	52000.0000
262	2019-01-07 00:00:00.000	2019-01-21 00:00:00.000	18	37495.0000
142	2019-01-05 00:00:00.000	2019-01-19 00:00:00.000	13	52000.0000
238	2019-01-04 00:00:00.000	2019-01-18 00:00:00.000	17	36835.0000

Solution Review

The *ORDER BY OrderDate DESC* retrieves the most recent orders on the top of the result set, while the *TOP 2 PERCENT* limits the results to 2% of the total number of rows. If 2% of the total rows happen to be a fraction, it will round up to the nearest whole number. We have 424 sales orders in the *SalesOrders* table, so when we use this SQL statement we retrieve 9 rows (8.48 rounded up to the nearest digit).

Notes

MySQL does not support the *PERCENT* keyword and so there is no simple solution for this question, but we will show you a technique to answer this type of question in a later lesson where we will show you how to summarize the results

Retrieving rows that match a predicate

A table can contain a large number of rows, but business users often need a subset of rows that match a specific criteria (i.e. a predicate). The *WHERE* clause in the *SELECT* statement allows you to filter rows based on a predicate that matches a specific criteria. A predicate can evaluate to *TRUE*, *FALSE* or *NULL*. When you use a *WHERE* clause in the *SELECT* statement, the predicate will be evaluated for each row of the table. Depending on the outcome of the predicate evaluation, the database engine will determine whether the corresponding row needs to be returned as below:

- *TRUE: the corresponding row of the table will be returned*
- *FALSE: the corresponding row of the table will not be returned*
- *NULL: the corresponding row of the table will not be returned*

The basic syntax for this *SELECT* statement is:

```
SELECT list of columns or expressions
FROM  table name
WHERE  predicate
ORDER BY order by column list;
```

If you want to see the results sorted in a specific order, please include an *ORDER BY* clause using the syntax shown above, otherwise you should exclude *ORDER BY* from the syntax above. When you exclude the *ORDER BY* clause from the above syntax, the database engine simply returns the rows from the database 'as is,' but if you include the *ORDER BY* clause, the database engine cannot simply return the resulting rows from the database—it has to sort the rows before returning them.

Hence, the *ORDER BY* clause can cause your query to perform more slowly. Therefore, it is recommended that you do not use the *ORDER BY* clause if you do not need your result in a particular order. Let's learn how to use the most common predicates (using comparison, *BETWEEN*, *IN*, *LIKE* and *IS NULL* operators) by solving some business problems.

Business Problem 7

Please give me a list of all male customers. Please show the identification number, name, email address, date of birth and gender of each.

Solution SQL – SQL Server

```
SELECT CustomerID, CONCAT(CustomerFirstName, ' ', CustomerLastName) AS Name, CustomerEmail AS Email,
       CustomerDateOfBirth AS BirthDate, CustomerGender AS Gender
FROM    Customers
WHERE   CustomerGender = 'Male';
```

SQL Result

CustomerID	Name	Email	BirthDate	Gender
1	Ricky Brown	RickBrown@SaleOnYourOwn.com	1970-01-01 00:00:00.000	Male
2	Adam Wilson	AdamWilson@SaleOnYourOwn.com	1975-02-01 00:00:00.000	Male
6	Robert Smith	RobertSmith@SaleOnYourOwn.com	1999-12-01 00:00:00.000	Male
7	Michael Jackson	MichaelJackson@SaleOnYourOwn.com	2000-02-01 00:00:00.000	Male
8	Ronald White	RonaldWhite@SaleOnYourOwn.com	1965-05-05 00:00:00.000	Male
15	Richard Martin	RichardMartin@SaleOnYourOwn.com	1976-07-25 00:00:00.000	Male
16	Robinson Clark	RobinsonClark@SaleOnYourOwn.com	1965-02-01 00:00:00.000	Male
18	Allen Hall	AllenHall@SaleOnYourOwn.com	1959-12-01 00:00:00.000	Male
19	King Smith	KingSmith@SaleOnYourOwn.com	1999-12-01 00:00:00.000	Male
20	Adam Green	AdamGreen@SaleOnYourOwn.com	1996-11-01 00:00:00.000	Male
21	Scott Baker	ScottBaker@SaleOnYourOwn.com	1968-02-01 00:00:00.000	Male
22	Ricky Ponting	RickyPonting@SaleOnYourOwn.com	1977-03-25 00:00:00.000	Male
23	Rick Strand	RickStrand@SaleOnYourOwn.com	1976-05-25 00:00:00.000	Male
29	Louis Hugo	LouisHugo@SaleOnYourOwn.com	1996-08-19 00:00:00.000	Male
30	Baldev Singh	BaldevSingh@SaleOnYourOwn.com	1996-08-19 00:00:00.000	Male
31	Akidul Islam	AkidulIslam@SaleOnYourOwn.com	1971-08-19 00:00:00.000	Male

Solution Review

The *CustomerGender = 'Male'* predicate in the *WHERE* clause allows you to retrieve only male customers from the *Customers* table. Here we have used the = operator to match the *CustomerGender* column's value with the string *'Male'*. You can do the same using the *LIKE* operator as well, i.e. you can get the same result by using a *CustomerGender LIKE 'Male'* predicate in the *WHERE* clause. The *CONCAT* function you see above has been used to generate the *Name* column from *CustomerFirstName* column, then a *blank space* and the *CustomerLastName* column. We have not used the *ORDER BY* clause, so you may see the data in a different order, but as long as your execution contains all of these 16 rows it should be good.

Business Problem 8

Please give me a list of our customers who are 50 years or older. Please show the identification number, name, email address, date of birth and gender of each. Please show all dates of birth in the day-month-year format.

Solution SQL – SQL Server

```
SELECT CustomerID, CustomerFirstName + ' ' + CustomerLastName AS [Name], CustomerEmail AS Email,
       FORMAT(CustomerDateOfBirth, 'dd-MM-yyyy') AS BirthDate, CustomerGender AS Gender
FROM Customers
WHERE CustomerDateOfBirth < DATEADD(yy, -50,DATEADD(dd,1,DATEDIFF(dd,0,GETDATE())));
```

Solution SQL – MySQL

SELECT CustomerID, CONCAT(CustomerFirstName, ' ', CustomerLastName) AS Name, CustomerEmail AS Email,
DATE_FORMAT(CustomerDateOfBirth, '%d-%m-%Y') AS BirthDate, CustomerGender AS Gender
FROM Customers
WHERE CustomerDateOfBirth < DATE_ADD(DATE_ADD(CURDATE(),INTERVAL 1 DAY),INTERVAL -50 YEAR);

SQL Result

CustomerID	Name	Email	BirthDate	Gender
8	Ronald White	RonaldWhite@SaleOnYourOwn.com	05-05-1965	Male
9	Adele Renton	AdeleRenton@SaleOnYourOwn.com	01-01-1962	Female
10	Emma Stephens	EmmaStephens@SaleOnYourOwn.com	01-02-1965	Female
11	Donna Moore	DonnaMoore@SaleOnYourOwn.com	01-02-1965	Female
16	Robinson Clark	RobinsonClark@SaleOnYourOwn.com	01-02-1965	Male
18	Allen Hall	AllenHall@SaleOnYourOwn.com	01-12-1959	Male

Solution Review

Assume that today's date is the *2nd of January, 2017*. The customers who were born on or before *2nd January 1967* will be at least 50 years old and we could have retrieved the customers list by specifying a *CustomerDateOfBirth < '1967-01-03'* predicate in the *WHERE* clause. Why did we not use *CustomerDateOfBirth <= '1967-01-02'*? Because it will not give you the desired result...it will exclude those who were born on January 2nd. The predicate *CustomerDateOfBirth <= '1967-01-02'* in expanded form is *CustomerDateOfBirth <= '1967-01-02 00:00:00.000'*. Any customers who were born between 12:01am and 11:59PM on the 2nd of January 1967 will be excluded, and that is why we have added one day to the 2nd of January and used the < operator instead of the <= operator. It's a fine detail, so we wanted to point it out so that you understand the difference.

To retrieve customers who were born on or before the 2nd of January 1967 is (with default date format), here's what our SQL will look like:

SELECT CustomerID, CustomerFirstName + ' ' + CustomerLastName AS [Name], CustomerEmail AS Email,
CustomerDateOfBirth AS BirthDate, CustomerGender AS Gender
FROM Customers
WHERE CustomerDateOfBirth < '1967-01-03';

In **SQL Server**, you can use the *GETDATE()* function to retrieve the current date and time, then the *DATEDIFF()* function to remove the time part from it, then the *DATEADD()* function to add one day to it and then the *DATEADD()* function again to subtract 50 years from it. The steps are as follows:

1. Use the *GETDATE()* function to return the current date and time (i.e. 2017-01-02 11:15:00 assuming the current date and time is 2nd January, 2017 at 11:15AM).
2. Remove the time part and add one day to it by using *DATEADD(dd, 1, DATEDIFF(dd, 0, GETDATE()))*. It will evaluate to 2017-01-03 00:00:00.
3. Subtract 50 years by using *DATEADD(yy, -50, DATEADD(dd, 1, DATEDIFF(dd, 0, GETDATE())))*. It will evaluate to 1967-01-03 00:00:00.

In **MySQL**, you can use the *CURDATE()* function to retrieve the current date, then the *DATE_ADD()* function to add one day to it and then the *DATE_ADD()* function again to subtract 50 years. The steps are:

1. Use the *CURDATE()* function to return the current date excluding the time part (i.e. 2017-01-02 assuming current date and time is 2nd January, 2017 at 11:15AM).
2. Add one day to it by using *DATE_ADD(CURDATE(), INTERVAL 1 DAY)*. It will evaluate to 2017-01-03.
3. Subtract 50 years by using *DATE_ADD (DATE_ADD(CURDATE(), INTERVAL 1 DAY), INTERVAL -50 YEAR)*. It will evaluate to 1967-01-03.

You may have noticed the format differences between MySQL and SQL Server. In SQL Server we used the *FORMAT* function with a *dd-MM-yyyy* format expression and the *DATE_FORMAT* function with *%d-%m-%Y* format expression in MySQL to show all dates in the *day-month-year* format.

Notes

The SQL example above was executed on 2nd January, 2017. Since you will be executing the SQL after 2nd January, 2017, you may receive different results.

Business Problem 9

What sales orders have been placed within the past 24 calendar months? Please show the order ID, order date, due date, delivery date (if the order has already been delivered), customer ID, gross value, discount and net value. Please show the report in descending order by order date and order ID.

Solution SQL – SQL Server

```
SELECT SalesOrderID AS OrderID, OrderDate, OrderDueDate AS DueDate, OrderDeliveryDate AS DeliveryDate,
       CustomerID, OrderTotal AS GrossValue, OrderDiscountTotal AS Discount, OrderTotal - OrderDiscountTotal AS NetValue
FROM SalesOrders
WHERE OrderDate >= DATEADD(mm, -24, DATEADD(dd, 1, EOMONTH(GETDATE())))
ORDER BY OrderDate DESC, SalesOrderID DESC;
```

Solution SQL – MySQL

```
SELECT SalesOrderID AS OrderID, OrderDate, OrderDueDate AS DueDate, OrderDeliveryDate AS DeliveryDate,
       CustomerID, OrderTotal AS GrossValue, OrderDiscountTotal AS Discount, OrderTotal - OrderDiscountTotal AS NetValue
FROM SalesOrders
WHERE OrderDate >= DATE_ADD(DATE_ADD(LAST_DAY(CURDATE()), INTERVAL 1 DAY), INTERVAL -24 MONTH)
ORDER BY OrderDate DESC, SalesOrderID DESC;
```

SQL Result

OrderID	OrderDate	DueDate	DeliveryDate	CustomerID	GrossValue	Discount	NetValue
310	2019-01-21 00:00:00	2019-02-04 00:00:00		20	2375	180	2195
382	2019-01-20 00:00:00	2019-01-25 00:00:00		26	1540	0	1540
394	2019-01-16 00:00:00	2019-01-21 00:00:00		27	2870	140	2730
190	2019-01-16 00:00:00	2019-01-30 00:00:00		15	50000	0	50000
286	2019-01-12 00:00:00	2019-01-26 00:00:00		19	38875	1380	37495
166	2019-01-09 00:00:00	2019-01-23 00:00:00		14	52000	0	52000
262	2019-01-07 00:00:00	2019-01-21 00:00:00		18	38875	1380	37495
142	2019-01-05 00:00:00	2019-01-19 00:00:00	2019-01-18 00:00:00	13	52000	0	52000
238	2019-01-04 00:00:00	2019-01-18 00:00:00	2019-01-18 00:00:00	17	38215	1380	36835
334	2019-01-02 00:00:00	2019-01-07 00:00:00	2019-01-07 00:00:00	22	23650	900	22750
118	2019-01-01 00:00:00	2019-01-15 00:00:00	2019-01-14 00:00:00	12	52000	0	52000
214	2018-12-30 00:00:00	2019-01-04 00:00:00	2019-01-04 00:00:00	16	4160	380	3780
94	2018-12-29 00:00:00	2019-01-12 00:00:00	2019-01-11 00:00:00	11	46800	0	46800
370	2018-12-27 00:00:00	2018-12-31 00:00:00	2018-12-31 00:00:00	25	1840	0	1840
35	2018-12-24 00:00:00	2019-01-07 00:00:00	2019-01-06 00:00:00	5	7080	160	6920

Solution Review

Only the first 15 rows have been shown in the SQL result section in order to minimize some spaces. We executed the query (*SELECT statement*) on the 4th of January 2019, so the orders that have been placed within the past 24 calendar months will be those that were placed on or after February 2017 (i.e. between February 2017 and January 2019). Therefore, we could have retrieved the same result by simply replacing the *WHERE* clause predicate with *OrderDate >= '2017-02-01'* like below:

SELECT SalesOrderID AS OrderID, OrderDate, OrderDueDate AS DueDate, OrderDeliveryDate AS DeliveryDate, CustomerID,
    OrderTotal AS GrossValue, OrderDiscountTotal AS Discount, OrderTotal - OrderDiscountTotal AS NetValue
FROM SalesOrders
WHERE OrderDate >= '2017-02-01'
ORDER BY OrderDate DESC, SalesOrderID DESC

The clock is always running, and 28 days later the current month is now February and the orders that have been placed within the past 24 calendar months will represent orders that have been placed from March 2017 to February 2019. To satisfy this requirement, the query should follow these steps:

1. Get today's date from the system (instead of using a fixed date literal that may not achieve the desired result).
2. Find the last day of current month, then add one day to it.
3. Then subtract 24 months from it.

This will provide the earliest placing date for orders.

In **SQL Server**, you can use the *GETDATE()* function to retrieve the current date and time, then the *EOMONTH()* function to manipulate current date and time to the last day of current month, then the *DATEADD()* function to add one day with it and then the *DATEADD()* function again to subtract 24 months from it. The steps are:

1. Use the *GETDATE()* function to return the current date and time i.e. *2019-01-04 11:15:00* (assuming current date and time is 4th January 2019 at 11:15AM)
2. Apply the *EOMONTH()* function to get the last day of the month by using *EOMONTH(GETDATE())*. It will evaluate to *2019-01-31 00:00:00*
3. Add one day to it to get the first day of next month by using *DATEADD(dd, 1, EOMONTH(GETDATE()))*. It will evaluate to *2019-02-01 00:00:00*
4. Subtract 24 months from it to get the earliest order date by using *DATEADD(mm, -24, DATEADD(dd, 1, EOMONTH(GETDATE())))*. It will evaluate to *2017-02-01 00:00:00*

In **MySQL**, you can use the *CURDATE()* function to retrieve the current date, then the *LAST_DAY()* function to manipulate the current date to the last day of current month, then the *DATE_ADD()* function to add one day with it, and finally the *DATE_ADD()* function again to subtract 24 months from it. The steps are:

1. Use the *CURDATE()* function to return the current date i.e. *2019-01-04* (assuming current date and time is 4th January 2019 at 11:15AM)
2. Apply the *LAST_DAY()* function to get last day of the month by using *LAST_DAY(CURDATE())* It will evaluate to *2019-01-31 00:00:00*
3. Add 1 day to it to get the first day of next month by using *DATE_ADD(LAST_DAY(CURDATE()), INTERVAL 1 DAY)*. It will evaluate to *2019-02-01 00:00:00*
4. Subtract 24 months from it to get the earliest order date by using *DATE_ADD (DATE_ADD(LAST_DAY(CURDATE()), INTERVAL 1 DAY), INTERVAL -24 MONTH)*. It will evaluate to *2017-02-01 00:00:00*.

ORDER BY OrderDate DESC, SalesOrderID DESC has been used at the end of the query to show the results in descending order by order date and order ID.

Notes

The SQL statement above was executed on the 4th January 2019. Since you will be executing the SQL statement after 4th January 2019, you may receive different results.

If you are using SQL Server and your version is earlier than 2012, the above SQL statement will not run, because only SQL Server 2012 and later versions support EOMONTH() function. But you can execute the SQL statement by replacing the WHERE clause's predicate with below:

```
OrderDate >= DATEADD(mm, -24, DATEADD(mm, DATEDIFF(mm, 0, GETDATE()), 0))
```

Business Problem 10

Which products have a standard sales price within the range of $120 to $200? Please retrieve each Product ID, name, standard sales price and Vendor ID for the report. Please sort the results in ascending order by Vendor ID.

Solution SQL

```
SELECT  ProductID, ProductName, StandardSalesPrice, VendorID
FROM Products
WHERE StandardSalesPrice BETWEEN 120 AND 200
ORDER BY VendorID
```

SQL Result

ProductID	ProductName	StandardSalesPrice	VendorID
46	Japanese Sanrio Hello Kitty Halloween Edge-of-the-Cup-Figure Completed Set 8pcs	120.0000	3
48	The Holy Family Statue Jesus Mary & Joseph	150.0000	6
24	Fairy Dolls 12 Packs	150.0000	7
32	Little Tikes Cook N Play Outdoor BBQ	200.0000	8
53	Artificial Cow Skull Wall Hanging	120.0000	9
54	Tibetan Buddhism Bronze Garuda Bird Caput God Old Wall Mask Buddha Ride Statue	200.0000	9

Solution Review

If the standard sales price is greater than or equal to $120 but less than or equal to $200, the predicate in the WHERE clause StandardSalesPrice BETWEEN 120 AND 200 will evaluate to TRUE and the product's details will be retrieved by the database engine, otherwise, the product will be left out. If you know the upper and lower limit of the values of a column or expression that you want to filter, the BETWEEN predicate in the WHERE clause can be used.

Business Problem 11

Which products offered by vendors 1, 3 & 9 are selling or used to sell? For each vendor that is selling products, please retrieve the Product ID, name, standard sales price and Vendor ID in your report. Please sort the results in ascending order by Vendor ID.

Solution SQL

```
SELECT  ProductID, ProductName, StandardSalesPrice, VendorID
FROM Products
WHERE VendorID IN (1,3,9)
ORDER BY VendorID ASC
```

SQL Result

ProductID	ProductName	StandardSalesPrice	VendorID
1	Ironman 3 Figures	310.0000	1
2	Magnetic Drawing Board	100.0000	1
3	Kids Batman Cape and Mask Dress Up Set	20.0000	1
4	My First Cash Register	60.0000	1
5	Vehicles Peg Puzzle	20.0000	1
44	Vintage Solid Brass Horse Statue Figurine	100.0000	3
45	Large Vintage Silver Plate And Wooden Altar Crucifix Religious Jesus Cross	50.0000	3
46	Japanese Sanrio Hello Kitty Halloween Edge-of-the-Cup-Figure Completed Set 8pcs	120.0000	3
53	Artificial Cow Skull Wall Hanging	120.0000	9
54	Tibetan Buddhism Bronze Garuda Bird Caput God Old Wall Mask Buddha Ride Statue	200.0000	9
55	Anime Astro Boy Figure Tetsuwan Atom Collection Toys	20.0000	9

Solution Review

Notice that the *VendorID* column represents which vendor is selling the product. Here we are looking for *VendorIDs 1, 3 & 9*, not the entire range from *1* to *9*. This is why we cannot use the *BETWEEN* predicate. We have some discrete values here, and the *IN* predicate is useful for discrete values. That is why we used the *VendorID IN (1, 3, 9)* predicate in the *WHERE* clause. If the *VendorID* of a product is *1, 3 or 9*, the predicate in the *WHERE* clause *VendorID IN (1, 3, 9)* will evaluate to *TRUE* and the product's details will be retrieved by the database engine, otherwise, the product will be left out.

Business Problem 12

Please give me the five most valuable sales orders that were due nearest to the end of the year 2017. For each, please provide the order ID, order date, due date, delivery date, customer ID, gross value, discount and net value.

Solution SQL – SQL Server

```
SELECT SalesOrderID AS OrderID, OrderDate, OrderDueDate AS DueDate, OrderDeliveryDate AS DeliveryDate,
      CustomerID, OrderTotal AS GrossValue, OrderDiscountTotal AS Discount, OrderTotal - OrderDiscountTotal AS NetValue
FROM SalesOrders
WHERE OrderDueDate < '2018-01-01'
ORDER BY NetValue DESC, OrderDueDate DESC
OFFSET 0 ROWS FETCH NEXT 5 ROWS ONLY;
```

Solution SQL – MySQL

```
SELECT SalesOrderID AS OrderID, OrderDate, OrderDueDate AS DueDate, OrderDeliveryDate AS DeliveryDate,
      CustomerID, OrderTotal AS GrossValue, OrderDiscountTotal AS Discount, OrderTotal - OrderDiscountTotal AS NetValue
FROM SalesOrders
WHERE OrderDueDate < '2018-01-01'
ORDER BY NetValue DESC, OrderDueDate DESC
LIMIT 5 OFFSET 0;
```

SQL Result

OrderID	OrderDate	DueDate	DeliveryDate	CustomerID	GrossValue	Discount	NetValue
150	2017-09-08 00:00:00	2017-09-22 00:00:00	2017-09-21 00:00:00	14	23040	0	23040
126	2017-09-04 00:00:00	2017-09-18 00:00:00	2017-09-17 00:00:00	13	23040	0	23040
102	2017-08-31 00:00:00	2017-09-14 00:00:00	2017-09-13 00:00:00	12	23040	0	23040
174	2017-09-15 00:00:00	2017-09-29 00:00:00	2017-09-28 00:00:00	15	21040	0	21040
78	2017-08-28 00:00:00	2017-09-11 00:00:00	2017-09-10 00:00:00	11	17840	0	17840

Solution Review

First of all, we need to exclude orders that were due after the end of the year 2017. This can be done by using the *OrderDueDate < '2018-01-01'* predicate in a *WHERE* clause to only include orders that were due before *1st January, 2018*. Then, to retrieve the most valuable orders within this period, we need to sort them in descending order based on their net values. If multiple orders have same net value, we can sort them in descending order based on their due date to get the orders nearest to the end of the year 2017. The *ORDER BY NetValue DESC, OrderDueDate DESC* clause will do that. Finally, we need to get the five rows from the top. *OFFSET 0* shows the results starting from the first row, then *LIMIT 5 (for MySQL)* and *FETCH NEXT 5 ROWS (for SQL Server)* limit the results to five rows only. If you are using SQL Server, you can also achieve the same result by using *TOP 5* keyword along with *ORDER BY* clause like below:

```
SELECT TOP 5 SalesOrderID AS OrderID, OrderDate, OrderDueDate AS DueDate, OrderDeliveryDate AS DeliveryDate,
       CustomerID, OrderTotal AS GrossValue, OrderDiscountTotal AS Discount, OrderTotal - OrderDiscountTotal AS NetValue
FROM SalesOrders
WHERE OrderDueDate < '2018-01-01'
ORDER BY NetValue DESC, OrderDueDate DESC;
```

Note

This business problem showed you how to use the *WHERE* clause along with the *TOP/LIMIT* keywords. The *WHERE* clause restricts the rows retrieving from table and the *TOP/LIMIT* keywords restrict the retrieved rows from showing to the user.

Business Problem 13

Please give me the details of all customers whose first name starts with '*Ric*'.

Solution SQL

```
SELECT   CustomerID, CustomerFirstName, CustomerLastName, CustomerEmail, CustomerGender
FROM     Customers
WHERE    CustomerFirstName LIKE 'Ric%'
```

SQL Result

CustomerID	CustomerFirstName	CustomerLastName	CustomerEmail	CustomerGender
1	Ricky	Brown	RickBrown@SaleOnYourOwn.com	Male
15	Richard	Martin	RichardMartin@SaleOnYourOwn.com	Male
22	Ricky	Ponting	RickyPonting@SaleOnYourOwn.com	Male
23	Rick	Strand	RickStrand@SaleOnYourOwn.com	Male

Solution Review

The percentage sign (%) wildcard represents zero, one, or more arbitrary characters. So, the predicate *CustomerFirstName LIKE 'Ric%'* in the *WHERE* clause will evaluate to *TRUE* if the *CustomerFirstName* column value matches with the pattern '*Ric%*' (i.e. any string that starts with *Ric* such as *Rick, Ricky* etc.). The *LIKE* operator is used to match the pattern here. Five of our customers' first names start with *Ric* and have been shown in the results.

Business Problem 14

Please give me the details of all customers whose first names start with *Ric* and consist of five characters.

Solution SQL

```
SELECT    CustomerID, CustomerFirstName, CustomerLastName, CustomerEmail, CustomerGender
FROM      Customers
WHERE     CustomerFirstName LIKE 'Ric__'
```

SQL Result

CustomerID	CustomerFirstName	CustomerLastName	CustomerEmail	CustomerGender
1	Ricky	Brown	RickBrown@SaleOnYourOwn.com	Male
22	Ricky	Ponting	RickyPonting@SaleOnYourOwn.com	Male

Solution Review

Each of the two underscore (_) wildcard characters represents exactly one arbitrary character. So, the pattern *'Ric__'* represents a string that starts with *Ric* and consists of five characters. In the previous business problem, you saw that we have four customers whose first name starts with *Ric* but only two of them consist of five characters. Those two have been retrieved by this SQL statement.

Business Problem 15

Please give me the details of all customers whose email address begin with *Rick* and end with *@SaleOnYourOwn.com*. They can consist of any number of characters.

Solution SQL

```
SELECT CustomerID, CustomerFirstName, CustomerLastName, CustomerEmail, CustomerGender
FROM Customers
WHERE CustomerEmail LIKE 'Rick%@SaleOnYourOwn.com'
```

SQL Result

CustomerID	CustomerFirstName	CustomerLastName	CustomerEmail	CustomerGender
1	Ricky	Brown	RickBrown@SaleOnYourOwn.com	Male
22	Ricky	Ponting	RickyPonting@SaleOnYourOwn.com	Male
23	Rick	Strand	RickStrand@SaleOnYourOwn.com	Male

Solution Review

The email addresses *RickBrown@SaleOnYourOwn.com*, *RickyPonting@SaleOnYourOwn.com* and *RickStrand@SaleOnYourOwn.com* match the pattern we're looking for, (*Rick%@SaleOnYourOwn.com*) where % has been represented by *Brown*, *Ponting* and *Strand*. So, these customers were retrieved by the above SQL statement.

Business Problem 16

Please give me the details of all customers whose names start with the letter 'R' or 'M' followed by the letter 'i'. Their names can consist of any number of characters.

Solution SQL – SQL Server

```
SELECT CustomerID, CustomerFirstName, CustomerLastName, CustomerEmail, CustomerGender
FROM Customers
WHERE CustomerFirstName LIKE '[RM]i%'
```

SQL Result

CustomerID	CustomerFirstName	CustomerLastName	CustomerEmail	CustomerGender
1	Ricky	Brown	RickBrown@SaleOnYourOwn.com	Male
7	Michael	Jackson	MichaelJackson@SaleOnYourOwn.com	Male
15	Richard	Martin	RichardMartin@SaleOnYourOwn.com	Male
22	Ricky	Ponting	RickyPonting@SaleOnYourOwn.com	Male
23	Rick	Strand	RickStrand@SaleOnYourOwn.com	Male
27	Millie	Moloney	MillieMoloney@SaleOnYourOwn.com	Female

Solution Review

MySQL doesn't support the brackets wildcard, so the above SQL statement can be executed on SQL Server, but not in MySQL. In SQL Server, [RM] represents the first character of the customer's first name and tells the database that it must only retrieve names that start with either 'R' or 'M'.

Business Problem 17

Please give me the details of all customers whose mobile numbers are not known to us.

Solution SQL

```
SELECT CustomerID, CustomerFirstName, CustomerLastName, CustomerPhoneNumber,
       CustomerMobileNumber, CustomerEmail, CustomerGender
FROM Customers
WHERE CustomerMobileNumber IS NULL;
```

SQL Result

Customer ID	Customer FirstName	Customer LastName	Customer PhoneNumber	Customer MobileNumber	CustomerEmail	Customer Gender
3	Crystal	Doslakoski	+61 3 333333333	NULL	CrystalDoslakoski@SaleOnYourOwn.com	Female
10	Emma	Stephens	+1 (312) 666-666666	NULL	EmmaStephens@SaleOnYourOwn.com	Female
20	Adam	Green	+1 (704) 333-33333333	NULL	AdamGreen@SaleOnYourOwn.com	Male
30	Baldev	Singh	+91 11 22222222	NULL	BaldevSingh@SaleOnYourOwn.com	Male

Solution Review

The predicate *CustomerMobileNumber IS NULL* evaluates to *TRUE* if the customer's mobile number is *NULL (i.e. unknown)*, otherwise it evaluates to *FALSE*. We have four customers whose mobile numbers are unknown. Notice that the *CustomerMobileNumber* column's values for each of these four customers whose mobile number data are *NULL*. If we change the *IS NULL* predicate to a comparison predicate with the = operator, the SQL statement will look like:

```
SELECT CustomerID, CustomerFirstName, CustomerLastName, CustomerPhoneNumber,
       CustomerMobileNumber, CustomerEmail, CustomerGender
FROM Customers
WHERE CustomerMobileNumber = NULL;
```

If you execute this SQL statement, it will not return any customers, because any mathematical operation on *NULL* value evaluates to *NULL*.

Business Problem 18

Please give me the details of all customers who do not have a mobile number.

Solution SQL

SELECT	CustomerID, CustomerFirstName, CustomerLastName, CustomerPhoneNumber,
	CustomerMobileNumber, CustomerEmail, CustomerGender
FROM	Customers
WHERE	CustomerMobileNumber = '';

SQL Result

Customer ID	Customer FirstName	Customer LastName	Customer PhoneNumber	Customer MobileNumber	CustomerEmail	Customer Gender
8	Ronald	White	+1 (312) 444-44444		RonaldWhite@SaleOnYourOwn.com	Male

Solution Review

Notice that we have used the equal to = operator to compare the *CustomerMobileNumber* column with an empty string ''.

Combining Multiple Result Sets Retrieved from a Table

The relational database is based on set theory. So, understanding basic set operation is important to solving complex business problems. From this point onwards, almost everything will be based on the set operation. Everything you have learned so far is in fact based on set operation, although you may not have realized it yet if it's been awhile since you studied it in school. Each table in a database represents a set where each row is a member of the set and each column is an attribute of that member. Therefore, you have already learned how to retrieve a whole set (i.e. all rows of a table) and a subset (i.e. a few rows from a table). Now you will learn how to deal with multiple sets. We will cover three set operations: *intersection*, *difference* and *union*. These operations are essential for understanding how to solve complex problems using SQL.

In order to understand intersection, difference and union with regard to set theory, let's look at an example. To illustrate, let's assume that we have two sets of people (A & B):

A = {Robert, Adam, Mili, Ashley, Tom}

B = {Adam, Rick, Baldev, Tom}

These two sets of people can be represented using a Venn diagram like the diagram on your right.

Intersection: The intersection of two sets is a set that consists of the common members that are present in both sets. *Adam* and *Tom* are the common members of set A and B. Therefore, the intersection of set *A* and *B* will be:

$$A \cap B = \{Adam, Tom\}$$

Difference: The difference between two sets is a set that consists of all members of the first set that are not present in the second set. *Robert, Adam, Mili, Ashley* and *Tom* are members of set A, but *Adam* and *Tom* are also member of set B. If you take out *Adam* and *Tom* from set A, the difference from set A to set B will be:

$$A \backslash B = \{Robert, Mili, Ashley\}$$

Adam, Rick, Baldev and *Tom* are members of set B, but *Adam* and *Tom* are also members of set A. If you take out *Adam* and *Tom* from set B, the difference from set B to set A will be:

$$B \backslash A = \{Rick, Baldev\}$$

Union: The union of two sets is a set that consists all members of the first set that are not present in the second set plus all members of the second set that are not present in the first set plus the common members which are present in both sets. In other words, if you take all members from both sets and remove the duplicates, then it becomes the union of both sets. Therefore, the union of set A and B in this case will include everyone:

$$A \cup B = \{Robert, Mili, Ashley, Rick, Baldev, Adam, Tom\}$$

Note

The order of members within a set does not have any impact on the set. For example, the set *{Adam, Tom}* is the same as the set *{Tom, Adam}*.

Now let's look at a real-life implementation of these set operations. If a business user asks for *a list of customers who were born in 1996*, you can execute the below SQL statement:

```
SELECT CustomerID, CONCAT(CustomerFirstName, ' ', CustomerLastName) AS Name,
       CustomerGender AS Gender, YEAR(CustomerDateOfBirth) AS YearOfBirth
FROM Customers
WHERE YEAR(CustomerDateOfBirth) = 1996 ORDER BY CustomerID
```

This SQL statement will give you the result below:

CustomerID	Name	Gender	YearOfBirth
14	Ashley Hawker	Female	1996
20	Adam Green	Male	1996
25	Bonnie Horne	Female	1996
26	Elle Moloney	Female	1996
27	Millie Moloney	Female	1996
28	Rowena Price	Female	1996
29	Louis Hugo	Male	1996
30	Baldev Singh	Male	1996

Indeed, our result is *a set of customers who were born in 1996* where each row represents a customer who is a member of the set. If another user asks for *a list of male customers*, you can execute the SQL statement below:

```
SELECT  CustomerID, CONCAT(CustomerFirstName, ' ', CustomerLastName) AS Name,
        CustomerGender AS Gender, YEAR(CustomerDateOfBirth) AS YearOfBirth
FROM Customers
WHERE CustomerGender = 'Male' ORDER BY CustomerID
```

This SQL statement will give you the below result:

CustomerID	Name	Gender	YearOfBirth
1	Ricky Brown	Male	1970
2	Adam Wilson	Male	1975
6	Robert Smith	Male	1999
7	Michael Jackson	Male	2000
8	Ronald White	Male	1965
15	Richard Martin	Male	1976
16	Robinson Clark	Male	1965
18	Allen Hall	Male	1959
19	King Smith	Male	1999
20	Adam Green	Male	1996
21	Scott Baker	Male	1968
22	Ricky Ponting	Male	1977
23	Rick Strand	Male	1976
29	Louis Hugo	Male	1996
30	Baldev Singh	Male	1996
31	Akidul Islam	Male	1971

This is a set of male customers where each row represents a customer who is a member of the set.

Now let's put these two sets (*customers who were born in 1996* and *all male customers*) one after another as in Fig 8.1 below:

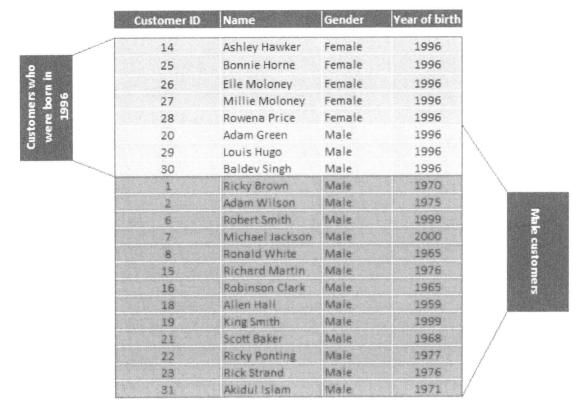

Customer ID	Name	Gender	Year of birth
14	Ashley Hawker	Female	1996
25	Bonnie Horne	Female	1996
26	Elle Moloney	Female	1996
27	Millie Moloney	Female	1996
28	Rowena Price	Female	1996
20	Adam Green	Male	1996
29	Louis Hugo	Male	1996
30	Baldev Singh	Male	1996
1	Ricky Brown	Male	1970
2	Adam Wilson	Male	1975
6	Robert Smith	Male	1999
7	Michael Jackson	Male	2000
8	Ronald White	Male	1965
15	Richard Martin	Male	1976
16	Robinson Clark	Male	1965
18	Allen Hall	Male	1959
19	King Smith	Male	1999
21	Scott Baker	Male	1968
22	Ricky Ponting	Male	1977
23	Rick Strand	Male	1976
31	Akidul Islam	Male	1971

Fig 8.1 - Two sets of customers with their subgroups

Here, the top five customers are members of the 1st set (*customers who were born in 1996*) only, the bottom thirteen customers are members of the 2nd set (*male customers*) only, and the middle three customers are members of both sets.

- If a business user wants *a list of male customers who were born in 1996*, the middle three rows represent this list, which is the intersection of these two sets—it will include *all customers who were born in 1996 and are male*.
- If a business user wants *a list of customers who were born in 1996 but are not male*, the top five rows represent this list. It is the *difference from the set of customers who were born in 1996 and the set of male customers*.
- If a business user wants *a list of male customers who were not born in 1996*, the bottom thirteen rows represent this list. It is the *difference from the set of male customers and the set of customers who were born in 1996*.
- If a business user wants *a list of customers who are either male or were born in 1996*, all rows i.e. all of top five, bottom thirteen and middle three rows represents the list which is the *union of both sets i.e. customers who were born in 1996 and male customers*.

Most of the RDBMS support three different ways to implement the intersection, difference and union operation:

Using keywords: We will discuss this now. Please note that some RDBMSs do not support all three operations through keyword

Using multiple predicates with AND/OR operators in the WHERE clause: We will discuss this later in this lesson.

Using Joins (INNER JOIN, LEFT JOIN, RIGHT JOIN & FILL JOIN): We will discuss this in later lessons.

The keyword for intersection operations: Most RDBMSs use the *INTERSECT* keyword to intersect two or more query result sets. The database engine provides the common rows that are returned by all *SELECT* statements. The basic syntax will be like below:

```
SELECT statement 1
INTERSECT
SELECT statement 2
................................
ORDER BY column list;
```

Please note that the *ORDER BY* clause can only be used at the end of the last *SELECT* statement, and the columns data type must be same or compatible with all *SELECT* statements. Also note that MySQL doesn't support the *INTERSECT* keyword.

Therefore, the SQL statement to retrieve *a list of male customers who were born in 1996* can be written as:

```
SELECT CustomerID, CONCAT(CustomerFirstName, ' ', CustomerLastName) AS Name,
       CustomerGender AS Gender, YEAR(CustomerDateOfBirth) AS YearOfBirth
FROM Customers
WHERE YEAR(CustomerDateOfBirth) = 1996
INTERSECT
SELECT CustomerID, CONCAT(CustomerFirstName, ' ', CustomerLastName) AS Name,
       CustomerGender AS Gender, YEAR(CustomerDateOfBirth) AS YearOfBirth
FROM Customers
WHERE CustomerGender = 'Male'
ORDER BY CustomerID;
```

The keyword for difference operations: To retrieve the difference between one query result set and another, the *EXCEPT/MINUS* keyword can be used. When you use the *EXCEPT/MINUS* keyword, the database engine removes all the rows from statement one's result set if they are present in statement two's result set, and it provides the remaining result set from statement one. If you use three statements, the database engine removes all the rows from the previous result set if they are present in statement three's result, and it provides the remaining result set. This process will continue until all select statements have finished execution. The basic syntax will be:

```
SELECT statement 1
EXCEPT
SELECT statement 2
................................
ORDER BY column list;
```

Please note that the *ORDER BY* clause can only be used at the end of the last *SELECT* statement and the column's data type must be the same or compatible across all *SELECT* statements. If you are using Oracle, please use *MINUS* instead of the *EXCEPT* keyword. MySQL doesn't support the *EXCEPT/MINUS* keyword.

The SQL statement to retrieve *a list of non-male customers who were born in 1996* can be written as:

```
SELECT CustomerID, CONCAT(CustomerFirstName, ' ', CustomerLastName) AS Name,
       CustomerGender AS Gender, YEAR(CustomerDateOfBirth) AS YearOfBirth
FROM Customers
WHERE YEAR(CustomerDateOfBirth) = 1996
EXCEPT
SELECT CustomerID,CONCAT(CustomerFirstName, ' ', CustomerLastName) AS Name,
       CustomerGender AS Gender, YEAR(CustomerDateOfBirth) AS YearOfBirth
FROM Customers
WHERE CustomerGender = 'Male'
ORDER BY CustomerID;
```

Similarly, the SQL statement to retrieve *a list of male customers who were not born in 1996* can be written as:

```
SELECT CustomerID, CONCAT(CustomerFirstName, ' ', CustomerLastName) AS Name,
       CustomerGender AS Gender, YEAR(CustomerDateOfBirth) AS YearOfBirth
FROM Customers
WHERE CustomerGender = 'Male'
EXCEPT
SELECT CustomerID, CONCAT(CustomerFirstName, ' ', CustomerLastName) AS Name,
       CustomerGender AS Gender, YEAR(CustomerDateOfBirth) AS YearOfBirth
FROM Customers
WHERE YEAR(CustomerDateOfBirth) = 1996
ORDER BY CustomerID;
```

The keyword for union operations:
To merge two or more query result sets, the *UNION/UNION ALL* keyword can be used. The *UNION ALL* keyword will show duplicate rows in the final result, while the *UNION* keyword provides only the unique rows in the final result. The basic syntax will be like below:

```
SELECT statement 1
UNION/UNION ALL
SELECT statement 2
..............................
ORDER BY column list;
```

Please note that the *ORDER BY* clause can only be used at the end of the last *SELECT* statement and the column's data type must be the same or compatible across all *SELECT* statements. Please use the *UNION ALL* keyword if you want to keep duplicate rows in your result, otherwise use the *UNION* keyword.

Therefore, the SQL statement to retrieve *a list of customers who are either male or were born in 1996 or both* can be written as:

```
SELECT CustomerID, CONCAT(CustomerFirstName, ' ', CustomerLastName) AS Name,
       CustomerGender AS Gender, YEAR(CustomerDateOfBirth) AS YearOfBirth
FROM Customers
WHERE CustomerGender = 'Male'
UNION
SELECT CustomerID, CONCAT(CustomerFirstName, ' ', CustomerLastName) AS Name,
       CustomerGender AS Gender, YEAR(CustomerDateOfBirth) AS YearOfBirth
FROM Customers
WHERE YEAR(CustomerDateOfBirth) = 1996
ORDER BY CustomerID;
```

Next, we'll learn how to use the *INTERSECT*, *EXCEPT/MINUS* and *UNION* operations by solving some business problems.

Business Problem 19

Please give me a list of products for vendor ID's 7 & 8. The list must include only the products that can be delivered in less than a week after the customer orders it. On the list, please show the product ID, product name, expected number of days needed for delivery, and the vendor ID for each product.

Solution SQL: SQL Server

```
SELECT    ProductID, ProductName, DaysToDeliver, VendorID
FROM      Products
WHERE     VendorID IN (7,8)

INTERSECT

SELECT    ProductID, ProductName, DaysToDeliver, VendorID
FROM      Products
WHERE     DaysToDeliver <= 7;
```

SQL Result

ProductID	ProductName	DaysToDeliver	VendorID
23	Avengers Titan Heroes Winter Soldier 12 Pack	5	7
24	Fairy Dolls 12 Packs	5	7
25	Friendship Bracelets Sets	5	7
26	Kids Avengers Thor Cape and Mask Dress Up Set	5	7
27	Electronic Toy Dishwasher	5	7
28	Fire Station Sound Puzzle	5	7
29	Super Hero Girls Playset	5	8
30	3D Magic Spinner Fairy Theme Pack	5	8
31	Kids Minions Cape and Mask Dress Up Set	5	8
32	Little Tikes Cook N Play Outdoor BBQ	5	8
33	Tools Sound Puzzle	5	8

Solution Review

The first *SELECT* statement uses a *VendorID IN (7, 8)* predicate, which means it will retrieve all products for vendors 7 & 8, but some of them can be delivered within a week and some of them can take more than a week.

The second *SELECT* statement uses a *DaysToDeliver <= 7* predicate, which means it will retrieve all products that can be delivered within a week, but some of them can be from vendors 7 & 8 and some of them can be from other vendors.

The *INTERSECT* keyword tells the database engine to provide only those common products retrieved by both of the *SELECT* statements that are products of vendor ID's 7 & 8 that can be delivered within a week.

Business Problem 20

Please give me a list of products for *vendor ID's 7 & 8* that may take more than a week to deliver from customer's order date. Please show each product's product ID, product name, expected number of days needed for delivery, and the vendor ID for each product.

Solution SQL: SQL Server

```
SELECT    ProductID, ProductName, DaysToDeliver, VendorID
FROM      Products
WHERE     VendorID IN (7,8)

EXCEPT

SELECT    ProductID, ProductName, DaysToDeliver, VendorID
FROM      Products
WHERE     DaysToDeliver <= 7;
```

SQL Result

ProductID	ProductName	DaysToDeliver	VendorID
34	Stunning Outdoor Wicker 10 Seater Dining Set	14	8
35	Bed Skirt (Queen, White, 15 Inch Fall)	14	8
36	Butter Knife 403 Stainless Steel Set	14	8

Solution Review

The first *SELECT* statement uses a *VendorID IN (7,8)* predicate, which means it will retrieve all the products for vendors 7 & 8. As was the case with *Business Problem 19*, this will not be enough to narrow the results. Some of the products can be delivered within a week, so we need to exclude those to solve our problem.

The second *SELECT* statement uses a *DaysToDeliver <= 7* predicate to retrieve all the products that can be delivered within a week. You would be right to guess that some of the results of this statement will include products from other vendors. But this is not relevant here—we just want to remove products from the results of the first *SELECT* statement from these results.

The *EXCEPT* keyword is used between these two *SELECT* statements to allow the database engine to exclude products from the first *SELECT* statement's results if they match the second *SELECT* statement's results. In other words, the products that can be delivered within seven days will be excluded from the products for vendors 7 & 8.

Alternatively, you can change the predicate from *DaysToDeliver <= 7* to *DaysToDeliver > 7* and use the *INTERSECT* keyword to achieve the same result. The SQL for this alternative solution will be:

```
SELECT    ProductID, ProductName, DaysToDeliver, VendorID
FROM      Products
WHERE     VendorID IN (7,8)

INTERSECT

SELECT    ProductID, ProductName, DaysToDeliver, VendorID
FROM      Products
WHERE     DaysToDeliver > 7;
```

Business Problem 21

Please give me a list of all the products for vendor ID's 7 & 8 as well as other vendor's products that may take more than a week to deliver. Please show the product ID, product name, expected number of days needed for delivery, and vendor ID for each product.

Solution SQL: SQL Server

```
SELECT    ProductID, ProductName, DaysToDeliver, VendorID
FROM      Products
WHERE     VendorID IN (7,8)

UNION

SELECT    ProductID, ProductName, DaysToDeliver, VendorID
FROM      Products
WHERE     DaysToDeliver > 7;
```

SQL Result

ProductID	ProductName	DaysToDeliver	VendorID
12	Dining Table and Chairs	14	2
20	5 seater modular couch with four cup holders	14	4
21	Sunbeam Microplush Heated Blanket with ComfortTech Controller	14	4
22	Round Woven Bread Roll Baskets	14	4
23	Avengers Titan Heroes Winter Soldier 12 Pack	5	7
24	Fairy Dolls 12 Packs	5	7
25	Friendship Bracelets Sets	5	7
26	Kids Avengers Thor Cape and Mask Dress Up Set	5	7
27	Electronic Toy Dishwasher	5	7
28	Fire Station Sound Puzzle	5	7

Solution Review

Here, the *UNION* operation merges two result sets produced by each of these two *SELECT* statements and merges any duplicate rows into single rows. If you want to keep all of the duplicate rows, then you can use *UNION ALL* instead of *UNION*. Only the first ten out of 24 rows have been displayed here to save space.

Using Multiple Predicates in a WHERE Clause

Now you know how to use the *INTERSECT*, *EXCEPT/MINUS* and *UNION* keywords between two *SELECT* statements. Let's carefully examine two *SELECT* statements we have used in the previous section:

First statement:

```
SELECT CustomerID, CONCAT(CustomerFirstName, ' ', CustomerLastName) AS Name,
       CustomerGender AS Gender, YEAR(CustomerDateOfBirth) AS YearOfBirth
FROM Customers
WHERE YEAR(CustomerDateOfBirth) = 1996;
```

Second statement:

```
SELECT CustomerID, CONCAT(CustomerFirstName, ' ', CustomerLastName) AS Name,
       CustomerGender AS Gender, YEAR(CustomerDateOfBirth) AS YearOfBirth
FROM Customers
WHERE CustomerGender = 'Male';
```

Everything is same between these two statements except the predicates in the *WHERE* clause. The first statement retrieves the rows where the predicate *YEAR(CustomerDateOfBirth) = 1996* evaluates to *TRUE*, and the second statement retrieves the rows where the *CustomerGender = 'Male'* predicate evaluates to *TRUE*. The *INTERSECT* operation retrieves those rows where both predicates evaluate to *TRUE*.

The same result can be achieved by combining both predicates with an *AND* operator in the *WHERE* clause. Therefore, the SQL statement below:

```
SELECT CustomerID, CONCAT(CustomerFirstName, ' ', CustomerLastName) AS Name,
       CustomerGender AS Gender, YEAR(CustomerDateOfBirth) AS YearOfBirth
FROM Customers
WHERE YEAR(CustomerDateOfBirth) = 1996;

INTERSECT

SELECT CustomerID, CONCAT(CustomerFirstName, ' ', CustomerLastName) AS Name,
       CustomerGender AS Gender, YEAR(CustomerDateOfBirth) AS YearOfBirth
FROM Customers
WHERE CustomerGender = 'Male';
```

...can also be written as:

```
SELECT CustomerID, CONCAT(CustomerFirstName, ' ', CustomerLastName) AS Name,
       CustomerGender AS Gender, YEAR(CustomerDateOfBirth) AS YearOfBirth
FROM Customers
WHERE YEAR(CustomerDateOfBirth) = 1996 AND CustomerGender = 'Male';
```

The AND operator: As you can see, you can do the *INTERSECT* operation by combining the *WHERE* clause's predicates with an *AND* operator. The difference between the *INTERSECT* operation and the *AND* operation is this:

The *INTERSECT* operation executes each query first and then decides which rows are common in both result sets. By contrast, the *AND* operator evaluates both predicates for each row and decides whether the row will be returned. It is important to understand what the evaluation result will be for the combined predicate when two predicates are combined with an *AND* operator.

The basic syntax for combining two predicates using an *AND* operator is:
Predicate 1 **AND** Predicate 2

You know that any predicate can be evaluated with either a *TRUE*, *FALSE* or *NULL* value.

- If both predicates evaluate to *TRUE*, then the combined predicate will evaluate to *TRUE* and the corresponding row will be returned.
- But if either of two predicates evaluates to *FALSE*, then the combined predicate will evaluate to *FALSE* and the corresponding row will not be returned.
- And if one predicate evaluates to *NULL* and the other predicate evaluates to either *NULL* or *TRUE*, then the combined predicate will evaluate to *NULL* and the corresponding row will not be returned.

We can summarize these evaluation results as you see below:

AND		Evaluation Result for Predicate 1		
		TRUE	FALSE	NULL
Evaluation Result for Predicate 2	TRUE	TRUE (Rows will be returned)	FALSE (Rows will not be returned)	NULL (Rows will not be returned)
	FALSE	FALSE (Rows will not be returned)	FALSE (Rows will not be returned)	FALSE (Rows will not be returned)
	NULL	NULL (Rows will not be returned)	FALSE (Rows will not be returned)	NULL (Rows will not be returned)

Now let's examine the *UNION* operation of the above two statements. The *UNION* operation returns rows where either of the two predicates evaluates to *TRUE*. The same result can be achieved by combining both predicates with an *OR* operator in the *WHERE* clause.

Therefore, the SQL statement:

```
SELECT CustomerID, CONCAT(CustomerFirstName, ' ', CustomerLastName) AS Name,
       CustomerGender AS Gender, YEAR(CustomerDateOfBirth) AS YearOfBirth
FROM Customers
WHERE YEAR(CustomerDateOfBirth) = 1996;

UNION

SELECT CustomerID, CONCAT(CustomerFirstName, ' ', CustomerLastName) AS Name,
       CustomerGender AS Gender, YEAR(CustomerDateOfBirth) AS YearOfBirth
FROM Customers
WHERE CustomerGender = 'Male';
```

...can also be written as:

```
SELECT CustomerID, CONCAT(CustomerFirstName, ' ', CustomerLastName) AS Name,
       CustomerGender AS Gender, YEAR(CustomerDateOfBirth) AS YearOfBirth
FROM Customers
WHERE YEAR(CustomerDateOfBirth) = 1996 OR CustomerGender = 'Male';
```

The OR operator: As you can see, you can do the *UNION* operation by combining a *WHERE* clause's predicates with an *OR* operator. The difference between the *UNION* operation and the *OR* operation is:

The *UNION* operation executes each query first, then merges both result sets, while the *OR* operator evaluates either the first predicate or both predicates for each row, and then decides whether the row will be returned. It is important to understand what the evaluation result will be for the combined predicate if two predicates are combined with an *OR* operator.

The basic syntax to combine two predicates using *OR* operator is:

```
Predicate 1 OR Predicate 2
```

This means that, when evaluating these two predicates:

- If either of the two predicates evaluates to *TRUE*, the combined predicate will evaluate to *TRUE* and the corresponding row will be returned (the RDBMS will not even bother to check the second predicate since the first predicate evaluated to *TRUE*).
- If both predicates evaluate to *FALSE*, the combined predicate will evaluate to *FALSE* and the corresponding row will not be returned.
- Or if one predicate evaluates to *NULL* and the other predicate evaluates to either *FALSE* or *NULL*, the combined predicate will evaluate to *NULL*, and the corresponding row will not be returned.

We can summarize these evaluation results as follows:

OR		Evaluation Result for Predicate 1		
		TRUE	FALSE	NULL
Evaluation Result for Predicate 2	**TRUE**	TRUE (Rows will be returned)	TRUE (Rows will be returned)	TRUE (Rows will be returned)
	FALSE	TRUE (Rows will be returned)	FALSE (Rows will not be returned)	NULL (Rows will not be returned)
	NULL	TRUE (Rows will be returned)	NULL (Rows will not be returned)	NULL (Rows will not be returned)

Now let's examine the *EXCEPT/MINUS* operation of the above two statements. The *EXCEPT/MINUS* operation returns rows from the first statement's result if they are not present in the second statement's result. In other words, each row in the final result should satisfy the first predicate but not the second predicate. We can achieve the same result by negating the second predicate with a *NOT* operator and then combining it with the first predicate using an *AND* operator in the *WHERE* clause. Therefore, the SQL statement:

```
SELECT CustomerID, CONCAT(CustomerFirstName, ' ', CustomerLastName) AS Name,
       CustomerGender AS Gender, YEAR(CustomerDateOfBirth) AS YearOfBirth
FROM Customers
WHERE YEAR(CustomerDateOfBirth) = 1996;

EXCEPT

SELECT CustomerID, CONCAT(CustomerFirstName, ' ', CustomerLastName) AS Name,
       CustomerGender AS Gender, YEAR(CustomerDateOfBirth) AS YearOfBirth
FROM Customers
WHERE CustomerGender = 'Male';
```

...can also be written as:

```
SELECT CustomerID, CONCAT(CustomerFirstName, ' ', CustomerLastName) AS Name,
       CustomerGender AS Gender, YEAR(CustomerDateOfBirth) AS YearOfBirth
FROM Customers
WHERE YEAR(CustomerDateOfBirth) = 1996 AND ( NOT CustomerGender = 'Male' );
```

The NOT operator: As you can see, you can do the *EXCEPT* operation by negating the second statement's predicate with a *NOT* operator and then combining it with the first statement's predicate using an *AND* operator in the *WHERE* clause. The basic syntax of the *NOT* operator is:

```
NOT Predicate
```

The *NOT* operator negates the predicate value (i.e. from *TRUE* to *FALSE* and *FALSE* to *TRUE*) but *NULL* data will be unchanged. We can summarize this evaluation results like below:

Evaluation Result for Predicate in WHERE Clause	
Original	**After applying NOT**
TRUE	FALSE (Rows will not be returned)
FALSE	TRUE (Rows will be returned)
NULL	NULL (Rows will not be returned)

When you use a *NOT* operator to negate a predicate, it can be written a few different ways. The table below shows how a *NOT* operator can be used with most commonly used predicates:

Original predicate	General form after negation	Simplified form after negation	Alternate form after negation
Expression 1 = Expression 2	NOT Expression 1 = Expression 2		Expression 1 <> Expression 2
Expression 1 <> Expression 2	NOT Expression 1 <> Expression 2		Expression 1 = Expression 2
Expression 1 < Expression 2	NOT Expression 1 < Expression 2		Expression 1 >= Expression 2
Expression 1 <= Expression 2	NOT Expression 1 <= Expression 2		Expression 1 > Expression 2
Expression 1 > Expression 2	NOT Expression 1 > Expression 2		Expression 1 <= Expression 2
Expression 1 >= Expression 2	NOT Expression 1 >= Expression 2		Expression 1 < Expression 2
Expression BETWEEN Value 1 AND Value 2	NOT Expression BETWEEN Value 1 AND Value 2	Expression NOT BETWEEN Value 1 AND Value 2	
Expression IN (Value 1, Value 2, ...)	NOT Expression IN (Value 1, Value 2, ...)	Expression NOT IN (Value 1, Value 2, ...)	
Expression LIKE pattern	NOT Expression LIKE pattern	Expression NOT LIKE pattern	
Expression IS NULL	NOT Expression IS NULL	Expression IS NOT NULL	

The order of execution for operators: So far, we have used multiple logical operators along with mathematical operators in a *WHERE* clause. We already discussed the execution order for mathematical operators in Lesson 6, but it's time to revisit the execution order with regard to using additional operators. When a database engine evaluates an expression, it starts with the operators with higher precedence and moves downward through those operators with lower precedence. In the case of multiple operators that do not have a higher or lower precedence to each other, they will be executed in order from left to right. In case of multiple parentheses being used, they will be executed from innermost to outermost. The table below shows the most frequently used operators and their order of execution within an expression or predicate:

Execution Order Level	Operator
1	() parenthesis
2	* (multiply), / (division), % (modulo), DIV
3	+ (add), - (subtract)
4	= (equal to), < (less than), <= (less than or equal to), > (greater than), >= (greater than or equal to), BETWEEN, IN, LIKE, IS NULL
5	NOT
6	AND
7	OR

Please note that the parentheses are not a real operator, but we have added it to the operator list because it can be used to prioritize an operator or a particular part of the expression with a higher precedence. Let's examine how the database engine evaluates the predicate for the previous SQL statement:

```
SELECT CustomerID, CONCAT(CustomerFirstName, ' ', CustomerLastName) AS Name,
       CustomerGender AS Gender, YEAR(CustomerDateOfBirth) AS YearOfBirth
FROM Customers
WHERE YEAR(CustomerDateOfBirth) = 1996  AND NOT CustomerGender = 'Male';
```

Here the predicate used in the *WHERE* clause is:

```
YEAR(CustomerDateOfBirth) = 1996  AND NOT CustomerGender = 'Male';
```

Therefore, the database engine will follow the steps below to evaluate the predicate for each row of the *Customers* table:

1. Evaluate YEAR(*CustomerDateOfBirth*)
2. Evaluate *result of step 1 = 1996*
3. Evaluate *CustomerGender = 'Male'*
4. Evaluate NOT *result of step 3*
5. Evaluate *Result of step* 2 AND *result of step 4*

If you carefully examine the steps, you can conclude that each predicate evaluates first before applying any *NOT/AND/OR* operators on them. Therefore, we can rewrite the predicate in either of the below forms:

```
(YEAR(CustomerDateOfBirth) = 1996)  AND (NOT CustomerGender = 'Male');
(YEAR(CustomerDateOfBirth) = 1996)  AND (NOT (CustomerGender = 'Male'));
```

The predicate evaluation tree can be graphically described as below:

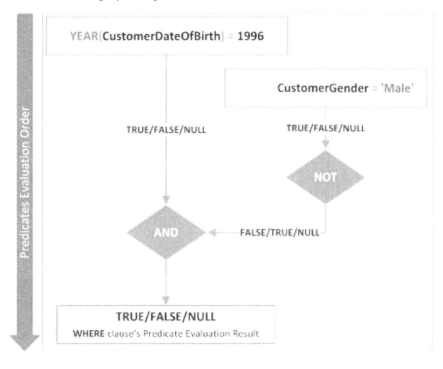

Let's add one more predicate with the original predicate:

```
YEAR(CustomerDateOfBirth) = 1996  AND NOT CustomerGender = 'Male' OR CustomerMobileNumber IS NULL;
```

We haven't enforced any evaluation priority here (i.e. parentheses haven't been used). So, the operators *AND, OR & NOT* will be evaluated as per their default order of evaluation, which is *NOT → AND → OR* and the predicate evaluation tree can be graphically described as below:

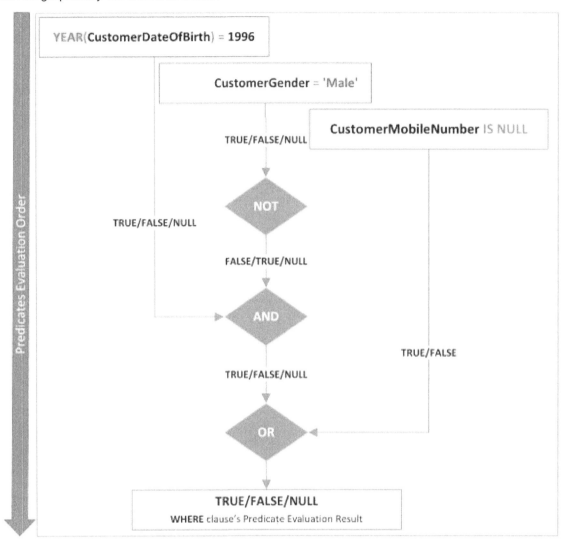

The database engine will negate the second predicate with a *NOT* operator, then apply an *AND* operator with the 1st predicate, and then apply an *OR* operator with the third predicate. If you use this in the *WHERE* clause of a *SELECT* statement, *the database engine will retrieve all non-male customers who were born in 1996 and all customers whose mobile numbers are unknown.*

Now let's see what happens when we add parentheses:

```
YEAR(CustomerDateOfBirth) = 1996  AND (NOT CustomerGender = 'Male' OR CustomerMobileNumber IS NULL);
```

We have just enforced an evaluation priority here by using parentheses. So, the operators within the () will be evaluated first. The resulting evaluation order of *AND, OR & NOT* will now be *NOT → OR → AND*, and the predicate evaluation tree for this can be graphically described as:

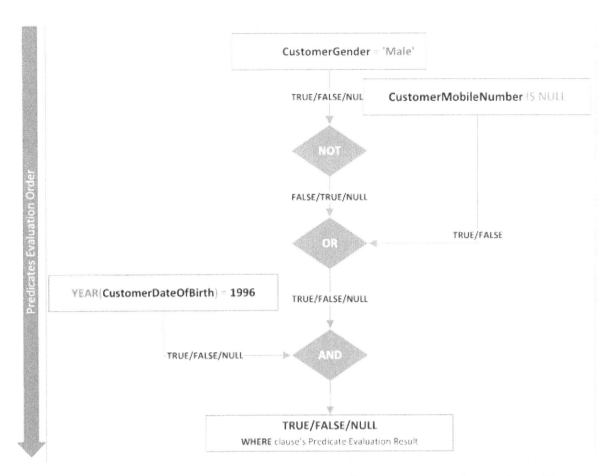

The database engine will negate the second predicate with a *NOT* operator, then apply an *OR* operator with the third predicate, and then apply *AND* operator with the first predicate. If you use this in the *WHERE* clause of a *SELECT* statement, *the database engine will retrieve all customers who were born in 1996 but either their mobile numbers are unknown or they are not male.*

Now move the parentheses after the *NOT* operator, as shown below:

```
YEAR(CustomerDateOfBirth) = 1996  AND NOT (CustomerGender = 'Male' OR CustomerMobileNumber IS NULL);
```

Here the evaluation order of *AND*, *OR* & *NOT* will be *OR* → *NOT* → *AND*, and the predicate evaluation tree can be graphically described as below:

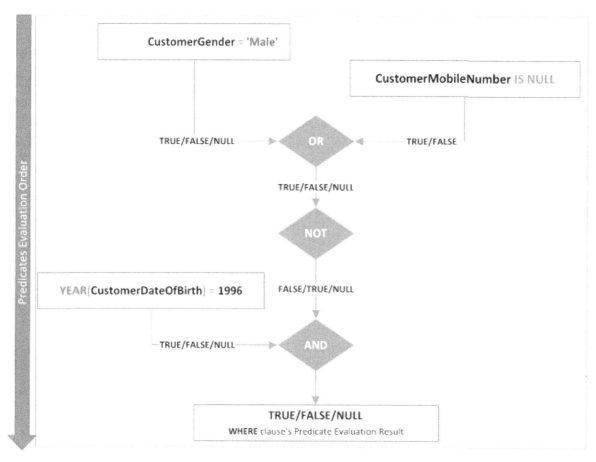

The database engine will apply an *OR* operator between the second and third predicates, then a *NOT* operator on the result, then an *AND* operator with the first predicate. If you use this in the *WHERE* clause of a *SELECT* statement, *the database engine will retrieve all non-male customers who were born in 1996 and their mobile numbers that are known to us.*

Note

As you can see, parentheses can change a result dramatically. Please use them carefully.

Now let's strengthen your understanding of the usages of the *AND*, *OR* & *NOT* operators by solving some business problems.

Business Problem 22

Please give me a list of all the products for Vendor ID's 7 & 8 that can be delivered within a week of a customer's initial order date. On your list, please show each product ID, product name, expected number of days needed for delivery, and vendor ID. This is almost the same as *Business Problem 19*, but in *Business Problem 19* we solved this problem by using the *INTERSECT* operator—which some RDBMSs (e.g. MySQL) do not support. For that reason, it's useful to know the alternative method we're about to show you, so please solve using the *AND* operator, which is widely supported among RDBMSs.

Solution SQL: SQL Server

```
SELECT ProductID, ProductName, DaysToDeliver, VendorID
FROM    Products
WHERE   VendorID IN (7,8) AND DaysToDeliver <= 7;
```

SQL Result

The result will be the same as *Business Problem 19.*

Solution Review

The database engine will evaluate the predicates *VendorID IN (7,8)* and *DaysToDeliver <= 7* for each row of the *Products* table. The first predicate will be *TRUE* if the vendor ID is either 7 or 8, otherwise it will be either *FALSE* or *NULL*, and the second predicate will be *TRUE* if days to deliver is less than or equal to 7, otherwise it will be *FALSE* or *NULL*. Since we have used the *AND* operator between the two predicates, the corresponding row will be returned only if both predicates become *TRUE*. Therefore, the *SELECT* statement will return a list of all products for vendor ID's 7 & 8 that can be delivered within a week.

Business Problem 23

Please give me a list of products for vendor ID's 7 & 8 that may take more than a week to deliver after a customer's initial order date. For each, please show the product ID, product name, expected number of days needed for delivery and vendor ID for each product on the list. This is same as *Business Problem 20*, but in *Business Problem 20* we solved it by using the *EXCEPT/MINUS* operator which some RDBMSs (e.g. MySQL) do not support. Please solve it using the more widely supported *AND* & *NOT* operators.

Solution SQL: SQL Server

```
SELECT ProductID, ProductName, DaysToDeliver, VendorID
FROM     Products
WHERE    VendorID IN (7,8) AND NOT DaysToDeliver <= 7;
```

SQL Result

You will receive the same result as *Business Problem 20*.

Solution Review

The database engine will evaluate the predicates *VendorID IN (7,8)* and *DaysToDeliver <= 7* for each row of *Products* table. The 1st predicate will be *TRUE* if the vendor ID is either 7 or 8, otherwise it will be either *FALSE* or *NULL*, and the *NOT* operator negates the 2nd predicate—in other words it will be *TRUE* if days to deliver is greater than 7, otherwise it will be *FALSE* or *NULL*. Therefore, the *SELECT* statement will return the list of products for vendor ID 7 & 8 that may take more than a week to deliver from customer's order date.

The predicate *NOT DaysToDeliver <= 7* can also be written as *DaysToDeliver > 7*. So, the above SQL statement can alternatively be written as:

```
SELECT ProductID, ProductName, DaysToDeliver, VendorID
FROM     Products
WHERE    VendorID IN (7,8) AND DaysToDeliver > 7;
```

Business Problem 24

Please give me a list that contains all the products for vendor ID's 7 & 8 as well as all products from other vendors that may take more than a week to deliver after a customer's initial order date. Please show the product ID, product name, expected number of days to deliver and vendor ID for each product on the list. This is same as *Business Problem 21*, but this time please solve it using the *OR* operator.

Solution SQL: SQL Server

```
SELECT ProductID, ProductName, DaysToDeliver, VendorID
FROM     Products
WHERE    VendorID IN (7,8) OR DaysToDeliver > 7;
```

SQL Result

You will receive the same result as *Business Problem 21*

Solution Review

The database engine will evaluate the predicates *VendorID IN (7,8)* and *DaysToDeliver > 7* for each row of the Products table. The 1st predicate will be *TRUE* if the vendor ID is either 7 or 8, otherwise it will be either *FALSE* or *NULL*, and the 2nd predicate will be *TRUE* if *DaysToDeliver* is greater than 7, otherwise it will be *FALSE* or *NULL*. Since we have used the *OR* operator between the two predicates, the corresponding row will be returned if either of the two predicates becomes *TRUE*. Therefore, the *SELECT* statement will return the list of products that contain all products for vendor ID's 7 & 8 as well as products from all other vendors that may take more than a week to deliver from customer's order date.

Using a Subquery within a Predicate in a WHERE Clause

Our database has a *SalesOrderProducts* table that stores each product of each sales order that is submitted by a customer. When a customer orders a product, the *ProductDeliveryDate* column in the *SalesOrderProducts* table stores no value until the product has been delivered to the customer. Once delivered, the *ProductDeliveryDate* column stores the actual delivery date. What if a business user asks you, *'Which products (listing ID's only) have been delivered to customers within the first three days of the year 2017?'* Based on your knowledge, you can easily write and execute the necessary SQL query:

```
SELECT ProductID
FROM SalesOrderProducts
WHERE ProductDeliveryDate >= '2017-01-01'
     AND ProductDeliveryDate < '2017-01-04';
```

...which will return the *ProductID's 25, 31, 49 and 58*.

Now, what if the business user asks you, *'Which of our vendors' products (ID's only) have been delivered to customers within the first three days of the year 2017?'* We know the *SalesOrderProducts* table does not have a *VendorID* column, but the *Products* table does. The *VendorID* column in *Products* table stores the ID for all vendors who supply our company's products. So, you can use the *ProductID* from the earlier query and write a query like the one below to provide you with the desired result:

```
SELECT VendorID
FROM  Products
WHERE ProductID IN (25,31,49,58);
```

Instead of executing the first query and using the result in the second query, RDBMSs allow you to replace the product list (that has been generated by the first query) with the first query as you see below:

```
SELECT VendorID
FROM Products
WHERE ProductID IN (
                SELECT ProductID
                FROM SalesOrderProducts
                WHERE ProductDeliveryDate >= '2017-01-01'
                     AND ProductDeliveryDate < '2017-01-04'
        );
```

Here, the query inside the *IN* predicate is called a subquery. If the business user is not happy with a result that only shows the ID's for vendors, you can get additional details about your vendors from the *Vendors* table and use the above query as a subquery:

```
SELECT VendorID, VendorName, VendorPhoneNumber, VendorEmail
FROM Vendors
WHERE VendorID IN (
                    SELECT VendorID
                    FROM Products
                    WHERE ProductID IN (
                                         SELECT ProductID
                                         FROM   SalesOrderProducts
                                         WHERE  ProductDeliveryDate >= '2017-01-01'
                                            AND ProductDeliveryDate < '2017-01-04'
                                        )
                  );
```

Here, the innermost query will be executed first, which will return *ProductIDs*. These *ProductIDs* will be used in the *WHERE* clause of the outer query which will return *VendorIDs*. These *VendorIDs* will then be used in the *WHERE* clause of the main query and will return each vendor's *ID*, *name*, *phone number* and *email address*. Since we're on the subject, let's talk about subqueries bit more before we go further.

Subquery: If you embed a query (a *SELECT* statement) within another query (a *SELECT* statement), this embedded query is called a subquery. Two types of subqueries are supported by almost all RDBMSs: the tabular subquery and the scalar subquery.

Tabular subquery: This is an embedded query that returns one or more columns and zero, one, or more rows of data. If a tabular subquery returns only one column, then it can be used in a *WHERE* clause predicate as per the earlier example. It can also be used in the *FROM* clause, which we will discuss in a later lesson. If a tabular subquery returns more than one column, it can only be used in a *FROM* and *JOIN* clause (which we will discuss further when we cover *FROM* with *JOIN* clauses).

Scalar subquery: This is an embedded query that returns one column and zero or one row of data. In other words, if an embedded query returns a single value or no value, it is called a scalar subquery. The scalar subquery is typically used with comparison operators in a *WHERE* clause or in a *SELECT* clause. When you use it in the *SELECT* clause, it will be executed once for each returning row. For example, let's assume that you want to retrieve every products in the database including their product names and vendor names. As you may recall, you can easily write a query to retrieve all stored product names, and you can write another query to retrieve all vendor names. The two queries will look like:

```
SELECT ProductName                          SELECT VendorName
FROM Products;                               FROM Vendors;
```

If you try to use the second query as a subquery in the *SELECT* clause of first query, the query may look like:

```
SELECT ProductName, ( SELECT VendorName
                      FROM Vendors
                    ) AS VendorName
FROM Products;
```

Unfortunately, trying to execute such a query will return an error because the subquery used in the *SELECT* clause is not a scalar subquery (the subquery will return multiple rows). To solve this, we need to change this subquery to return only one row for each product. To do so, we can include a *WHERE* clause predicate:

```
SELECT  ProductName, ( SELECT VendorName
                       FROM Vendors
                       WHERE Vendors.VendorID = Products.VendorID
                     ) AS VendorName
FROM Products;
```

Here, *Products.VendorID* represents the *VendorID* column in the *Products* table. This is called a two-part naming convention, which is *TableName.ColumnName*. When two tables use the same column name and both columns are used in a query, you have to use the two-part naming convention, otherwise the database engine will be confused. Here, for each resulting row from *Products* table, the subquery will match its *VendorID* with the *VendorID* from *Vendors* table and return only the corresponding vendor's name. Here's what the graphical representation of the execution process looks like:

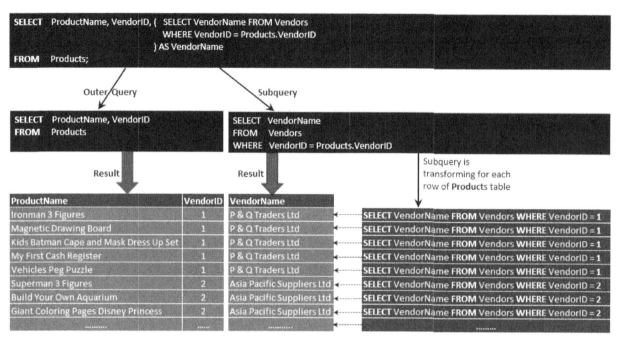

Note

In a subquery, when you are using a column name from outside (i.e. from an outer query), you have to use the two-part name, otherwise, just the column name should be OK. For example, the above subquery is retrieving data from the *Vendors* table. Therefore, the *VendorID* column from the *Vendors* table can be written either as *VendorID* or *Vendors.VendorID* because this table is being used in the *FROM* clause of this subquery, but the *VendorID* from the *Products* table must be written as *Products.VendorID*. Therefore, the above query can also be written like below:

```
SELECT  ProductName, ( SELECT VendorName
                FROM Vendors
                WHERE VendorID = Products.VendorID
              ) AS VendorName
FROM Products;
```

Let's solve some business problems to practice using subqueries.

Business Problem 25

Which of our customers live in Australia? For each customer, please show their ID, name, email address ID and postal address ID.

Solution SQL: SQL Server

```
SELECT  CustomerID, CustomerFirstName AS FirstName,CustomerLastName AS LastName,
        CustomerEmail AS Email, CustomerAddressID AS PostalAddressID
FROM Customers
WHERE CustomerAddressID IN ( SELECT AddressID FROM Addresses
                        WHERE Country LIKE 'Australia');
```

SQL Result

CustomerID	FirstName	LastName	Email	PostalAddressID
1	Ricky	Brown	RickBrown@SaleOnYourOwn.com	1
2	Adam	Wilson	AdamWilson@SaleOnYourOwn.com	2
3	Crystal	Doslakoski	CrystalDoslakoski@SaleOnYourOwn.com	5
4	Melanie	Bowell	KerrynWhite@SaleOnYourOwn.com	6
5	Sophie	Smith	SophieSmith@SaleOnYourOwn.com	8
16	Robinson	Clark	RobinsonClark@SaleOnYourOwn.com	41

Solution Review

Here, the country column is in the *Addresses* table but the customer's other details are in the *Customers* table. The subquery *SELECT AddressID FROM Addresses WHERE Country LIKE 'Australia'* will return a list of *AddressIDs* from the *Addresses* table for Australia and pass them to the *WHERE* clause of the outer query, and then the outer query check if any *CustomerAddressID* matches with the list and retrieve those customers that match. The graphical representation of this execution processes will look like below:

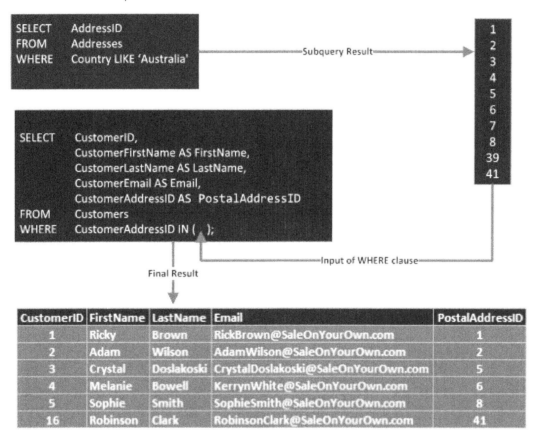

Please note that the *LIKE* operator can be replaced with equal to = operator and the *IN* operator can be replaced with = *ANY* operator in the above query. So, you can rewrite the query like:

```
SELECT CustomerID, CustomerFirstName AS FirstName, CustomerLastName AS LastName,
       CustomerEmail AS Email, CustomerAddressID AS PostalAddressID
FROM Customers
WHERE CustomerAddressID = ANY ( SELECT AddressID FROM  Addresses WHERE  Country LIKE 'Australia');
```

Notice that the full addresses of our customers are not shown by the above query. If you want to show customers' full addresses, please have a look at the next business problem.

Business Problem 26

Which customers live in Australia? For each, please show the ID, name, full postal address and email address.

Solution SQL: SQL Server

```
SELECT CustomerID, CustomerFirstName AS FirstName, CustomerLastName AS LastName, CustomerEmail AS Email,
        (       SELECT CONCAT(StreetAddress, ', ', City, ', ', StateProvince, ', ', Country)
                FROM Addresses
                WHERE Addresses.AddressID = Customers.CustomerAddressID
        ) AS PostalAddress
FROM Customers
WHERE CustomerAddressID IN (     SELECT AddressID
                                 FROM Addresses
                                 WHERE Country LIKE 'Australia'
                            );
```

SQL Result

CustomerID	FirstName	LastName	Email	PostalAddress
1	Ricky	Brown	RickBrown@SaleOnYourOwn.com	475 Flinders Lane, Melbourne, Victoria, Australia
2	Adam	Wilson	AdamWilson@SaleOnYourOwn.com	211 La Trobe Street, Melbourne, Victoria, Australia
3	Crystal	Doslakoski	CrystalDoslakoski@SaleOnYourOwn.com	455 George Street, Sydney, New South Wales, Australia
4	Melanie	Bowell	KerrynWhite@SaleOnYourOwn.com	412-414 George Street, Sydney, New South Wales, Australia
5	Sophie	Smith	SophieSmith@SaleOnYourOwn.com	159-175 Church Street, Parramatta, New South Wales, Australia
16	Robinson	Clark	RobinsonClark@SaleOnYourOwn.com	2000 Moreland Road, Fawkner, Victoria, Australia

Solution Review

Here, the requirements are almost same as the previous question, and the only difference is you need to show the full postal address instead of numbers from *PostalAddressID*. Notice that we have used the query from the previous question and replaced the *SELECT* clause's *CustomerAddressID* column with the below subquery: :

```
SELECT CONCAT(StreetAddress, ', ', City, ', ', StateProvince, ', ', Country)
FROM Addresses
WHERE Addresses.AddressID = Customers.CustomerAddressID
```

Since this subquery is used in the *SELECT* clause, it will be executed once for each row, and each row's *CustomerAddressID* (i.e. the *PostalAddressID* from the previous result) will be passed to the subquery's *WHERE* clause predicate.

Practice Business Problems

Here are some more practice business problems for you to solve for the topics we've covered in this lesson. As always, the solutions to this lesson's practice problems can be found in *Appendix A* and we have also provided them for you at the following Google Drive links:

SQL Server:
https://drive.google.com/open?id=1ww1HeWmUZdEw6ritzMmmMx6_AyRDmaC3

MySQL:
https://drive.google.com/open?id=1GL_0oatasdY2vHUrGigBf1is14iSfmnP

Practice Business Problem 1

Please give me a list of the countries where our employees, customers and vendors are located.

Practice Business Problem 2

Please give me ten sample products and show me the ID, name, standard unit price, unit discount and net unit price for each.

Practice Business Problem 3

Please show me the ten most expensive products (based on their net unit price) with the ID, name, standard unit price, unit discount and net unit price for each.

Practice Business Problem 4

Please give me a list of all female employees. Please show the ID number, name, phone number, mobile number, email address, gender and date of birth for each.

Practice Business Problem 5

Please give me a list of products whose IDs are less than or equal to 15. Please show the ID, name and standard sales price for each result.

Practice Business Problem 6

Please give me a list of products with IDs that are greater than 15. Please show the ID, name and standard sales price for each.

Practice Business Problem 7

Which customers have registered on the website within the past five years? Please provide each Customer ID, name, phone number, mobile number, email address, date of birth, gender and registration date in the report. All dates should be formatted as a 1- or 2-digit day followed by blank space followed by abbreviated month name followed by blank space followed by 4 digit year(e.g. 5 Mar 2015).

Practice Business Problem 8

Which sales orders have a net value within a range of $30,000 to $40,000? For each sales order that falls within this range, retrieve the order ID, order date, due date, delivery date, customer ID, gross value, discount and net value. Please sort the results in descending order by delivery date and order ID.

Practice Business Problem 9

Which sales orders were due to be delivered on the 2nd, 3rd and 6th of February, 2017? For each sales order, please provide the order ID, order date, due date, delivery date, customer ID, gross value, discount and net value. Please sort the results in ascending order by delivery date and order ID.

Practice Business Problem 10

Please give me the details of all customers whose last name ends with 'son'.

Practice Business Problem 11

Please show me all orders that have not yet been delivered. For each result, please provide the order ID, order date, due date, delivery date, customer ID, gross value, discount and net value of each order.

Practice Business Problem 12

Please give me a list of all customers who were born between the years 1995 and 2000 and have first names that start with the letter 'R'. For each customer, please provide the ID number, name, gender and year of birth. Please show the list in ascending order by *CustomerID*.

Practice Business Problem 13

Please give me a list of all customers who were born between the year of 1995 and 2000 and whose first names **do not** start with the letter 'R'. For each customer, please provide the ID number, name, gender and year of birth. Please show the list in ascending order by *CustomerID*.

Practice Business Problem 14

Please give me a list of all customers who were either born between the year of 1995 and 2000, or whose first name starts with the letter 'R'. For each customer, please provide the ID number, name, gender and year of birth. Please show the list in ascending order by *CustomerID*.

Lesson Summary

In this lesson, you learned different techniques to retrieve a subset of rows from a table. You have seen that only those rows that meet a predicate can be retrieved from a table. You have also seen how to remove duplicate rows from a result set. In summary:

- Using the *DISTINCT* keyword in a *SELECT* clause removes any duplicate rows from the result set.
- SQL Server uses the *OFFSET-FETCH* clause at the end of a *SELECT* statement or *TOP N* keyword in the *SELECT* clause to perform a *TOP-N* or *BOTTOM-N* analysis.
- MySQL uses the *LIMIT-OFFSET* clause at the end of a *SELECT* statement to perform a *TOP-N* or *BOTTOM-N* analysis.
- When you use a predicate in the *WHERE* clause, only the rows that satisfy the predicate will be returned by the *SELECT* statement.
- The *AND*, *OR* and *NOT* operators can be used to combine multiple predicates.
- When you use an *INTERSECT* keyword between two queries, it will return the common rows returned by both queries.
- When you use the *EXCEPT/MINUS* keyword between two queries, it will return those rows from the first query that are not returned by the second query.
- When you use a *UNION/UNION ALL* keyword between two queries, it will return all rows returned by both queries.
- When you use a subquery in the *WHERE* clause predicate, it will give you the power to solve complex business problems.

Lesson 9

Summarizing Retrieved Rows from a Table

```
NEW SQL STATEMENTS AND KEYWORDS COVERED IN THIS LESSON:

COUNT()                          SELECT...FROM...GROUP BY
AVG()                            SELECT...FROM...GROUP BY...ORDER BY
SUM()                            SELECT...FROM...WHERE...GROUP BY
MIN()                            SELECT...FROM...WHERE...GROUP BY...ORDER BY
MAX()                            SELECT...FROM...WHERE...GROUP BY...HAVING
                                 SELECT...FROM...WHERE...GROUP BY...HAVING...ORDER BY
```

Lesson Objective

So far you have learned the techniques necessary to retrieve detailed information and filter that information to suit a user's needs. This detailed information is very useful to those who are involved in day-to-day business operations, but they are rarely useful for senior managers. Senior managers often ask 'big picture' questions—i.e. they want you to summarize information for the business so they can make strategic decisions. This lesson will show you some techniques to summarize data retrieved from a single table so that you can answer these 'big picture' questions. You will learn:

- How to summarize all rows
- How to summarize rows by groups
- How to summarize a subset of rows
- How to summarize a subset of rows by groups
- How to limit summarized results

Code Samples

As in previous lessons, you will be asked to solve business problems in this lesson that require you to write SQL codes and execute them in your database, and you can find that code at the links below.

SQL Server:
https://drive.google.com/open?id=1W8xsb3MdM0Nbtl418mHeYxWvuHqlmzJN

MySQL:
https://drive.google.com/open?id=1d-WCITgF-rK2kOrsHNiYO3nolFc7kntX

The Fundamentals of Summarizing Data – Aggregate Functions

As we mentioned, you'll present a lot of value to senior managers wanting to take a big picture look at their business if you can answer questions like:

- *How many new customers have we added this year?*
- *What are our most (or least) profitable products this year?*
- *What are the total sales for this month?*

Simply retrieving detailed rows won't be good enough to answer these types of questions. True, you can aggregate detailed rows using a spreadsheet, website or any other front-end application, but to do this you would need to transfer these rows from the database server to your front-end computer or application server, and that will take up a lot of network bandwidth and slow-down your system.

Let's assume your company has processed 1 million sales orders this month. If you want to answer the third question above using a spreadsheet, you will need to download all 1 million orders from the database server to your computer, then summarize all these orders to get the total sales for this month. Downloading 1 million orders will take time. Wouldn't it be great if the database server could summarize all 1 million orders and return you only the total sales figures? That is where the aggregate function excels.

SQL standards provide you with some aggregate functions that will allow you to summarize detailed data and answer these types of questions. Almost all RDBMSs support the aggregate functions *COUNT(), SUM(), AVG(), MIN()* and *MAX()*. All of these functions typically aggregate a set of values from a column or column expression and return a single value.

To learn the behaviours of these functions, we'll discuss each aggregate function using an arbitrary example before moving on to the real business cases.

Assume that we have a customer table in our database that contains name, country and age columns:

Name	Country	Age
Rick	Australia	38
Tom	UK	25
Robert		21
Mili	USA	
Ben	India	32
Adam	USA	40
Peter	UK	24

You'll notice that we have seven customers. We know the names for all, but *Robert* hasn't disclosed his country and *Mili* hasn't disclosed her age. Let's see how the following SQL aggregate functions would apply to the data in the table above:

COUNT(): *COUNT()* will return the number of rows that exist in the table. It can be used in three ways: *COUNT(*)*, *COUNT(Column Name)* and *COUNT(DISTINCT Column Name)*.

COUNT(*): *COUNT(*)* will return the number of rows in the table. If you apply a *COUNT(*)* function to the above table, it will return '7'. This function allows you to answer a question like:

How many customers we have?

COUNT(Column Name): This function will return the number of rows in the table that has a value for the column. In other words, NULL values will not be counted. The third row for the *Country* column in the above table doesn't have a value (i.e. it contains *NULL*) because only six out of seven customers disclosed their country. Therefore, *COUNT(Country)* will return '6'. Since all rows in the name column have values, *COUNT(Name)* will return '7'. Notice that *COUNT(*)* and *COUNT(Name)* both return '7', which means if each row in a column has values, then you can use the either of the above functions. This function allows you to answer a question like:

How many customers disclosed the country where they live?

COUNT(DISTINCT Column Name): This function will return the number of unique values for the column in the table. *NULL* values will also not be counted here. The *Country* column in the above table contains four unique values: *Australia, UK* (twice), *USA* (twice) and *India*. Therefore, *COUNT(DISTINCT Country)* will return '4'. This function allows you to answer a question like:

How many different countries are our customers located in?

SUM(Column Name): This function will return a total of the values for the column in the table. *NULL* values will be ignored here too. The total age for all of the customers is:

$$38 + 25 + 21 + 32 + 40 + 24 = 180$$

Therefore, *SUM(Age)* will return *180*. This function allows you to answer a question like:

What is the total age of our customers?

AVG(Column Name): This function will return the average value for the column in the table. *NULL* values will be ignored here too. The *AVG()* function can be represented as:

$$AVG(Column\ Name) = \frac{SUM(Column\ Name)}{COUNT(Column\ Name)}$$

Therefore:

$$AVG(Age) = \frac{SUM(Age)}{COUNT(Age)} = \frac{180}{6} = 30$$

i.e. *AVG(Age)* will return *30*. This function allows you to answer a question like:

What is the average age of our customers?

MAX(Column Name): This will return the maximum value of the column in the table. *NULL* values will be ignored here too. Therefore, *MAX(Age)* will return *'40'*. This function allows you to answer a question like:

What is the age of our oldest customer?

MIN(Column Name): This will return the minimum value of the column in the table. *NULL* values will be ignored here too. Therefore, *MIN(Age)* will return *'21'*. This function allows you to answer a question like:

What is the age of our youngest customer?

Now let's move on to our business case and see some practical aggregate functions uses.

Summarizing All the Rows of a Table

Let's look at the below questions from business users:

- *How many countries do our customers live in?*
- *What is the average age of our customers?*
- *How many products do we have?*
- *What are the unit prices of our cheapest and expensive products?*
- *How much revenue has our company earned since we started business?*

If you want to answer these questions, you need to know how to use aggregate functions in a *SELECT* statement like the one you see below:

```
SELECT aggregate function 1, aggregate function 2, ..........
FROM table name;
```

Business Problems 1 - 4 will show you how to do that by summarizing all the rows of a table.

Business Problem 1

How many products do we have? Please provide the output column with a name like ***NumberOfProducts***.

Solution SQL

```
SELECT COUNT(*) AS NumberOfProducts
FROM Products;
```

SQL Result

NumberOfProducts
66

Solution Review

We haven't used the *WHERE* clause here; therefore, the *COUNT(*)* function counts the number of rows from the *Products* table, then returns the result. We used the *AS* keyword to provide the resulting column with a name: *NumberOfProducts*. The *ProductID* column is the primary key of the *Products* table, which is to say it has a value for every row. Therefore, the query can be re-written as below:

```
SELECT COUNT(ProductID) AS NumberOfProducts
FROM Products;
```

Business Problem 2

How many sales orders have we received since the inception of the company? Please put together a list with the following questions, providing each resulting item with a unique name:

- The number of sales orders,
- The total gross value of all sales
- The total amount of discounts given
- The total net value of all sales
- The average gross value of all sales

Solution SQL

```
SELECT COUNT(*) AS NumberOfOrders, SUM(OrderTotal) AS TotalGrossValue, SUM(OrderDiscountTotal) AS TotalDiscount,
        SUM(OrderTotal - OrderDiscountTotal) AS TotalNetValue, AVG(OrderTotal) AS AverageGrossValue
FROM SalesOrders;
```

SQL Result

NumberOfOrders	TotalGrossValue	TotalDiscount	TotalNetValue	AverageGrossValue
424	4420052.0000	232892.0000	4187160.0000	10424.650943

Solution Review

This *SalesOrders* table stores all sales order information since the inception of the company, where the *OrderTotal* column represents the gross value for all orders and *OrderDiscountTotal* represents the discounts given for the orders. There is no column for net value in the *SalesOrders* table, but it can be calculated by subtracting *OrderDiscountTotal* from *OrderTotal* i.e. *OrderTotal - OrderDiscountTotal*, which is a calculated column or column expression. Here's a breakdown of the steps:

First, *SUM(OrderTotal)* will return the sum of all values for the *OrderTotal* column. Next, *SUM(OrderDiscountTotal)* will return the sum of all the values for the *OrderDiscountTotal* column and *AVG(OrderTotal)* will return average all the values for the *OrderTotal* column. Like *'column'*, you can also use *'calculated column'* or *'column expression'* in the *SUM()* function. Therefore, *SUM(OrderTotal - OrderDiscountTotal)* will return the sum of the net values for all orders. We have used *AS* keyword to provide column aliases and all columns have been separated by commas (*,*). You can use as many aggregate functions as you want within a query.

Business Problem 3

What are the unit prices of our cheapest and most expensive products? Please ignore the discount amount and consider only the standard price. Please provide each resulting item with a name.

Solution SQL

```
SELECT MIN(StandardSalesPrice) AS CheapestProductPrice, MAX(StandardSalesPrice) AS MostExpensiveProductPrice
FROM Products;
```

SQL Result

CheapestProductPrice	MostExpensiveProductPrice
10.0000	6000.0000

Solution Review

Here, *MIN(StandardSalesPrice)* will return the lowest standard selling price among all products and *MAX(StandardSalesPrice)* will return the highest standard selling price among all products. The *AS* keyword has been used here to provide the column name for the lowest selling price as *CheapestProductPrice* and the highest selling price as *MostExpensiveProductPrice*.

Business Problem 4

What are the unit prices of our cheapest and most expensive products? Please provide each resulting item with a name.

Solution SQL

```
SELECT MIN ( StandardSalesPrice - (   CASE  WHEN SalesDiscountPercentage <> 0
                                            THEN StandardSalesPrice * SalesDiscountPercentage/100
                                      ELSE SalesDiscountAmount
                               END
                                  )
            ) AS CheapestProductPrice,
       MAX ( StandardSalesPrice - (   CASE  WHEN SalesDiscountPercentage <> 0
                                            THEN StandardSalesPrice * SalesDiscountPercentage/100
                                      ELSE SalesDiscountAmount
                               END
                                  )
            ) AS MostExpensiveProductPrice
FROM Products;
```

SQL Result

CheapestProductPrice	MostExpensiveProductPrice
10.0000000000	5800.0000000000

Solution Review

Recall that the below expression will return the net selling price for any product (please see *Business Problem 10* in *Lesson 7* for details):

```
StandardSalesPrice - ( CASE   WHEN SalesDiscountPercentage <> 0 THEN StandardSalesPrice * SalesDiscountPercentage/100
                              ELSE SalesDiscountAmount
                       END
                     )
```

The *MIN()* function will return the lowest selling price of all products in our database, while the *MAX()* function will return the highest selling price. As you are hopefully aware by now, the *AS* keyword allows us to provide our column names, *CheapestProductPrice* and *MostExpensiveProductPrice*.

Summarizing All the Rows in a Table by Groups

Here are some more questions you may be asked in in real-world business situations:

- *How many of our customers live in each country?*
- *What is the average age of our customers of each gender?*
- *How many products do we have for each category?*
- *What are the prices for each vendor's cheapest and most expensive products?*
- *What was our total revenue for each year we were in business?*

To answer these types of questions, you need to know how to divide all of a table's rows into groups, then summarize each group. To do this you need to use an additional clause, *'GROUP BY'*, in your *SELECT* statement with the aggregate functions as in the example below:

```
SELECT    column 1, column 2, aggregate function 1, aggregate function 2, ..........
FROM      table name
GROUP BY  column 1, column 2, ........
ORDER BY  column 1, column 2, .......;
```

Note

The columns you use in a *GROUP BY* clause must be present in the *SELECT* clause. If you want your results in a particular order, you must use an *ORDER BY* clause. If the order is not important, you can ignore this clause. The *ORDER BY* clause can use any column (including the aggregate column) from the *SELECT* list.

Let's practice this concept by solving some more business problems.

Business Problem 5

How many products do we have in each subcategory? Please show the *ProductSubcategoryID* and the corresponding number of products in each *ProductSubcategoryID*.

Solution SQL

```
SELECT ProductSubCategoryID, COUNT(*) AS NumberOfProducts
FROM Products
GROUP BY ProductSubCategoryID;
```

SQL Result

ProductSubCategoryID	NumberOfProducts
1	9
2	6
3	11
4	6
5	3
6	3
7	3
8	5
9	5
10	4
11	3
12	3
13	3
14	1
15	1

Solution Review

This *Products* table has a *ProductSubcategoryID* column that stores the identification number of each subcategory under which a particular product is sold. We used the *ProductSubcategoryID* column in a *GROUP BY* clause, which means the database engine will sort all of the *Products* table rows by their *ProductSubcategoryIDs*, then divide the rows related to each *ProductSubcategoryID* into separate logicals group. The *COUNT(*)* function in the *SELECT* clause above then counts the number of rows in each logical group and returns them with their corresponding *ProductSubcategoryIDs*. Notice that the same column was used in both the *SELECT* and *GROUP BY* clause. As we noted above, the database engine would return an error if we had not done so.

Since the *ProductID* column has a value for every row in the table, you can also re-write the query like so:

```
SELECT ProductSubCategoryID, COUNT(ProductID) AS NumberOfProducts
FROM Products
GROUP BY ProductSubCategoryID;
```

Business Problem 6

Please show the same information as in *Business Problem 5*, but this time please order the results in descending order by the number of products in each subcategory.

Solution SQL

```
SELECT ProductSubCategoryID, COUNT(ProductID) AS NumberOfProducts
FROM Products
GROUP BY ProductSubCategoryID
ORDER BY NumberOfProducts DESC;
```

SQL Result

ProductSubCategoryID	NumberOfProducts
3	11
1	9
2	6
4	6
8	5
9	5
10	4
11	3
12	3
13	3
5	3
6	3
7	3
14	1
15	1

Solution Review

For this problem, we used the aggregated column *NumberOfProducts* in the *ORDER BY* clause to sort the aggregated results by the *NumberOfProducts*. Alternatively, you can use the aggregate function *COUNT(ProductID)* in the *ORDER BY* clause like you see below:

```
SELECT ProductSubCategoryID, COUNT(ProductID) AS NumberOfProducts
FROM     Products
GROUP BY ProductSubCategoryID
ORDER BY COUNT(ProductID) DESC;
```

Note

When you use the *GROUP BY* clause in a query, you cannot use any column or column expression in the *ORDER BY* clause if the column(s) in question do not exist in the *SELECT* list. If, on the other hand, you are not using the *GROUP BY* clause, you can use *any* column in the *ORDER BY* clause from the table even if it doesn't exist in the *SELECT* list.

Business Problem 7

Please put together a list giving the following information:

How many sales orders have we received each year since our company opened its doors for business? Please give us a report showing these sales orders divided into rows by the year they were ordered. For each year, show the number of orders made, the total gross value, total of discounts given, and total net value. Please also provide each resulting column with a name.

Solution SQL

```
SELECT YEAR(OrderDate) AS YearOfOrder, COUNT(*) AS NumberOfOrders, SUM(OrderTotal) AS TotalGrossValue,
       SUM(OrderDiscountTotal) AS TotalDiscount, SUM(OrderTotal - OrderDiscountTotal) AS TotalNetValue
FROM SalesOrders
GROUP BY YEAR(OrderDate);
```

SQL Result

YearOfOrder	NumberOfOrders	TotalGrossValue	TotalDiscount	TotalNetValue
2017	207	1419464.0000	84015.0000	1335449.0000
2018	206	2648188.0000	143517.0000	2504671.0000
2019	11	352400.0000	5360.0000	347040.0000

Solution Review

Let's break down what we just did. First of all, *YEAR(OrderDate)* will return the year each order was made. The column expression *YEAR(OrderDate)* in the *GROUP BY* clause means the database engine will evaluate the expression and sort all rows from the *Products* table by their evaluated values of *YEAR(OrderDate)*, then divide the rows related to each order year into a separate logical group, then finally apply the aggregate functions (*COUNT* and *SUM*). Notice that the same column expression has been used in both the *SELECT* and the *GROUP BY* clause, otherwise, the database engine would return an error.

Note

Can you use an aliased column name in the *GROUP BY* clause? The answer is No. In the above query you cannot use the alias you designated with the *AS* keyword, '*YearOfOrder*', instead of *YEAR(OrderDate)* in the *GROUP BY* clause. Why? Traditional programming languages evaluate their code from top to bottom and left to right, but each SQL query processor evaluates its code in a special order known as the logical query processing order.

So, far you have learned the following keywords/clauses of a query:

- SELECT
- FROM
- WHERE
- ORDER BY
- GROUP BY
- DISTINCT
- TOP/OFFSET-FETCH/LIMIT-OFFSET

The logical processing order of these keywords/clauses is:

FROM → WHERE → GROUP BY → SELECT → DISTINCT → ORDER BY → TOP/OFFSET-FETCH/LIMIT-OFFSET.

Notice that the *SELECT* clause will be evaluated after the GROUP BY clause. Therefore, the aliased column name will not be available to the *GROUP BY* clause at the time the RDBMS evaluates it, and *that* is why you can't use the aliased column name in a *GROUP BY* clause.

Business Problem 8

We want to see a month-by-month breakdown of the number of sales orders we received since we started business. What were the total gross values, total discounts, total net values and average gross values for all our sales orders? Please provide each resulting item with a name. Please show the results in the ascending order by year of order and month of year. Each month should be designated by its number on the calendar.

Solution SQL

```
SELECT YEAR(OrderDate) AS YearOfOrder, MONTH(OrderDate) AS MonthOfYear, COUNT(*) AS NumberOfOrders,
        SUM(OrderTotal) AS TotalGrossValue, SUM(OrderDiscountTotal) AS TotalDiscount,
        SUM(OrderTotal - OrderDiscountTotal) AS TotalNetValue, AVG(OrderTotal) AS AverageGrossValue
FROM SalesOrders
GROUP BY YEAR(OrderDate), MONTH(OrderDate)
ORDER BY YearOfOrder, MonthOfYear;
```

SQL Result

YearOfOrder	MonthOfYear	NumberOfOrders	TotalGrossValue	TotalDiscount	TotalNetValue	AverageGrossValue
2017	1	5	20200.0000	1710.0000	18490.0000	4040.000000
2017	2	15	75080.0000	6885.0000	68195.0000	5005.333333
2017	3	25	104750.0000	6907.0000	97843.0000	4190.000000
2017	4	19	98130.0000	5560.0000	92570.0000	5164.736842
2017	5	19	121030.0000	3295.0000	117735.0000	6370.000000
2017	6	17	112730.0000	9755.0000	102975.0000	6631.176470
2017	7	27	144018.0000	9110.0000	134908.0000	5334.000000
2017	8	16	139510.0000	6620.0000	132890.0000	8719.375000
2017	9	16	153980.0000	4340.0000	149640.0000	9623.750000
2017	10	16	151340.0000	13627.0000	137713.0000	9458.750000
2017	11	17	118676.0000	7736.0000	110940.0000	6980.941176
2017	12	15	180020.0000	8470.0000	171550.0000	12001.333333
2018	1	17	211906.0000	6586.0000	205320.0000	12465.058823
2018	2	13	145930.0000	13175.0000	132755.0000	11225.384615
2018	3	24	180034.0000	11790.0000	168244.0000	7501.416666
2018	4	19	200210.0000	10410.0000	189800.0000	10537.368421
2018	5	17	286546.0000	6586.0000	279960.0000	16855.647058
2018	6	15	191180.0000	17150.0000	174030.0000	12745.333333
2018	7	21	194592.0000	12711.0000	181881.0000	9266.285714
2018	8	16	216590.0000	11582.0000	205008.0000	13536.875000
2018	9	13	319100.0000	6310.0000	312790.0000	24546.153846
2018	10	14	234650.0000	20445.0000	214205.0000	16760.714285
2018	11	17	189280.0000	12442.0000	176838.0000	11134.117647
2018	12	20	278170.0000	14330.0000	263840.0000	13908.500000
2019	1	11	352400.0000	5360.0000	347040.0000	32036.363636

Solution Review

The column expressions *YEAR(OrderDate)* and *MONTH(OrderDate)* will return the year and month for each order, respectively. We have used both column expressions in the *GROUP BY* clause, which means the rows will be grouped by their year of order, and within each group they will be sub-grouped by their month of order, and after that the database engine will apply the aggregate functions. The *ORDER BY* clause ensures the results to be displayed in ascending order by year of order, then by month of year.

Business Problem 9

What are the unit prices for each vendor's cheapest and expensive products? Please show the vendor list in ascending order from the cheapest product to the most expensive product.

Solution SQL

```
SELECT VendorID,
    MIN ( StandardSalesPrice –
            ( CASE WHEN SalesDiscountPercentage <> 0 THEN StandardSalesPrice * SalesDiscountPercentage/100
                ELSE SalesDiscountAmount  END ) ) AS CheapestProductPrice,
    MAX ( StandardSalesPrice –
            ( CASE WHEN SalesDiscountPercentage <> 0 THEN StandardSalesPrice * SalesDiscountPercentage/100
                ELSE SalesDiscountAmount END ) ) AS MostExpensiveProductPrice
FROM     Products
GROUP BY VendorID
ORDER BY CheapestProductPrice ASC;
```

SQL Result

VendorID	CheapestProductPrice	MostExpensiveProductPrice
5	10.0000000000	2850.0000000000
10	10.0000000000	5800.0000000000
4	18.0000000000	5000.0000000000
7	20.0000000000	400.0000000000
8	20.0000000000	4000.0000000000
9	20.0000000000	180.0000000000
1	20.0000000000	290.0000000000
2	20.0000000000	2000.0000000000
3	50.0000000000	120.0000000000
6	100.0000000000	2800.0000000000

Solution Review

You may have noticed that, for this task, we added a *GROUP BY VendorID* within the query in *Business Problem 4*, which instructs the database engine to group the products as per their *VendorID* and calculate the minimum and maximum prices within each group. The *ORDER BY* clause shown here ensures the results to be displayed in ascending order of cheapest product to most expensive.

Retrieving the First N Rows from Summarized Results

Next, we'll show you how to anser common business user questions such as:

- *Who are our top five most valuable customers?*
- *Give me a list of the top ten countries where most of our customers live in.*
- *What are our top three categories that have the least number of products?*
- *Give me the two vendors who are selling the least expensive products.*

If you analyze the first question you would probably agree with me that you can use the following steps to answer it:

1. Calculate the net value of each sales order from the *SalesOrders* table by subtracting *OrderDiscountTotal* from *OrderTotal*.
2. Group all the sales orders from the *SalesOrders* table by their *CustomerID*.
3. Aggregate each group by their net value that generate a list of *CustomerIDs* with their total net values.
4. Sort the aggregated results in descending order by their total net value.
5. Return the first five customers from the sorted results.

You may be thinking that you can achieve this by creating a SQL query combining what you have already learned in *this lesson* and *Lesson 8*. If so, you are right! You learned in *Lesson 8* how to return the first N rows from detailed results using the *TOP* keyword in a *SELECT* clause or the *OFFSET-FETCH* clause in SQL Server and *LIMIT-OFFSET* clause in MySQL. The database engine applies this clause to the final results and returns only the specified number of rows from the final result set. Therefore, these clauses can also be used to retrieve the first N rows from the summarized results, as you see below:

SQL Server:

```
SELECT  CustomerID, SUM(OrderTotal - OrderDiscountTotal) AS TotalNetValue
FROM       SalesOrders
GROUP BY CustomerID
ORDER BY TotalNetValue DESC
OFFSET 0 ROWS FETCH NEXT 5 ROWS ONLY;
```

Alternatively, you can use the *TOP* keyword:

```
SELECT TOP 5 CustomerID, SUM(OrderTotal - OrderDiscountTotal) AS TotalNetValue
FROM      SalesOrders
GROUP BY CustomerID
ORDER BY TotalNetValue DESC;
```

MySQL:

```
SELECT  CustomerID, SUM(OrderTotal - OrderDiscountTotal) AS TotalNetValue
FROM      SalesOrders
GROUP BY CustomerID
ORDER BY TotalNetValue DESC
LIMIT 5 OFFSET 0;
```

The following diagram visually represents these execution steps and their results:

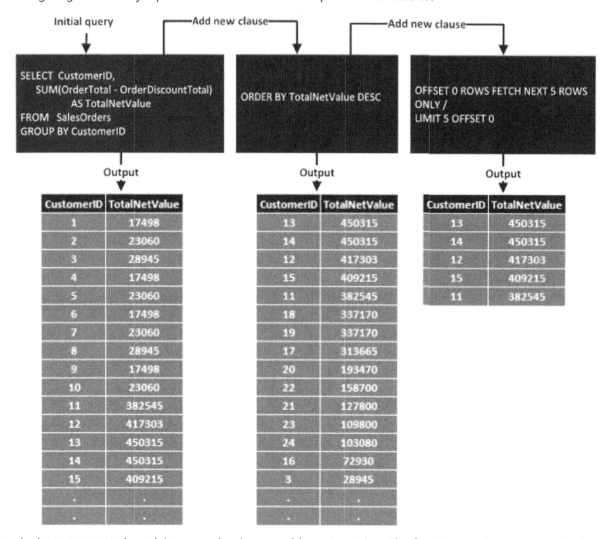

Let's apply these concepts by solving some business problems to retrieve the first N rows from summarized results.

Business Problem 10

Please give me the top 3 subcategories that have the most number of products. Please show the *ProductSubcategoryID* and the corresponding number of products for each *ProductSubcategoryID*.

Solution SQL – SQL Server:

```
SELECT ProductSubCategoryID, COUNT(ProductID) AS NumberOfProducts
FROM     Products
GROUP BY ProductSubCategoryID
ORDER BY NumberOfProducts DESC
OFFSET 0 ROWS FETCH NEXT 3 ROWS ONLY;
```

Solution SQL - MySQL:

```
SELECT ProductSubCategoryID, COUNT(ProductID) AS NumberOfProducts
FROM     Products
GROUP BY ProductSubCategoryID
ORDER BY NumberOfProducts DESC
LIMIT 3 OFFSET 0;
```

SQL Result

ProductSubCategoryID	NumberOfProducts
3	11
1	9
4	6

Solution Review

If you recall *Business Problem 6's* result, it showed 15 subcategories with their corresponding number of products. In *Business Problem 6*, *SubcategoryID 3* had the highest number of products, then *SubcategoryID 1*, then *SubcategoryID 2* & *SubcategoryID 4* have the same number of products.

In this query we have instructed the query processor to return first the (top) three rows and that is why only one subcategory ID from 2 & 4 has been returned by the query processor.

If you are using SQL Server, you can also use the *TOP* keyword instead of *OFFSET-FETCH* clause:

```
SELECT TOP 3 ProductSubCategoryID, COUNT(ProductID) AS NumberOfProducts
FROM     Products
GROUP BY ProductSubCategoryID
ORDER BY NumberOfProducts DESC;
```

Business Problem 11

Please show me the three vendors who are selling our least expensive products. Please show the vendors by *VendorID* and the price of each vendor's least expensive product.

Solution SQL - SQL Server:

```
SELECT VendorID,
     MIN ( StandardSalesPrice –
              ( CASE WHEN SalesDiscountPercentage <> 0 THEN StandardSalesPrice * SalesDiscountPercentage/100
                       ELSE SalesDiscountAmount  END ) ) AS CheapestProductPrice
FROM     Products
GROUP BY VendorID
ORDER BY CheapestProductPrice ASC
OFFSET 0 ROWS FETCH NEXT 3 ROWS ONLY;
```

Solution SQL - MySQL:

```
SELECT VendorID,
     MIN ( StandardSalesPrice –
                ( CASE WHEN SalesDiscountPercentage <> 0 THEN StandardSalesPrice * SalesDiscountPercentage/100
                     ELSE SalesDiscountAmount  END ) ) AS CheapestProductPrice
FROM      Products
GROUP BY VendorID
ORDER BY CheapestProductPrice ASC
LIMIT 3 OFFSET 0;
```

SQL Result

VendorID	CheapestProductPrice
5	10.0000000000
10	10.0000000000
4	18.0000000000

Solution Review

If you recall *Business Problem 9's* result, it shows all 10 vendors with their least and most expensive product's prices. In *Business Problem 9, VendorIDs 5 & 10* are tied for having the least expensive product, then *VendorID 4* has the next least expensive product.

In this query, we have instructed query processor to give first (top) three rows and that is why the *VendorIDs* from *5, 10 & 4* have been returned by the query processor.

If you are using SQL Server, you can also use *TOP* keyword instead of *OFFSET-FETCH* clause like below:

```
SELECT TOP 3 VendorID,
     MIN ( StandardSalesPrice –
                ( CASE WHEN SalesDiscountPercentage <> 0 THEN StandardSalesPrice * SalesDiscountPercentage/100
                     ELSE SalesDiscountAmount  END ) ) AS CheapestProductPrice
FROM      Products
GROUP BY VendorID
ORDER BY CheapestProductPrice ASC;
```

Retrieving Summarized Rows that Match One or More Predicates

You already know how to group and aggregate all rows from a table. Now it's time to learn how to filter the aggregated results. To answer questions like the ones below, you need to group & aggregate all rows from a table, then filter those aggregated results that match certain conditions:

- *Give me a list of customers who bought more than $400,000 in products from us.*
- *Give me a list of the countries where at least ten of our customers live in.*
- *Give me a list of the categories that have less than 20 products.*
- *Give me a list of vendors who are selling products with unit prices less than $20.*

Let us analyse the first question. You can use the following steps to answer it:

1. Generate a list of all customers with their total net values, i.e. the total amount they have ordered.
2. Filter the list that matches a comparison predicate like total net value > 400000

With the knowledge you have learned so far, you can easily write a query for Step 1:

```
SELECT  CustomerID, SUM(OrderTotal - OrderDiscountTotal) AS TotalNetValue
FROM      SalesOrders
GROUP BY CustomerID
```

You may be thinking that you should add a *WHERE* clause like *WHERE TotalNetValue > 400000* to the above query and that should give the answer to the first question, but that would not work. Recall the logical processing order of different clauses and keywords we mentioned earlier in this lesson:

FROM → WHERE → GROUP BY → SELECT → DISTINCT → ORDER BY → TOP/OFFSET-FETCH/LIMIT-OFFSET.

Notice that the *WHERE* clause will be evaluated before the *GROUP BY* clause. The *TotalNetValue* will be calculated by the aggregate function *SUM()* which will be evaluated with the *GROUP BY* clause, but the *GROUP BY* clause will be evaluated after the *WHERE* clause by the query processor. Therefore, *TotalNetValue* will not exist as far as the database is concerned until after the *WHERE* clause is processed, and that is why you cannot use any aggregated value in the *WHERE* clause.

The good news is that all mainstream RDBMSs provide a *HAVING* clause to apply a predicate on aggregated values. The syntax of a *SELECT* statement after including the *HAVING* clause is:

```
SELECT     column 1, column 2, aggregate function 1, aggregate function 2, ..........
FROM       table name
GROUP BY column 1, column 2, ........
HAVING predicate1 AND/OR predicate 2 .......
ORDER BY column 1, column 2, .......;
```

...where each predicate contains columns or aggregate functions using either the *SELECT* or *GROUP BY* clauses or literals or literal expressions. After adding the *HAVING* clause, the logical processing order of clauses and keywords will be

FROM → WHERE → GROUP BY → HAVING → SELECT → DISTINCT → ORDER BY → TOP/OFFSET-FETCH/LIMIT-OFFSET

Now you know that you can use the *HAVING* clause instead of the *WHERE* clause to satisfy Step 2 above. In that case, it would be *HAVING SUM(OrderTotal - OrderDiscountTotal) > 400000*. Therefore, the full query for the first question would be:

```
SELECT  CustomerID, SUM(OrderTotal - OrderDiscountTotal) AS TotalNetValue
FROM SalesOrders
GROUP BY CustomerID
HAVING SUM(OrderTotal - OrderDiscountTotal) > 400000;
```

If you want to sort the results by *TotalNetValue*, you can add an *ORDER BY* clause:

```
SELECT  CustomerID, SUM(OrderTotal - OrderDiscountTotal) AS TotalNetValue
FROM SalesOrders
GROUP BY CustomerID
HAVING SUM(OrderTotal - OrderDiscountTotal) > 400000
ORDER BY TotalNetValue DESC;
```

You can add more predicates in the *HAVING* clause. For example, if you want *a list of customers who have bought more than $400,000 and whose CustomerID is less than 14*, you can add one more predicates, like so:

```
SELECT  CustomerID, SUM(OrderTotal - OrderDiscountTotal) AS TotalNetValue
FROM SalesOrders
GROUP BY CustomerID
HAVING SUM(OrderTotal - OrderDiscountTotal) > 400000 AND CustomerID < 14
ORDER BY TotalNetValue DESC;
```

You can also use a subquery in the *HAVING* clause's predicate. For example, if you want *a list of customers, each of whom generates more than 10% of our revenue*, you can write a subquery to return 10% of our revenue, then pass the subquery in the *HAVING* clause's predicate:

```
SELECT  CustomerID, SUM(OrderTotal - OrderDiscountTotal) AS TotalNetValue
FROM SalesOrders
GROUP BY CustomerID
HAVING SUM(OrderTotal - OrderDiscountTotal) > (SELECT SUM(OrderTotal - OrderDiscountTotal)*0.1 FROM SalesOrders)
ORDER BY TotalNetValue DESC;
```

The subquery *SELECT SUM(OrderTotal - OrderDiscountTotal)*0.1 FROM SalesOrders* will return 10% of total revenue.

You can also exclude an aggregate function from a *SELECT* clause to generate a list based on aggregated filter and use the query as a subquery in another query's *WHERE* clause. For example, if you want *a list of customer details for those who bought more than $400,000*, you can use the above query as a subquery in the *WHERE* clause of a query which returns customers' details like you see below:

```
SELECT CustomerID, CONCAT(CustomerFirstName, '', CustomerLastName) AS Name,
       CustomerEmail AS Email, CustomerAddressID AS PostalAddressID
FROM Customers
WHERE CustomerID IN (   SELECT CustomerID
                        FROM SalesOrders
                        GROUP BY CustomerID
                        HAVING SUM(OrderTotal - OrderDiscountTotal) > 400000
                    );
```

The following business problems will give you a chance to practice these concepts further.

Business Problem 12

Please give me a list of all subcategories that have less than three products. Please show the *ProductSubcategoryID* and corresponding number of products for each *ProductSubcategoryID*.

Solution SQL

```
SELECT ProductSubCategoryID, COUNT(*) AS NumberOfProducts
FROM Products
GROUP BY ProductSubCategoryID
HAVING COUNT(ProductID) < 3;
```

SQL Result

ProductSubCategoryID	NumberOfProducts
14	1
15	1

Solution Review

Notice that we have added the *HAVING* clause to the query of *Business Problem 5* to filter the summarized rows with a number of products less than three. The subcategories 14 & 15 have less than three products and all other subcategories have three or more products. Therefore, the query will return these two subcategories.

Business Problem 13

Please give me a list of the vendors who are selling products with unit prices less than $20. Please show the *VendorID* and their least expensive product's price. Please show the list in ascending order by the least expensive product's price.

Solution SQL

```
SELECT    VendorID,
          MIN ( StandardSalesPrice -
                     (
                          CASE
                               WHEN SalesDiscountPercentage <> 0
                                    THEN StandardSalesPrice * SalesDiscountPercentage/100
                               ELSE SalesDiscountAmount
                          END
                     )
               ) AS CheapestProductPrice
FROM Products
GROUP BY VendorID
HAVING    MIN( StandardSalesPrice -
                     (
                          CASE
                               WHEN SalesDiscountPercentage <> 0
                                    THEN StandardSalesPrice * SalesDiscountPercentage/100
                               ELSE SalesDiscountAmount
                          END
                     )
               ) < 20
ORDER BY CheapestProductPrice ASC;
```

SQL Result

VendorID	CheapestProductPrice
5	10.0000000000
10	10.0000000000
4	18.0000000000

Solution Review

Notice that we have added a *HAVING* clause to the query of *Business Problem 9* to filter the summarized rows whose cheapest product prices are less than $20. Vendor 4, 5 & 10's cheapest product prices are less than $20, and all other vendors are selling products at unit prices of $20 or more. The *ORDER BY* clause shows the final result in ascending order by the cheapest product's prices.

Business Problem 14

Which products have sold in quantities of 500 or more? Please show the identification number, name, quantity in stock and *VendorID* for these products. Please show these products in descending order by the number of units in stock.

Solution SQL

```
SELECT ProductID, ProductName, StockQuantity, VendorID
FROM Products
WHERE ProductID IN (    SELECT ProductID
                        FROM SalesOrderProducts
                        GROUP BY ProductID
                        HAVING SUM(ProductQuantity) > 500  )
ORDER BY StockQuantity DESC;
```

SQL Result

ProductID	ProductName	StockQuantity	VendorID
16	Colour Wonder Markers and Paper - Disney Princess	500	4
17	Kids Superman Cape and Mask Dress Up Set	100	4
18	Electronic Toy Toaster	100	4
10	Electronic Toy Microwave	100	2
14	Puppy In My Pocket	20	4
7	Build Your Own Aquarium	20	2

Solution Review

Take a look at the query below:

```
SELECT ProductID, SUM(ProductQuantity)
FROM SalesOrderProducts
GROUP BY ProductID
HAVING SUM(ProductQuantity) > 500
```

This query will return the products (*ProductIDs* and number of quantities sold) that have been sold in quantities of 500 or more. Notice that we have removed the aggregate function *SUM(ProductQuantity)* from the *SELECT* clause and used the query as a subquery within the *IN* predicate of the outer query, which means the subquery will return only the list of *ProductIDs*, and this list will be used by *IN* predicate.

Summarizing a Subset of Rows from a Table

In Lesson 8 you learned that you can use a *WHERE* clause predicate to retrieve a subset of rows from a table, and earlier in this lesson you learned that you can use an aggregate function in the *SELECT* clause to summarize all the rows from a table. If you use both the *WHERE* clause and aggregate function within a query, the *WHERE* clause's predicate filters the rows and returns a subset of rows that match the predicate, then the subset of rows will be aggregated by the aggregate functions. This will allow you to answer questions like:

- *What is the average age of our customers living in Australia?*
- *How many countries are we selling in that have male customers?*
- *How many products are we currently selling?*
- *What are the prices of the most expensive products that our premium vendors are selling?*
- *How much revenue did we earn in 2016?*

The syntax for solving such questions would look like:

```
SELECT aggregate function 1, aggregate function 2, ..........
FROM      table name
WHERE predicate1 AND/OR predicate 2 .......;
```

Let's learn this by solving some business problems.

Business Problem 15

How many products are we currently selling? Please name the result *NumberOfProducts*.

Solution SQL

```
SELECT COUNT(ProductID) AS NumberOfProducts
FROM Products
WHERE IsActive = 1;
```

SQL Result

NumberOfProducts
64

Solution Review

The *IsActive* column in the *Products* table indicates whether a product is currently selling or not. If *IsActive = 1*, the corresponding product is currently available for sale. We have used a *WHERE* clause here which means that the database engine will return all rows whose *IsActive* column's values are *1*, then *COUNT(Product)* counts them. Notice that we have just added the *WHERE* clause to the *Business Problem 1*. You can also use the wildcard (*) in the aggregate function and rewrite the query like below:

```
SELECT COUNT(*) AS NumberOfProducts
FROM Products
WHERE IsActive = 1;
```

Business Problem 16

How many sales orders did we receive in 2017? What was the combined total gross value, total discount, total net value and average gross value for these orders? Please provide each resulting item with a name.

Solution SQL

```
SELECT    COUNT(*) AS NumberOfOrders,
          SUM(OrderTotal) AS TotalGrossValue,
          SUM(OrderDiscountTotal) AS TotalDiscount,
          SUM(OrderTotal - OrderDiscountTotal) AS TotalNetValue,
          AVG(OrderTotal) AS AverageGrossValue
FROM      SalesOrders
WHERE     YEAR(OrderDate) = 2017;
```

SQL Result

NumberOfOrders	TotalGrossValue	TotalDiscount	TotalNetValue	AverageGrossValue
207	1419464.0000	84015.0000	1335449.0000	6857.314009

Solution Review

We used the *YEAR(OrderDate) = 2017* predicate in the *WHERE* clause to retrieve only the orders that were placed in 2017, then we used the same aggregate functions from *Business Problem 2* to summarize 2017's orders.

Summarizing a Subset of Rows by Groups from a Table

You already know that the *WHERE* clause allows you to retrieve a subset of rows from a table and the *GROUP BY* clause along with aggregate functions allow you to summarize rows by groups. All mainstream RDBMSs allow you to use both the *WHERE* and *GROUP BY* clauses within a query to summarize a subset of rows from a table. This allows you to answer questions like:

- *How many of our male customers live in each country?*
- *What is the average age of our American customers for each gender?*
- *How many products with a standard price greater than $100 do we have in each category?*
- *What are the prices for each vendor's cheapest and expensive products?*
- *How much revenue did we earn each year from orders that didn't use our discount?*

The SQL syntax to answer such questions would look like:

SELECT column 1, column 2, aggregate function 1, aggregate function 2, ……….
FROM table name
WHERE predicate1 AND/OR predicate 2 …….
GROUP BY column 1, column 2, ……..
ORDER BY column 1, column 2, …….;

Let's learn this by solving some business problems.

Business Problem 17

How many products with a standard price greater than $100 do we have for each subcategory? Please show the *ProductSubcategoryID* and corresponding number of products for each *ProductSubcategoryID*. Please show the result in descending order by number of products.

Solution SQL

SELECT ProductSubCategoryID, COUNT(ProductID) AS NumberOfProducts
FROM Products
WHERE StandardSalesPrice > 100
GROUP BY ProductSubCategoryID
ORDER BY NumberOfProducts DESC

SQL Result

ProductSubCategoryID	NumberOfProducts
1	8
8	5
11	3
12	3
13	3
5	2
6	2
7	1
3	1

Solution Review

This query is similar than *Business Problem 5*. We have added a *WHERE* clause with the predicate *StandardSalesPrice > 100* which instructs database engine to return only the products whose standard prices are more than $100 before counting them within their subcategories. We have also added an *ORDER BY* clause to sort the results. We have designated a column alias in the *ORDER BY* clause, but you can also use the aggregate function like our query shown below:

SELECT   ProductSubCategoryID, COUNT(ProductID) AS NumberOfProducts
FROM   Products
WHERE   StandardSalesPrice > 100
GROUP BY ProductSubCategoryID
ORDER BY COUNT(ProductID) DESC;

Business Problem 18

Show me a list of all the sales orders we received each year, broken down by month. Please include only those orders where the customer received no discount. Also, include the total gross value, total net value and average gross value for each. Please give each resulting column a name and show the results in ascending order by year of order and month of year.

Solution SQL

```
SELECT    YEAR(OrderDate) AS YearOfOrder, MONTH(OrderDate) AS MonthOfYear,
          COUNT(*) AS NumberOfOrders,
          SUM(OrderTotal) AS TotalGrossValue,
          SUM(OrderTotal - OrderDiscountTotal) AS TotalNetValue,
          AVG(OrderTotal) AS AverageGrossValue
FROM      SalesOrders
WHERE     OrderDiscountTotal = 0
GROUP BY YEAR(OrderDate), MONTH(OrderDate)
ORDER BY YearOfOrder, MonthOfYear;
```

SQL Result

YearOfOrder	MonthOfYear	NumberOfOrders	TotalGrossValue	TotalNetValue	AverageGrossValue
2017	2	2	590.0000	590.0000	295.000000
2017	3	3	2930.0000	2930.0000	976.666666
2017	4	4	17270.0000	17270.0000	4317.500000
2017	5	5	61640.0000	61640.0000	12328.000000
2017	6	3	3160.0000	3160.0000	1053.333333
2017	7	4	7400.0000	7400.0000	1850.000000
2017	8	3	41640.0000	41640.0000	13880.000000
2017	9	4	67780.0000	67780.0000	16945.000000
2017	10	2	1330.0000	1330.0000	665.000000
2017	11	2	1710.0000	1710.0000	855.000000
2017	12	3	56390.0000	56390.0000	18796.666666
2018	1	4	89720.0000	89720.0000	22430.000000
2018	2	2	1700.0000	1700.0000	850.000000
2018	3	2	2200.0000	2200.0000	1100.000000
2018	4	4	36620.0000	36620.0000	9155.000000
2018	5	5	149180.0000	149180.0000	29836.000000
2018	6	2	2070.0000	2070.0000	1035.000000
2018	7	2	2690.0000	2690.0000	1345.000000
2018	8	2	41130.0000	41130.0000	20565.000000
2018	9	5	178360.0000	178360.0000	35672.000000
2018	10	2	2440.0000	2440.0000	1220.000000
2018	11	2	3180.0000	3180.0000	1590.000000
2018	12	4	51640.0000	51640.0000	12910.000000
2019	1	5	207540.0000	207540.0000	41508.000000

Solution Review

This question is similar to *Business Problem 8*. The only difference here is that you need to exclude orders where the customer received a discount. To do so, we added a *WHERE* clause with the predicate *OrderDiscountTotal = 0*, which will be evaluated by the query processor and return only those sales orders that didn't receive discounts before being summarized by the query processor.

Summarizing a Subset of Rows and Retrieving the First N Rows from Those Summarized Results

Sometimes you need to retrieve a subset of rows from a table, then summarize them by groups, then sort the summarized results, and finally return the first N rows from it. You can satisfy this type of requirement by adding the *TOP* keyword in a *SELECT* clause or *OFFSET-FETCH* clause for SQL Server and *LIMIT-OFFSET* clause for MySQL with the query you have learned earlier in this lesson. The *OFFSET-FETCH/LIMIT-OFFSET* clause will always be used at the end of the *SELECT* statement. This will allow you to answer the questions like:

- *Who are our top five most valuable American customers?*
- *What are our top three categories with the least number of products from our standard vendors (i.e. vendors who are not in our Gold or Diamond categories)?*
- *Give me the top two vendors who sell the most products where each unit price is (excluding discounts) at least $100.*

The next business problem will show you how to answer these types of questions.

Business Problem 19

Please give me a list of the top 3 subcategories that include the highest number of products from our vendors and whose identification number is below 5. Please show the *ProductSubcategoryID* and corresponding number of products for each *ProductSubcategoryID*.

SQL Solution - SQL Server:

```
SELECT ProductSubCategoryID, COUNT(ProductID) AS NumberOfProducts
FROM      Products
WHERE     VendorID < 5
GROUP BY ProductSubCategoryID
ORDER BY NumberOfProducts DESC, ProductSubCategoryID ASC
OFFSET 0 ROWS FETCH NEXT 3 ROWS ONLY;
```

SQL Solution - MySQL:

```
SELECT ProductSubCategoryID, COUNT(ProductID) AS NumberOfProducts
FROM      Products
WHERE     VendorID < 5
GROUP BY ProductSubCategoryID
ORDER BY NumberOfProducts DESC, ProductSubCategoryID ASC
LIMIT 3 OFFSET 0;
```

SQL Result

ProductSubCategoryID	NumberOfProducts
3	6
1	5
2	3

Solution Review

For *Business Problem 10*, we retrieved a list of subcategories that included the highest number of products (all vendors' products). Here, we need to retrieve the same data yet only include products from *VendorIDs 1 – 4* in our result. The *WHERE* clause predicate *VendorIDs < 5* returns only the products for *VendorIDs 1 – 4* before applying the aggregate function. In that scenario, *SubcategoryID 3* has the highest number of products, *SubcategoryID 1* has the second highest, and *SubcategoryID 2* & *SubcategoryID 4* have the same number of products.

In this query, we instructed the processor to return the first (top) three rows, and that is why only one *SubcategoryID* from *2 – 4* was returned by the query processor here. If you execute the query multiple times, sometimes you may get *SubcategoryID 2*, and sometimes you may get *SubcategoryID 4*. To make the result consistent every time it is executed, we have added *SubcategoryID* as a secondary sort column in the *ORDER BY* clause.

If you are using SQL Server, you can also use *TOP* keyword instead of *OFFSET-FETCH* clause like below:

```
SELECT TOP 3 ProductSubCategoryID, COUNT(ProductID) AS NumberOfProducts
FROM Products
WHERE VendorID < 5
GROUP BY ProductSubCategoryID
ORDER BY NumberOfProducts DESC, ProductSubCategoryID ASC;
```

Retrieving a Summarized Subset of Rows by Groups that Match One or More Predicates

All mainstream RDBMSs allow you to use the *WHERE*, *GROUP BY* and *HAVING* clauses within a single query. The *WHERE* clause produces a subset of rows from a table, then the *GROUP BY* clause summarizes them by groups, and the *HAVING* clause filters the summarized rows and returns the limited number of rows that satisfies the filtering condition (i.e. the *HAVING* clause's predicate). This allows you to answer the questions like:

- *How many of our male customers live in each country? Please include a country on the list only if it has more than 10 male customers.*
- *For each category, how many products do we have whose standard price is above $100? Please show only the categories that have a number of products greater than 5.*
- *How much revenue did we earn for each month from orders that weren't discounted? Only include months where our monthly revenue was greater than $50,000.*

The SQL syntax for solving such questions will look like:

```
SELECT    column 1, column 2, aggregate function 1, aggregate function 2, ..........
FROM      table name
WHERE predicate1 AND/OR predicate 2 .......
GROUP BY column 1, column 2, ........
HAVING predicate 1 AND/OR predicate 2 .......
ORDER BY column 1, column 2, .......;
```

Let's practice this by solving some business problems.

Business Problem 20

How many products do we have whose standard price is above $100? Please show the *ProductSubcategoryID* and a corresponding number of products for each *ProductSubcategoryID* only if the number of products is 5 or more.

Solution SQL

```
SELECT    ProductSubCategoryID, COUNT(ProductID) AS NumberOfProducts
FROM      Products
WHERE     StandardSalesPrice > 100
GROUP BY ProductSubCategoryID
HAVING COUNT(ProductID) >= 5
ORDER BY NumberOfProducts DESC;
```

SQL Result

ProductSubCategoryID	NumberOfProducts
1	8
8	5

Solution Review

This query is similar to *Business Problem 17*. This time around, we added a *HAVING* clause with the predicate *COUNT(ProductID) >= 5* to *Business Problem 17*'s query, which instructs the database engine to return only those rows from the summarized rows whose product count is greater than or equal to 5.

Business Problem 21

Show me a list of all the sales orders we received each year ordered by month. Please include only those orders where the customer received no discount. Also, include the total gross value, total net value and average gross value for each. Please provide each resulting item with a name and show only the months where there were more than four undiscounted orders. Please show the results in ascending order by year of order and month of year.

Solution SQL

```
SELECT  YEAR(OrderDate) AS YearOfOrder,  MONTH(OrderDate) AS MonthOfYear,
        COUNT(*) AS NumberOfOrders, SUM(OrderTotal) AS TotalGrossValue,
        SUM(OrderTotal - OrderDiscountTotal) AS TotalNetValue, AVG(OrderTotal) AS AverageGrossValue
FROM    SalesOrders
WHERE   OrderDiscountTotal = 0
GROUP BY YEAR(OrderDate), MONTH(OrderDate)
HAVING COUNT(*) > 4
ORDER BY YearOfOrder, MonthOfYear;
```

SQL Result

YearOfOrder	MonthOfYear	NumberOfOrders	TotalGrossValue	TotalNetValue	AverageGrossValue
2017	5	5	61640.0000	61640.0000	12328.000000
2018	5	5	149180.0000	149180.0000	29836.000000
2018	9	5	178360.0000	178360.0000	35672.000000
2019	1	5	207540.0000	207540.0000	41508.000000

Solution Review

You may notice that this problem is similar to *Business Problem 18*. The difference here is that you need to include only the months where more than four orders were not discounted. Therefore, we have added a *HAVING* clause with the predicate *COUNT(*) > 4* which will return only the rows from the summarized results that include more than four orders.

Business Problem 22

Which products did we deliver to customers in 2017 that generated more than $140,000 in total revenue? For each product, please give me the identification number, the number of orders that has been delivered, and the total revenue generated by each of these products. Please show the results in descending order by total revenue.

Solution SQL

```
SELECT    ProductID, COUNT(SalesOrderID) AS NumberOfOrders,
          SUM ( ProductQuantity * ProductUnitPrice – ProductQuantity * ProductUnitPriceDiscount ) AS TotalRevenue
FROM      SalesOrderProducts
WHERE     YEAR(ProductDeliveryDate) = 2017
GROUP BY  ProductID
HAVING    SUM(ProductQuantity * ProductUnitPrice – ProductQuantity * ProductUnitPriceDiscount) > 140000
ORDER BY  TotalRevenue DESC;
```

SQL Result

ProductID	NumberOfOrders	TotalRevenue
7	49	192600.0000
14	49	144900.0000

Solution Review

In the example above, the *WHERE* clause's predicate selects only those sales orders that have been delivered in 2017, then the *GROUP BY* clause groups those results together by *ProductID* and applies the *COUNT()* and *SUM()* functions to each group of rows and generates a summarized row for each *ProductID*. Finally, the *HAVING* clause's predicate excludes all rows whose total revenues are less than or equal to $140,000.

Lesson Summary

In this lesson, you have learned different techniques you can use to summarize whole or subset of data from a table. You have also seen how you can summarize data by groups and how to filter the summarized result. In summary:

- *COUNT(), SUM(), AVG(), MIN()* and *MAX()* are the most commonly used aggregate functions to summarize results. All modern RDBMSs support these functions.
- When you use aggregate functions in the *SELECT* clause, then use the *FROM* clause (and no other clauses), then the query will summarize all of the rows from a table and return a single row result.
- When you add a *GROUP BY* clause to the query just mentioned, then the query will summarize all rows from a table by groups and return one row result for each group.
- When you add a *HAVING* clause to the earlier query, then the query will return only those summarized rows that satisfy the *HAVING* clause's predicate.
- When you add a *WHERE* clause to any one of the earlier queries, then the query will first filter the rows from the table that satisfy the *WHERE* clause's predicate, then execute the original query on the filtered rows.
- You are not allowed to use a column alias in a *HAVING* clause.
- If you want to sort your result to any of the earlier query, simply add an *ORDER BY* clause.

Section C
Retrieving Business Insights from Multiple Tables

Section Overview

Let's look at what you've learned so far in this book. So far you know how to:

- Design a database
- Add data into a database
- Update or remove existing data from a database
- Write query to retrieve all rows or rows that match specific conditions
- Summarize all rows in a table or summarize rows by groups
- Return summarized rows that match specific conditions
- Display the final result set in a specific order

You also know how to join multiple result sets using *INTERSECT*, *EXCEPT/MINUS* and *UNION* keywords. These are most of the techniques that you need to know to interact with your database and solve business problems. But all of the techniques you have applied up to this point have only required data from a single table, which only contains data related to a single subject. Though you can solve a fair amount of business problems by retrieving and manipulating data from a single table, you will often be asked to do tasks that require you to retrieve data from multiple tables. These tables are usually related in some way. Customers place orders, vendors sell products, relationship managers interact with vendors, etc.

You already know how to join multiple similar result sets from a single table, but now you'll learn how to join *dissimilar* result sets as well as similar result sets coming from different tables. All mainstream RDBMSs support the *JOIN* keyword as part of a *FROM* clause. This combination is useful for linking two dissimilar result sets or tables if they have one or more similar columns. *JOIN* links two tables or result sets and provides a logical table that contains all of the columns from both tables/result sets.

Fig C-1 is a diagram showing what happens when you join multiple table together using the *JOIN* keyword.

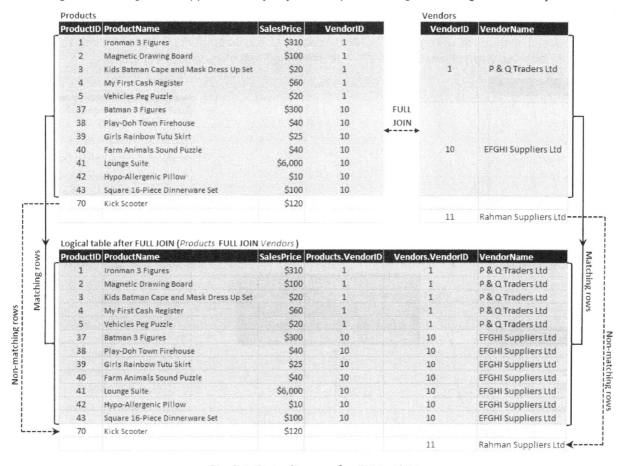

Fig C-1: Data diagram for FULL JOIN

In the above diagram, the *Products* table has a *VendorID* column that represents the vendors who sell them and the *Vendors* table has *VendorID* as its primary key. Therefore, when you instruct a database engine to do a *FULL JOIN* between the *Products* and *Vendors* tables based on their *VendorID* columns, it will provide a logical table that contains:

- All rows from the **Products** table with their corresponding vendor details if **VendorID** is available in the **Vendors** table
- All rows from the **Products** table whose **VendorID** is either unknown or not available in the **Vendors** table. It will leave this vendor information empty/NULL
- All rows from the **Vendors** table if they haven't started selling any products yet (i.e. that vendor's VendorID is not available in the **Products** table). The database will leave product information empty/NULL for these vendors

The *Kick Scooter* is a notable example. This is our company's own product and that is why the *VendorID* is empty in the *Products* table. Therefore, vendor-related columns are left *NULL/empty* for *Kick Scooter* product in the logical table. Also, the row for *Rahman Suppliers Ltd* has missing information as well. This company has just been listed as a vendor but hasn't started selling any products yet. Therefore, all product-related columns are currently *NULL/empty* for *Rahman Suppliers Ltd*.

Please note that '*empty*' means *NULL* in the above tables.

You may have noticed that, for illustration purposes, we have shown only four columns from the *Products* table and two columns from the *Vendors* table in the above diagram. Hence the logical table produced by the *JOIN* contains *6 (4+2)* columns. But in our business case, the *Products* and *Vendors* tables have *12* and *10* columns, respectively. Hence the logical table produced by the *JOIN* will contain *22 (12+10)* columns. The diagram Fig C-2 shows a visual representation of how the logical table has been generated by a *JOIN* between the *Products* and *Vendors* tables:

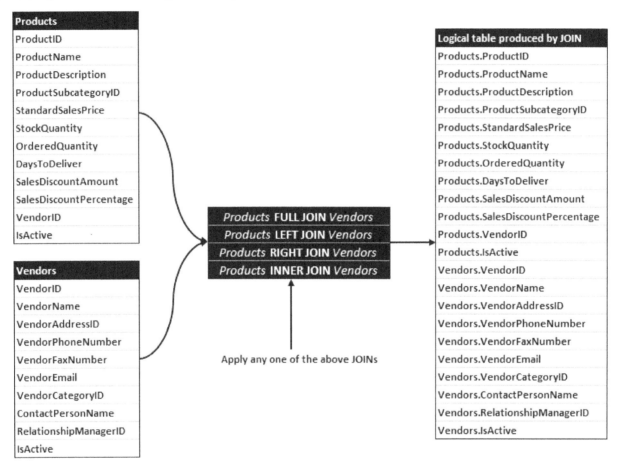

Fig C-2: Logical table transformation diagram for JOINs

Variations of the JOIN Keyword
SQL supports four common variations of *JOIN*, all of which we'll discuss briefly in this lesson:

- FULL JOIN
- LEFT JOIN
- RIGHT JOIN
- INNER JOIN

FULL JOIN: As explained in the example above, *FULL JOIN* will return all rows from two tables and their corresponding matching rows will be shown if available, otherwise they will be *NULL* in the non-matching side of the logical table.

LEFTJOIN: This operation will return all of the rows from the left side table (*Products*) with their corresponding matching rows from the right side table (*Vendors*), but the rows that do not match the key values on the right side table will be *NULL* on the corresponding right side column in the logical table. In the above example, if you use *LEFT JOIN* instead of *FULL JOIN*, the logical table will include all rows except the last row which is not present on the left side table (i.e. *Products*) in Fig C-1. So, the transformation of logical table will be like Fig C-3 below:

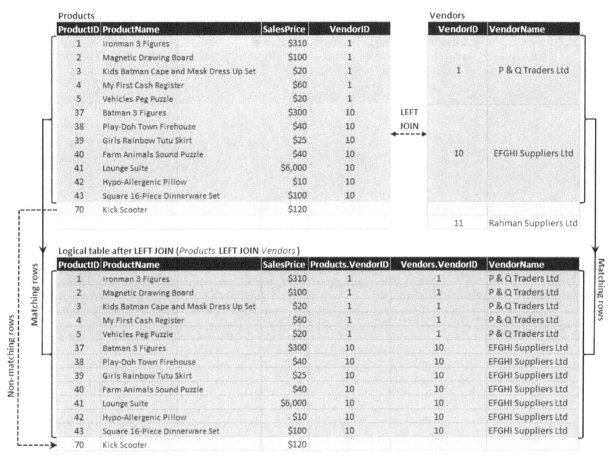

Fig C-3: Data diagram for LEFT JOIN

RIGHT JOIN: This will return all of the rows from the right side table with their corresponding matching rows from the first/left side table, but the rows that do not match the key values of the first/left side table will appear *NULL* on the corresponding left side columns of the logical table. Specifically, *ProductID 70* will not be shown in the result. In the above example described in Fig C-1, if you use *RIGHT JOIN* instead of *FULL JOIN*, the logical table will include all rows except the row just before the last row which is not present in the second/right side table (i.e. *Vendors*). So, the logical table will be like the one we show below (Fig C-4):

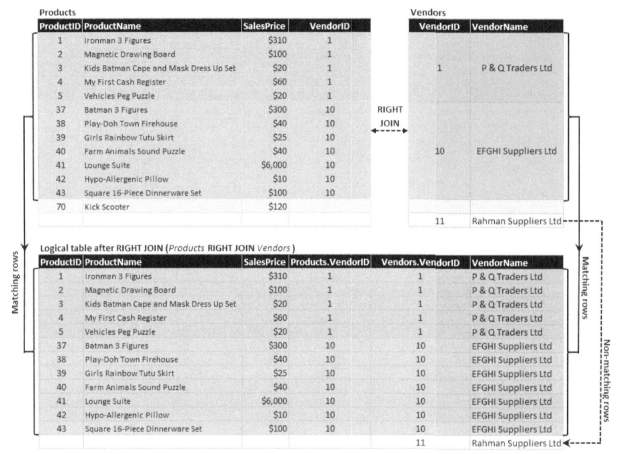

Fig C-4: Data diagram for RIGHT JOIN

INNER JOIN: This will return all of the rows from the first/left side table with their corresponding matching rows from the second/right side table. The rows that do not match the key values of the second/right side table will not be included in the logical table. In the above example described in Fig C-1, if you use *INNER JOIN* instead of *FULL JOIN*, the logical table will include all rows except the last two (one of these rows does not have any vendor IDs that match with the right side table, and the other row has no corresponding products in the left side table). So, the new logical table will be like Fig C-5 you see here:

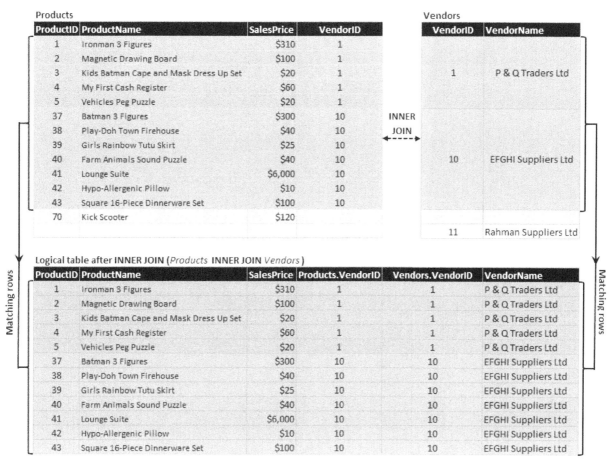

Fig C-5: Data diagram for INNER JOIN

JOIN typically occurs between the *primary key* and *foreign key*, but it doesn't have to. As long as two columns have compatible data types (i.e. numeric vs. numeric, date vs. date or string vs. string) you can use them in a *JOIN* predicate.

In this section, you will learn how to use various types of *JOIN* operations including *UNION* to solve a complex business problem that requires retrieving data from multiple tables.

Lesson 10
Retrieving and Summarizing Data from Multiple Tables Using Inner Join

---

NEW SQL STATEMENTS AND KEYWORDS COVERED IN THIS LESSON:

- CROSS JOIN → SELECT...FROM...CROSS JOIN
- INNER JOIN → SELECT...FROM...INNER JOIN...(Optional Clauses)

Lesson Objective

We'll start off this lesson by discussing *CROSS JOIN*, then show you some valuable ways to use *INNER JOIN*:

- To retrieve all rows or a subset of matching rows from multiple tables
- To summarize all or a subset of matching rows from multiple tables
- To filter summarized results coming from multiple tables

Code Samples

You can find the SQL code solutions for the examples and business problems in this lesson at the following link:
https://drive.google.com/open?id=1TriEJBpxlHm9I25g3TcuLDgf5cuUl-Ny

Retrieving a Cartesian Products of Rows from Two Tables

When you combine the rows from one table with those of another table, the combined result set is what is known as the *Cartesian product* of the two original sets of data. 'Cartesian product' is a set theory term, and in the SQL world it refer to the merging of rows using a *CROSS JOIN* between two tables. Most mainstream RDBMSs have implemented *CROSS JOIN* in the two ways shown below:

Option 1:

```
SELECT column list from both tables
FROM table1 CROSS JOIN table2;
```

Option 2:

```
SELECT column list from both tables
FROM table1, table2;
```

You can either use the *CROSS JOIN* keyword between two tables in a *FROM* clause or you can completely skip the step by using *JOIN*. The number of rows returned after the *CROSS JOIN* between *Table1* and *Table2* will be the number of rows in *Table1* multiplied by the number of rows in *Table2*.

The below diagram illustrates *CROSS JOIN* in action:

Table1

Column1	Column2
11	AA1
12	BB1
13	CC1

Table2

Column1	Column2
21	AA2
22	BB2

Cartesian product after cross join between Table1 & Table2

Table1Column1	Table1Column2	Table2Column1	Table2Column2
11	AA1	21	AA2
11	AA1	22	BB2
12	BB1	21	AA2
12	BB1	22	BB2
13	CC1	21	AA2
13	CC1	22	BB2

The query to create the above diagram can be written in one of the two ways you see below:

Option 1:

```
SELECT    Table1.Column1 AS Table1Column1, Table1.Column2 AS Table1Column2,
          Table2.Column1 AS Table2Column1, Table2.Column2 AS Table2Column2
FROM      Table1 CROSS JOIN Table2;
```

Option 2:

```
SELECT    Table1.Column1 AS Table1Column1, Table1.Column2 AS Table1Column2,
          Table2.Column1 AS Table2Column1, Table2.Column2 AS Table2Column2
FROM      Table1, Table2;
```

Here, we have used all the columns from both tables. If you do not need all the columns, you would simply list the specific columns you need in the *SELECT* clause. Please note that you must use the *Table Name.Column Name* format instead of just column name in the *SELECT* list if both tables have the same column name. If this is not the case, you can just use column name. It is recommended to always use the *Table Name.Column Name* format when you are using multiple tables in a query.

Table alias: Since it is recommended that you use the column name in the *Table Name.Column Name* format, some statements may become very long. Fortunately, you can shorten the table name by using a table alias. As with column aliases, you can use the *AS* keyword to rename a *table name*—in this case, to make it shorter. Please note that if you alias a table, you must use that table alias instead of its table name in every part of the query. For example, you alias *Table1* as *t1* and *Table2* as *t2*, the above query may look like below:

```
SELECT    t1.Column1 AS Table1Column1, t1.Column2 AS Table1Column2,
          t2.Column1 AS Table2Column1, t2.Column2 AS Table2Column2
FROM      Table1 AS t1 CROSS JOIN Table2 AS t2;
```

Since *CROSS JOIN* returns a significantly large number of rows, it can be detrimental to your database server. Therefore, please use it carefully and only when the tables are relatively small and there are no better alternatives.

Note

When you use two tables in the *FROM* clause and forget to mention a *JOIN*, the database engine treats them as a *CROSS JOIN*. Therefore, if you are not doing a *CROSS JOIN*, please explicitly specify the *JOIN* type in the *FROM* clause (or add a predicate in *WHERE* clause that links between two tables).

Let's solve a business problem using *CROSS JOIN*.

Business Problem 1

Please give me all combinations of our employees and vendors. Please show the IDs and names of our employees and vendors.

Solution SQL

```
SELECT EmployeeID, CONCAT(EmployeeFirstName, ' ', EmployeeLastName) AS EmployeeName, VendorID, VendorName
FROM Employees CROSS JOIN Vendors
```

SQL Result

EmployeeID	EmployeeName	VendorID	VendorName
1	Ben Wild	1	P & Q Traders Ltd
1	Ben Wild	2	Asia Pacific Suppliers Ltd
1	Ben Wild	3	UVWXYZ Suppliers Ltd
1	Ben Wild	4	JKLMN Suppliers Ltd
1	Ben Wild	5	Vision 2020 Electronics Ltd
1	Ben Wild	6	PQRST Suppliers Ltd
1	Ben Wild	7	A & B Traders Ltd
1	Ben Wild	8	Things for Future Generations Ltd
1	Ben Wild	9	ABCDE Suppliers Ltd
1	Ben Wild	10	EFGHI Suppliers Ltd
1	Ben Wild	11	Rahman Suppliers Ltd
2	Tony Abbot	1	P & Q Traders Ltd
2	Tony Abbot	2	Asia Pacific Suppliers Ltd
2	Tony Abbot	3	UVWXYZ Suppliers Ltd

Solution Review

Please note that we have only shown the first 14 of 44 rows. When you execute the query yourself, you should get 44 rows (and now you can see for yourself just how large these joined tables can be!). We have four employees in the *Employees* table and eleven vendors in *Vendors* table. You can verify the number of employees and vendors by executing the following queries:

```
SELECT * FROM Employees;
SELECT * FROM Vendors;
```

Therefore, the total number of rows the *CROSS JOIN* should return is $4 \times 11 = 44$. Please note that this is not an example from our business case, but merely an example to illustrate the usage of *CROSS JOIN*. We'll show you how to use *CROSS JOIN* to solve business case problems later in this lesson.

Retrieving All Matching Rows from Two Tables

Few tables have similar data in a real-world relational database, but you would be hard-pressed to find a table that isn't related to other tables in the database in some way. Two tables are usually related to each other through their primary and foreign keys.

So then, if you want to retrieve any data from two tables that share one or more columns (typically their primary and foreign key columns), you can specify these similar columns in an *INNER JOIN* predicate with the *FROM* clause:

```
SELECT output column list
FROM table1
INNER JOIN table2
    ON          table1.column expression1 OPERATOR table2.column expression1
        AND/OR table1.column expression2 OPERATOR table2.column expression2
```

In the example above, '*OPERATOR*' can be any operator that returns a *Boolean* value (i.e. *TRUE/FALSE/NULL*). The most commonly used operators are = (equal to), < (less than), <= (less than or equal to), > (greater than), >= (greater than or equal to), *BETWEEN*, *IN* and *LIKE*.

The best way to understand this is to walk through an example. *ProductCategories*, *ProductSubCategories* and *Products* are three tables in our business case database that represent our product catalogue. Here's what a relationship diagram of these three tables would look like:

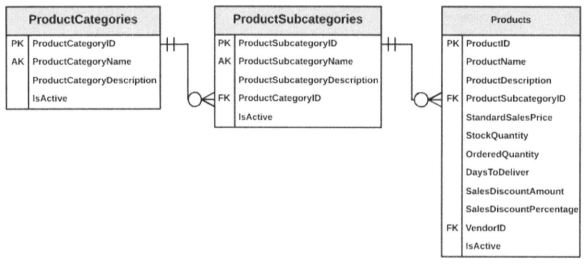

If you want to retrieve a list of product subcategories along with their categories, you can join the *ProductCategories* and *ProductSubCategories* tables based on the *ProductCategoryID* column and retrieve your intended columns from these two tables. The query will look like:

```
SELECT    ProductCategories.ProductCategoryName,
          ProductSubCategories.ProductSubCategoryID,
          ProductSubCategories.ProductSubCategoryName
FROM ProductCategories
INNER JOIN ProductSubCategories
    ON ProductCategories.ProductCategoryID = ProductSubCategories.ProductCategoryID;
```

Here, the *INNER JOIN* predicate *ProductCategories.ProductCategoryID = ProductSubCategories.ProductCategoryID* is matching the value of *ProductCategoryID* for every row of the *ProductSubCategories* table with the value of *ProductCategoryID* of the *ProductCategories* table. If it matches, then the database engine will retrieve the corresponding *ProductCategoryName* from the *ProductCategories* table. If it doesn't match, it will skip the row.

If you want to do the same task while using a table alias, the query can be re-written like below:
```
SELECT  PC.ProductCategoryName, PSC.ProductSubCategoryID, PSC.ProductSubCategoryName
FROM ProductCategories AS PC
INNER JOIN ProductSubCategories AS PSC
        ON PC.ProductCategoryID = PSC.ProductCategoryID;
```

You can also use both tables in the *FROM* clause and replace the *INNER JOIN* predicate with the *WHERE* clause predicate. Therefore, the query can be re-written as below:
```
SELECT     PC.ProductCategoryName, PSC.ProductSubCategoryID, PSC.ProductSubCategoryName
FROM       ProductCategories AS PC, ProductSubCategories AS PSC
WHERE      PC.ProductCategoryID = PSC.ProductCategoryID;
```

Please note that this query is supported by most RDBMSs, but it is not recommended as of the latest SQL standards. The latest SQL standards prefer the *INNER JOIN* predicate instead of the *WHERE* clause predicate for linking two tables. The diagram below illustrates how *INNER JOIN* maps data from two tables to produce the output of the above query(for illustration purposes, only *'Collectables'* and *'Home and Garden'* are shown here, so if you want to see the full, detailed result please execute the query yourself):

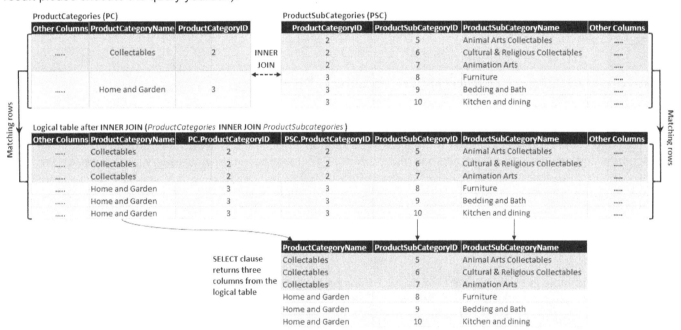

Equijoin: In the above example, the equal to *(=)* operator has been used in the *INNER JOIN* predicate—i.e. the equal to *(=)* operator has been used to join two tables. This is referred to as *EQUIJOIN*, and it can be either an *INNER JOIN* or *OUTER JOIN* as long as the equal to *(=)* operator is being used.

Let's solve a business problem using *INNER JOIN*.

Business Problem 2

Please give me a list of all our customers. Please show every customer's ID, name and postal address.

Solution SQL

```
SELECT c.CustomerID, CONCAT(c.CustomerFirstName, ' ', c.CustomerLastName) AS Name,
      CONCAT(a.StreetAddress, ', ', a.City, ', ', a.StateProvince, ', ', a.Country) AS PostalAddress
FROM Customers AS c
INNER JOIN Addresses AS a ON c.CustomerAddressID = a.AddressID;
```

SQL Result

CustomerID	Name	PostalAddress
1	Ricky Brown	475 Flinders Lane, Melbourne, Victoria, Australia
2	Adam Wilson	211 La Trobe Street, Melbourne, Victoria, Australia
3	Crystal Doslakoski	455 George Street, Sydney, New South Wales, Australia
4	Melanie Bowell	412-414 George Street, Sydney, New South Wales, Australia
5	Sophie Smith	159-175 Church Street, Parramatta, New South Wales, Australia
6	Robert Smith	9600 Firdale Avenue, Edmonds, Washington, United States
7	Michael Jackson	102 5th Ave S, Edmonds, Washington, United States
8	Ronald White	134 Parkplace Center, Kirkland, Washington, United States

Solution Review

Since the *CustomerAddressID* column of the *Customers* table is a foreign key that refers to the primary key of the *Addresses* table, the *INNER JOIN* predicate *c.CustomerAddressID = a.AddressID* links the *Customers* table with the *Addresses* table and returns detailed columns for our customers' postal addresses. The *CONCAT()* function has been used to populate the postal address from the *StreetAddress*, *City*, *StateProvince* and *Country* columns.

Please note that we only show 8 out of 32 customers in our example, but you should get 32 rows after execution of the query.

Retrieving All Matching Rows from More Than Two Tables

You have just learned how to use *INNER JOIN* to retrieve rows that match a predicate between two tables. If you want to retrieve matching rows between more than two tables, you can add an additional *INNER JOIN* clause for every additional table. Regarding our example from the previous section, if you want to get a list of products along with their subcategories and categories, you can add one more *INNER JOIN* clause to the previous query, as you see below:

```
SELECT PC.ProductCategoryName, PSC.ProductSubCategoryName, P.ProductID, P.ProductName
FROM ProductCategories AS PC
INNER JOIN ProductSubCategories AS PSC
    ON PC.ProductCategoryID = PSC.ProductCategoryID
INNER JOIN Products AS P
    ON PSC.ProductSubCategoryID = P.ProductSubCategoryID;
```

Here, the *Products* table is linked with the *ProductSubCategories* table by its foreign key, *ProductSubCategoryID*. With the previous query, we have added the last two lines of code: another *INNER JOIN* to the *Products* table based on the *ProductSubCategoryID*. Think of the previous query's result set as a logical table that is then joining with the *Products* table to providing the final results. For illustration, take a look at the snapshot we created below of the final query result for the *Home and Garden* category (for a full query result, please execute the query):

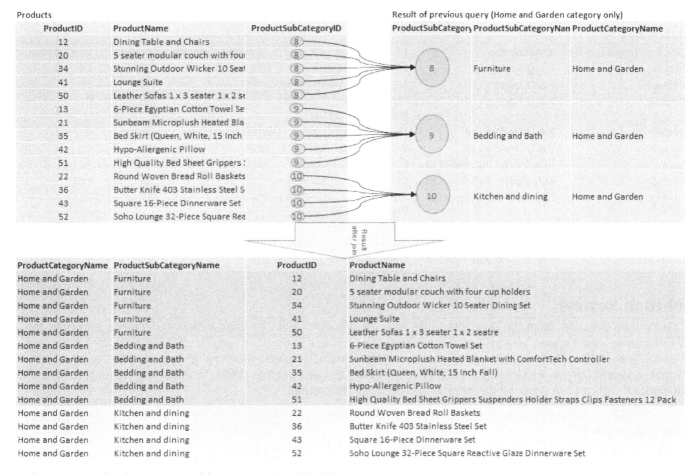

Products

ProductID	ProductName	ProductSubCategoryID
12	Dining Table and Chairs	8
20	5 seater modular couch with four	8
34	Stunning Outdoor Wicker 10 Seat	8
41	Lounge Suite	8
50	Leather Sofas 1 x 3 seater 1 x 2 se	8
13	6-Piece Egyptian Cotton Towel Se	9
21	Sunbeam Microplush Heated Bla	9
35	Bed Skirt (Queen, White, 15 Inch	9
42	Hypo-Allergenic Pillow	9
51	High Quality Bed Sheet Grippers :	9
22	Round Woven Bread Roll Baskets	10
36	Butter Knife 403 Stainless Steel S	10
43	Square 16-Piece Dinnerware Set	10
52	Soho Lounge 32-Piece Square Rea	10

Result of previous query (Home and Garden category only)

ProductSubCategory	ProductSubCategoryNan	ProductCategoryName
8	Furniture	Home and Garden
9	Bedding and Bath	Home and Garden
10	Kitchen and dining	Home and Garden

Result after join

ProductCategoryName	ProductSubCategoryName	ProductID	ProductName
Home and Garden	Furniture	12	Dining Table and Chairs
Home and Garden	Furniture	20	5 seater modular couch with four cup holders
Home and Garden	Furniture	34	Stunning Outdoor Wicker 10 Seater Dining Set
Home and Garden	Furniture	41	Lounge Suite
Home and Garden	Furniture	50	Leather Sofas 1 x 3 seater 1 x 2 seatre
Home and Garden	Bedding and Bath	13	6-Piece Egyptian Cotton Towel Set
Home and Garden	Bedding and Bath	21	Sunbeam Microplush Heated Blanket with ComfortTech Controller
Home and Garden	Bedding and Bath	35	Bed Skirt (Queen, White, 15 Inch Fall)
Home and Garden	Bedding and Bath	42	Hypo-Allergenic Pillow
Home and Garden	Bedding and Bath	51	High Quality Bed Sheet Grippers Suspenders Holder Straps Clips Fasteners 12 Pack
Home and Garden	Kitchen and dining	22	Round Woven Bread Roll Baskets
Home and Garden	Kitchen and dining	36	Butter Knife 403 Stainless Steel Set
Home and Garden	Kitchen and dining	43	Square 16-Piece Dinnerware Set
Home and Garden	Kitchen and dining	52	Soho Lounge 32-Piece Square Reactive Glaze Dinnerware Set

Let's solve another business problems using *INNER JOIN*.

Business Problem 3

Please give me a list of our products with their corresponding vendor details and the categories of the vendors they belong to. On the list, please show the vendor name & the category they belong to as well as each product ID, product name, available quantity, unit price and unit discount.

Solution SQL

```
SELECT    VendCat.VendorCategoryName, Vend.VendorName, Prod.ProductName,
          Prod.StockQuantity - Prod.OrderedQuantity AS AvailableQuantity,
          Prod.StandardSalesPrice AS UnitPrice,
          CASE
               WHEN Prod.SalesDiscountPercentage <> 0
                    THEN Prod.StandardSalesPrice * Prod.SalesDiscountPercentage/100
               ELSE Prod.SalesDiscountAmount
          END AS UnitDiscount
FROM      Products AS Prod
INNER JOIN Vendors AS Vend
     ON Prod.VendorID = Vend.VendorID
INNER JOIN VendorCategories AS VendCat
     ON Vend.VendorCategoryID = VendCat.VendorCategoryID;
```

SQL Result

VendorCategoryName	VendorName	ProductName	AvailableQuantity	UnitPrice	UnitDiscount
Regular	P & Q Traders Ltd	Ironman 3 Figures	93	310	20
Regular	P & Q Traders Ltd	Magnetic Drawing Board	100	100	20
Regular	P & Q Traders Ltd	Kids Batman Cape and Mask Dress Up Set	100	20	0
Regular	P & Q Traders Ltd	My First Cash Register	100	60	0
Regular	P & Q Traders Ltd	Vehicles Peg Puzzle	100	20	0
Diamond	Asia Pacific Suppliers Ltd	Superman 3 Figures	120	320	20
Diamond	Asia Pacific Suppliers Ltd	Build Your Own Aquarium	20	1000	100
Diamond	Asia Pacific Suppliers Ltd	Giant Coloring Pages Disney Princess	500	30	3
Diamond	Asia Pacific Suppliers Ltd	Kids Spiderman Cape and Mask Dress Up Set	100	20	0
Diamond	Asia Pacific Suppliers Ltd	Electronic Toy Microwave	70	100	0

Solution Review

The first *INNER JOIN* links the *Products* table with the *Vendors* table by their *VendorID* columns and gets the *VendorName* and *VendorCategoryID* columns from the *Vendors* table. The second *INNER JOIN* then links this *VendorCategoryID* to the *VendorCategoryID* column of the *VendorCategories* table and gets the *VendorCategoryName* from the *VendorCategories* table. The *CASE-END* operator has been used to calculate the unit price (please refer to *Business Problem 10* in *Lesson 7* for more details on how this is done).

Again, the figure above is for example purposes and so we have only shown 10 out of the 66 products you should get after executing the query.

Filtering matching data using derived tables

By now you know that you can use a subquery in *WHERE*, *SELECT* and *HAVING* clauses. You might be thinking that, since each query returns a tabular result set, we can use them in the *FROM* clause like a table. The answer is yes, you *can* use a subquery in *FROM* and *INNER JOIN* clauses. When you use a subquery in a *FROM* or *INNER JOIN* clause, it treats them as a virtual table. We call this virtual table a *derived table*. In a real-world scenario, you often need to join multiple large tables to satisfy the business query, but rarely will you need the whole table's data. For this reason, derived tables are very useful for retrieving a subset of data from single or multiple tables before joining them with another table.

In the previous topic, you learned that a query like the one below will return all products with their categories and subcategories (i.e. all rows from the *Products* table with their category name from the *ProductCategories* table and their subcategory name from the *ProductSubcategories* table):

```
SELECT  PC.ProductCategoryName, PSC.ProductSubCategoryName, P.ProductID, P.ProductName
FROM ProductCategories AS PC
INNER JOIN ProductSubCategories AS PSC ON PC.ProductCategoryID = PSC.ProductCategoryID
INNER JOIN Products AS P ON PSC.ProductSubCategoryID = P.ProductSubCategoryID;
```

The figure below outlines a detailed processing flow of how the logical table is generated by *INNER JOINs* and how the columns being returned by the *SELECT* clause will be organized (shows only column names):

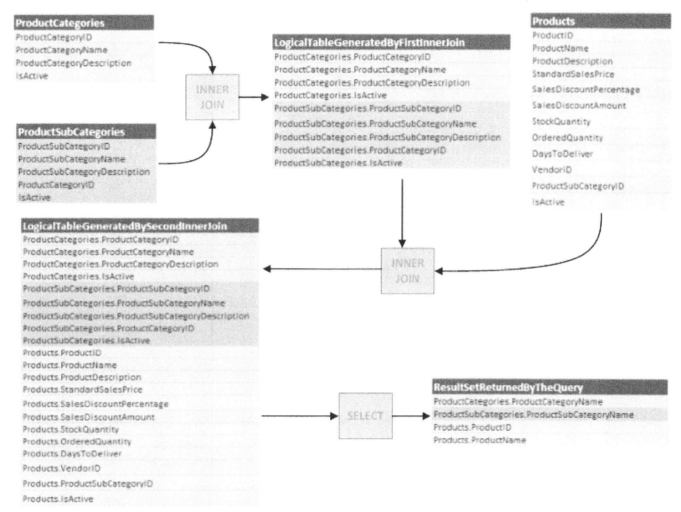

Notice that not all the columns are used in the actual query. The columns that are used from the *ProductCategories* table are:

- *ProductCategoryID* (used in the *INNER JOIN* clause)
- *ProductCategoryName* (used in the final result)

And the columns that are used from the *ProductSubCategories* table are:

- *ProductSubCategoryID* (used in the *INNER JOIN* clause)
- *ProductSubCategoryName* (used in the final result)
- *ProductCategoryID* (used in the *INNER JOIN* clause)

And the columns that are used from the *Products* table are:

- *ProductID* (used in final result)
- *ProductName* (used in final result)
- *ProductSubCategoryID* (used in *INNER JOIN* clause)

You may have noticed that there are two logical tables with lots of columns have been generated by the two *INNER JOINs*. Sometimes a large logical table can cause a query to perform slowly. Let's see how we can reduce the size of a logical table to increase performance.

The three queries below will return all rows from the *ProductCategories*, *ProductSubCategories* and *Products* tables but not the whole list of columns. These will show only the columns you need for the above query:

Query 1:

```
SELECT    ProductCategoryID, ProductCategoryName
FROM      ProductCategories;
```

Query 2:

```
SELECT    ProductSubCategoryID, ProductSubCategoryName, ProductCategoryID
FROM      ProductSubCategories;
```

Query 3:

```
SELECT    ProductID, ProductName, ProductSubCategoryID
FROM      Products;
```

If you replace the *ProductCategories*, *ProductSubCategories* and *Products* tables in the initial query with *Query 1*, *Query 2* and *Query 3* respectively, it will return exactly the same results as the initial query, and the query will look like below:

```
SELECT  PC.ProductCategoryName, PSC.ProductSubCategoryName, P.ProductID, P.ProductName
FROM (    SELECT ProductCategoryID, ProductCategoryName
          FROM      ProductCategories
       ) AS PC
INNER JOIN (   SELECT ProductSubCategoryID, ProductSubCategoryName, ProductCategoryID
               FROM      ProductSubCategories
          ) AS PSC ON PC.ProductCategoryID = PSC.ProductCategoryID
INNER JOIN (   SELECT ProductID, ProductName, ProductSubCategoryID
               FROM      Products
          ) AS P ON PSC.ProductSubCategoryID = P.ProductSubCategoryID;
```

Here we have used *Query 1*, *Query 2* and *Query 3* as subqueries instead of tables in the *FROM* and *INNER JOIN* clauses. Therefore, these subqueries are treated as derived tables. This query returns the same results but processes fewer columns, which accounts for the increased performance. See below to see a detailed processing flow of our most recent logical table:

The above query processes fewer columns but returns all matching rows from the three tables. If instead you want to return a subset of rows, you can do this by adding a *WHERE* clause predicate to the subqueries.

Let's see an example. Assume that a business

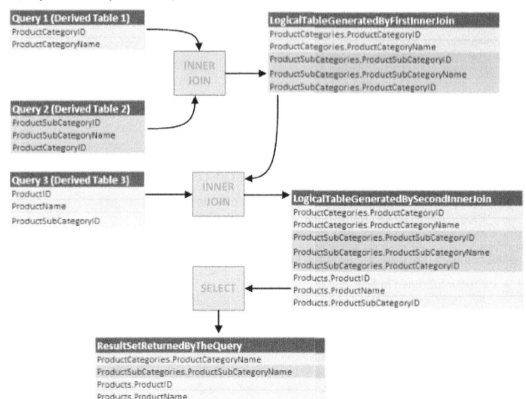

user asks for *a list of products in the Home and Garden category including their subcategories*. If you add *ProductCategoryName = 'Home and Garden'* as a *WHERE* clause predicate in *Query 1*, then it will return exactly the information the business user is asking for. The query for this would be:

```
SELECT  PC.ProductCategoryName, PSC.ProductSubCategoryName, P.ProductID, P.ProductName
FROM (    SELECT ProductCategoryID, ProductCategoryName
          FROM      ProductCategories
          WHERE     ProductCategoryName = 'Home and Garden'
       ) AS PC
INNER JOIN (    SELECT ProductSubCategoryID, ProductSubCategoryName, ProductCategoryID
                FROM      ProductSubCategories
           ) AS PSC ON PC.ProductCategoryID = PSC.ProductCategoryID
INNER JOIN (    SELECT ProductID, ProductName, ProductSubCategoryID
                FROM      Products
           ) AS P ON PSC.ProductSubCategoryID = P.ProductSubCategoryID;
```

Moving on, let's solve some business problems to brush-up your skills with *INNER JOIN* and *derived tables*:

Business Problem 4

Please give me a list of our Canadian customers. Please show every customer's ID, name and postal address.

Solution SQL

```
SELECT    c.CustomerID, CONCAT(c.CustomerFirstName, ' ', c. CustomerLastName) AS Name,
          CONCAT(a.StreetAddress, ', ', a.City, ', ', a.StateProvince, ', ', a.Country) AS PostalAddress
FROM Customers AS c
INNER JOIN
    (
          SELECT AddressID, StreetAddress, City, StateProvince, Country
          FROM      Addresses
          WHERE     Country = 'Canada'
    ) AS a ON c.CustomerAddressID = a.AddressID;
```

SQL Result

CustomerID	Name	PostalAddress
18	Allen Hall	701 W Georgia St, Vancouver, British Columbia, Canada
19	King Smith	650 W 41st Ave, Vancouver, British Columbia, Canada
20	Adam Green	1150 Douglas St, Victoria, British Columbia, Canada
21	Scott Baker	1245 Dupont St, Toronto, Ontario, Canada
22	Ricky Ponting	1309 Carling Ave, Ottawa, Ontario, Canada

Solution Review

You may notice that this query is almost same as *Business Problem 2*, except we replaced the *Addresses* table with the subquery below:

```
SELECT AddressID, StreetAddress, City, StateProvince, Country
FROM Addresses
WHERE Country = 'Canada'
```

Sure enough, this subquery returns only *Canadian* addresses from the *Addresses* table, which are then matched with the *CustomerAddressID* column of the *Customers* table.

Business Problem 5

Please give me a list of all our products with their corresponding vendor details for our *Diamond* category vendors. Please show the vendor name & the category they belong to as well as the product ID, product name, available quantity, unit price and unit discount for each product these vendors sell.

Solution SQL

```
SELECT VendCat.VendorCategoryName, Vend.VendorName, Prod.ProductName,
       Prod.StockQuantity - Prod.OrderedQuantity AS AvailableQuantity,
       Prod.StandardSalesPrice AS UnitPrice,
       CASE
           WHEN Prod.SalesDiscountPercentage <> 0
               THEN Prod.StandardSalesPrice * Prod.SalesDiscountPercentage/100
           ELSE Prod.SalesDiscountAmount
       END AS UnitDiscount
FROM      Products AS Prod
INNER JOIN Vendors AS Vend ON Prod.VendorID = Vend.VendorID
INNER JOIN ( SELECT  VendorCategoryID, VendorCategoryName
             FROM   VendorCategories
             WHERE VendorCategoryName = 'Diamond'
           ) AS VendCat ON Vend.VendorCategoryID = VendCat.VendorCategoryID;
```

SQL Result

VendorCategory Name	VendorName	ProductName	AvailableQuantity	UnitPrice	UnitDiscount
Diamond	Asia Pacific Suppliers Ltd	Superman 3 Figures	120	320	20
Diamond	Asia Pacific Suppliers Ltd	Build Your Own Aquarium	20	1000	100
Diamond	Asia Pacific Suppliers Ltd	Giant Coloring Pages Disney Princess	500	30	3
Diamond	Asia Pacific Suppliers Ltd	Kids Spiderman Cape and Mask Dress Up Set	100	20	0
Diamond	Asia Pacific Suppliers Ltd	Electronic Toy Microwave	70	100	0
Diamond	Asia Pacific Suppliers Ltd	Ravensburger Muscle Cars Puzzle	100	30	0
Diamond	Asia Pacific Suppliers Ltd	Dining Table and Chairs	-9	2000	0
Diamond	Asia Pacific Suppliers Ltd	6-Piece Egyptian Cotton Towel Set	100	30	4
Diamond	JKLMN Suppliers Ltd	Puppy In My Pocket	20	500	50
Diamond	JKLMN Suppliers Ltd	Minecraft Series Mini Figures 6 Pack	50	100	10
Diamond	JKLMN Suppliers Ltd	Colour Wonder Markers and Paper - Disney Princess	500	20	2
Diamond	JKLMN Suppliers Ltd	Kids Superman Cape and Mask Dress Up Set	100	20	0
Diamond	JKLMN Suppliers Ltd	Electronic Toy Toaster	100	80	0
Diamond	JKLMN Suppliers Ltd	Dragon Wooden Jigsaw	80	20	0
Diamond	JKLMN Suppliers Ltd	5 seater modular couch with four cup holders	-9	5000	0
Diamond	JKLMN Suppliers Ltd	Sunbeam Microplush Heated Blanket with ComfortTech Controller	80	100	0
Diamond	JKLMN Suppliers Ltd	Round Woven Bread Roll Baskets	70	20	0

Solution Review

Here we have created a similar statement to our SQL in *Business Problem 3*, but this time we replaced the *VendorCategories* table with a subquery:

```
SELECT VendorCategoryID, VendorCategoryName
FROM VendorCategories
WHERE VendorCategoryName = 'Diamond'
```

This subquery instructs the database engine to limit the products to only those sold by our *Diamond* category vendors.

Filtering Matching Data Using the WHERE Clause

You learned earlier how to retrieve data from multiple tables that matches a specific predicate by using a *WHERE* clause predicate within a subquery. You can do the same function by adding the *WHERE* clause predicate in the outer query, and the syntax for this is:

```
SELECT output column list
FROM table1
INNER JOIN table2
        ON table1.column expression1 OPERATOR table2.column expression1
            AND/OR table1.column expression2 OPERATOR table2.column expression2
        ..................................................................................................
WHERE predicate 1 AND/OR predicate 2.......................................................;
```

Let's review the query we just discussed to return a list of all *'Home and Garden'* category products including their subcategories. With the skills you have gained so far, you can return the list by executing one of three queries.

Query 1:

```
SELECT  PC.ProductCategoryName, PSC.ProductSubCategoryName, P.ProductID, P.ProductName
FROM (
        SELECT ProductCategoryID, ProductCategoryName
        FROM      ProductCategories
        WHERE     ProductCategoryName = 'Home and Garden'
    )    AS PC
INNER JOIN (
        SELECT ProductSubCategoryID, ProductSubCategoryName, ProductCategoryID
        FROM      ProductSubCategories
    ) AS PSC ON PC.ProductCategoryID = PSC.ProductCategoryID
INNER JOIN (
        SELECT ProductID, ProductName, ProductSubCategoryID
        FROM      Products
    ) AS P ON PSC.ProductSubCategoryID = P.ProductSubCategoryID;
```

Query 2:

```
SELECT  PC.ProductCategoryName, PSC.ProductSubCategoryName, P.ProductID, P.ProductName
FROM (
        SELECT ProductCategoryID, ProductCategoryName
        FROM      ProductCategories
        WHERE     ProductCategoryName = 'Home and Garden'
    )    AS PC
INNER JOIN (
        SELECT ProductSubCategoryID, ProductSubCategoryName, ProductCategoryID
        FROM      ProductSubCategories
    ) AS PSC ON PC.ProductCategoryID = PSC.ProductCategoryID
INNER JOIN Products AS P ON PSC.ProductSubCategoryID = P.ProductSubCategoryID;
```

Query 3

```
SELECT  PC.ProductCategoryName, PSC.ProductSubCategoryName, P.ProductID, P.ProductName
FROM (
        SELECT ProductCategoryID, ProductCategoryName
        FROM    ProductCategories
        WHERE   ProductCategoryName = 'Home and Garden'
    )   AS PC
INNER JOIN ProductSubCategories AS PSC ON PC.ProductCategoryID = PSC.ProductCategoryID
INNER JOIN Products AS P ON PSC.ProductSubCategoryID = P.ProductSubCategoryID;
```

Here's a breakdown of each of these queries and how they are different:

- *Query 1* will generate the smallest logical table. Therefore, it will perform better than *Query 2* and *Query 3*, but it is the largest query and difficult to read.
- *Query 2* will generate a logical table that is smaller than Query 3 but larger than *Query 1*. Therefore, it will perform a little better than *Query 3* but not as well as *Query 1*.
- *Query 3* will generate the largest logical table. Therefore, it will perform worse than *Query 1* and *Query 2*, but it is the smallest query and very easy to read.

For a beginning SQL programmer, *Query 3* may be easier to parse, but it is the worst performing one of the three. If performance is an issue, we recommend *Query 1*. Please do not worry too much about this dilemma at this moment. For now, we suggest you keep learning different methods until you have a strong grasp of the various methods for accomplishing real-world tasks—and the advantages and disadvantages of each.

As far as database performance is concerned, your queries will not be the only factor. That also depends on factors like indexes, database or server settings, etc. A proper index can make all of the above queries perform well (and we will discuss indexing in *Lesson 18*).

Moving on, here's a way to make *Query 3* simpler by removing the subquery and moving the *WHERE* clause to the end of the main query. The revised query will return exactly the same result and will be easiest to read. See below:

```
SELECT  PC.ProductCategoryName, PSC.ProductSubCategoryName, P.ProductID, P.ProductName
FROM ProductCategories AS PC
INNER JOIN ProductSubCategories AS PSC ON PC.ProductCategoryID = PSC.ProductCategoryID
INNER JOIN Products AS P ON PSC.ProductSubCategoryID = P.ProductSubCategoryID
WHERE    ProductCategoryName = 'Home and Garden';
```

Let's solve some business problems to explore filtering an *INNER JOIN's* results using the *WHERE* clause:

Business Problem 6

Please give me our *Canadian* customers list as you did in *Business Problem 4*, but this time use a *WHERE* clause instead of a subquery. Please show every customer with their ID, name and postal address.

Solution SQL

```
SELECT c.CustomerID, CONCAT(c.CustomerFirstName, ' ', c.CustomerFirstName) AS Name,
    CONCAT(a.StreetAddress, ', ', a.City, ', ', a.StateProvince, ', ', a.Country) AS PostalAddress
FROM Customers AS c
INNER JOIN Addresses AS a ON c.CustomerAddressID = a.AddressID
WHERE a.Country = 'Canada';
```

SQL Result

The result will be the same as *Business Problem 4*.

Solution Review

The *INNER JOIN* predicate *Customers.CustomerAddressID = Addresses.AddressID* will link the *Customers* table with the *Addresses* table and produce a logical table that contains all the rows from *Customers* table that have matching *AddressIDs* in the *Addresses* table (this logical table contains all the columns from both tables). Next, the *WHERE* clause predicate *Addresses.Country = 'Canada'* will filter the generated rows from this logical table and return only those rows whose *Country* is *Canada*. Finally, the *SELECT* clause specifies only the columns, as per user requirement.

Business Problem 7

Please give me a list of our products and their corresponding vendor details for our *Diamond* category vendors. Please show the vendor name & the category they belong to as well as the product ID, product name, available quantity, unit price and unit discount for each product these vendors sell. The solution here will be similar to *Business Problem 5*, but please use a *WHERE* clause this time instead of a subquery.

Solution SQL

```
SELECT VendCat.VendorCategoryName, Vend.VendorName, Prod.ProductName,
       Prod.StockQuantity - Prod.OrderedQuantity AS AvailableQuantity, Prod.StandardSalesPrice AS UnitPrice,
    CASE      WHEN Prod.SalesDiscountPercentage <> 0
                  THEN Prod.StandardSalesPrice * Prod.SalesDiscountPercentage/100
           ELSE Prod.SalesDiscountAmount
    END AS UnitDiscount
FROM      Products AS Prod
INNER JOIN Vendors AS Vend ON Prod.VendorID = Vend.VendorID
INNER JOIN VendorCategories AS VendCat ON Vend.VendorCategoryID = VendCat.VendorCategoryID
WHERE     VendCat.VendorCategoryName = 'Diamond';
```

SQL Result

The result will be the same as *Business Problem 5*.

Solution Review

The difference between this problem and *Business Problem 5* is that we have added *VendorCategories .VendorCategoryName = 'Diamond'* as a *WHERE* clause predicate. This predicate instructs the database engine to filter the rows and return only the rows whose *VendorCategoryName* column is equal to *'Diamond'*.

Summarizing Matching Data

So far in this lesson you have learned how to retrieve all the rows from multiple tables using *INNER JOIN* and then how to filter joined rows using the *WHERE* clause predicate. In *Lesson 9*, you learned how to summarize results (rows) using aggregate functions along with the *GROUP BY* and *HAVING* clauses. You also know that when you use *INNER JOIN* it generates a logical table. So, you can use this logical table and apply aggregate functions along with *GROUP BY* and *HAVING* clauses to summarize them. The syntax for this will be like below:

```
SELECT column 1, column 2, aggregate function 1, aggregate function 2, ……….
FROM table1
INNER JOIN table2
       ON table1.column expression1 OPERATOR table2.column expression1
           AND/OR table1.column expression2 OPERATOR table2.column expression2
       ............................................................
WHERE predicate 1 AND/OR predicate 2……………………
GROUP BY column 1, column 2…………………….
HAVING predicate 1 AND/OR predicate 2…………………….;
```

In this topic you will learn how to use the aggregate function along with the *INNER JOIN, GROUP BY* and *HAVING* clauses to retrieve summarized data from multiple tables that share some common columns or expressions. Let's look at the query you learned earlier in this lesson that returns *a list of products along with their subcategories and categories*:

```
SELECT  PC.ProductCategoryName, PSC.ProductSubCategoryName, P.ProductID, P.ProductName
FROM ProductCategories AS PC
INNER JOIN ProductSubCategories AS PSC ON PC.ProductCategoryID = PSC.ProductCategoryID
INNER JOIN Products AS P ON PSC.ProductSubCategoryID = P.ProductSubCategoryID;
```

The above query will return tabular results. You should think of the result as a logical table and apply the aggregate function to it along with the *GROUP BY* and *HAVING* clauses in the similar ways as you did in *Lesson 9*. Almost every RDBMS supports this.

Now if you want to know *how many products each subcategory has along with each product's category name*, you can apply the *COUNT()* aggregate function on *ProductID* and the *GROUP BY* on both *ProductCategoryName* and *ProductSubCategoryName* like you see below:

```
SELECT  PC.ProductCategoryName, PSC.ProductSubCategoryName, COUNT(P.ProductID) AS NumberOfProducts
FROM ProductCategories AS PC
INNER JOIN ProductSubCategories AS PSC ON PC.ProductCategoryID = PSC.ProductCategoryID
INNER JOIN Products AS P ON PSC.ProductSubCategoryID = P.ProductSubCategoryID
GROUP BY PC.ProductCategoryName, PSC.ProductSubCategoryName;
```

The query will return this result:

ProductCategoryName	ProductSubCategoryName	NumberOfProducts
Toys	Action Figures and Playsets	9
Collectables	Animal Arts Collectables	3
Collectables	Animation Arts	3
Toys	Arts and Crafts	6
Home and Garden	Bedding and Bath	5
Toys	Costumes and Pretend Playsets	11
Collectables	Cultural & Religious Collectables	3
Computers and Tablets	Desktops	3
Home and Garden	Furniture	5
Home and Garden	Kitchen and dining	4
Computers and Tablets	Laptops	3
Fashion and clothing	Men's clothing	1
Toys	Puzzles	6
Computers and Tablets	Tablets	3
Fashion and clothing	Women's clothing	1

Now if you want to see only the subcategories that have more than five products, you can add the *HAVING* clause predicate *COUNT(P.ProductID) > 5* to the above query like we show below:

```
SELECT  PC.ProductCategoryName, PSC.ProductSubCategoryName, COUNT(P.ProductID) AS NumberOfProducts
FROM ProductCategories AS PC
INNER JOIN ProductSubCategories AS PSC ON PC.ProductCategoryID = PSC.ProductCategoryID
INNER JOIN Products AS P ON PSC.ProductSubCategoryID = P.ProductSubCategoryID
GROUP BY PC.ProductCategoryName, PSC.ProductSubCategoryName
HAVING COUNT(P.ProductID) > 5;
```

The query will return this result:

ProductCategoryName	ProductSubCategoryName	NumberOfProducts
Toys	Action Figures and Playsets	9
Toys	Arts and Crafts	6
Toys	Costumes and Pretend Playsets	11
Toys	Puzzles	6

You can even exclude rows from the logical table before summarizing them. For example, if you want to know *how many products each subcategory has whose standard prices (excluding discounts) are more than $100 and also show their category names*, you can add the *WHERE* clause predicate `P.StandardSalesPrice > 100` to the previous query. The *WHERE* clause predicate excludes products whose standard prices are less than or equal to $100 before applying a *COUNT()* aggregate function on the *ProductID* and before applying *GROUP BY* on the *ProductCategoryName* and *ProductSubCategoryName* columns. The query for this will be like below:

```
SELECT  PC.ProductCategoryName, PSC.ProductSubCategoryName, COUNT(P.ProductID) AS NumberOfProducts
FROM ProductCategories AS PC
INNER JOIN ProductSubCategories AS PSC ON PC.ProductCategoryID = PSC.ProductCategoryID
INNER JOIN Products AS P ON PSC.ProductSubCategoryID = P.ProductSubCategoryID
WHERE P.StandardSalesPrice > 100
GROUP BY PC.ProductCategoryName, PSC.ProductSubCategoryName;
```

And the query will return this result:

ProductCategoryName	ProductSubCategoryName	NumberOfProducts
Toys	Action Figures and Playsets	8
Collectables	Animal Arts Collectables	2
Collectables	Animation Arts	1
Toys	Costumes and Pretend Playsets	1
Collectables	Cultural & Religious Collectables	2
Computers and Tablets	Desktops	3
Home and Garden	Furniture	5
Computers and Tablets	Laptops	3
Computers and Tablets	Tablets	3

You can also apply an aggregate filter on the above query to exclude some of the aggregated rows. For example, if you want *a list of subcategories who have at least five products whose standard prices are more than $100*, you can add the *HAVING* clause predicate `COUNT(P.ProductID) >= 5` to the above query. The *HAVING* clause predicate will exclude the rows that have less than five products from the above result set. The query will look like below:

```
SELECT  PC.ProductCategoryName, PSC.ProductSubCategoryName, COUNT(P.ProductID) AS NumberOfProducts
FROM ProductCategories AS PC
INNER JOIN ProductSubCategories AS PSC ON PC.ProductCategoryID = PSC.ProductCategoryID
INNER JOIN Products AS P ON PSC.ProductSubCategoryID = P.ProductSubCategoryID
WHERE P.StandardSalesPrice > 100
GROUP BY PC.ProductCategoryName, PSC.ProductSubCategoryName
HAVING COUNT(P.ProductID) >= 5;
```

And it will return the following result:

ProductCategoryName	ProductSubCategoryName	NumberOfProducts
Toys	Action Figures and Playsets	8
Home and Garden	Furniture	5

Let's solve some business problems to practice the skills you've just learned about summarizing matching data retrieved from multiple tables:

Business Problem 8

How many customers do we have in each country?

Solution SQL

```
SELECT a.Country, COUNT(CustomerID) AS NumberOfCustomers
FROM Customers AS c
INNER JOIN Addresses a ON c.CustomerAddressID = a.AddressID
GROUP BY a.Country;
```

SQL Result

Country	NumberOfCustomers
Australia	6
Bangladesh	1
Canada	5
China	1
France	1
Germany	2
India	1
United Kingdom	4
United States	11

Solution Review

The *INNER JOIN* predicate *Customers.CustomerAddressID = Addresses.AddressID* will generate a logical table that contains all rows from *Customers* table with their matching rows from *Addresses* table, and then the *GROUP BY* clause will group the logical table's rows by their country. Lastly, the *COUNT()* function counts the number of rows within each group.

Business Problem 9

How many female customers do we have in each country?

Solution SQL

```
SELECT a.Country, COUNT(CustomerID) AS NumberOfCustomers
FROM Customers AS c
INNER JOIN Addresses a ON c.CustomerAddressID = a.AddressID
WHERE c.CustomerGender = 'Female'
GROUP BY a.Country;
```

SQL Result

Country	NumberOfCustomers
Australia	3
China	1
Germany	2
United Kingdom	3
United States	7

Solution Review

In this case, the *WHERE* predicate *Customers.CustomerGender = 'Female'* includes only the *female customers* before aggregating the rows.

Business Problem 10

Out of all the products we delivered to our customers in 2017, which ones generated more than $140,000 in total revenue? Please give me the product name, how many delivered orders included each product and the total revenue generated by each product.

Solution SQL

```
SELECT p.ProductName, COUNT(so.SalesOrderID) AS NumberOfOrders,
    SUM(so.ProductQuantity * so.ProductUnitPrice
        - so.ProductQuantity * so.ProductUnitPriceDiscount) AS TotalProductRevenue
FROM SalesOrderProducts AS so
INNER JOIN Products AS p ON so.ProductID = p.ProductID
WHERE  YEAR(so.ProductDeliveryDate) = 2017
GROUP BY p.ProductName
HAVING SUM(so.ProductQuantity * so.ProductUnitPrice - so.ProductQuantity * so.ProductUnitPriceDiscount) > 140000;
```

SQL Result

ProductName	NumberOfOrders	TotalProductRevenue
Build Your Own Aquarium	49	192600.0000
Puppy In My Pocket	49	144900.0000

Solution Review

This question is similar to *Business Problem 22* in *Lesson 9*. In *Lesson 9*, the user was happy to have only the identification number of each product shown, but this time the user wants to see the name of each product. This data is not available in the *SalesOrderProducts* table, so we used *INNER JOIN* to link our *SalesOrderProducts* table with the *Products* table, which gave us the *product name* column from the *Products* table.

Business Problem 11

We would like another report showing which of our products sold in 2017 generated more than $140,000 revenue. This time, please give me the percentage of revenue generated by each product in addition to the product name, number of orders we delivered in 2017, and total revenue generated by each product. Please sort the output in descending order by the revenue generated by the products.

Solution SQL

```
SELECT ProductSales.ProductName, ProductSales.NumberOfOrders, ProductSales.TotalProductRevenue,
    ( ProductSales.TotalProductRevenue * 100 / TotalSales.TotalCompanyRevenue ) AS PercentageOfTotal
FROM (
        SELECT  p.ProductName, COUNT(so.SalesOrderID) AS NumberOfOrders,
        SUM ( so.ProductQuantity * so.ProductUnitPrice
            - so.ProductQuantity * so.ProductUnitPriceDiscount) AS TotalProductRevenue
        FROM SalesOrderProducts AS so
        INNER JOIN Products AS p ON so.ProductID = p.ProductID
        WHERE YEAR(so.ProductDeliveryDate) = 2017
        GROUP BY p.ProductName
        HAVING SUM (so.ProductQuantity * so.ProductUnitPrice
                – so.ProductQuantity * so.ProductUnitPriceDiscount) > 140000
    ) AS ProductSales
CROSS JOIN (
        SELECT SUM ( ProductQuantity * ProductUnitPrice
                    - ProductQuantity * ProductUnitPriceDiscount ) AS TotalCompanyRevenue
        FROM SalesOrderProducts
        WHERE YEAR(ProductDeliveryDate) = 2017
    ) AS TotalSales
ORDER BY TotalProductRevenue DESC;
```

SQL Result

ProductName	NumberOfOrders	TotalProductRevenue	PercentageOfTotal
Build Your Own Aquarium	49	192600.0000	15.076568
Puppy In My Pocket	49	144900.0000	11.342652

Solution Review

Notice that this question is similar to *Business Problem 10*, but you need to retrieve the total company revenue for the year 2017 to calculate the percentage. The query shown below returns the total company revenue for 2017:

```
SELECT SUM ( ProductQuantity * ProductUnitPrice
                - ProductQuantity * ProductUnitPriceDiscount ) AS TotalCompanyRevenue
FROM SalesOrderProducts
WHERE YEAR(ProductDeliveryDate) = 2017
```

If you use the whole query from *Business Problem 10* in the *FROM* clause as a derived table and *CROSS JOIN* it with the above query as another derived table, the total company revenue will be distributed to each resulting row as you see below:

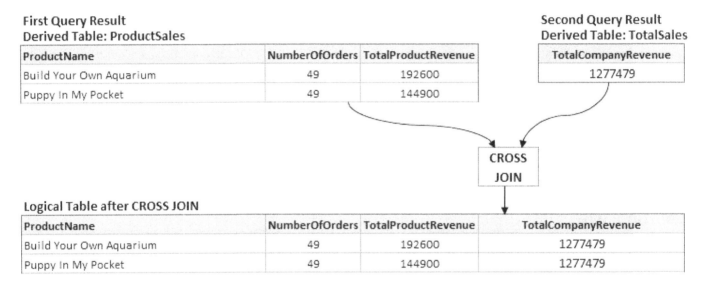

The percentage of total revenue has then been calculated from the *TotalProductRevenue* and *TotalCompanyRevenue* columns of the logical table after the *CROSS JOIN* by using the formula below that has been used in the *SELECT* clause:

$$PercentageOfTotal = \frac{TotalProductRevenue}{TotalCompanyRevenue} \times 100$$

Note

Business users often want to analyze detailed data or item-wise summarized data with the final summary and they need the detail and summary side-by-side. The *CROSS JOIN* is one good way to do this. Some example problems that can be solved with *CROSS JOIN* are:

- *Finding employee sales along with total sales*
- *Showing country sales along with total sale*
- *Showing product details along with most/least expensive product's details etc.*

Lesson Summary

In this lesson you have learned the SQL statements to retrieve data from two or more dissimilar tables:

- *CROSS JOIN* will return all the combinations of rows between two tables, and there is no need for common columns to join the tables. *CROSS JOIN* is very useful when you want to show detailed rows along with a set of summarized values.
- Using *INNER JOIN* between two tables will produce a logical table that consists of all columns and all rows from both the tables that match the *JOIN* predicate(s).
- In case of multiple *INNER JOINs* within a query, the RDBMS executes the first *INNER JOIN* between the first two tables and produces the first logical table, which is then combined with the third table by way of *INNER JOIN* to produce the second logical table and so on, like in the diagram below:

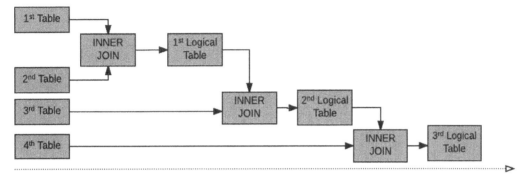

- The *WHERE* clause predicate applies to the final logical table produced from *INNER JOINs* and returns rows that satisfy the predicates.
- You should specify only your desired columns from the final logical table in the *SELECT* clause.
- The *GROUP BY* clause applies to the final logical table to summarize the data and the *HAVING* clause filters the summarized data.
- Instead of using a table you can use subquery that will act as a derived table. This derived table can be used to filter both columns and/or rows before the *INNER JOIN*.

Lesson 11

Retrieving and summarizing data from multiple tables using Outer Join

NEW SQL STATEMENTS AND KEYWORDS COVERED IN THIS LESSON:

- LEFT OUTER JOIN → SELECT...FROM...LEFT OUTER JOIN...(Optional Clauses)
- RIGHT OUTER JOIN → SELECT...FROM...RIGHT OUTER JOIN...(Optional Clauses)

Lesson Objective

With the knowledge you have gained so far, you can retrieve any and all matching rows that exist among two, three, or even more tables, but sometimes you may need to retrieve non-matching rows to do other operations on the results of this type of operation in the same query. For most RDBMSs, *OUTER JOIN* is a way to do that. This lesson will show you different ways to use *OUTER JOIN*:

- To retrieve all or a subset of rows from a table with their matching rows from another table
- To summarize retrieved results
- To filter summarized results

Code Samples

For this lesson, you can find the SQL code solutions for the examples and business problems at the following link:
https://drive.google.com/open?id=1iAlw2jckNIciPrEirpvgn7IbHLCgTY6m

Retrieving All the Rows from a Table with the Matching Rows from Another Table

If you want to retrieve all data from a table along with the matching data from another table, RDBMSs allow you to do so using *LEFT/RIGHT OUTER JOIN*. The basic syntax of *OUTER JOIN* is:

```
SELECT output column list
FROM table1
LEFT/RIGHT OUTER JOIN table2
    ON table1.column expression1 OPERATOR table2.column expression1
        AND/OR table1.column expression2 OPERATOR table2.column expression2
```

Here, the operator can be any operator that returns a *Boolean* value, i.e. *TRUE/FALSE/NULL*. The most commonly used operators are = (equal to), < (less than), <= (less than or equal to), > (greater than), >= (greater than or equal to), *BETWEEN*, *IN* and *LIKE*.

The best way to understand this is to practice an example. Our *VendorCategories*, *Vendors* and *Products* tables store the vendor categories, vendor details and products details respectively. Each vendor belongs to a category and each product is sold by a vendor. Here's what the relationship diagram for these tables would look like:

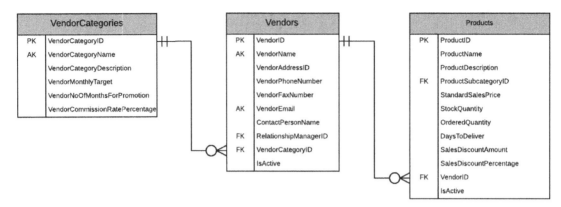

If you want to retrieve a list of vendors along with the products they are selling, you can do a *LEFT JOIN* between the *Vendors* and *Products* tables based on the *VendorID* column and retrieve your intended columns from these two tables. The query will look like below:

```
SELECT    Vendors.VendorName,
          Products.ProductID,
          Products.ProductName,
          Products.StockQuantity
FROM      Vendors
LEFT OUTER JOIN Products
          ON Vendors.VendorID = Products.VendorID;
```

The *OUTER* keyword is optional and you can omit it, as we have below:

```
SELECT    Vendors.VendorName,
          Products.ProductID,
          Products.ProductName,
          Products.StockQuantity
FROM      Vendors
LEFT JOIN Products
          ON Vendors.VendorID = Products.VendorID;
```

The *LEFT JOIN* predicate *Vendors.VendorID = Products.VendorID* compares the *VendorID* column values of each row of the *Vendors* table with the *VendorID* column values of each row of the *Products* table. If all of their columns match, both tables will be returned as a row of the logical table. If a *VendorID* only presents in the *Vendors* table, the *LEFT JOIN* still returns the row but the columns for the *Products* table will be *NULL* (*empty/unknown*).

Fig 11.1 gives you a visual idea of *LEFT JOIN* in action:

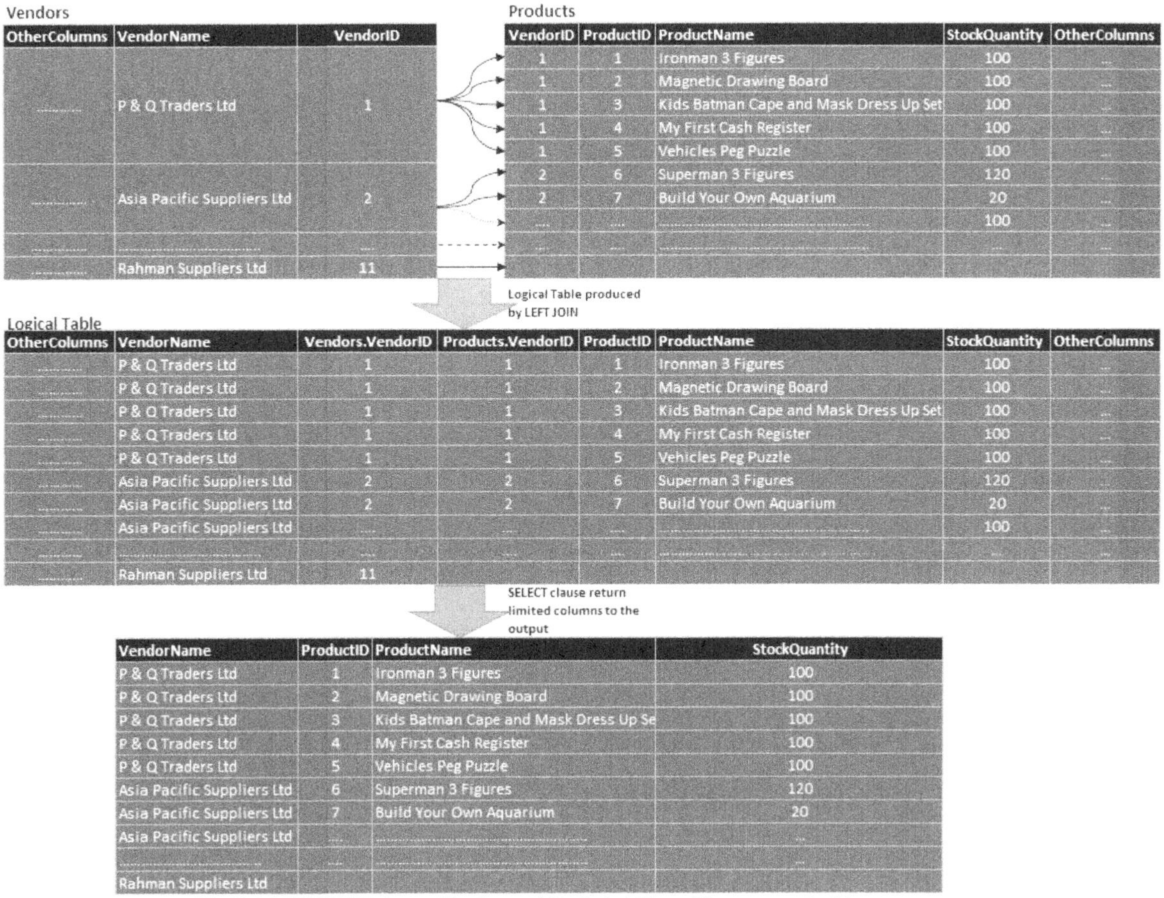

Fig 11.1: LEFT JOIN between Vendors and Products tables with some sample data

Notice that, for the first row of the *Vendors* table, the *LEFT JOIN* predicate *Vendors.VendorID = Products.VendorID* evaluates to *TRUE* for the first five rows of the *Products* table, and so five rows have been produced for *VendorID 1* in the logical table (please look at the first five rows in the logical table). For the last row, however, the *LEFT JOIN* predicate evaluates to *FALSE* for every row in the *Products* table (i.e. none of them have *VendorID 11*) and therefore one row has been populated with only columns from *Vendors* table and *NULL* (*empty*) for the other columns. The *SELECT* clause then returns the rows from the logical table with only the specified columns.

If you use a table alias, the query can be re-written like you see below:

```
SELECT v.VendorName, p.ProductID, p.ProductName, p.StockQuantity
FROM Vendors AS v
LEFT OUTER JOIN Products AS p
    ON v.VendorID = p.VendorID;
```

RIGHT JOIN is similar to *LEFT JOIN* with the only difference being that *LEFT JOIN* returns all rows from the table on the left side and matching rows from the right side, while the *RIGHT JOIN* returns all rows from the right side and matching rows from the left side. If you swap the position of the tables and replace *LEFT JOIN* with *RIGHT JOIN*, both queries will return exactly same results. Therefore, the query below will return exactly the same results as the above query:

```
SELECT v.VendorName, p.ProductID, p.ProductName, p.StockQuantity
FROM Products AS p
RIGHT OUTER JOIN Vendors AS v
    ON p.VendorID = v.VendorID;
```

Notes

- If each row of the left-side table has at least one matching row in the right-side table, the *LEFT JOIN* and *INNER JOIN* will return exactly the same results.
- If each row of the right-side table has at least one matching row in the left-side table, the *RIGHT JOIN* and *INNER JOIN* will return exactly the same results.
- The *OUTER* keyword is optional here (so you can remove it).

The following business problem will give you a chance to practice using *LEFT/RIGHT OUTER JOIN*.

Business Problem 1

We'd like to know what feedback (if any) that our customers are giving. Please give me a list of our customers and their feedback (if any). Please show each customers' last name, first name, the product ID on which they have provided feedback, the numerical feedback rating they gave, and the actual text of the feedback. Please sort the output in ascending order by our customer's last names.

Solution SQL

```
SELECT c.CustomerLastName AS LastName, c.CustomerFirstName AS FirstName, cf.ProductID,
       cf.CustomerFeedbackRating AS FeedbackRating, cf.CustomerFeedback AS FeedbackText
FROM Customers AS c
LEFT OUTER JOIN CustomerFeedbacks AS cf ON c.CustomerID = cf.CustomerID
ORDER BY c.CustomerLastName;
```

SQL Result

LastName	FirstName	ProductID	FeedbackRating	FeedbackText
Baker	Scott	NULL	NULL	NULL
Bowell	Melanie	3	5	Excellent service and product quality is very good
Brown	Ricky	2	5	Excellent service and product quality is very good
Clark	Robinson	NULL	NULL	NULL
Doslakoski	Crystal	3	4	Excellent service but product quality is not very good
Green	Adam	NULL	NULL	NULL
Hall	Allen	NULL	NULL	NULL
Hawker	Ashley	NULL	NULL	NULL

Solution Review

Here, *LEFT OUTER JOIN* links the *Customers* table with the *CustomerFeedbacks* table by their *CustomerID* columns and gets all feedback provided by each customer (*ProductID, CustomerFeedbackRating* and *CustomerFeedback* columns) from the *CustomerFeedbacks* table. For those customers who provided feedback for multiple products, multiple rows will be returned, while for those customers who have not provided any feedback, the *ProductID, CustomerFeedbackRating* and *CustomerFeedback* columns will return *NULL* values.

For example, the customer ID for *Scott Baker* does not exist in the *CustomerFeedbacks* table and that is why the *ProductID, FeedbackRating* and *FeedbackText* columns are *NULL* for him in the result. Please note that we have opted to show only 8 out of 32 customers who gave feedback in the SQL Result section. You should get 32 rows after executing the query.

You can swap the position of the tables and use *RIGHT OUTER JOIN* instead of *LEFT OUTER JOIN*. If you do, it will return exactly the same results. Here's what that query would look like:

```
SELECT  c.CustomerLastName AS LastName, c.CustomerFirstName AS FirstName, cf.ProductID,
     cf.CustomerFeedbackRating AS FeedbackRating, cf.CustomerFeedback AS FeedbackText
FROM CustomerFeedbacks AS cf
RIGHT OUTER JOIN Customers AS c ON c.CustomerID = cf.CustomerID
ORDER BY c.CustomerLastName;
```

If you want to replace *NULL* with *N/A* in your result, you can use the *ISNULL* function. This function accepts two parameters: if the first parameter is *NOT NULL* then it will return the first parameter, otherwise it will return the second parameter. The datatypes for both parameters must be the same.

Using this method, you would re-write the query as follows to show *N/A* instead of *NULL* in the result:

```
SELECT c.CustomerLastName AS LastName, c.CustomerFirstName AS FirstName,
     ISNULL(CAST(cf.ProductID AS VARCHAR(10)), 'NA') AS ProductID,
     ISNULL(CAST(cf.CustomerFeedbackRating AS VARCHAR(10)), 'NA') AS FeedbackRating,
     ISNULL(cf.CustomerFeedback, 'NA') AS FeedbackText
FROM Customers AS c
LEFT OUTER JOIN CustomerFeedbacks AS cf ON c.CustomerID = cf.CustomerID
ORDER BY c.CustomerLastName;
```

Both the *ProductID* and *CustomerFeedbackRating* columns are numeric and that is why we used the *CAST* function to convert the datatype to string before passing them to the *ISNULL* function. Since the *CustomerFeedback* column is already in a string, there is no need to use the *CAST* function on it.

Notes

Regarding the *CAST()* function—as you can see in *Business Problem 1*, there are scenarios where we need to convert one type of value to another data type. The *CAST()* function converts a value from one data type to another convertible data type, and the syntax is:

```
CAST ( value to be converted AS target data type)
```

You can always convert numbers or dates to strings, but you may not always be able to convert strings to dates or numbers. Some examples:

CAST(25 AS VARCHAR(10)) = '25': here, the number 25 has been converted to a string, '25'
CAST('25' AS INT) = 25: here, the string '25' has been converted to the number 25
CAST('Abc' AS INT) = Error: here, the string 'Abc' cannot be converted to a number.

Retrieving All of the Rows from a Table with Matching Rows from Two or More Tables

In an earlier topic, you learned how to use *LEFT/RIGHT OUTER JOIN* to retrieve all rows from a table along with those rows that match a predicate with another table, but if you want to do the same with *more than one table*, you can simply add an additional *LEFT/RIGHT OUTER JOIN* clause for every additional table. To make things a little easier, we'll stick with the previous topic's example.

This time, if you want to add the *VendorCategories* table (i.e. if you want to get *a list of vendors along with the products they are selling and the categories they belong to*), you can add one more *LEFT OUTER JOIN* clause to the previous query. The new query would look like this:

```
SELECT  v.VendorName, p.ProductID, p.ProductName, p.StockQuantity, vc.VendorCategoryName
FROM Vendors AS v
LEFT OUTER JOIN Products AS p
     ON v.VendorID = p.VendorID
LEFT OUTER JOIN VendorCategories AS vc
     ON v.VendorCategoryID = vc.VendorCategoryID;
```

Here, the *Vendors* table is linked with *VendorCategories* table by its foreign key: *VendorCategoryID*. In the above query, we added the last two lines of code. Specifically, we added another *LEFT OUTER JOIN* with the *VendorCategories* table based on *VendorCategoryID*. Think of the first *LEFT OUTER JOIN* as producing a logical table (same as the logical table in Fig 11.1) that is then performing a *LEFT OUTER JOIN* with the *VendorCategories* table and providing the final result.

Fig 11.2 shows a snapshot of the final query result :

VendorName	ProductID	ProductName	StockQuantity	VendorCategoryName
P & Q Traders Ltd	1	Ironman 3 Figures	100	Regular
P & Q Traders Ltd	2	Magnetic Drawing Board	100	Regular
P & Q Traders Ltd	3	Kids Batman Cape and Mask Dress Up Set	100	Regular
P & Q Traders Ltd	4	My First Cash Register	100	Regular
P & Q Traders Ltd	5	Vehicles Peg Puzzle	100	Regular
Asia Pacific Suppliers Ltd	6	Superman 3 Figures	120	Diamond
Asia Pacific Suppliers Ltd	7	Build Your Own Aquarium	20	Diamond
Asia Pacific Suppliers Ltd	....	....	...	Diamond
....	....	....	...	...
Rahman Suppliers Ltd				Gold

Fig 11.2: LEFT JOIN between Vendors, Products and VendorCategories tables with some sample data

Since each vendor always belongs to a category, the rows from the earlier logical table always have a matching row in the *VendorCategories* table and that is why all of the rows in the final result have *VendorCategoryName*. Therefore, in this particular scenario, if you replace the last *LEFT OUTER JOIN* with *INNER JOIN*, it will return the same result and the query will look like the one you see below:

```
SELECT v.VendorName, p.ProductID, p.ProductName, p.StockQuantity, vc.VendorCategoryName
FROM Vendors AS v
LEFT OUTER JOIN Products AS p
    ON v.VendorID = p.VendorID
INNER JOIN VendorCategories AS vc
    ON v.VendorCategoryID = vc.VendorCategoryID;
```

This means that you can use different types of joins within the same query. Let's solve a business problem using multiple joins with the same and/or multiple types.

Business Problem 2

Please give me a customer list including any feedback they gave us and the country & city where they are living. Please show each customer's last name, first name, city, country, and also include the product ID they provided feedback for (if any), the feedback rating and the actual text of the feedback. For those customers who have not yet provided feedback, please show '- -' in the corresponding rows in the *ProductID*, *FeedBackRating* and *FeedBackText* columns. Please sort the output in ascending order by country, city and last name.

Solution SQL

```
SELECT c.CustomerLastName AS LastName, c.CustomerFirstName AS FirstName,
    ISNULL(CAST(cf.ProductID AS VARCHAR(10)), '--') AS ProductID,
    ISNULL(CAST(cf.CustomerFeedbackRating AS VARCHAR(10)), '--') AS FeedbackRating,
    ISNULL(cf.CustomerFeedback, '--') AS FeedbackText,
    a.City, a.Country
FROM Customers AS c
LEFT OUTER JOIN CustomerFeedbacks AS cf ON c.CustomerID = cf.CustomerID
LEFT OUTER JOIN Addresses AS a ON c.CustomerAddressID = a.AddressID
ORDER BY a.Country, a.City, c.CustomerLastName;
```

SQL Result

LastName	FirstName	ProductID	FeedbackRating	FeedbackText	City	Country
Clark	Robinson	--	--	--	Fawkner	Australia
Brown	Ricky	2	5	Excellent service and product quality is very good	Melbourne	Australia
Wilson	Adam	--	--	--	Melbourne	Australia
Smith	Sophie	4	4	Service was not good but product quality is very good	Parramatta	Australia
Bowell	Melanie	3	5	Excellent service and product quality is very good	Sydney	Australia
Doslakoski	Crystal	3	4	Excellent service but product quality is not very good	Sydney	Australia
Islam	Akidul	--	--	--	Dhaka	Bangladesh
Ponting	Ricky	--	--	--	Ottawa	Canada

Solution Review

Here's what we did to accomplish this task. First, we used *LEFT OUTER JOIN* to link the *Customers* table with the *CustomerFeedbacks* table by the *CustomerID* columns. We did this to produce a logical table that contains all the columns from both tables and all the rows from the *Customers* table (including their feedback from the *CustomerFeedbacks* table). This logical table then links with the *Addresses* table to produce our final and complete logical table. This logical table contains all the columns from the first logical table and *Addresses* table as well as all the rows from the first logical table and their addresses from *Addresses* table. The *SELECT* clause lists the columns that you need to retrieve from the final logical table and the *ORDER BY* clause lists the columns that you need to sort by. The *ISNULL* function replaces the *NULL* result with --. You should get 32 rows after executing the query, but we have only shown 8 here to keep our result at a reasonable size for demonstration purposes.

Filtering Data Returned from Multiple Tables Using the WHERE Clause

In this topic we will show you how to use a *WHERE* clause predicate to filter results produced by the *INNER/LEFT/RIGHT JOINs* we have recently shown you how to perform. The basic syntax for this is:

```
SELECT output column list
FROM table1
INNER/LEFT/RIGHT JOIN table2
      ON table1.column expression1 OPERATOR table2.column expression1
          AND/OR table1.column expression2 OPERATOR table2.column expression2
..............................................................................................
WHERE predicate 1 AND/OR predicate 2................................................................
```

We previously showed you a query that retrieves a list of vendors along with the products they are selling (if any), but if you want *a list of vendors who have not yet started selling any products*, you use our earlier query's result and choose to select only the rows from that result that have no values in product-related columns (e.g. *ProductID, ProductName* etc.). To do so, you can simply add the *WHERE* clause predicate *ProductID IS NULL* in the earlier query like the one below:

```
SELECT v.VendorName, p.ProductID, p.ProductName, p.StockQuantity
FROM Vendors AS v
LEFT OUTER JOIN Products AS p
      ON v.VendorID = p.VendorID
WHERE p.ProductID IS NULL;
```

Similarly, if you want *a list of vendors who have started selling products*, you can simply change the *WHERE* clause predicate to *ProductID IS NOT NULL*, the query will be like below:

```
SELECT v.VendorName, p.ProductID, p.ProductName, p.StockQuantity
FROM Vendors AS v
LEFT OUTER JOIN Products AS p
    ON v.VendorID = p.VendorID
WHERE p.ProductID IS NOT NULL;
```

If you want only the vendor's information and want a unique list, you can remove the columns from the *Products* table from our *SELECT* clause, and then add a *DISTINCT* keyword to make the list unique. Optionally, you can add even more columns to the *SELECT* clause from the *Vendors* table like you see below:

```
SELECT DISTINCT v.VendorID, v.VendorName, v.VendorEmail
FROM Vendors AS v
LEFT OUTER JOIN Products AS p
    ON v.VendorID = p.VendorID
WHERE p.ProductID IS NOT NULL;
```

Business Problem 3 will give you another opportunity to practice filtering results from a *LEFT/RIGHT/INNER JOIN* using *WHERE* clause.

Business Problem 3

Please give me a list of our United States customers who have not yet provided any feedback. Please show every customer's city of residence, first name and last name. Please sort the list by city and first name.

Solution SQL

```
SELECT a.City, c.CustomerFirstName AS FirstName, c.CustomerLastName AS LastName
FROM Customers AS c
LEFT OUTER JOIN CustomerFeedbacks AS cf ON c.CustomerID = cf.CustomerID
LEFT OUTER JOIN Addresses AS a ON c.CustomerAddressID = a.AddressID
WHERE a.Country LIKE 'United States' AND cf.CustomerFeedbackRating IS NULL
ORDER BY a.City, c.CustomerFirstName;
```

SQL Result

City	FirstName	LastName
Edmonds	Robert	Smith
Kirkland	Adele	Renton
San Antonio	Lauren	McIntosh
San Diego	Emma	Stephens
San Francisco	Chelsea	Hillman
San Gabriel	Ashley	Hawker

Solution Review

This is similar to *Business Problem 2*, but in this case instead of showing all customers, you need to show only our United States customers who have not yet provided any feedback. The *WHERE* clause predicate *a.Country LIKE 'United States'* will include only the customers who are in United States and the other predicate *cf.CustomerFeedbackRating IS NULL* will include only the customers who haven't provided any feedback yet. The *AND* operator between these two predicates will ensure that the only customers who will be shown are those who have satisfied both predicates.

Since *AddressID* in a mandatory column in the *Customers* table, each customer will always have a related row in the *Addresses* table. Therefore, the *LEFT OUTER JOIN* and *INNER JOIN* will return the same results in this case. So if you replace the second *LEFT OUTER JOIN* with *INNER JOIN* as shown below, the query will return exactly the same results:

```
SELECT a.City, c.CustomerFirstName AS FirstName, c.CustomerLastName AS LastName
FROM Customers AS c
LEFT OUTER JOIN CustomerFeedbacks AS cf ON c.CustomerID = cf.CustomerID
INNER JOIN Addresses AS a ON c.CustomerAddressID = a.AddressID
WHERE a.Country LIKE 'United States' AND cf.CustomerFeedbackRating IS NULL
ORDER BY a.City, c.CustomerFirstName;
```

Summarizing Data from Multiple Tables

In *Lesson 10*, you learned how to summarize rows returned by *INNER JOIN* using aggregate functions along with the *GROUP BY* and *HAVING* clauses. You also know that, regardless of the type or combination of *JOIN* that you use, SQL will ultimately return a logical table. So, the summarization process will be same as *Lesson 10*, but the problem we will be solving here is a bit different. The syntax we will use is:

```
SELECT column 1, column 2, aggregate function 1, aggregate function 2, ...................
FROM table1
INNER/LEFT OUTER/RIGHT OUTER JOIN table2
        ON table1.column expression1 OPERATOR table2.column expression1
            AND/OR table1.column expression2 OPERATOR table2.column expression2
.............................................................................................................
WHERE predicate 1 AND/OR predicate 2.........................................................................
GROUP BY column 1, column 2................................................................................
HAVING predicate 1 AND/OR predicate 2.....................................................................;
```

Let's walk through a real-life business example. Assume that your marketing department would like to assess what impact it would have on company sales for the last quarter of 2017 if those current customers who didn't purchase any products had in fact purchased products at the same rate as your paying customers that quarter. They are essentially asking you to provide the following statistics for the last quarter of 2017:

- The total number of customers
- The number of customers who purchased products
- The total sales amount (based on order date)
- The average sales amount per customer who purchased products this quarter
- The average sales amount per customer who may or may not have purchased any products this quarter

Based on the knowledge you have gained so far, you can retrieve or calculate each of these necessary statistical items separately. Since this is a somewhat complex task, let's start off by looking at a diagram of what this collected data would look like (Fig 11.3 below):

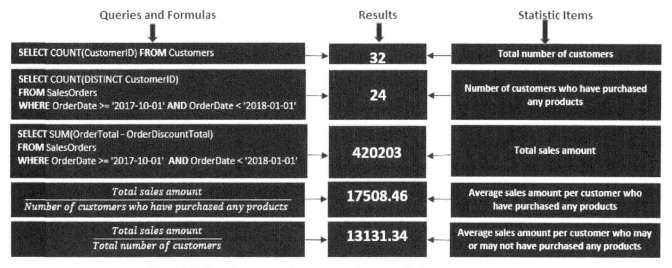

Fig 11.3: Retrieve or calculate each statistic items separately

You may be thinking that you can provide these statistics using *INNER JOIN* as you learned in *Lesson 10*. Let's see what such a query might look like:

```
SELECT    COUNT(c.CustomerID) as TotalNumberOfCustomers,
          COUNT(so.CustomerID) AS NumberOfCustomersWhoPurchasedProducts,
          SUM(so.OrderNetTotal) AS TotalSalesAmount,
          AVG(so.OrderNetTotal) AS AverageSalesAmountPerPurchasedCustomer,
          SUM(so.OrderNetTotal)/COUNT(c.CustomerID) AS AverageSalesAmountPerCustomer
FROM Customers c
INNER JOIN (
          SELECT CustomerID,
          SUM(OrderTotal - OrderDiscountTotal) AS OrderNetTotal
          FROM SalesOrders
          WHERE OrderDate >= '2017-10-01' AND OrderDate < '2018-01-01'
          GROUP BY CustomerID
     ) AS so ON c.CustomerID = so.CustomerID;
```

And the query result would look like:

TotalNumberOf Customers	NumberOfCustomers WhoPurchasedProducts	TotalSalesAmount	AverageSalesAmount PerPurchasedCustomer	AverageSalesAmount PerCustomer
24	24	420203.0000	17508.458333	17508.458333

You might have noticed that we have a small problem here. The total number of customers is the same as the number of customers who have purchased one or more products, and the average sales amount per customer who purchased products is the same as the average sales amount per customer who may or may not have purchased any products.

This is obviously not our desired result. So, why did we return (incorrect) duplicate values for the total number of customers and the number of customers who have purchased products? The reason this happened is because the *INNER JOIN* does not include non-matching customers into the logical table. The derived table after the *INNER JOIN* contains the customers who have purchased products in the last quarter of 2017. We know eight customers did not purchase any products in this quarter. Therefore, after the *INNER JOIN*, the logical table will not include these customers. That means the logical table will have only 24 customers who have purchased products in the last quarter of 2017, and that is why the above query returns the same value for both the total number of customers and the number of customers who have purchased. So, we now know what went wrong, but how can we fix it?

To solve this problem, we need to find a way to include the eight customers who didn't make any purchases last quarter of 2017 in our logical table   *LEFT JOIN* will allow us to do exactly that.

If you replace *INNER JOIN* with *LEFT OUTER JOIN* (or simply *LEFT JOIN)* in the above query, the logical table will return all 32 customers, but 27 of them will have valid values for *OrderNetTotal* and eight of them will have *NULL* values. Therefore, the query will return exactly the results you are looking for. The appropriate query will be:

```
SELECT    COUNT(c.CustomerID) as TotalNumberOfCustomers,
          COUNT(so.CustomerID) AS NumberOfCustomersWhoPurchasedProducts,
          SUM(so.OrderNetTotal) AS TotalSalesAmount,
          AVG(so.OrderNetTotal) AS AverageSalesAmountPerPurchasedCustomer,
          SUM(so.OrderNetTotal)/COUNT(c.CustomerID) AS AverageSalesAmountPerCustomer
FROM Customers c
LEFT OUTER JOIN (
          SELECT CustomerID,
          SUM(OrderTotal - OrderDiscountTotal) AS OrderNetTotal
          FROM SalesOrders
          WHERE OrderDate >= '2017-10-01' AND OrderDate < '2018-01-01'
          GROUP BY CustomerID
     ) AS so ON c.CustomerID = so.CustomerID;
```

And the query result we are looking for will return, as you can see below:

TotalNumberOf Customers	NumberOfCustomers WhoPurchasedProducts	TotalSalesAmount	AverageSalesAmount PerPurchasedCustomer	AverageSalesAmount PerCustomer
32	24	420203.0000	17508.458333	13131.343750

Now, if you want to return the same statistics, but this time specific for each country, you can add another *INNER JOIN* with the *Addresses* table and apply *GROUP BY* on the *Country* column like below:

```
SELECT    a.Country, COUNT(c.CustomerID) as TotalNumberOfCustomers,
          COUNT(so.CustomerID) AS NumberOfCustomersWhoPurchasedProducts,
          SUM(so.OrderNetTotal) AS TotalSalesAmount,
          AVG(so.OrderNetTotal) AS AverageSalesAmountPerPurchasedCustomer,
          SUM(so.OrderNetTotal)/COUNT(c.CustomerID) AS AverageSalesAmountPerCustomer
FROM Customers c
INNER JOIN Addresses AS a ON c.CustomerAddressID = a.AddressID
LEFT OUTER JOIN (
          SELECT CustomerID,
          SUM(OrderTotal - OrderDiscountTotal) AS OrderNetTotal
          FROM SalesOrders
          WHERE OrderDate >= '2017-10-01' AND OrderDate < '2018-01-01'
          GROUP BY CustomerID
     ) AS so ON c.CustomerID = so.CustomerID
GROUP BY a.Country;
```

The country-specific query result will be like below:

Country	TotalNumberOf Customers	NumberOfCustomers WhoPurchasedProducts	TotalSales Amount	AverageSalesAmount PerPurchasedCustomer	AverageSalesAmount PerCustomer
Australia	6	3	18120	6040.00	3020.00
Bangladesh	1	1	1440	1440.00	1440.00
Canada	5	5	109385	21877.00	21877.00
China	1	1	3360	3360.00	3360.00
France	1	1	1160	1160.00	1160.00
Germany	2	2	1080	540.00	540.00
India	1	1	3360	3360.00	3360.00
United Kingdom	4	4	33970	8492.50	8492.50
United States	11	6	248328	41388.00	22575.27

Now if you want to see only the countries where some customers haven't purchased any products for the quarter, you can add a *HAVING* clause predicate *COUNT(c.CustomerID) <> COUNT(so.CustomerID)* to the above query, and the new query will look like this:

```
SELECT      a.Country, COUNT(c.CustomerID) as TotalNumberOfCustomers,
            COUNT(so.CustomerID) AS NumberOfCustomersWhoPurchasedProducts,
            SUM(so.OrderNetTotal) AS TotalSalesAmount,
            AVG(so.OrderNetTotal) AS AverageSalesAmountPerPurchasedCustomer,
            SUM(so.OrderNetTotal)/COUNT(c.CustomerID) AS AverageSalesAmountPerCustomer
FROM Customers c
INNER JOIN Addresses AS a ON c.CustomerAddressID = a.AddressID
LEFT OUTER JOIN (
            SELECT CustomerID,
            SUM(OrderTotal - OrderDiscountTotal) AS OrderNetTotal
            FROM SalesOrders
            WHERE OrderDate >= '2017-10-01' AND OrderDate < '2018-01-01'
            GROUP BY CustomerID
      ) AS so ON c.CustomerID = so.CustomerID
GROUP BY a.Country
HAVING COUNT(c.CustomerID) <> COUNT(so.CustomerID);
```

The new query result will be narrowed down to exactly what we're looking for:

Country	TotalNumberOf Customers	NumberOfCustomers WhoPurchasedProducts	TotalSales Amount	AverageSalesAmount PerPurchasedCustomer	AverageSalesAmount PerCustomer
Australia	6	3	18120	6040.00	3020.00
United States	11	6	248328	41388.00	22575.27

You can even exclude rows from the logical table before summarizing them. For example, if you want to return the original statistics but for male customers only, you can add the *WHERE* clause predicate *c.CustomerGender LIKE 'Male'* in the previous query. The *WHERE* clause predicate excludes non-male customers before applying the aggregate, and then new query will be:

```
SELECT      a.Country, COUNT(c.CustomerID) as TotalNumberOfCustomers,
            COUNT(so.CustomerID) AS NumberOfCustomersWhoPurchasedProducts,
            SUM(so.OrderNetTotal) AS TotalSalesAmount,
            AVG(so.OrderNetTotal) AS AverageSalesAmountPerPurchasedCustomer,
            SUM(so.OrderNetTotal)/COUNT(c.CustomerID) AS AverageSalesAmountPerCustomer
FROM Customers c
INNER JOIN Addresses AS a ON c.CustomerAddressID = a.AddressID
LEFT OUTER JOIN (
            SELECT CustomerID,
            SUM(OrderTotal - OrderDiscountTotal) AS OrderNetTotal
            FROM SalesOrders
            WHERE OrderDate >= '2017-10-01' AND OrderDate < '2018-01-01'
            GROUP BY CustomerID
      ) AS so ON c.CustomerID = so.CustomerID
WHERE c.CustomerGender LIKE 'Male'
GROUP BY a.Country;
```

And here is the query result:

Country	TotalNumberOf Customers	NumberOfCustomers WhoPurchasedProducts	TotalSales Amount	AverageSalesAmount PerPurchasedCustomer	AverageSalesAmount PerCustomer
Australia	3	1	10390	10390.00	3463.33
Bangladesh	1	1	1440	1440.00	1440.00
Canada	5	5	109385	21877.00	21877.00
France	1	1	1160	1160.00	1160.00
India	1	1	3360	3360.00	3360.00
United Kingdom	1	1	15970	15970.00	15970.00
United States	4	1	33655	33655.00	8413.75

You can also apply another aggregate filter to exclude some of the aggregated rows. For example, if you want to exclude countries where all male customers have bought products from this result, you can add a *HAVING* clause predicate *COUNT(c.CustomerID) <> COUNT(so.CustomerID)* to the above query like below:

```
SELECT    a.Country, COUNT(c.CustomerID) as TotalNumberOfCustomers,
          COUNT(so.CustomerID) AS NumberOfCustomersWhoPurchasedProducts,
          SUM(so.OrderNetTotal) AS TotalSalesAmount,
          AVG(so.OrderNetTotal) AS AverageSalesAmountPerPurchasedCustomer,
          SUM(so.OrderNetTotal)/COUNT(c.CustomerID) AS AverageSalesAmountPerCustomer
FROM Customers c
INNER JOIN Addresses AS a ON c.CustomerAddressID = a.AddressID
LEFT OUTER JOIN (
          SELECT CustomerID,
          SUM(OrderTotal - OrderDiscountTotal) AS OrderNetTotal
          FROM SalesOrders
          WHERE OrderDate >= '2017-10-01' AND OrderDate < '2018-01-01'
          GROUP BY CustomerID
     ) AS so ON c.CustomerID = so.CustomerID
WHERE c.CustomerGender LIKE 'Male'
GROUP BY a.Country
HAVING COUNT(c.CustomerID) <> COUNT(so.CustomerID);
```

The query result will be like below:

Country	TotalNumberOf Customers	NumberOfCustomers WhoPurchasedProducts	TotalSales Amount	AverageSalesAmount PerPurchasedCustomer	AverageSalesAmount PerCustomer
Australia	3	1	10390	10390	3463.333333
United States	4	1	33655	33655	8413.750000

Let's solve some business problems to practice summarizing data from multiple tables.

Business Problem 4

In which countries do our customers that have not yet provided any feedback on a product? Show the countries by name and show the number of customers per country who haven't provided feedback.

Solution SQL

```
SELECT a.Country, COUNT(DISTINCT c.CustomerID) AS NumberOfCustomers
FROM Customers AS c
INNER JOIN Addresses AS a ON c.CustomerAddressID = a.AddressID
LEFT OUTER JOIN CustomerFeedbacks AS cf ON c.CustomerID = cf.CustomerID
WHERE cf.CustomerFeedbackRating IS NULL
GROUP BY a.Country;
```

SQL Result

Country	NumberOfCustomers
Australia	2
Bangladesh	1
Canada	5
China	1
France	1
Germany	2
India	1
United Kingdom	4
United States	6

Solution Review

The steps the database engine goes through when executing this query are as follows:

1. First, the *INNER JOIN* predicate *c.CustomerAddressID = a.AddressID* will generate a logical table that contains all columns from both tables and all rows from the *Customers* table along with their addresses from the *Addresses* table.
2. Next, the *LEFT OUTER JOIN* predicate will link the first logical table with the *CustomerFeedbacks* table via their *CustomerID* columns. This will generate another logical table that contains all of the columns and matching rows from both tables along with those that do not match from the first logical table. It will also include the *NULL* values in the *CustomerFeedbacks* table columns for those rows that do not match.
3. Next, the *WHERE* clause predicate *cf.CustomerFeedbackRating IS NULL* selects only those rows from the final logical table whose *CustomerFeedbackRating* column's value is *NULL*.
4. Next, the *GROUP BY* clause groups the selected rows by their country and the *COUNT()* function counts the number of rows within each group.

Since one customer may provide multiple feedback comments, the *DISTINCT* keyword allows us to avoid one customer being counted multiple times.

Business Problem 5

Please give me a list of countries where more than four customers have not yet provided any feedback. Please provide the country name along with the number of customers per country.

Solution SQL

```
SELECT a.Country, COUNT(DISTINCT c.CustomerID) AS NumberOfCustomers
FROM Customers AS c
INNER JOIN Addresses AS a ON c.CustomerAddressID = a.AddressID
LEFT OUTER JOIN CustomerFeedbacks AS cf ON c.CustomerID = cf.CustomerID
WHERE cf.CustomerFeedbackRating IS NULL
GROUP BY a.Country
HAVING COUNT(DISTINCT c.CustomerID) > 4;
```

SQL Result

Country	NumberOfCustomers
Canada	5
United States	6

Solution Review

To answer this question we only need to include the countries from the result of the earlier question (*Business Problem 4*) that have a value greater than four in *NumberOfCustomers*. The *HAVING* clause predicate *COUNT(DISTINCT c.CustomerID) > 4* will do this for us.

Lesson Summary

In this lesson you have learned the SQL statements necessary to retrieve data from two or more dissimilar tables:

- Using *LEFT/RIGHT OUTER JOIN* between two tables produces a logical table consisting of all the columns and rows from both tables if they satisfy the *JOIN* predicate(s). It will also include all rows that do not satisfy the *JOIN* predicate(s) from one table (the left-side table for *LEFT OUTER JOIN* and the right-side table for *RIGHT OUTER JOIN*).
- Multiple types of *JOINs (LEFT/RIGHT/INNER)* can be used within the same query.
- In the case of more than one *JOIN* within a query, the RDBMS executes the first *JOIN* between the first two tables and produces the first logical table. This logical table is then merged with the third table by *JOIN*, which produces the second logical table and so on, like in the following diagram:

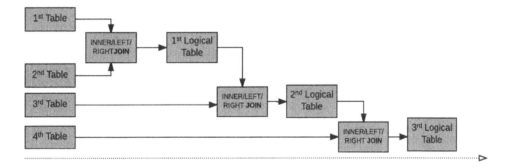

- The *WHERE* clause predicate applies to the final logical table produced from the *JOIN* and returns the rows that satisfy the predicate.
- You can use the *SELECT* clause to specify only your desired columns from the final logical table.
- The *GROUP BY* clause can be applied to the final logical table to summarize the data and if you use a *HAVING* clause in conjunction, it will filter the summarized data.

Lesson 12
Retrieving and Summarizing Data from Multiple Tables Using UNION

NEW SQL STATEMENTS AND KEYWORDS COVERED IN THIS LESSON:

- UNION JOIN → SELECT...Other Clauses...UNION/UNION ALL...SELECT...Other Clauses

---

Lesson Objective

By now, you know how to retrieve data from dissimilar tables that have at least one common column, but what if you need to merge two or more dissimilar tables or result sets that do not have any common columns? This lesson will show you how the *UNION* operation combines two or more dissimilar tables or result sets, and how to summarize the final result.

Code Samples

For this lesson, you can find the SQL code solutions for the examples and business problems at the following link: https://drive.google.com/open?id=1hBCQjd9HMVPeCNQ88NAiot-pioH1CqV1

Retrieving All of the Rows from Two or More Dissimilar Tables

You learned how to combine two or more similar result sets from a single table back in *Lesson 8*. The technique we will cover in this lesson is quite similar, except the query we will be using here is more complex and involves multiple tables. You'll see how this will become useful when you see this in practice with some real-world business problems. For now, let's look at the basic syntax of *UNION*:

```
SELECT statement 1
UNION ALL
SELECT statement 2
UNION ALL
SELECT statement 3
...............................
ORDER BY column list;
```

Each *SELECT* statement will execute on its own, combine the results, then eliminate any duplicate results if you use *UNION* instead of *UNION ALL*. Finally, the statement will apply the *ORDER BY* clause. Each *SELECT* statement can be as complex as you want, but a *UNION* operation has two restrictions:

- The *ORDER BY* clause is optional here, but if you want to use the *ORDER BY* clause, then it has to be at end of the last *SELECT* statement.
- Every *SELECT* statement must have the same number of columns and they must have compatible data types.

So, if you want *a list of vendors, customers and employees that includes their contact details in three separate lists*, you can execute the three queries shown below:

Query 1:

```
SELECT VendorName AS Name, VendorEmail AS Email, VendorPhoneNumber AS ContactNumber
FROM Vendors;
```

Query 2:

```
SELECT CONCAT(CustomerFirstName, ' ', CustomerLastName) AS Name,
     CustomerEmail AS Email, CustomerPhoneNumber AS ContactNumber
FROM Customers;
```

Query 3:

```
SELECT  CONCAT(EmployeeFirstName, ' ', EmployeeLastName) AS Name,
     EmployeeEmail AS Email, EmployeePhoneNumber AS ContactNumber
FROM Employees;
```

Let's explore the *UNION* operation by looking at an example. Assume that your company is celebrating its 50th birthday and you want to send a gift to every vendor, customer and employee. In preparation, you need to provide a list that contains all vendors, customers and employees and includes their contact details. Since *Query 1*, *Query 2* and *Query 3* all have three columns and each column's datatype is a string, you can use the *UNION* keyword to combine the results of these three queries:

```
SELECT VendorName AS Name, VendorEmail AS Email, VendorPhoneNumber AS ContactNumber
FROM Vendors

UNION

SELECT CONCAT(CustomerFirstName, ' ', CustomerLastName) AS Name,
     CustomerEmail AS Email, CustomerPhoneNumber AS ContactNumber
FROM Customers

UNION

SELECT CONCAT(EmployeeFirstName, ' ', EmployeeLastName) AS Name,
     EmployeeEmail AS Email, EmployeePhoneNumber AS ContactNumber
FROM Employees;
```

If an employee bought a product from the company, he/she will be in both the *Employees* and *Customers* tables, and that is why we used *UNION* instead of *UNION ALL* to remove any duplicates. If you want to keep the duplicate, you can use *UNION ALL* here.

Filtering Data Returned from Multiple Dissimilar Tables

In the previous topic, you saw an example of how to combine and retrieve all rows from multiple dissimilar tables using *UNION/UNION ALL*. This topic will show you how to use a *WHERE* clause predicate to filter the result produced by a *UNION* operation.

Let's learn this by continuing with the previous example. The query in the previous topic retrieves a list that contains all vendors, customers and employees with their contact details, but if you want *a list that contains only the vendors, customers and employees (and their contact details) who are located in the USA*, you can get such a list in two different ways:

Option 1:

Join each of the three queries with the *Addresses* table and use the *WHERE* clause predicate *Country LIKE 'United States'* to retrieve only the vendors/customers/employees who are located in the USA.

The query would look like:

```
SELECT v.VendorName AS Name, v.VendorEmail AS Email, v.VendorPhoneNumber AS ContactNumber
FROM Vendors AS v
INNER JOIN Addresses AS a ON v.VendorAddressID = a.AddressID
WHERE a.Country LIKE 'United States'

UNION

SELECT  CONCAT(c.CustomerFirstName, ' ', c.CustomerLastName) AS Name,
        c.CustomerEmail AS Email, c.CustomerPhoneNumber AS ContactNumber
FROM Customers AS c
INNER JOIN Addresses AS a ON c.CustomerAddressID = a.AddressID
WHERE a.Country LIKE 'United States'

UNION

SELECT  CONCAT(e.EmployeeFirstName, ' ', e.EmployeeLastName) AS Name,
        e.EmployeeEmail AS Email, e.EmployeePhoneNumber AS ContactNumber
FROM Employees AS e
INNER JOIN Addresses AS a ON e.EmployeeAddressID = a.AddressID
WHERE    a.Country LIKE 'United States';
```

Option 2:

In **option 1**, we first filtered each SQL statement to return the resulting rows for the USA, then combined the three filtered result sets using a *UNION* operation. Here we will do it the opposite way:

- Add the *AddressID* column to the *SELECT* clause of each statement
- Combine three unfiltered result sets using a *UNION* operation
- Use this combined result set as a derived table and join it with *Addresses* table
- Apply the *WHERE* clause predicate *Country LIKE 'United States'* to retrieve only the vendors/customers/employees who are located in USA.

When we put all these steps in practice, the query will look like what you see below:

```
SELECT Persons.Name, Persons.Email, Persons.ContactNumber
FROM (
        SELECT VendorName AS Name, VendorEmail AS Email, VendorPhoneNumber AS ContactNumber,
            VendorAddressID AS AddressID
        FROM Vendors

        UNION

        SELECT CONCAT(CustomerFirstName, ' ', CustomerLastName) AS Name, CustomerEmail AS Email,
            CustomerPhoneNumber AS ContactNumber, CustomerAddressID AS AddressID
        FROM Customers

        UNION

        SELECT CONCAT(EmployeeFirstName, ' ', EmployeeLastName) AS Name, EmployeeEmail AS Email,
            EmployeePhoneNumber AS ContactNumber, EmployeeAddressID AS AddressID
        FROM Employees
    ) AS Persons
INNER JOIN Addresses ON Persons.AddressID = Addresses.AddressID
WHERE Addresses.Country LIKE 'United States';
```

Summarizing Data Returned from Multiple Dissimilar Tables

As you know, aggregate functions allow us to summarize detailed rows and return one summarized row. You also know that aggregate functions combined correctly with a *GROUP BY* clause summarize detailed rows by groups and return one summarized row for each group. Also, you have learned that the *HAVING* clause allows us to return only those summarized rows that satisfy the *HAVING* clause's predicate. Now let's continue expanding your knowledge of these summarization techniques. To make things easier, we'll continue using the example from the previous topic.

You know you can provide *a list that contains all customers and employees with their respective contact details* by executing this query:

```
SELECT CONCAT(CustomerFirstName, ' ', CustomerLastName) AS Name,
        CustomerEmail AS Email, CustomerPhoneNumber AS ContactNumber
FROM Customers

UNION

SELECT CONCAT(EmployeeFirstName, ' ', EmployeeLastName) AS Name,
        EmployeeEmail AS Email, EmployeePhoneNumber AS ContactNumber
FROM Employees;
```

What if a business user asks you, *'How many customers and employees do we have altogether?'* To answer this, you need to count the number of rows produced by the above query. To do this, you can use the whole query in a *FROM* clause of another query as a derived table and apply a *COUNT* aggregate function. See below:

```
SELECT COUNT(Persons.Name) AS NumberOfContacts
FROM (
        SELECT CONCAT(CustomerFirstName, ' ', CustomerLastName) AS Name,
                CustomerEmail AS Email, CustomerPhoneNumber AS ContactNumber
        FROM Customers

        UNION

        SELECT CONCAT(EmployeeFirstName, ' ', EmployeeLastName) AS Name,
                EmployeeEmail AS Email, EmployeePhoneNumber AS ContactNumber
        FROM Employees
    ) AS Persons;
```

Now, what if the user asks you a slightly different question: *'How many customers and employees we have all together in the USA?'* This time, you need include only the customers and employees located in the USA *before* applying the *COUNT* aggregate function. You can do this in two ways, and both are similar to the solutions we showed you in the previous topic.

Option 1:

Filter each *SELECT* statement using a *WHERE* clause, then combine the results using a *UNION* operator, and finally apply a *COUNT* aggregate function to the combined results:

```
SELECT COUNT(Persons.Name) AS NumberOfContacts
FROM (
        SELECT CONCAT(c.CustomerFirstName, ' ', c.CustomerLastName) AS Name,
            c.CustomerEmail AS Email, c.CustomerPhoneNumber AS ContactNumber
        FROM Customers AS c
        INNER JOIN Addresses AS a ON c.CustomerAddressID = a.AddressID
        WHERE a.Country LIKE 'United States'

        UNION

        SELECT CONCAT(EmployeeFirstName, ' ', EmployeeLastName) AS Name,
            EmployeeEmail AS Email, EmployeePhoneNumber AS ContactNumber
        FROM Employees AS e
        INNER JOIN Addresses AS a ON e.EmployeeAddressID = a.AddressID
        WHERE a.Country LIKE 'United States'
    ) AS Persons;
```

Option 2:

Combine the results of each *SELECT* statement using a *UNION* operator, then filter the combined results using a *WHERE* clause, and finally apply a *COUNT* aggregate function to the filtered results:

```
SELECT COUNT(Persons.Name) AS NumberOfContacts
FROM (
        SELECT CONCAT(CustomerFirstName, ' ', CustomerLastName) AS Name, CustomerEmail AS Email,
            CustomerPhoneNumber AS ContactNumber, CustomerAddressID AS AddressID
        FROM Customers

        UNION

        SELECT CONCAT(EmployeeFirstName, ' ', EmployeeLastName) AS Name, EmployeeEmail AS Email,
            EmployeePhoneNumber AS ContactNumber, EmployeeAddressID AS AddressID
        FROM Employees
    ) AS Persons
INNER JOIN Addresses ON Persons.AddressID = Addresses.AddressID
WHERE    Addresses.Country LIKE 'United States';
```

If the user wants to know *how many customers and employees the company has all together in each country*, you should not filter for a specific country as seen in the above query. Instead, you need to add a *Country* column to each of the *SELECT* lists so that you can use the column in the *GROUP BY* clause and the *SELECT* list of the outer query. Your query for achieving this result will look like:

```
SELECT Persons.Country, COUNT(Persons.Name) AS NumberOfContacts
FROM (
        SELECT CONCAT(c.CustomerFirstName, ' ', c.CustomerLastName) AS Name,
            c.CustomerEmail AS Email, c.CustomerPhoneNumber AS ContactNumber, a.Country
        FROM Customers AS c
        INNER JOIN Addresses AS a ON c.CustomerAddressID = a.AddressID

        UNION

        SELECT CONCAT(EmployeeFirstName, ' ', EmployeeLastName) AS Name,
            EmployeeEmail AS Email, EmployeePhoneNumber AS ContactNumber, a.Country
        FROM Employees AS e
        INNER JOIN Addresses AS a ON e.EmployeeAddressID = a.AddressID
    ) AS Persons
GROUP BY Persons.Country;
```

Now, if the user wants to know *which countries have more than four contacts (including customers and employees),* you can add a *HAVING* clause predicate, *COUNT(Persons.Name) > 4*, to the above query to filter out the countries that have 0, 1, 2, 3, or 4 contacts:

```
SELECT Persons.Country, COUNT(Persons.Name) AS NumberOfContacts
FROM (
        SELECT CONCAT(c.CustomerFirstName, ' ', c.CustomerLastName) AS Name,
            c.CustomerEmail AS Email, c.CustomerPhoneNumber AS ContactNumber, a.Country
        FROM Customers AS c
        INNER JOIN Addresses AS a ON c.CustomerAddressID = a.AddressID

        UNION

        SELECT CONCAT(EmployeeFirstName, ' ', EmployeeLastName) AS Name,
            EmployeeEmail AS Email, EmployeePhoneNumber AS ContactNumber, a.Country
        FROM Employees AS e
        INNER JOIN Addresses AS a ON e.EmployeeAddressID = a.AddressID
    ) AS Persons
GROUP BY Persons.Country
HAVING COUNT(Persons.Name) > 4;
```

Lesson Summary

In this lesson, you learned the various usages of *UNION* operations in a variety of different queries. Keep in mind that:

- If multiple *SELECT* statements return the same number of columns with compatible datatypes, the results can be combined together using *UNION/UNION ALL* operators.
- *UNION* removes any duplicate rows and *UNION ALL* keeps duplicate rows.
- To filter detailed rows, a *WHERE* clause can be applied either on individual *SELECT* statements before the *UNION* operation, or on the derived table after the *UNION* operation.
- After generating the combined results, you can use the results as a derived table and apply aggregate functions and/or a *GROUP BY* clause and/or a *HAVING* clause on them.

Lesson 13
Working with Views

Lesson Objective

If you're wondering, *'Why we are discussing **views** in a section titled **Retrieving Business Insights from Multiple Tables**?'* As you may have noticed, as soon you start joining multiple tables, the queries tend to quickly become big and complex—and sometimes very hard to follow if you are not a computer. Using *views* allows us to simplify these large and complex queries significantly, and that is why now is a great time to discuss them. This lesson will show you:

- What a view is
- How to create them
- How to modify them
- How to remove them
- What the use cases for them are
- What the limitations of them are

Code Samples

You can find this lesson's SQL code solutions for all examples and business problems at the following link:
https://drive.google.com/open?id=170-jNSqMb4q3IRNnflp0kuDR_ckVwU15

What Is a View?

When you execute a query it returns a result set that is effectively a *'virtual table'*, and if you give it a name, this result set can be used just as if it is an existing table. This named query is what is known as a *database view*, or simply a *view*.

A *view* can be used the same way as a table in *SELECT, INSERT, UPDATE* and *DELETE* operations, although there are some restrictions to the ways *INSERT, UPDATE* and *DELETE* operations can be performed on them. Nevertheless, the syntax is exactly same as with a table. When you use a view within a query, the query processor expands the view name with the actual query, which therefore becomes a derived table for the outer query. You can use a view inside another view as well. In fact, you can nest the view as many times as you want, but this can lead to performance issues, as you can imagine. Therefore, if you are nesting the view, please test your queries before using them in your application.

Note

All mainstream RDBMSs allow naming a query.

How to Create a View?

The basic syntax to create a view is:
```
CREATE VIEW view name
AS
SELECT Statement;
```

If you want to create the view **ProductsView** for the whole **Products** table, the SQL statement will be like you see below:

```
CREATE VIEW ProductsView
AS
SELECT * FROM Products;
```

For example, if you want to *create a view that contains a list of products with their corresponding vendor and category details (vendor name, vendor category, product ID, product name, stock quantity, ordered quantity, standard sales price, sales discount percentage and sales discount amount)*, the SQL statement would be:

```
CREATE VIEW ProductsWithVendors
AS
SELECT VendCat.VendorCategoryName, Vend.VendorName, Prod.ProductID, Prod.ProductName, Prod.StockQuantity,
       Prod.OrderedQuantity, Prod.StandardSalesPrice, Prod.SalesDiscountPercentage, Prod.SalesDiscountAmount
FROM Products AS Prod
INNER JOIN Vendors AS Vend
    ON Prod.VendorID = Vend.VendorID
INNER JOIN VendorCategories AS VendCat
    ON Vend.VendorCategoryID = VendCat.VendorCategoryID;
```

The view represents the *virtual table* of the *SELECT* statement. Therefore, if you execute *SELECT * FROM ProductsWithVendors*, then it will return exactly the same result as the actual query. You can also add a *WHERE* clause in the *SELECT* statement to restrict data access. For example, if your company has a group of people who act as customer service liaisons for *Diamond* category vendors, you can create a view for them by adding the *WHERE* clause predicate *VendorCategoryName = 'Diamond'* to the previous view, as you see below:

```
CREATE VIEW ProductsWithVendorsV1
AS
SELECT  VendCat.VendorCategoryName, Vend.VendorName, Prod.ProductID, Prod.ProductName, Prod.StockQuantity,
       Prod.OrderedQuantity, Prod.StandardSalesPrice, Prod.SalesDiscountPercentage, Prod.SalesDiscountAmount
FROM Products AS Prod
INNER JOIN Vendors AS Vend
    ON Prod.VendorID = Vend.VendorID
INNER JOIN VendorCategories AS VendCat
    ON Vend.VendorCategoryID = VendCat.VendorCategoryID
WHERE VendCat.VendorCategoryName = 'Diamond';
```

You can also add calculated columns to the *SELECT* clause in the view, but each calculated column must have a name (i.e. you must make an alias for each calculated column):

```
CREATE VIEW ProductsWithVendorsV2
AS
SELECT VendCat.VendorCategoryName, Vend.VendorName, Prod.ProductID, Prod.ProductName,
       Prod.StockQuantity - Prod.OrderedQuantity AS AvailableQuantity,
       Prod.StandardSalesPrice AS UnitPrice,
       CASE
            WHEN Prod.SalesDiscountPercentage <> 0
                THEN Prod.StandardSalesPrice * Prod.SalesDiscountPercentage/100
            ELSE Prod.SalesDiscountAmount
       END AS UnitDiscount
FROM Products AS Prod
INNER JOIN Vendors AS Vend
    ON Prod.VendorID = Vend.VendorID
INNER JOIN VendorCategories AS VendCat
    ON Vend.VendorCategoryID = VendCat.VendorCategoryID;
```

Therefore, if you execute *SELECT * FROM ProductsWithVendorsV2*, it will return exactly the same result as the actual query. You can add any clause except an *ORDER BY* clause to the *SELECT* statement in the view.

How to Modify a View?

You cannot modify part of a query; the whole query must be replaced. Since a view effectively represents a query, if you want to modify it, you can simply replace the *CREATE* keyword with an *ALTER* keyword in the *CREATE VIEW* statement and re-write the query as per your needs. The basic syntax to modify a view is:

```
ALTER VIEW view name
AS
SELECT Statement;
```

So, if you want to remove the *ProductID* column from the *ProductsWithVendors* view, the SQL statement would look like:

```
ALTER VIEW ProductsWithVendors
AS
SELECT  VendCat.VendorCategoryName, Vend.VendorName, Prod.ProductName, Prod.StockQuantity, Prod.OrderedQuantity,
        Prod.StandardSalesPrice, Prod.SalesDiscountPercentage, Prod.SalesDiscountAmount
FROM Products AS Prod
INNER JOIN Vendors AS Vend
    ON Prod.VendorID = Vend.VendorID
INNER JOIN VendorCategories AS VendCat
    ON Vend.VendorCategoryID = VendCat.VendorCategoryID;
```

You can even modify the query to be completely different:

```
ALTER VIEW ProductsWithVendors
AS
SELECT  VendCat.VendorCategoryName, Vend.VendorName, COUNT(Prod.ProductID) AS TotalProducts
FROM Products AS Prod
INNER JOIN Vendors AS Vend
    ON Prod.VendorID = Vend.VendorID
INNER JOIN VendorCategories AS VendCat
    ON Vend.VendorCategoryID = VendCat.VendorCategoryID
GROUP BY VendCat.VendorCategoryName, Vend.VendorName;
```

How to Remove a View?

If a view is not being used, you should remove it from the database. The basic syntax to remove a view is:

```
DROP VIEW view name;
```

If you want to remove view *ProductsWithVendors*, the SQL statement will be like below:

```
DROP VIEW ProductsWithVendors;
```

What Business Uses Are There for Views?

Now you know what views are and how to create them, but why do you need them? Here are some use cases where views can play an important role:

Views can be used to provide a process-oriented look at the underlying data structure for end-users: Within an organization, lots of people work with data, but only a few of them (yourself included) know details such as the normalized-form of a relational database, how many tables exist in the database, how to join tables and so on. There will be times when the user needs to see certain results on a regular basis, but without requesting a specific report from you or other colleagues whose job it is to manage SQL in the database. It will make your job a whole lot easier if you can create views that these less-skilled business users can simply use.

Consider the *ProductsWithVendorsV2* view that virtually stores products along with their vendor details. If you want to retrieve a list of products with their vendor details, you can simply execute a *SELECT * FROM ProductsWithVendorsV2* query. In doing so, all the major attributes related to products and vendors are stored within a view (virtual table). As you know, if a business user wants to see how many units of a product are in stock at a given time, someone (you) needs to write a SQL statement to subtract the ordered quantity from the stock quantity. If you create a view, however, then you do not need to do this calculation anymore. More importantly, you need to write a complex expression to get the unit discount value, but if you create a view for this purpose, then you do not need to do it anymore.

In conclusion, the business user does not need to know the technical details if you create one or more views to suit their needs. All of the calculations and business rules can be encapsulated within the view, and users can simply use it.

Views can significantly simplify complex query: Most business requirements are related to one or more business process. You follow the process-oriented approach to create views with all of the complex calculations embedded within them that allow your queries only to retrieve data from views, which in turn provide you with the following benefits:

- Making complex queries simple and more readable
- Allows you to reuse the same calculations and joins
- Complex calculations and joins can be done by more proficient database professionals, thereby increasing performance and reducing the chances of user error

Let's look at an example. Assume that you have to provide *a list of vendors with their category names and average discount values per product they offer to customers*. If you use previously created view *ProductsWithVendorsV2*, the query will simply look like below:

```
SELECT  VendorCategoryName,VendorName, AVG(UnitDiscount) AS AverageUnitDiscount
FROM ProductsWithVendorsV2
GROUP BY VendorCategoryName,VendorName;
```

Without using view, however, one of the ways the same query can be written like below:

```
SELECT VendCat.VendorCategoryName, Vend.VendorName,
    AVG (
            CASE
                WHEN Prod.SalesDiscountPercentage <> 0
                    THEN Prod.StandardSalesPrice * Prod.SalesDiscountPercentage/100
                ELSE Prod.SalesDiscountAmount
            END
        ) AS AverageUnitDiscount
FROM Products AS Prod
INNER JOIN Vendors AS Vend
    ON Prod.VendorID = Vend.VendorID
INNER JOIN VendorCategories AS VendCat
    ON Vend.VendorCategoryID = VendCat.VendorCategoryID
GROUP BY VendCat.VendorCategoryName, Vend.VendorName;
```

Comparing these two queries, it's clear to see how much simpler the first query is. And if the requirements get more complex, the query using views gets even simpler. Assume that you need to provide *the same list but only for those vendors whose average discount value per product is above $20*. The first query will look like:

```
SELECT  VendorCategoryName,VendorName, AVG(UnitDiscount) AS AverageUnitDiscount
FROM ProductsWithVendorsV2
GROUP BY VendorCategoryName,VendorName
HAVING AVG(UnitDiscount) > 20;
```

...while the second query will look like:

```
SELECT VendCat.VendorCategoryName, Vend.VendorName,
    AVG (
            CASE
                WHEN Prod.SalesDiscountPercentage <> 0
                    THEN Prod.StandardSalesPrice * Prod.SalesDiscountPercentage/100
                ELSE Prod.SalesDiscountAmount
            END
        ) AS AverageUnitDiscount
FROM        Products AS Prod
INNER JOIN Vendors AS Vend
    ON Prod.VendorID = Vend.VendorID
INNER JOIN VendorCategories AS VendCat
    ON Vend.VendorCategoryID = VendCat.VendorCategoryID
GROUP BY VendCat.VendorCategoryName, Vend.VendorName
HAVING    AVG (
                CASE
                    WHEN Prod.SalesDiscountPercentage <> 0
                        THEN Prod.StandardSalesPrice * Prod.SalesDiscountPercentage/100
                    ELSE Prod.SalesDiscountAmount
                END
            ) > 20;
```

Views can be used as a security feature to allow access only to a subset of rows of the underlying tables: Let's start with an example view *ProductsWithVendorsV1*, which is used to see *Diamond category* vendors and their product details. It may be that you only want users who interact with *Diamond category* vendors to be able to access data for these particular vendors. If you only grant these users access to the view pertaining to *Diamond category* vendor data, you will effectively restrict them from accessing the underlying tables where other vendor data can be found. In a relational database all data related to each subject (sales, products catalogue, skillsets of employees etc.) is stored in a table, but users are generally restricted to accessing data for their own territories or departments. Views facilitate these requirements.

The Limitations of Views

Limitations vary between RDBMSs as far as creating and using views is concerned, but there are some limitations that all mainstream RDBMSs share. Some of these are:

- The name of the view must be unique within a database schema. Therefore, you cannot use a name that has been used by other database objects (e.g. table, view, stored procedure etc.).
- You cannot use an *ORDER BY* clause in the *SELECT* statement used in the view.
- Most RDBMSs support the *INSERT*, *UPDATE* and *DELETE* operations on a view, but there may be limitations for these operations. These limitations vary between RDBMSs, so please check your RDBMS's documentation for details.
- Since views function like a table, each column in a view must have a unique name.

Lesson Summary

This lesson has briefly shown you how views can empower your SQL knowledge to simplify complex queries and secure your data:

- The *CREATE/ALTER/DROP VIEW* statements allow you to add/modify/remove views in your database.
- The usage of a filtered query in a view allows you to provide access to the subset of data to the underlying tables for a user or group of users.
- Most RDBMSs do not allow the *ORDER BY* clause to be used inside the view.
- The usage of a complex but re-usable query as a view can significantly simplify your operations.
- You can create a view within another view, a process called nesting. If desired, the RDBMS even allows you to nest a view inside another view, and then nest those views inside yet another view, and so on. RDBMSs differ on the maximum number of views they allow you to nest inside a view, so please check your RDBMS documentation for details). When you nest a view inside another view, please keep in mind that this can cause performance issues. For this reason, please test your query before using it in your application.

Lesson 14
Comparing Data Between Rows Within the Same Table or Result Set Using Self-Join

Lesson Objective

With the knowledge you have gained so far, you know how to compare and apply operators on rows between different tables, but what if you need to compare and/or do operations on the different rows within the same table? An example of this would be for *the relationship between an employee and his/her manager* (who is also an employee). If you want to compare or do other operations between employees and their managers, you have to do the operation between rows within the same table. This is a type of join called a *'self-join'*. All mainstream RDBMSs support self-joins for these types of operation.

In this lesson, you will learn what self-join is, how it can help you to solve some business problems, and some alternative solutions for certain problems.

Code Samples

For this lesson, you can find the SQL code solutions for the examples and business problems at the following link:
https://drive.google.com/open?id=1ygHSNLaYfeWPCdQWm_p2ebPe66s05CCq

What is Self-Join?

When you use an alias for a table, you know that you must use the alias (not the table name) for all references to the table within the query. That means that an alias can be treated like a virtual table. Therefore, you can use the same table two or more times with different aliases, and that it will be treated like the same table with two or more virtual tables. You can use any type of *JOIN (LEFT/RIGHT/INNER)* between those virtual tables. This type of join between the same tables is called *self-join,* and it allows you to answer questions like:

- *Please give me a list of employees along with the manager's details of each.*
- *Please give me a list of customers who have bought both product ID 53 & product 55.*
- *Please give me a list of customers who bought product ID 53 but not product ID 55.*
- *Please give me a list of customers who have bought either product ID 53 or 55, but not both.*

The basic syntax of self-join is:

```
SELECT output column list
FROM table1 AS alias1
LEFT/RIGHT/INNER JOIN table1 AS alias2
    ON alias1.column expression1 OPERATOR alias2.column expression1
        AND/OR alias1.column expression2 OPERATOR alias2.column expression2
```

Fig 14.1 represents a classic example of self-join. Here, the *ManagerID* is joined with the *EmployeeID* of the same table to get details for these employees' managers.

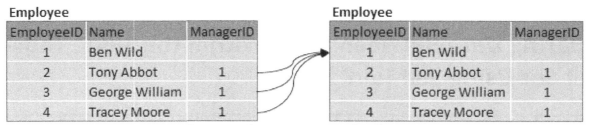

Fig 14.1: Classic example of self-join

Retrieving Data in Parent-child Relationships from the Same Table

As you know, employees and their managers have a child-parent relationship, but each manager is also an employee. Therefore, the *EmployeeID* and *ManagerID* within the *Employees* table have a one-to-many (primary key – foreign key) relationship. If you want to get *a list of employees along with their manager's details,* you can perform *INNER JOIN* on the *EmployeeID* of one instance of the *Employees* table with the *ManagerID* of another instance of the *Employees* table like you see below:

```
SELECT e1.EmployeeID, CONCAT(e1.EmployeeFirstName,' ', e1.EmployeeLastName) AS EmployeeName,
       e1.ManagerID, CONCAT(e2.EmployeeFirstName,' ', e2.EmployeeLastName) AS ManagerName
FROM Employees e1
INNER JOIN Employees e2 ON e1.ManagerID = e2.EmployeeID;
```

The result of this query will be:

EmployeeID	EmployeeName	ManagerID	ManagerName
2	Tony Abbot	1	Ben Wild
3	George William	1	Ben Wild
4	Tracey Moore	1	Ben Wild

Since *Ben Wild* does not have a manager, he has not appeared on the list on his own row as an employee (he only appears on the manager column only). If you want *Ben Wild* to appear on his own row as an employee, you can replace the *INNER JOIN* with a *LEFT JOIN* like below:

```
SELECT e1.EmployeeID, CONCAT(e1.EmployeeFirstName,' ', e1.EmployeeLastName) AS EmployeeName,
       e1.ManagerID, CONCAT(e2.EmployeeFirstName,' ', e2.EmployeeLastName) AS ManagerName
FROM Employees e1
LEFT JOIN Employees e2 ON e1.ManagerID = e2.EmployeeID;
```

The result for this query will be:

EmployeeID	EmployeeName	ManagerID	ManagerName
1	Ben Wild	NULL	
2	Tony Abbot	1	Ben Wild
3	George William	1	Ben Wild
4	Tracey Moore	1	Ben Wild

Retrieving Data Without Parent-child Relationships from the Same Table

With what you have learned so far, you can join two or more tables to return attribute values for two or more subjects, and you can also aggregate values from a group of rows returned from one or more tables, but how do you compare the attribute values between rows within a group? The self-join allows you to compare attribute values between rows within each group. Learning how to do this will empower you to answer questions that require checking the correlation between rows within the same dataset (table/derived table/view).

For now, let's execute the SQL statement below to create a view that contains all customers and the products they bought:

```
CREATE VIEW CustomerProducts
AS
SELECT DISTINCT c.CustomerID, CONCAT(c.CustomerFirstName, ' ', c.CustomerLastName) AS CustomerName,
    c.CustomerEmail, sop.ProductID
FROM Customers AS c
INNER JOIN SalesOrders AS so ON c.CustomerID = so.CustomerID
INNER JOIN SalesOrderProducts AS sop ON so.SalesOrderID = sop.SalesOrderID;
```

If you execute this *SELECT * FROM CustomerProducts* statement, it will return 460 rows. Here's a partial list of what that result will look like:

CustomerID	CustomerName	CustomerEmail	ProductID
1	Ricky Brown	RickBrown@SaleOnYourOwn.com	1
1	Ricky Brown	RickBrown@SaleOnYourOwn.com	6
1	Ricky Brown	RickBrown@SaleOnYourOwn.com	33
2	Adam Wilson	AdamWilson@SaleOnYourOwn.com	3
2	Adam Wilson	AdamWilson@SaleOnYourOwn.com	4
4	Melanie Bowell	KerrynWhite@SaleOnYourOwn.com	1
4	Melanie Bowell	KerrynWhite@SaleOnYourOwn.com	2
4	Melanie Bowell	KerrynWhite@SaleOnYourOwn.com	6

For illustration purposes, let assume the above table represents the whole result set. If you are asked which customers have bought *ProductIDs 1* and *6*, you need to check the product IDs between the first three rows for *CustomerID 1*, followed by the next two rows for *CustomerID 2*, and then the next three rows for *CustomerID 4*. This is where the self-join will become very handy.

Let's start with an example where self-join will play a vital role to fulfil business requirements. Assume that your company is going to start a target-based sales campaign focusing on existing customers and has already analysed their buying patterns and identified different groups of customers to whom the campaign will offer promotions. You have been asked to provide the following audiences: lists of customer groups who have bought:

- A list of customers who have bought *product ID 53* and *Product ID 55*
- A list of customers who have bought *product ID 53*, but not *product ID 55*
- A list of customers who have bought only *product IDs 53 & 55* and no other products
- A list of customers who have bought either *product ID 53* or *55*, but not both

Let's analyse the SQL statements you need to execute each of these requirements.

Return a List of Customers Who Have Bought ProductID 53 and ProductID 55

There are multiple ways you can write the SQL to provide *a list of customers who have bought both ProductID 55 and ProductID 55* (customers who have bought other products should not be excluded, but they must have at least bought these two). To demonstrate, we will show you two solutions here: one using self-join and the other using an aggregate function.

Solution – using self-join: The diagram below shows one of the ways to obtain our desired list:

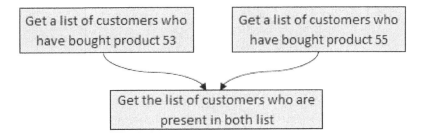

You have already learned that you can execute *Query 1* below to get *a list of customers who have bought ProductID 53:*

Query 1:
```
SELECT CustomerName, CustomerEmail, CustomerID
FROM CustomerProducts
WHERE ProductID = 53;
```

Similarly, you can execute *Query 2* as seen below to get *a list of customers who have bought ProductID 55:*

Query 2:
```
SELECT CustomerID, CustomerName, CustomerEmail
FROM CustomerProducts
WHERE ProductID = 55;
```

If you place the results of the first and second queries side by side, it will look like Fig 14.2 shown here:

Product53

CustomerName	CustomerEmail	CustomerID
Ricky Brown	RickBrown@SaleOnYourOwn.com	1
Melanie Bowell	KerrynWhite@SaleOnYourOwn.com	4
Robert Smith	RobertSmith@SaleOnYourOwn.com	6
Adele Renton	AdeleRenton@SaleOnYourOwn.com	9
Donna Moore	DonnaMoore@SaleOnYourOwn.com	11
Emily Maddicks	EmilyMaddicks@SaleOnYourOwn.com	12
Chelsea Hillman	ChelseaHillman@SaleOnYourOwn.com	13
Ashley Hawker	AshleyHawker@SaleOnYourOwn.com	14
Richard Martin	RichardMartin@SaleOnYourOwn.com	15
Akidul Islam	AkidulIslam@SaleOnYourOwn.com	31
Caroline Tran	CarolineTran@SaleOnYourOwn.com	32

Product55

CustomerID	CustomerName	CustomerEmail
2	Adam Wilson	AdamWilson@SaleOnYourOwn.com
5	Sophie Smith	SophieSmith@SaleOnYourOwn.com
7	Michael Jackson	MichaelJackson@SaleOnYourOwn.com
10	Emma Stephens	EmmaStephens@SaleOnYourOwn.com
11	Donna Moore	DonnaMoore@SaleOnYourOwn.com
12	Emily Maddicks	EmilyMaddicks@SaleOnYourOwn.com
13	Chelsea Hillman	ChelseaHillman@SaleOnYourOwn.com
14	Ashley Hawker	AshleyHawker@SaleOnYourOwn.com
15	Richard Martin	RichardMartin@SaleOnYourOwn.com
31	Akidul Islam	AkidulIslam@SaleOnYourOwn.com

Fig 14.2: Joining product 53 customers with product 55 customers to get the customers who bought both product 53 & 55

Notice that *CustomerIDs 11, 12, 13, 14, 15* and *31* exist in both result sets. This means they have bought both *Product ID 53* and *ProductID 55*. Therefore, if you join these two result sets using *INNER JOIN* on matching *CustomerIDs*, it will return only those customers who exist in both result sets (those who have bought both *Product ID 53* and *Product ID 55*). So, the query will look like:

Query 3:
```
SELECT  Product53.CustomerID, Product53.CustomerName, Product53.CustomerEmail
FROM (
          -- Customers who have bought product 53
          SELECT CustomerID, CustomerName, CustomerEmail
          FROM CustomerProducts
          WHERE ProductID = 53
    ) AS Product53
INNER JOIN (
          -- Customers who have bought product 55
          SELECT CustomerID, CustomerName, CustomerEmail
          FROM CustomerProducts
          WHERE ProductID = 55
    ) AS Product55 ON Product53.CustomerID = Product55.CustomerID;
```

And the result will be:

CustomerID	CustomerName	CustomerEmail
11	Donna Moore	DonnaMoore@SaleOnYourOwn.com
12	Emily Maddicks	EmilyMaddicks@SaleOnYourOwn.com
13	Chelsea Hillman	ChelseaHillman@SaleOnYourOwn.com
14	Ashley Hawker	AshleyHawker@SaleOnYourOwn.com
15	Richard Martin	RichardMartin@SaleOnYourOwn.com
31	Akidul Islam	AkidulIslam@SaleOnYourOwn.com

Notice that the derived tables *Product53* and *Product55* both represent subsets of the *CustomerProducts* view. The above query joins the derived table *Product53* with another derived table, *Product55*, effectively joining one instance of the *CustomerProducts* view with another instance of the *CustomerProducts* view. This is one form of a *self-join* operation. Since you are using an equal to (=) operator in both the *INNER JOIN* and the *WHERE* clause predicates, you can move the *WHERE* clauses to the outer query and combined both predicates by an *AND* operator like you see below:

Query 3 – Simplified:
```
SELECT  Product53.CustomerID, Product53.CustomerName, Product53.CustomerEmail
FROM CustomerProducts AS Product53
INNER JOIN CustomerProducts AS Product55
      ON Product53.CustomerID = Product55.CustomerID
WHERE Product53.ProductID = 53
      AND Product55.ProductID = 55;
```

Solution – using the aggregate function: This
diagram demonstrates another way to get our desired list:

You know that you can use an *IN (53, 55)* operator in the *WHERE* clause of *Query 1* or *Query 2* (like below) to get *the list of customers who have bought Product ID 53, 55 or both*:

Query 4:
```
SELECT CustomerID, CustomerName, CustomerEmail, ProductID
FROM CustomerProducts
WHERE ProductID IN (53,55);
```

We added *ProductID* here in the *SELECT* list so that we can use it in the *COUNT* function. Fig 14.3 below shows you the result of this query:

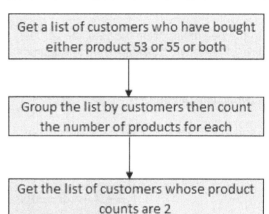

CustomerID	CustomerName	CustomerEmail	ProductID	
1	Ricky Brown	RickBrown@SaleOnYourOwn.com	53	
4	Melanie Bowell	KerrynWhite@SaleOnYourOwn.com	53	
6	Robert Smith	RobertSmith@SaleOnYourOwn.com	53	53 Only
9	Adele Renton	AdeleRenton@SaleOnYourOwn.com	53	
32	Caroline Tran	CarolineTran@SaleOnYourOwn.com	53	
11	Donna Moore	DonnaMoore@SaleOnYourOwn.com	53	
11	Donna Moore	DonnaMoore@SaleOnYourOwn.com	55	
12	Emily Maddicks	EmilyMaddicks@SaleOnYourOwn.com	53	
12	Emily Maddicks	EmilyMaddicks@SaleOnYourOwn.com	55	
13	Chelsea Hillman	ChelseaHillman@SaleOnYourOwn.com	53	
13	Chelsea Hillman	ChelseaHillman@SaleOnYourOwn.com	55	both 53 & 55
14	Ashley Hawker	AshleyHawker@SaleOnYourOwn.com	53	
14	Ashley Hawker	AshleyHawker@SaleOnYourOwn.com	55	
15	Richard Martin	RichardMartin@SaleOnYourOwn.com	53	
15	Richard Martin	RichardMartin@SaleOnYourOwn.com	55	
31	Akidul Islam	AkidulIslam@SaleOnYourOwn.com	53	
31	Akidul Islam	AkidulIslam@SaleOnYourOwn.com	55	
2	Adam Wilson	AdamWilson@SaleOnYourOwn.com	55	
5	Sophie Smith	SophieSmith@SaleOnYourOwn.com	55	
7	Michael Jackson	MichaelJackson@SaleOnYourOwn.com	55	55 Only
10	Emma Stephens	EmmaStephens@SaleOnYourOwn.com	55	

Fig 14.3: Customers who have bought either product 53, or 55 or both

If you count the *product IDs* by each customer as a group, the product count for the customers who have bought either *ProductID 53* or *ProductID 55* will be one, but the product count for the customers who have bought both 53 or 55 will be two. Then, if you keep only the customers whose product counts are two, you will obtain your desired list. Therefore, the query will be like you see below:

Query 5:
```
SELECT CustomerID, CustomerName, CustomerEmail
    --, COUNT(ProductID) AS NumberOfProducts
FROM CustomerProducts
WHERE ProductID IN (53,55)
GROUP BY CustomerID, CustomerName, CustomerEmail
HAVING COUNT(ProductID) = 2;
```

Notes

In the beginning of the second line of *Query 5*, you may have noticed that we have used '--'. This means the second line of code will be skipped by the database engine. Most of the latest RDBMS versions allow you to skip using an aggregate function in the *SELECT* list. If your RDBMS does not support skipping aggregate functions in the *SELECT* list, you will need to un-comment the section *COUNT(ProductID) AS NumberOfProducts* by removing '--' from the second line of code.

Return a List of Customers Who Have Bought Product ID 53 but Not Product ID 55

The diagram below shows the steps to get *a list of customers who bought product ID 53 but not product ID 55:*

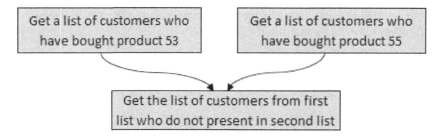

Notice that this diagram is similar to the self-join solution of the earlier example, but here, instead of returning the customers who exist in both result sets, it will return the customers from the first result set (*Product53*) who do not exist in the second result set (*Product55*). You know that when you use the *LEFT JOIN* in *Query 3* instead of *INNER JOIN*, if a customer is present in the *Product53* result set but not present in the *Product55* result set, then the corresponding columns for *Product55* will return as *NULL*—i.e. *Product55.CustomerID* will be *NULL*. Therefore, if we replace *INNER JOIN* with *LEFT JOIN* in *Query 3* and add a *WHERE* clause like *WHERE Product55.CustomerID IS NULL*, we will get the desired result. The query for this operation will look like the one you see below:

Query 6:
```
SELECT  Product53.CustomerID, Product53.CustomerName, Product53.CustomerEmail
FROM (          -- Customers who have bought product 53
                SELECT CustomerID, CustomerName, CustomerEmail
                FROM CustomerProducts
                WHERE ProductID = 53
        ) AS Product53
LEFT JOIN (     -- Customers who have bought product 55
                SELECT CustomerID, CustomerName, CustomerEmail
                FROM CustomerProducts
                WHERE ProductID = 55
        ) AS Product55 ON Product53.CustomerID = Product55.CustomerID
WHERE Product55.CustomerID IS NULL;
```

And the result will be:

CustomerID	CustomerName	CustomerEmail
1	Ricky Brown	RickBrown@SaleOnYourOwn.com
4	Melanie Bowell	KerrynWhite@SaleOnYourOwn.com
6	Robert Smith	RobertSmith@SaleOnYourOwn.com
9	Adele Renton	AdeleRenton@SaleOnYourOwn.com
32	Caroline Tran	CarolineTran@SaleOnYourOwn.com

Return a List of Customers Who Have Only Bought ProductIDs 53 & 55 (And No Other Products)

This diagram shows the steps to get *a list of customers who bought Product ID 53 & 55 but no other products*:

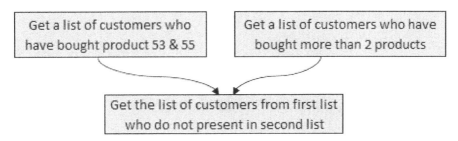

We know that our original *Query 3, simplified Query 3*, and *Query 5* will all return *a list of customers who bought Product ID 53 and 55*. We also know that it will include customers who may also have bought other products. In this case, we need to find a way to exclude customers who have bought other products from the list (that means anyone who has purchased more than two products). First off, let's find out how to return a list of customers who bought more than two products. If you remove the *WHERE* clause from *Query 5* and replace the *HAVING* clause operator from = to >, as shown below, then the database engine will return the list we're looking for in this step:

Query 7:
```
SELECT CustomerID, CustomerName, CustomerEmail
FROM CustomerProducts
GROUP BY CustomerID, CustomerName, CustomerEmail
HAVING COUNT(ProductID) > 2;
```

In the earlier example you learned that you can use *LEFT JOIN* with the *WHERE* clause predicate *CustomerID IS NULL* to allow you to exclude customers from the first list if they are present in the second list. If you replace the first query in *Query 6* with either *Query 3* (or our simplified Query 3 or Query 5) and replace the second query with Query 7, then your SQL will return *the list of customers who only bought Product IDs 53 and 55*. You can see what this query will look like below (we have used the *simplified Query 3* statement here, but we welcome you to try the other two queries yourself):

Query 8:
```
SELECT Product53_55.CustomerID, Product53_55.CustomerName, Product53_55.CustomerEmail
FROM (          -- Customers who have bought at least product 53 & 55
           SELECT Product53.CustomerID, Product53.CustomerName, Product53.CustomerEmail
           FROM CustomerProducts AS Product53
           INNER JOIN CustomerProducts AS Product55 ON Product53.CustomerID = Product55.CustomerID
           WHERE Product53.ProductID = 53 AND Product55.ProductID = 55
     ) AS Product53_55
LEFT JOIN (     -- Customers who have bought more than 2 products
           SELECT CustomerID, CustomerName, CustomerEmail
           FROM CustomerProducts
           GROUP BY CustomerID, CustomerName, CustomerEmail
           HAVING COUNT(ProductID) > 2
     ) AS TwoProducts ON Product53_55.CustomerID = TwoProducts.CustomerID
WHERE TwoProducts.CustomerID IS NULL;
```

Similar to the *simplified Query 3*, you can move the first query's *WHERE* clause predicates to the outer query to make *Query 8* simpler, like below:

Query 8 - Simplified:

```
SELECT  Product53.CustomerID, Product53.CustomerName, Product53.CustomerEmail
FROM CustomerProducts AS Product53
INNER JOIN CustomerProducts AS Product55 ON Product53.CustomerID = Product55.CustomerID
LEFT JOIN (
                -- Customers who have bought more than 2 products
                SELECT CustomerID, CustomerName, CustomerEmail
                FROM CustomerProducts
                GROUP BY CustomerID, CustomerName, CustomerEmail
                HAVING COUNT(ProductID) > 2
        ) AS TwoProducts ON Product55.CustomerID = TwoProducts.CustomerID
WHERE Product53.ProductID = 53
        AND Product55.ProductID = 55
        AND TwoProducts.CustomerID IS NULL;
```

The result will be:

CustomerID	CustomerName	CustomerEmail
31	Akidul Islam	AkidulIslam@SaleOnYourOwn.com

Return a List of Customers Who Have Bought Either Product ID 53 or 55 (But Not Both)

Earlier in this lesson, you saw the SQL statement that returns *a list of customers who have bought both Product IDs 53 and 55, but here we are looking for the customers who have bought Product ID 53 or 55 (not both)*. Again, we'll show you two ways to find the solution—one of which uses self-join, and the other uses an aggregate function.

Solution – using self-join: The diagram below shows one of the ways to get *the list of customers who have bought either Product ID 53 or 55*:

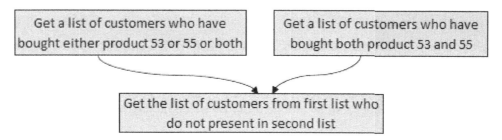

We know that either *Query 3*, the simplified version of *Query 3*, or *Query 5* will return *a list of customers who have bought both Product IDs 53 and 55*. We also know that *Query 4* returns *a list of customers who have bought either Product ID 53 or 55—or both*. Similar to the previous example, you can use *Query 4 LEFT JOIN* with either *Query 3*, the *simplified Query 3*, or *Query 5* with a *WHERE* clause to return the desired list.

Below, we used the *simplified Query 3*, so please try other two queries to practice different ways to achieve this solution:

```
SELECT  Product53_55_Both.CustomerID, Product53_55_Both.CustomerName, Product53_55_Both.CustomerEmail
FROM (     -- Customers who bought either product 53 or 55 or both
           SELECT CustomerID, CustomerName, CustomerEmail
           FROM CustomerProducts
           WHERE ProductID IN (53,55)
       ) AS Product53_55_Both
LEFT JOIN (       -- Customers who bought both products 53 & 55
              SELECT Product53.CustomerID, Product53.CustomerName, Product53.CustomerEmail
              FROM CustomerProducts AS Product53
              INNER JOIN CustomerProducts AS Product55 ON Product53.CustomerID = Product55.CustomerID
              WHERE Product53.ProductID = 53 AND Product55.ProductID = 55
          ) AS ProductBoth ON Product53_55_Both.CustomerID = ProductBoth.CustomerID
WHERE ProductBoth.CustomerID IS NULL;
```

Solution – using the aggregate function: If you look at *Query 5* from the earlier example, you should notice that we used the *HAVING* clause predicate *COUNT(ProductID) = 2*, and it returned only those customers who bought both products. In this example we needed to return the customers who bought either product. This can be done by changing the *HAVING* clause predicate to *COUNT(ProductID) = 1* as you see below:

```
SELECT CustomerID, CustomerName, CustomerEmail
FROM CustomerProducts
WHERE ProductID IN (53,55)
GROUP BY CustomerID, CustomerName, CustomerEmail
HAVING COUNT(ProductID) = 1;
```

The result will be like you see below:

CustomerID	CustomerName	CustomerEmail
1	Ricky Brown	RickBrown@SaleOnYourOwn.com
2	Adam Wilson	AdamWilson@SaleOnYourOwn.com
4	Melanie Bowell	KerrynWhite@SaleOnYourOwn.com
5	Sophie Smith	SophieSmith@SaleOnYourOwn.com
6	Robert Smith	RobertSmith@SaleOnYourOwn.com
7	Michael Jackson	MichaelJackson@SaleOnYourOwn.com
9	Adele Renton	AdeleRenton@SaleOnYourOwn.com
10	Emma Stephens	EmmaStephens@SaleOnYourOwn.com
32	Caroline Tran	CarolineTran@SaleOnYourOwn.com

Lesson Summary

This lesson has given you a brief explanation how self-join can be useful for returning statistics of interrelated data within same table or result set:

- You can use *INNER/LEFT/RIGHT JOIN* within the same table/result set to return organizational hierarchical data.
- Using *INNER JOIN* between two instances of the same table/result set to return a list of entities who participated in both occurrences of one or more attributes.
- Using *LEFT/RIGHT JOIN* between two instances of the same table/result set returns a list of entities that have participated as either occurrences of one or more attributes.

Section D
Programming with SQL

Lesson 15
Working with Flow-control Statements

Lesson Objective

The knowledge you have gained so far enables you to perform a task or set of tasks with SQL statements. Now we're going to show you how to write even more sophisticated SQL statements that will only perform a task—or set of tasks— if it satisfies a specific condition, otherwise it will perform a different task (or set of tasks). This lesson will cover some commonly used flow-control statements and how they can help you to solve complex business problems.

Code Samples

You can find the SQL code solutions for the examples and business problems in this lesson at the following link:
https://drive.google.com/open?id=1S7IYjVBVJISPvafQgl5k_FMLtxPubcmq

Flow-control statements in SQL

All mainstream RDBMSs support flow-control statements to control the flow of execution of SQL statements within a batch or stored procedures. Some RDBMs (e.g. MySQL) only support flow-control statements within the stored procedures or functions, not in simple batches. In this lesson, we will show you the syntax for SQL Server only, but in a later lesson we will show you the MySQL syntax as well when we discuss the stored procedures or functions. The most widely used flow-control statements for controlling the execution of SQL statements within a batch are the:
- *IF* statement
- *WHILE* statement

Simple IF statements

The *IF* statement allows you to execute a SQL statement if it satisfies a *predicate/boolean expression*. The syntax differs widely between RDBMSs, so we will stick to showing you the SQL Server version here, which is:
```
IF predicate/condition
    SQL statement;
```

Here, if the *predicate/condition* evaluates to *TRUE*, then the SQL statement will be executed. If it's not *TRUE*, it will do nothing.

Let's solve a business problem to learn how to use a simple *IF* statement.

Business Problem 1

A new customer partially completed his registration form with the following details:

UserID: BenThomas
Email: BenThomas@SaleOnYourOwn.com
Password: BenT1234

Your application needs to add this new customer's login details only if the user ID does not already exist in the *Logins* table. Write the SQL batch your application needs to execute to perform this task.

Solution SQL

```
IF NOT EXISTS ( SELECT UserID FROM Logins WHERE UserID = 'BenThomas')
     INSERT INTO Logins(UserID, Password, Email)
     VALUES ('BenThomas', 'BenT1234', 'BenThomas@SaleOnYourOwn.com');
```

Solution Review

The steps of this solution are illustrated in the diagram below:

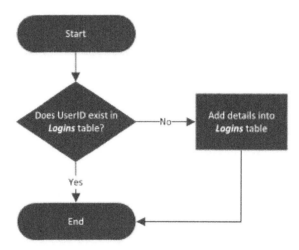

The *EXISTS (SELECT statement)* function will evaluate to *TRUE* if the *SELECT statement* returns one or more rows, otherwise it will evaluate to *FALSE*. Therefore, *EXISTS (SELECT UserID FROM Logins WHERE UserID = 'BenThomas')* will evaluate to *TRUE* if *BenThomas* exists in the *Logins* table, otherwise it will evaluate to *FALSE*. We have added *NOT* before *EXISTS*, which will reverse the Boolean result. Therefore, *NOT EXISTS (SELECT UserID FROM Logins WHERE UserID = 'BenThomas')* will evaluate to *TRUE* if *BenThomas* does not exist in the *Logins* table, and then the *INSERT* statement will be executed to add the details of *BenThomas* into the *Logins* table (otherwise it will evaluate to *FALSE* and the *INSERT* statement will not be executed).

Simple IF..ELSE Statements

An *IF..ELSE* statement allows you to execute a SQL statement if it satisfies a *predicate/Boolean expression*, otherwise it will execute another SQL statement. The basic syntax for this is:

```
IF predicate/condition
     SQL statement 1
ELSE
     SQL statement 2;
```

Here, if the predicate/condition evaluates to *TRUE*, then *SQL statement 1* will be executed; otherwise *SQL statement 2* will be executed.

Business Problem 2 will show you how to use a simple *IF..ELSE*.

Business Problem 2

This is essentially the same as *Business Problem 1* except you would like your application to notify the user saying *'This UserID has already been used, please try with different UserID'* if the user ID already exists in the *Logins* table. What SQL batch will your application need to execute to perform the task?

Solution SQL

```
IF NOT EXISTS ( SELECT UserID FROM Logins WHERE UserID = 'BenThomas')
      INSERT INTO Logins(UserID, Password, Email)
      VALUES ('BenThomas', 'BenT1234', 'BenThomas@SaleOnYourOwn.com');
ELSE
      SELECT 'This UserID has already been used, please try with different UserID ';
```

Solution Review

The steps of the solution will follow those you see here:

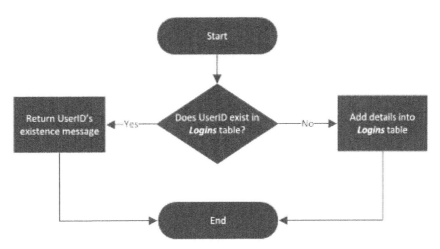

The *NOT EXISTS (SELECT UserID FROM Logins WHERE UserID = 'BenThomas')* will evaluate to *TRUE* if *BenThomas* does not exist in the *Logins* table, and next the *INSERT* statement will execute to add the details of *BenThomas* into the *Logins* table. If *BenThomas* exists, it will evaluate to *FALSE* and the *SELECT* statement will execute to return the message *'This UserID has already been used, please try with different UserID'* to the user. You can perform the same task by removing the *NOT* from the *IF* predicate and swapping the *INSERT* and *SELECT* statements like you below:

```
IF EXISTS ( SELECT UserID FROM Logins WHERE UserID = 'BenThomas')
      SELECT 'This UserID has already been used, please try with different UserID ';
ELSE
      INSERT INTO Logins(UserID, Password, Email)
      VALUES ('BenThomas', 'BenT1234', 'BenThomas@SaleOnYourOwn.com');
```

Executing Multiple Statements within an IF..ELSE Statement

You saw in the previous two topics how an *IF* statement allows you to execute a SQL statement if it satisfies the predicate (and hopefully you have an idea what will occur if it does not). So then, what if you want to execute multiple statements instead of single statement? The *BEGIN...END* flow-control statement allows you to execute a list of SQL statements as a group. Below, we will show you the syntax to execute a list of SQL statements if a specific condition is satisfied. In this case, if that condition isn't satisfied, it will execute a different list of SQL statements:

```
IF predicate/condition
    BEGIN
        First list of SQL statements;
    END
ELSE
    BEGIN
        Second list of SQL statements;
    END
```

Here, if the predicate/condition evaluates to *TRUE*, then the first list of SQL statements will be executed otherwise the second list of SQL statements will be executed. If any of the two lists contain just one statement, you don't have to use *BEGIN...END* for that section.

Let's solve *Business Problem 3* to learn the usage of multiple statements within an *IF..ELSE* statement.

Business Problem 3

A new customer has partially completed her registration form with her login and credit card details:

UserID	AngelaWatson	Password	AngelaW1234
Email	AngelaWatson @SaleOnYourOwn.com		

CreditCardNumber	344444444444445555	CardHolderName	Angela Watson
CreditCardType	Master Card	CreditCardExpiryMonth	12
CreditCardExpiryYear	2016		

Your application needs to add the login and credit card details only if they do not already exist in the *Logins* and *CreditCards* tables, respectively (i.e. if those details are already in the system, they should not be duplicated). What SQL batch does your application need to execute to perform this task?

Solution SQL

```
IF NOT EXISTS ( SELECT UserID FROM Logins WHERE UserID = 'AngelaWatson')
    -- UserID does not exist in Logins table and it needs to be added
    BEGIN
        -- Adding login details into Logins table
        INSERT INTO Logins(UserID, Password, Email)
        VALUES ('AngelaWatson', 'AngelaW1234', 'AngelaWatson@SaleOnYourOwn.com');

        --Checking if credit card exists in CreditCards table
        IF NOT EXISTS (  SELECT CreditCardID FROM CreditCards WHERE CreditCardNumber = '344444444444445555' )

            -- CreditCardNumber does not exist in CreditCards table and it needs to be added
            BEGIN
                -- Adding credit card details into CreditCards table
                INSERT INTO CreditCards   (CreditCardNumber, CardHolderName, CreditCardType,
                                CreditCardExpiryMonth, CreditCardExpiryYear)
                VALUES ('344444444444445555', 'Angela Watson', 'Master Card', 12, 2016);
            END
    END
ELSE
    BEGIN
        SELECT 'This UserID has already been used, please try with different UserID ';
    END
```

Solution Review

Here is a diagram to show the steps of the solution:

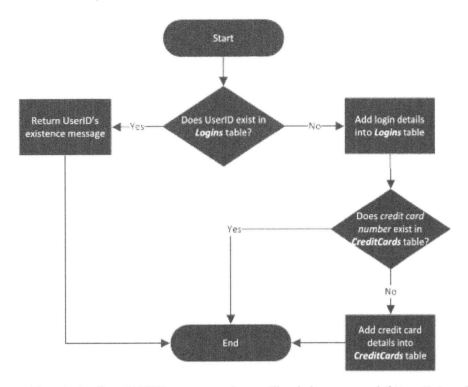

Similar to *Business Problem 2*, the first *INSERT* statement here will only be executed if UserID *AngelaWatson* does not exist in the *Logins* table. The second *IF* statement checks for the existence of credit card number, *344444444444445555*, and if the credit card number does not exist in the *CreditCards* table, the second *INSERT* statement will be executed to add her credit card details into the *CreditCards* table.

Notice that we have multiple statements after the first *IF* statement, therefore they have to be written them within the *BEGIN...END* block. After the *ELSE* we have only one *SELECT* statement and we have also written it within a *BEGIN...END* block, but you can skip that here if you want. The second *IF* statement also has an *INSERT* statement, so you can skip the *BEGIN...END* there as well. If you skip these optional *BEGIN...END* flow-control blocks, the query will look like: :

```
IF NOT EXISTS ( SELECT UserID FROM Logins WHERE UserID = 'AngelaWatson')
        -- UserID does not exist in Logins table and it needs to be added
    BEGIN
            -- Adding login details into Logins table
        INSERT INTO Logins(UserID, Password, Email)
        VALUES ('AngelaWatson', 'AngelaW1234', 'AngelaWatson@SaleOnYourOwn.com');

        --Checking if credit card exists in CreditCards table
        IF NOT EXISTS ( SELECT CreditCardID FROM CreditCards WHERE CreditCardNumber = '344444444444445555' )
                -- CreditCardNumber does not exist in CreditCards table and it needs to be added
                -- Adding credit card details into CreditCards table
            INSERT INTO CreditCards (CreditCardNumber, CardHolderName,CreditCardType,
                    CreditCardExpiryMonth, CreditCardExpiryYear)
            VALUES ('344444444444445555', 'Angela Watson', 'Master Card', 12, 2016);
    END
ELSE
        SELECT 'This UserID has already been used, please try with different UserID ';
```

Business Problem 4

Here are the complete login, credit card, address and other personal details for a new customer:

UserID: AmandaBaker
Email: AmandaBaker@SaleOnYourOwn.com
Password: AmandaB1234

CreditCardNumber: 42222222222222223333
CardHolderName: Amanda Baker
CreditCardType: Visa
CreditCardExpiryMonth: 01
CreditCardExpiryYear: 2017

CustomerFirstName: Amanda
CustomerLastName: Baker
StreetAddress: 10117 Edmonds Way
City: Edmonds
StateProvince: Washington
Country: United States
ZipPostalCode: 98020
CustomerPhoneNumber: +1 (312) 333-333335

Your application should add the login details if they do not already exist, otherwise the application should return a message telling the user the details are duplicate info and they must enter different information. If the credit card and address details do not exist in the database, the application should add them and store their newly generated IDs (auto-generated surrogate keys) into variables for the use of foreign key values in the *Customers* table, otherwise SQL should get the *CreditCardID* and *AddressID* from those tables and store them in variables for the use of foreign key values in the *Customers* table. Finally, the customer's details and their *CreditCardID* and *AddressID* should be added into the *Customers* table by the application. What SQL batch your application need to execute to perform these tasks?

Solution SQL

```
IF NOT EXISTS ( SELECT UserID FROM Logins WHERE UserID = 'AmandaBaker')
    BEGIN
        -- Declaring variables to store CreditCardID and AddressID
        DECLARE @CreditCardID INT, @AddressID INT;
        -- Adding login details into Logins table
        INSERT INTO Logins(UserID, Password, Email)
        VALUES('AmandaBaker', 'AmandaB1234', 'AmandaBaker@SaleOnYourOwn.com');
        IF NOT EXISTS ( SELECT CreditCardID FROM CreditCards WHERE CreditCardNumber = '42222222222222223333' )
            BEGIN
                -- Adding credit card details into CreditCards table
                INSERT INTO CreditCards (CreditCardNumber, CardHolderName, CreditCardType,
                                        CreditCardExpiryMonth, CreditCardExpiryYear)
                VALUES ('42222222222222223333', 'Amanda Baker', 'Visa', 01, 2017);
                -- Storing CreditCardID for newly added CreditCardNumber into variable @CreditCardID
                SELECT @CreditCardID = SCOPE_IDENTITY();
            END
        ELSE
            BEGIN
                -- Storing the CreditCardID into the variable @CreditCardID
                SELECT @CreditCardID = CreditCardID FROM CreditCards
                WHERE CreditCardNumber = '42222222222222223333';
            END
        IF NOT EXISTS ( SELECT AddressID FROM Addresses
                    WHERE StreetAddress = '10117 Edmonds Way' AND ZipOrPostalCode = '98020' )
            BEGIN
                -- Adding address details into Addresses table
                INSERT INTO Addresses (StreetAddress, City, StateProvince, Country, ZipOrPostalCode)
                VALUES ('10117 Edmonds Way', 'Edmonds', 'Washington', 'United States', '98020');
                -- Storing AddressID for newly added address into the variable @AddressID
                SELECT @AddressID = SCOPE_IDENTITY();
            END
        ELSE
            BEGIN
                -- Storing the AddressID into the variable @AddressID
                SELECT @AddressID = AddressID FROM Addresses
                WHERE StreetAddress = '10117 Edmonds Way' AND ZipOrPostalCode = '98020'
            END
        --Adding customer's details into Customers table
        INSERT INTO Customers(CustomerFirstName, CustomerLastName, CustomerAddressID,
                        CustomerPhoneNumber, CustomerEmail, CustomerCreditCardID)
        VALUES ('Amanda', 'Baker', @AddressID, '+1 (312) 333-333335',
                'AmandaBaker@SaleOnYourOwn.com',@CreditCardID);
    END
ELSE
    BEGIN
        SELECT 'This UserID has already been used, please try with different UserID ';
    END
```

Solution Review

Here is a diagram to show the steps of this solution:

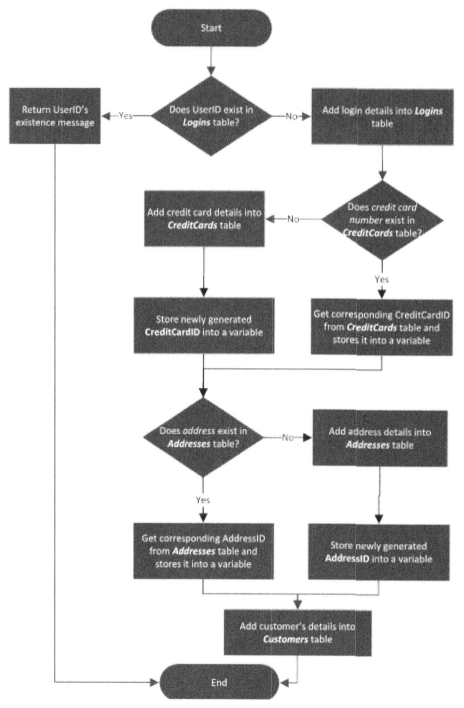

The steps here are similar to *Business Problem 3*. This time, however, in order to add a row in the *Customers* table you need the *CreditCardID* and *AddressID*. These have been auto-generated after adding the customer's credit card and address details into the *CreditCards* and *Addresses* tables, respectively. Therefore, after adding a new row into the *CreditCards* and *Addresses* tables, we have temporarily stored the newly generated IDs into two variables: *@CreditCardID* and *@AddressID*. These are then passed as values into the *Customers* table's row.

Simple WHILE Statements

The *IF* statement allows you to execute a batch of SQL statements only one time if it satisfies a predicate, but what if you want to execute that batch of SQL statements repeatedly until the predicate becomes false? The solution is to use a *WHILE* flow-control statement. Again, we're only showing the SQL Server version of syntax here for demonstration purposes. The basic syntax is as below:

```
WHILE predicate/condition
    BEGIN
        SQL statement list
    END
```

Here, if the predicate/condition evaluates to *TRUE*, all SQL statements within the *BEGIN...END* block will be executed, then the database engine will go back and re-evaluate the predicate/condition again. If it evaluates to *TRUE* again, all SQL statements within the *BEGIN...END* block will be executed again, and so on. This process will continue until the predicate/condition evaluates to *FALSE*. Once this occurs, it starts executing any statements after the *END* keyword. However, if there are no more statements after the *END* keyword it will simply finish the execution. This diagram illustrates the execution process of this *WHILE* statement.

Business Problem 5 will demonstrate this simple *WHILE* statement in action.

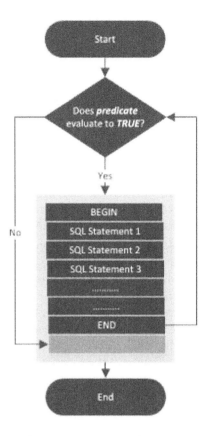

Business Problem 5

Your company has decided to increase the standard sales price of all products by 5% until the average standard sales price become at least $650. What SQL (or SQL batch) do you need to execute to perform this task?

Solution SQL

```
WHILE (SELECT AVG(StandardSalesPrice) FROM Products) < 650
    BEGIN
        UPDATE Products SET StandardSalesPrice = StandardSalesPrice * 1.05;
    END
```

Solution Review

The diagram below shows the steps of the solution:

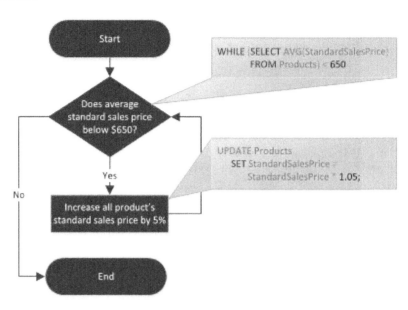

The *WHILE* predicate *'SELECT AVG(StandardSalesPrice) FROM Products) < 650'* will check if the average standard sales price is below $650. If so, the *WHILE* predicate evaluates to *TRUE* and will execute the *BEGIN...END* block (i.e. it will execute *UPDATE Products SET StandardSalesPrice = StandardSalesPrice * 1.05* and then go back to evaluate the *WHILE* predicate again, and so on). But if the *WHILE* predicate evaluates to *FALSE*, it skips the *BEGIN ...END* block.

How do you know that the *UPDATE* statement in the SQL solution is executing repeatedly until the *WHILE* predicate becomes *FALSE*? You can verify this by executing the *UPDATE* statements multiple times within a batch and check the average standard sales price before and after each *UPDATE*:

```
BEGIN TRANSACTION

-- First Iteration
SELECT AVG(StandardSalesPrice) AS InitialAveragePrice FROM Products;
UPDATE Products SET StandardSalesPrice = StandardSalesPrice * 1.05;
SELECT AVG(StandardSalesPrice) AS AveragePriceAfterFirstIteration FROM Products;

-- Second Iteration
UPDATE Products SET StandardSalesPrice = StandardSalesPrice * 1.05;
SELECT AVG(StandardSalesPrice) AS AveragePriceAfterSecondIteration FROM Products;

-- Third Iteration
UPDATE Products SET StandardSalesPrice = StandardSalesPrice * 1.05;
SELECT AVG(StandardSalesPrice) AS AveragePriceAfterThirdIteration FROM Products;

ROLLBACK TRANSACTION
```

The result will look like:

InitialAveragePrice
572.257575

AveragePriceAfterFirstIteration
600.870454

AveragePriceAfterSecondIteration
630.913977

AveragePriceAfterThirdIteration
662.459686

Notice that the initial average standard sales price starts at $572.257575. After executing the *UPDATE* statement once, the average standard sales price will become $600.870454, then the second *UPDATE* statement will result in the price being $630.913977, and the third (and final) *UPDATE* statement will bring the average standard sales price to $662.459686, which is greater than $650.

The *BEGIN...END* block of our SQL solution (i.e. the *UPDATE* statement) should execute three times before the final average standard sales price becomes $662.459686. Once this has occurred, the *WHILE* statement should finish its execution. If you now execute the SQL solution, you will see that it will indeed execute the *UPDATE* statement three-times, which causes the average standard sales price become $662.459686. This test verifies that our *WHILE* statement is working properly.

Using the WHILE Statement for Complex Flow Control

The *WHILE* statement allows you to keep executing a list of SQL statements within a *BEGIN...END* block as long as the predicate/condition evaluates to *TRUE*, but what if you want to skip executing one or more statements within the *BEGIN...END* block or the whole block based on other conditions? The answer is to use the *BREAK* and *CONTINUE* keywords within the *WHILE* statement. Here's what the basic syntax for this would look like:

```
WHILE predicate/condition1
    BEGIN
        SQL statement list 1
        IF predicate/condition2
            BEGIN
                SQL statement list 2 along with BREAK/CONTINUE keyword
            END
        ELSE
            BEGIN
                SQL statement list 3 along with BREAK/CONTINUE keyword
            END
    END
```

Business Problem 6 will demonstrate the *WHILE* statement with the *BREAK/CONTINUE* keywords.

Business Problem 6

Your company has decided to decrease the standard sales prices of all products by 5% until the average standard sales price becomes $500 or just below that. There is a stipulation here, however: the minimum standard price should *never* drop down below $9.50 per unit. What SQL statement (or SQL batch) do you need to execute to perform this task?

Solution SQL

```
WHILE (SELECT AVG(StandardSalesPrice) FROM Products) > 500
    BEGIN
        IF (SELECT MIN(StandardSalesPrice * 0.95) FROM Products) >= 9.50
            BEGIN
                UPDATE Products  SET StandardSalesPrice = StandardSalesPrice * 0.95;
                CONTINUE;
            END
        ELSE
            BREAK;
    END
```

Solution Review

Here is a diagram to show the steps of the solution:

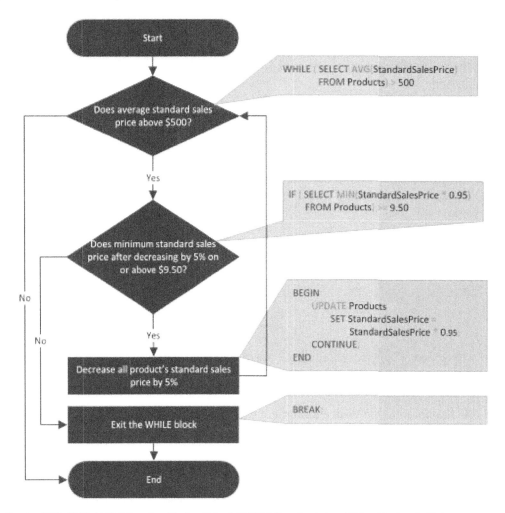

The *WHILE* predicate *(SELECT AVG(StandardSalesPrice) FROM Products) > 500* will check if the average standard sales price is above $500. If the *WHILE* predicate evaluates to *TRUE* then execute the *BEGIN...END* block. Within the *BEGIN...END* block, the *IF* predicate *(SELECT MIN (StandardSalesPrice * 0.95) FROM Products) >= 9.50* will check if the minimum standard price is still at or above $9.50 after all of the standard sales prices are decreased by 5%. If the *IF* predicate evaluates to *TRUE*, it will execute the inner *BEGIN...END* block—i.e. the *UPDATE* and *CONTINUE* statements then go back to execute the *WHILE* predicate again. When the *IF* predicate evaluates to *FALSE*, then it will execute the *BREAK* statement which serves to finish the execution of the *WHILE* statement.

Lesson Summary

This lesson has shown you how flow-control statements can help you to solve complex business problems:

- The *IF* statement allows you to execute a SQL statement or a batch of SQL statements if it satisfies a predicate.
- The *IF..ELSE* statement allows you to execute a SQL statement or a batch of SQL statements if it satisfies a predicate, otherwise it will execute another SQL statement or another batch of statements.
- The *WHILE* statement allows you to execute a SQL statement or a batch of SQL statements repeatedly until a specific predicate evaluates to FALSE.
- You can combine the *IF* and *WHILE* statements to solve complex problems.

Lesson 16
Working with Stored Procedures

Lesson Objective

You now have the knowledge to write a SQL statement or batch of SQL statements to perform tasks both simple and complex, ranging from producing reports to data manipulation to various combinations of all. But what if you want to reuse your SQL statement or batch of SQL statements over and over again? Based on what you learned in *Lesson 13*, you might be thinking that you can use views for that purpose. You are partly right, but views support only one *SELECT* statement. For this reason, they will not help you if you want to reuse a task with one or more *SELECT/INSERT/UPDATE/DELETE* operations or flow-control operations. That's why we're going to spend this lesson showing you how to save a SQL batch into your RDBMS so that you can reuse it again and again. This is known as a *stored procedure*. Here's what we'll be discussing:

- What stored procedures are
- How to create them
- How to execute them
- How to remove them
- Some real-world uses for them

Code Samples

You can find this lesson's SQL code solutions at the following links:

SQL Server:
https://drive.google.com/open?id=1oCH8WxMUk3DWoXq54hppntp79LSA1qlh

MySQL:
https://drive.google.com/open?id=1A6Daou3ZAGbG0nosFjEPdkprjZCD2DMR

What is a Stored Procedure?

Saving a SQL statement or batch of SQL statements with a name within your RDBMS enables you to reuse it. Most mainstream RDBMSs allow you to save your SQL statements or batches with a name. Once named and saved, it is what we call a stored procedure. Let's look at the SQL batch we created back in *Lesson 15* to add *Ben Thomas's* customer login details into the *Logins* table (this batch is from *Business Problem 1* in *Lesson 15*):

Batch 1:
```
IF NOT EXISTS ( SELECT UserID FROM Logins WHERE UserID = 'BenThomas')

     INSERT INTO Logins(UserID, Password, Email)
     VALUES ('BenThomas', 'BenT1234', 'BenThomas@SaleOnYourOwn.com');
```

This SQL batch first checks the existence of UserID *BenThomas* in the *Logins* table, and if it doesn't exist it will add a new row into the *Logins* table with *Ben Thomas's* details. The other SQL batch adds login details for another customer, *Angela Watson*, into the *Logins* table (this batch is from *Business Problem 2* in *Lesson 15*):

Batch 2:

```
IF NOT EXISTS ( SELECT UserID FROM Logins WHERE UserID = 'AngelaWatson')

    INSERT INTO Logins(UserID, Password, Email)
    VALUES ('AngelaWatson', 'AngelaW1234', 'AngelaWatson@SaleOnYourOwn.com');
```

Notice that the only differences between *Batch 1* and *Batch 2* are the *UserID*, *Password* and *Email* values. Therefore, if you want to add another customer's login details, you need to create another similar batch with the same differences. But if you declare variables for *UserID*, *Password* and *Email* and use these variables instead of values inside the batch, then you do not need to change the batch for every new customer. You will just need to reset the values for the variables. The SQL Server version of this code would look like:

Batch 3:

```
DECLARE @UserID VARCHAR(50), @Password NVARCHAR(50), @Email VARCHAR(50);
SELECT @UserID = 'BenThomas', @Password = 'BenT1234', @Email = 'BenThomas@SaleOnYourOwn.com';

IF NOT EXISTS ( SELECT UserID FROM Logins WHERE UserID = @UserID)

    INSERT INTO Logins(UserID, Password, Email)
    VALUES (@UserID, @Password, @Email);
```

As you know, variable names in SQL Server start with '@'. The first statement declares (defines) three variables with the names *@UserID*, *@Password* and *@Email*. The second statement assigns (sets) the values *BenThomas*, *BenT1234* and *BenThomas@SaleOnYourOwn.com* to the variables *@UserID*, *@Password* and *@Email*, respectively. Now, if you want to add *Angela Watson's* login details into the *Logins* table, you only need to re-assign her values *AngelaWatson*, *AngelaW1234* and *AngelaWatson@SaleOnYourOwn.com* to the variables *@UserID*, *@Password* and *@Email* respectively, in the second statement. No code in the actual batch needs to be changed. When you save *Batch 3* as a stored procedure, these variables will act as parameters, and each time you execute the stored procedure you can pass different values for those parameters.

To sum up this explanation, understand that a stored procedure is a named batch that allows users/applications to pass parameters to perform a specific task without rewriting a new SQL statement each time.

How to Create a Stored Procedure

The basic syntax for creating stored procedures varies between RDBMSs, and we will demonstrate this concept by showing you how to create a new stored procedure in *SQL Server* and *MySQL*. If you are using another RDBMS, please refer to your documentation for the proper syntax.

Creating stored procedures in SQL Server

The basic syntax to create a stored procedure in SQL Server is:

```
CREATE PROCEDURE stored procedure name
    parameters definitions
AS
BEGIN
    One or more SQL statements;
END;
```

The parameters are optional and the name of each parameter must start with @ as with variables. A parameter can be either an *INPUT* or *OUTPUT*. When an application executes/calls a stored procedure, it has to pass a value for each *INPUT* parameter, and the *OUTPUT* parameters return values to the calling application. Defining a parameter is similar to defining a variable, but here you do not need use the *DECLARE* keyword. However, you will need to add the *OUTPUT* keyword for the *OUTPUT* parameters. Remember: if the stored procedure consists of only one SQL statement, *BEGIN...END* becomes optional. The name of the stored procedure must be unique within the database/schema like views or tables. Let's look at some examples.

Creating a simple stored procedure to access subset of rows from tables: For this example, we will show you how to create a stored procedure that will return a list of products for our *Diamond* category vendors. We will include the following attributes: vendor name, vendor category name, product ID, product name, stock quantity, quantity of items ordered, standard sales price, sales discount percentage and sales discount amount. The SQL statement needed to do all this will look like the one you see below (let's call it *ProductsForDiamondVendors*):

```
CREATE PROCEDURE ProductsForDiamondVendors
AS
BEGIN
    SELECT  VendCat.VendorCategoryName, Vend.VendorName, Prod.ProductID,Prod.ProductName, Prod.StockQuantity,
        Prod.OrderedQuantity, Prod.StandardSalesPrice, Prod.SalesDiscountPercentage, Prod.SalesDiscountAmount
    FROM Products AS Prod
    INNER JOIN Vendors AS Vend ON Prod.VendorID = Vend.VendorID
    INNER JOIN VendorCategories AS VendCat ON Vend.VendorCategoryID = VendCat.VendorCategoryID
    WHERE VendCat.VendorCategoryName = 'Diamond';
END
```

When you execute the *CREATE PROCEDURE* statement above, it will create the procedure *ProductsForDiamondVendors* within your database. Once this is set up, it will always execute the same query when an application calls the stored procedure. Notice that only one *SELECT* statement has been used in this stored procedure, so you do not need to use *BEGIN...END* here. Without *BEGIN...END*, the *CREATE PROCEDURE* statement would look like:

```
CREATE PROCEDURE ProductsForDiamondVendors
AS
SELECT VendCat.VendorCategoryName, Vend.VendorName, Prod.ProductID, Prod.ProductName, Prod.StockQuantity,
    Prod.OrderedQuantity, Prod.StandardSalesPrice, Prod.SalesDiscountPercentage, Prod.SalesDiscountAmount
FROM Products AS Prod
INNER JOIN Vendors AS Vend ON Prod.VendorID = Vend.VendorID
INNER JOIN VendorCategories AS VendCat ON Vend.VendorCategoryID = VendCat.VendorCategoryID
WHERE VendCat.VendorCategoryName = 'Diamond';
```

Creating stored procedure with an input parameter to access subset of rows from tables: If your application needs to return the same information but for your *Regular* or *Gold* categories of vendors, you could certainly create two more procedures like the one we just showed you, but a more efficient way to provide access to each category of vendors would be to use a parameter as you can see illustrated in the figure below:

Provide a generic name to the earlier stored procedure

```
CREATE PROCEDURE ProductsForAVendorCategory
        @VendorCategoryName varchar(20)
AS
BEGIN
        SELECT    VendCat.VendorCategoryName, Vend.VendorName, Prod.ProductID, Prod.ProductName,
                  Prod.StockQuantity, Prod.OrderedQuantity, Prod.StandardSalesPrice,
                  Prod.SalesDiscountPercentage, Prod.SalesDiscountAmount
        FROM      Products AS Prod
        INNER JOIN Vendors AS Vend
                  ON Prod.VendorID = Vend.VendorID
        INNER JOIN VendorCategories AS VendCat
                  ON Vend.VendorCategoryID = VendCat.VendorCategoryID
        WHERE VendCat.VendorCategoryName = @VendorCategoryName
END
```

A parameter added in the earlier stored procedure

The literal value 'Diamond' has been replaced with the parameter in the earlier stored procedure

Creating stored procedure with input parameters to add data into tables: If you want to create a stored procedure (let's call it *AddLoginDetails*) to add any new customer's login details into the *Logins* table, you can use the SQL statements from *Batch 3* (just simply use the variables as parameters):

```
CREATE PROCEDURE AddLoginDetails
      @UserID VARCHAR(50),
      @Password NVARCHAR(50),
      @Email VARCHAR(50)
AS
BEGIN
      IF NOT EXISTS ( SELECT UserID FROM Logins WHERE UserID = @UserID)
            INSERT INTO Logins(UserID, Password, Email) VALUES (@UserID, @Password, @Email);
END;
```

Let's look at a complex business process to illustrate this. When a new customer submits his/her registration details, the application has to add login, credit card and address details into the *Logins, CreditCards* and *Addresses* tables, and then the application adds the IDs from these newly added details (with some additional details) into the *Customers* table. The whole process for this was described in *Business Problem 4* in *Lesson 15*, so you could certainly use the SQL batch from that problem to create a stored procedure. You'll see we have done this below, and we called ours *AddCustomerRegistrationDetails*.

As you can see, this is a very useful procedure for adding all of your new customer registration details:

```
CREATE PROCEDURE AddCustomerRegistrationDetails
        @UserID VARCHAR(50), @Password NVARCHAR(50), @Email VARCHAR(50), @CreditCardNumber VARCHAR(20),
        @CardHolderName VARCHAR(50), @CreditCardType VARCHAR(25), @CreditCardExpiryMonth INT,
        @CreditCardExpiryYear INT, @StreetAddress VARCHAR(100), @ZipOrPostalCode VARCHAR(20), @City VARCHAR(25),
        @StateProvince VARCHAR(25), @Country VARCHAR(25), @CustomerFirstName VARCHAR(20),
        @CustomerLastName VARCHAR(20), @CustomerPhoneNumber VARCHAR(25), @CustomerEmail VARCHAR(50)
AS
BEGIN
    IF NOT EXISTS (SELECT UserID FROM Logins WHERE UserID = @UserID)
        BEGIN
            DECLARE @CreditCardID INT, @AddressID INT;

            -- Adding login details into Logins table
            INSERT INTO Logins(UserID, Password, Email)
            VALUES (@UserID, @Password, @Email);

            -- Adding credit card details into CreditCards table
            IF NOT EXISTS ( SELECT CreditCardID FROM CreditCards WHERE CreditCardNumber = @CreditCardNumber )
                BEGIN
                    INSERT INTO CreditCards (CreditCardNumber, CardHolderName,CreditCardType,
                                            CreditCardExpiryMonth, CreditCardExpiryYear)
                    VALUES (@CreditCardNumber, @CardHolderName, @CreditCardType,
                            @CreditCardExpiryMonth, @CreditCardExpiryYear);
                    SELECT @CreditCardID = SCOPE_IDENTITY();
                END
            ELSE
                SELECT @CreditCardID = CreditCardID FROM CreditCards
                WHERE CreditCardNumber = @CreditCardNumber;

            -- Adding address details into Addresses table
            IF NOT EXISTS ( SELECT AddressID FROM Addresses
                            WHERE StreetAddress = @StreetAddress AND ZipOrPostalCode = @ZipOrPostalCode )
                BEGIN
                    INSERT INTO Addresses (StreetAddress, City, StateProvince, Country, ZipOrPostalCode)
                    VALUES (@StreetAddress, @City, @StateProvince, @Country, @ZipOrPostalCode);
                    SELECT @AddressID = SCOPE_IDENTITY();
                END
            ELSE
                SELECT @AddressID = AddressID FROM Addresses
                WHERE StreetAddress = @StreetAddress AND ZipOrPostalCode = @ZipOrPostalCode

            --Adding customer's details into Customers table
            INSERT INTO Customers(CustomerFirstName, CustomerLastName,CustomerAddressID,
                            CustomerPhoneNumber, CustomerEmail, CustomerCreditCardID)
            VALUES (@CustomerFirstName, @CustomerLastName, @AddressID,
                    @CustomerPhoneNumber, @CustomerEmail, @CreditCardID);
        END
    ELSE
        SELECT 'This UserID has already been used, please try with different UserID ';
END
```

Creating stored procedure with input and output parameters to add data into tables: When a customer submits an order, the application has to return a receipt number for it. In *Lesson 5* you learned how to process an order using a SQL batch, and you can probably guess by now that you can use the same batch to create a stored procedure to process the customer's order. To do so, you need to define each detail of the order as an input parameter and the receipt number as output parameter. The *OUTPUT* keyword must be used in the parameter definition if you want to use the parameter as an output parameter. The statement below demonstrates how to create a stored procedure capable of processing a maximum of two products in an order:

```
CREATE PROCEDURE AddSalesOrderDetails
        @OrderDate DATETIME,
        @OrderDueDate DATETIME,
        @CustomerID INT,
        @OrderTotal DECIMAL(18,4),
        @OrderDiscountTotal DECIMAL(18,4),
        @OrderBillingAddressID INT,
        @OrderShippingAddressID INT,
        @OrderCreditCardID INT,
        @ProductID1 INT,
        @ProductQuantity1 INT,
        @ProductUnitPrice1 DECIMAL(18,4),
        @ProductUnitPriceDiscount1 DECIMAL(18,4),
        @ProductID2 INT,
        @ProductQuantity2 INT,
        @ProductUnitPrice2 DECIMAL(18,4),
        @ProductUnitPriceDiscount2 DECIMAL(18,4),
        @SalesOrderID INT OUTPUT
AS
BEGIN

    /*Adding sales order summary into SalesOrders table*/
    INSERT INTO SalesOrders ( OrderDate, OrderDueDate, CustomerID, OrderTotal, OrderDiscountTotal,
        OrderBillingAddressID, OrderShippingAddressID, OrderCreditCardID)
    VALUES ( @OrderDate, @OrderDueDate, @CustomerID,@OrderTotal, @OrderDiscountTotal,
        @OrderBillingAddressID, @OrderShippingAddressID, @OrderCreditCardID );

    /*Assigning previously added identity number into @SalesOrderID parameter*/
    SELECT @SalesOrderID = SCOPE_IDENTITY();

    /*Adding products details of the sales order into SalesOrderProducts table*/
    INSERT INTO SalesOrderProducts ( SalesOrderID, ProductID, ProductQuantity, ProductUnitPrice, ProductUnitPriceDiscount)
    VALUES (@SalesOrderID, @ProductID1, @ProductQuantity1, @ProductUnitPrice1, @ProductUnitPriceDiscount1);
    INSERT INTO SalesOrderProducts ( SalesOrderID, ProductID, ProductQuantity, ProductUnitPrice, ProductUnitPriceDiscount)
    VALUES (@SalesOrderID, @ProductID2, @ProductQuantity2, @ProductUnitPrice2, @ProductUnitPriceDiscount2);
END;
```

Notice that both products have a set of parameters (*@ProductID1, @ProductQuantity1, @ProductUnitPrice1, @ProductUnitPriceDiscount1*) and (*@ProductID2, @ProductQuantity2, @ProductUnitPrice2, @ProductUnitPriceDiscount2*). If you want to support more than two products within same order, you need to add an additional set of parameters and also an additional *INSERT* statement for each new product in the *SalesOrderProducts* table. After the first *INSERT* statement, a new *SalesOrderID* will be generated. A *SCOPE_IDENTITY()* function has been used to catch the *SalesOrderID* (which is the receipt number for the order) and store it into the output parameter *@SalesOrderID*. Therefore, using the output parameter above, your application can get this receipt number and provide it to the customer. The value of the output parameter *@SalesOrderID* can also be set using the *SET* command like below:

```
SET @SalesOrderID = SCOPE_IDENTITY();
```

Creating a stored procedure with an input to modify data from tables: When a vendor ships a product, it reports the shipment date via your application. Here, your application can execute a stored procedure by passing the *@SalesOrderID*, *@ProductID* and *@ShipDate* parameters to update the shipment date for a given product of that order.

Below, we show you how to create a stored procedure for this purpose, and we have named it *UpdateSalesOrderProductsShipdate*:

```
CREATE PROCEDURE UpdateSalesOrderProductsShipdate
        @SalesOrderID INT,
        @ProductID INT,
        @ShipDate DATETIME
AS
BEGIN
        IF EXISTS (  SELECT * FROM SalesOrderProducts
                    WHERE SalesOrderID = @SalesOrderID
                    AND ProductID = @ProductID )
            UPDATE SalesOrderProducts
                SET ProductShipDate = @ShipDate
            WHERE SalesOrderID = @SalesOrderID AND ProductID = @ProductID;
        ELSE
            SELECT 'SalesOrderID or ProductID does not exist. Please try with correct IDs'
END
```

The stored procedure we have created checks whether the *SalesOrderID* and *ProductID* provided by the vendor are correct before it updates the shipment date. If it finds the *SalesOrderID* and *ProductID* in the *SalesOrderProducts* table, it will modify the corresponding *ProductShipDate* column, otherwise it will return an error message saying the *'SalesOrderID or ProductID does not exist. Please try with correct IDs'*.

Creating stored procedures in MySQL

The basic syntax to create a stored procedure in MySQL is:

```
DELIMITER delimiter character

CREATE PROCEDURE stored procedure name
        (   parameters definitions )
    BEGIN
            One or more SQL statements;
    END delimiter character


DELIMITER ;
```

We should take a moment to talk about delimiters. Since the default delimiter character semicolon (;) must be used to end the individual SQL statement, the MySQL processor will be confused if the same delimiter is used for the stored procedures (or any other routine program). So you need to change the default delimiter character to something else (e.g. //) that will not be used within any SQL statement in the stored procedure's routine. The parameters are optional for MySQL and SQL Server, but in MySQL you do not need to start the name of the parameters with @. Instead, just use a unique name within the stored procedure. A parameter can be either an *INPUT* or *OUTPUT*. When an application executes/calls a stored procedure, it has to pass a value for each INPUT parameter, but the *OUTPUT* parameters return values to the calling application. Defining a parameter is similar to defining a variable, but you do not need to use a *DECLARE* keyword. You do need to add the *OUT* keyword for the *OUTPUT* parameters before the parameter name. As with other situations, if the stored procedure consists of only one SQL statement, the usage of *BEGIN...END* becomes optional. The name of the stored procedure must be unique within a database/schema like views or tables.

Let's look at how *MySQL* code differs from the earlier stored procedures.

The MySQL code for creating the stored procedure *ProductsForDiamondVendors:*

```
-- Change the default delimiter to //
DELIMITER //

CREATE PROCEDURE ProductsForDiamondVendors ()

    BEGIN

        SELECT    VendCat.VendorCategoryName, Vend.VendorName, Prod.ProductID,
                  Prod.ProductName, Prod.StockQuantity, Prod.OrderedQuantity,
                  Prod.StandardSalesPrice, Prod.SalesDiscountPercentage, Prod.SalesDiscountAmount
        FROM Products AS Prod
        INNER JOIN Vendors AS Vend
                ON Prod.VendorID = Vend.VendorID
        INNER JOIN VendorCategories AS VendCat
                ON Vend.VendorCategoryID = VendCat.VendorCategoryID
        WHERE VendCat.VendorCategoryName = 'Diamond';

    END //

-- Change the default delimiter back to ;
DELIMITER ;
```

Notice that we changed the default delimiter to '*//*' at the start of the code. After the *END* keyword we used our new '*//*' delimiter, and at end of the code we changed the default delimiter back to '*;*'. We have also used parentheses () at the end of the stored procedure name (in SQL Server the *AS* keyword is used instead of parentheses).

The MySQL code for creating the stored procedure *ProductsForAVendorCategory:*

```
DELIMITER //

CREATE PROCEDURE ProductsForAVendorCategory
        (
              pVendorCategoryName varchar(20)
        )

    BEGIN

        SELECT    VendCat.VendorCategoryName, Vend.VendorName, Prod.ProductID,
                  Prod.ProductName,Prod.StockQuantity,Prod.OrderedQuantity,
                  Prod.StandardSalesPrice, Prod.SalesDiscountPercentage, Prod.SalesDiscountAmount
        FROM Products AS Prod
        INNER JOIN Vendors AS Vend ON Prod.VendorID = Vend.VendorID
        INNER JOIN VendorCategories AS VendCat ON Vend.VendorCategoryID = VendCat.VendorCategoryID
        WHERE VendCat.VendorCategoryName = pVendorCategoryName;

    END //

DELIMITER ;
```

Notice that the parameter name does not start with @ as it would in SQL Server, but we have changed the parameter name to *pVendorCategoryName* to avoid confusion with the column name. If you wish, you can keep the parameter name same as the column name.

The MySQL code for creating the stored procedure *AddLoginDetails:*

```
DELIMITER //

CREATE PROCEDURE AddLoginDetails
        (
                pUserID varchar(50),
                pPassword VARCHAR(50),
                pEmail VARCHAR(50)
        )
    BEGIN

        DECLARE ExistingUserID VARCHAR(50);
        SELECT UserID into ExistingUserID FROM Logins WHERE UserID = pUserID;

        IF ExistingUserID IS NULL
            THEN
                    INSERT INTO Logins (UserID, Password, Email) VALUES (pUserID, pPassword, pEmail);
        END IF;

    END //

DELIMITER ;
```

Unlike *SQL Server*, *MySQL* does not support the *NOT EXISTS* (sub query) in the *IF* statement. To achieve the same result we have declared a variable called *ExistingUserID*, then inserted the subquery result into the variable *ExistingUserID*, and then we used this variable in the *IF* statement. If the *pUserID* exists in the *Logins* table, the *ExistingUserID* will contain the same value as *pUserID*, which is *NOT NULL*, otherwise it will contain a *NULL* value. Another point to note here is that the *IF* statement's *MySQL* syntax is different from *SQL Server*, as you can see below:

SQL Server:
```
IF predicate
      SQL batch
ELSE
      SQL Batch
```

MySQL:
```
IF predicate
      THEN
            SQL batch;
      ELSE
            SQL Batch;
END IF;
```

The MySQL code for creating the stored procedure *AddCustomerRegistrationDetails:*

```
DELIMITER //
CREATE PROCEDURE AddCustomerRegistrationDetails
    (       pUserID varchar(50), pPassword NVARCHAR(50), pEmail VARCHAR(50), pCreditCardNumber VARCHAR(20),
            pCardHolderName VARCHAR(50), pCreditCardType VARCHAR(25), pCreditCardExpiryMonth INT,
            pCreditCardExpiryYear INT, pStreetAddress VARCHAR(100), pZipOrPostalCode VARCHAR(20),
            pCity VARCHAR(25), pStateProvince VARCHAR(25), pCountry VARCHAR(25), pCustomerFirstName VARCHAR(20),
            pCustomerLastName VARCHAR(20), pCustomerPhoneNumber VARCHAR(25),pCustomerEmail VARCHAR(50)   )
    BEGIN
        DECLARE ExistingUserID VARCHAR(50);
        SELECT UserID into ExistingUserID FROM Logins WHERE UserID = pUserID;
        IF ExistingUserID IS NULL
            THEN
                BEGIN
                    DECLARE ExistingCreditCardID INT;
                    DECLARE ExistingAddressID INT;

                    INSERT INTO Logins(UserID, Password, Email) VALUES (pUserID, pPassword, pEmail);

                    SELECT CreditCardID INTO ExistingCreditCardID FROM CreditCards
                    WHERE CreditCardNumber = pCreditCardNumber;
                    IF ExistingCreditCardID IS NULL
                        THEN
                            BEGIN
                                INSERT INTO CreditCards (CreditCardNumber, CardHolderName, CreditCardType,
                                        CreditCardExpiryMonth, CreditCardExpiryYear)
                                VALUES (pCreditCardNumber, pCardHolderName, pCreditCardType,
                                        pCreditCardExpiryMonth, pCreditCardExpiryYear);
                                -- Storing CreditCardID for newly added CreditCardNumber into variable ExistingCreditCardID
                                SELECT LAST_INSERT_ID() INTO ExistingCreditCardID;
                            END;
                    END IF;

                    SELECT AddressID INTO ExistingAddressID FROM Addresses
                    WHERE StreetAddress = pStreetAddress AND ZipOrPostalCode = pZipOrPostalCode;
                    IF ExistingAddressID IS NULL
                        THEN
                            BEGIN
                                INSERT INTO Addresses (StreetAddress, City, StateProvince, Country, ZipOrPostalCode)
                                VALUES (pStreetAddress, pCity, pStateProvince, pCountry, pZipOrPostalCode);
                                SELECT LAST_INSERT_ID() INTO ExistingAddressID;
                            END;
                    END IF;

                    INSERT INTO Customers(CustomerFirstName, CustomerLastName, CustomerAddressID,
                            CustomerPhoneNumber, CustomerEmail, CustomerCreditCardID)
                    VALUES (pCustomerFirstName, pCustomerLastName, ExistingAddressID,pCustomerPhoneNumber,
                            CustomerEmail, ExistingCreditCardID);
                END;
            ELSE
                BEGIN
                    SELECT 'This UserID has already been used, please try with different UserID ';
                END;
        END IF;
    END //
DELIMITER ;
```

Here we have used nested *IF* statements. Most of the *THEN* and *ELSE* instances use more than one SQL statement, and they are included within the *BEGIN...END* blocks.

The MySQL code for creating the stored procedure *AddSalesOrderDetails:*

```
-- Change the delimiter to //
DELIMITER //

CREATE PROCEDURE AddSalesOrderDetails
    (
        pOrderDate DATETIME, pOrderDueDate DATETIME, pCustomerID INT, pOrderTotal DECIMAL(18,4),
        pOrderDiscountTotal DECIMAL(18,4), pOrderBillingAddressID INT,pOrderShippingAddressID INT,
        pOrderCreditCardID INT, pProductID1 INT, pProductQuantity1 INT,pProductUnitPrice1 DECIMAL(18,4),
        pProductUnitPriceDiscount1 DECIMAL(18,4), pProductID2 INT, pProductQuantity2 INT,
        pProductUnitPrice2 DECIMAL(18,4), pProductUnitPriceDiscount2 DECIMAL(18,4), OUT pSalesOrderID INT
    )
    BEGIN
        /*Adding sales order summary into SalesOrders table*/
        INSERT INTO SalesOrders ( OrderDate, OrderDueDate, CustomerID, OrderTotal, OrderDiscountTotal,
            OrderBillingAddressID, OrderShippingAddressID, OrderCreditCardID )
        VALUES (pOrderDate, pOrderDueDate, pCustomerID, pOrderTotal, pOrderDiscountTotal, pOrderBillingAddressID,
            pOrderShippingAddressID, pOrderCreditCardID);

        /* Assigning previously added identity number into pSalesOrderID parameter*/
        SET pSalesOrderID = LAST_INSERT_ID();

        /* Adding products details of the sales order into SalesOrderProducts table*/
        INSERT INTO SalesOrderProducts(SalesOrderID, ProductID, ProductQuantity,
            ProductUnitPrice, ProductUnitPriceDiscount)
        VALUES (pSalesOrderID, pProductID1, pProductQuantity1, pProductUnitPrice1, pProductUnitPriceDiscount1);
        INSERT INTO SalesOrderProducts(SalesOrderID, ProductID, ProductQuantity,
            ProductUnitPrice, ProductUnitPriceDiscount)
        VALUES (pSalesOrderID, pProductID2, pProductQuantity2, pProductUnitPrice2, pProductUnitPriceDiscount2);
    END //

-- Change the delimiter back to ;
DELIMITER ;
```

After the first *INSERT* statement, a new *SalesOrderID* will be generated. The *LAST_INSERT_ID()* function has been used to catch the newly generated *SalesOrderID* (which is the receipt number for the order) and the *SET* command stores it into the output parameter *pSalesOrderID*. From this parameter, your application can get this receipt number and provide it to the customer. In *MySQL*, the *OUT* keyword is used to identify a parameter as an output parameter. Notice that we used the *OUT* keyword before the *pSalesOrderID* parameter name in the parameter definition.

The MySQL code for creating the stored procedure *UpdateSalesOrderProductsShipdate:*

```
-- Change the delimiter to //
DELIMITER //

CREATE PROCEDURE UpdateSalesOrderProductsShipdate (pSalesOrderID INT, pProductID INT, pShipDate DATETIME)
    BEGIN
        -- Declaring variables to store CreditCardID and AddressID
        DECLARE ExistingSalesOrderID INT;
        SELECT SalesOrderID INTO ExistingSalesOrderID  FROM SalesOrderProducts
        WHERE SalesOrderID = pSalesOrderID AND ProductID = pProductID;

        -- Updating ship date
        IF ExistingSalesOrderID IS NOT NULL
            THEN
                UPDATE SalesOrderProducts SET ProductShipDate = pShipDate
                WHERE SalesOrderID = pSalesOrderID AND ProductID = pProductID;
            ELSE
                SELECT 'SalesOrderID or ProductID does not exist. Please try with correct IDs';
        END IF;
    END //

-- Change the delimiter back to ;
DELIMITER ;
```

Unlike *SQL Server, MySQL* does not support the *EXISTS* function. To work around this, we declared a variable called *ExistingSalesOrderID*. Then the following:

```
SELECT SalesOrderID INTO ExistingSalesOrderID FROM SalesOrderProducts
WHERE SalesOrderID = pSalesOrderID  AND ProductID = pProductID
```

...will return the *SalesOrderID* into the variable if it exists, otherwise the variable's value will remain *NULL*. If the variable's value is *NOT NULL*, it will execute the *UPDATE* statement to set the shipment date, otherwise it will return an error message saying the *'SalesOrderID or ProductID does not exist. Please try with correct IDs.'*

How to Call/Execute a Stored Procedure

As you have seen, you can write a complex routine within a stored procedure. Your company's senior programmers can embed complex business logic within a SQL batch (routine) and save them as stored procedures, and the junior programmers can simply call them as needed. Now, how exactly can you call a stored procedure after it has been created in your database? The syntax to call a stored procedure would look like:

SQL Server:
```
EXECUTE stored procedure name parameter name 1 = parameter value 1, parameter name 2 = parameter value 2,.....................;
```

Or
```
EXECUTE stored procedure name parameter value 1, parameter value 2,.............................................................................................;
```

MySQL:
```
CALL stored procedure name (parameter value 1, parameter value 2.....................................................................................................);
```

If you want to see the list of products for *Diamond* category vendors, instead of writing the whole query you can simply call the *ProductsForDiamondVendors* stored procedure as we demonstrate below:

SQL Server:
```
EXECUTE ProductsForDiamondVendors;
```

MySQL:
```
CALL ProductsForDiamondVendors;
```

The stored procedure *ProductsForDiamondVendors* does not have any parameters, so calling the stored procedure becomes very simple here: just use *EXECUTE/CALL* followed by the stored procedure name. But if a stored procedure has input parameters, you must supply these input parameters from the calling program. For example, if you want to use the stored procedure *ProductsForAVendorCategory* instead of *ProductsForDiamondVendors* to retrieve the list of products for *Diamond* category vendors, you have to supply the *Diamond* value to the *VendorCategoryName* parameter:

SQL Server:

Option 1:
```
EXECUTE ProductsForAVendorCategory 'Diamond';
```

Option 2:
```
EXECUTE ProductsForAVendorCategory @VendorCategoryName = 'Diamond';
```

MySQL:
```
CALL ProductsForAVendorCategory ('Diamond');
```

If the stored procedure has an output parameter, you need to supply a variable to store the value of the output parameter so that your calling application can use that value. For example, let's say a customer submits an order with the below details:

Customer ID	1	Order Date	1/04/2017	Order Due Date	5/04/2017
Billing Address ID	2	Shipping Address ID	2	Credit Card ID	1

Product ID	Quantity	Unit Price	Unit Discount	Product Total	Product Discount Total
1	1	$100	$0	$100	$0
2	2	$550	$15	$1100	$30
Order Total				$1200	$30

Your application need to add these details into the *SalesOrders* and *SalesOrderProducts* tables and then provide the receipt number back to the customer as a reference. In your application, you can easily perform this task by calling the stored procedure *AddSalesOrderDetails* with all the details as input parameters and a variable as an output parameter which will store the receipt number. Here's what that would look like:

SQL Server:

Option 1:
```
DECLARE @ReceiptNo INT;
EXECUTE AddSalesOrderDetails '2017-04-01','2017-04-05', 1, 1200,30,2,2,1,1,1,100,0,2,2,550,15,@ReceiptNo OUTPUT;
SELECT @ReceiptNo;
```

Option 2:
```
DECLARE @ReceiptNo INT;
EXECUTE AddSalesOrderDetails
    @OrderDate = '2017-04-01', @OrderDueDate = '2017-04-05', @CustomerID = 1, @OrderTotal =1200,
    @OrderDiscountTotal =30, @OrderBillingAddressID =2, @OrderShippingAddressID =2, @OrderCreditCardID =1,
    @ProductID1 =1, @ProductQuantity1 =1, @ProductUnitPrice1 =100, @ProductUnitPriceDiscount1 =0,
    @ProductID2 =2, @ProductQuantity2 =2, @ProductUnitPrice2 =550,@ProductUnitPriceDiscount2 =15,
    @ReceiptNo OUTPUT;
SELECT @ReceiptNo;
```

MySQL:
```
CALL AddSalesOrderDetails ('2017-05-01','2017-05-05', 3, 1200,30,2,2,1,3,1,100,0,4,2,550,30,@ReceiptNo);
SELECT @ReceiptNo;
```

In *SQL Server* you need to declare the variable *@ReceiptNo* before using it as output parameter, but remember that in *MySQL* you do not need to declare the variable *@ReceiptNo*. Unlike a regular variable in *MySQL*, you need to start the variable name with @ when you use the variable as an output parameter.

How to Remove a Stored Procedure

If a stored procedure is no longer being used, you should remove it from the database. The basic syntax to remove a stored procedure is:

```
DROP PROCEDURE stored procedure name;
```

If you want to remove the stored procedure *ProductsForDiamondVendors*, the SQL statement would be:

```
DROP PROCEDURE ProductsForDiamondVendors;
```

Real-world Uses for Stored Procedures

Now you know what stored procedures are and how to create them, but why do you need them? Stored procedures encapsulate complex business logic within a simple and easy to read name. This in turn gives you a huge range of use cases. Here are a few cases where stored procedures can play an important role:

Stored procedures can be used to improve data integrity by reducing human errors: Most of the stored procedures we wrote earlier in this lesson have a long routine of codes. Your organization's senior programmers can write the stored procedures just one time and test them to be sure they function properly, and then others can simply call these proven procedures whenever needed. This can significantly reduce the risk of less experienced users adding incorrect data into tables. The less often your programmers need to write long routines of code, the less likely someone will end up introducing an error.

Stored procedures can be used to improve performance: Stored procedures are stored in the database in compiled form. If you execute a stored procedure instead of a SQL statement/routine, there are two ways it can improve your application's performance:

- The RDBMS's query processor does not need to compile the SQL statement/routine
- Your application does not need to send the long SQL routine over the network: it just needs to send a short procedure call.

Stored procedures can significantly reduce application changes: Stored procedures can be used to encapsulate complex business logic. Therefore, when the business logic changes, in most cases you do not need to change your application. Instead, you can support the existing business logic by modifying the stored procedures. Sometimes there is a need to modify the table structures, and in this case you can simple modify the stored procedures to adapt to these types of changes.

Stored procedures can be used as effective security features: Some companies grant access to the tables to only a few administrators, while all other users and applications access table data via stored procedures. In a setup such as this, you only need to grant permission to execute the stored procedures, which decreases unwanted access to the underlying tables and data. It also reduces the risk of data corruptions.

Lesson Summary

This lesson has briefly shown how stored procedures can empower you to simplify complex SQL batches and add another layer of security to your data:

- *CREATE/DROP PROCEDURE* statements allow you to add/remove stored procedures from your database.
- Since the semicolon (;) is the default delimiter in MySQL, you now know how to use the *DELIMITER* keyword to change the delimiter for the stored procedure before a *CREATE PROCEDURE* statement.
- The *EXECUTE/CALL* statement allows you to call the stored procedure from your application.
- Stored procedures can be used to reduce application changes, improve application performance and secure your tables.

Lesson 17
Working with Triggers

Lesson Objective

With the knowledge you have gained so far, you can instruct your preferred RDBMS to do a range of specific operation(s), but what if you want your RDMBS to perform a task automatically when a specific operation occurs in the database? This is where *triggers* come to rescue, allowing you to do prepare automatic operations for various uses. This lesson will show you:

- What triggers are
- What triggers can be used for
- How to create and remove them

Code Samples

You can find the SQL code solutions for the examples and business problems in this lesson at the following links:

SQL Server:
https://drive.google.com/open?id=1KlFhQULbMhtJmd1QGEV3FbsZS3dLVOTN

MySQL:
https://drive.google.com/open?id=1x3bUBZD03R4fXIihaWUcSNx4hiU0FdKL

What Are Triggers?

Like a stored procedure, a trigger is a batch of SQL statements or routines that are stored within a database. Stored procedures are stored independently within the database, but each trigger is always attached to a specific table. You have to call a stored procedure's routine if you want to execute it, whereas a trigger will execute automatically as the result of an *INSERT*, *UPDATE* or *DELETE* operation on the table the trigger has been attached to. In its simplest form, a trigger is a SQL routine that executes automatically as a result of the *INSERT*, *UPDATE* or *DELETE* operation on a particular table.

Why Do We Need Triggers?

Before we start creating triggers, let's review why you even need them. Here are some use cases where triggers can play an important role:

Triggers can improve data integrity by automatically updating their related tables: Summarized or calculated attributes often change based on transactional events. For example, the *Product* table has both *StockQuantity* and *OrderedQuantity* columns that store the current number of units in stock (**StockQuantity**) and any outstanding orders (*OrderedQuantity*) for each product. As soon as a customer places an order to buy one or more units of a product, we have to increase the corresponding *OrderedQuantity* by one or more. Similarly as soon as a vendor ships one or more units of a product to a customer, we have to decrease the corresponding *StockQuantity* to match that order. If we don't do this necessary bookkeeping, the *OrderedQuantity* and *StockQuantity* tables will not represent the correct values. You may have already noticed that when we added a customer's data in the earlier lessons we added one row in the *SalesOrder* table and added one or more rows in the *SalesOrderProducts* table, but we didn't increase the corresponding *OrderedQuantity* value for each product in the *Products* table. To resolve this issue, we can create a trigger on the

SalesOrderProducts table that will automatically fire after an *INSERT* of a row to the *SalesOrderProducts* table. The trigger will go to work and *UPDATE* the corresponding *OrderedQuanity* value of the *Products* table. Similarly, we can create another trigger for the *SalesOrderProducts* table which will automatically execute after an *UPDATE* of a *ShipDate* column of a row from the *SalesOrderProducts* table. This trigger will *UPDATE* the corresponding *StockQuanity* value to the *Products* table.

Triggers can be used to audit and log data manipulation activities: Data is the most valuable asset for every business. Accidental changes to data can constitute a big loss. For example, if you decrease the *StandardSalesPrice* of a product below the actual production cost, or increase the *SalesDiscountPercentage/SalesDiscountAmount* of the product above the production cost, this could lead to a loss for the company. So it is very important to log these changes for auditing purposes. To log changes of sensitive data, we can create a trigger on the *Products* table which will automatically fire after any *UPDATE* of a row and add the changes to an audit table. These changes could include the old value along with new value, the time the change occurred and perhaps who made the change.

Triggers can be used to archive deleted rows: Just as it's important to audit data manipulation, your company may want to archive the entire row for auditing purposes when someone deletes a row from a table. For example, when someone abuses the customer feedback function, we need to remove the feedback from the *CustomerFeedbacks* table, but for auditing purposes we need to keep the last state of the feedback, the time of deletion, and who wrote the feedback. We can create a trigger on the *CustomerFeedbacks* table which can automatically execute after any *DELETE* action of a row from the *CustomerFeedbacks* table and archive the previous state of the row into an audit table.

Triggers can be used to apply complex validation before data manipulation activities: Companies often create triggers to ensure the overall data integrity of a power user's intentional or unintentional changes. For example, you can create a trigger to update the *IsActive* flag instead of deleting a product from *Products* table, or you can create a trigger to validate the *StockQuantity* before any *UPDATE* action on the column.

How to Create a Trigger?

Next, we will show you how you can create triggers starting with the basic syntax, then show you some different types of triggers you might need for various use cases.

Basic syntax of triggers in SQL Server

As you may have guessed, the basic syntax to create a trigger varies between RDBMSs, so you'll need to refer to your documentation if you're not using *SQL Server* or *MySQL* to follow along with this lesson. The basic syntax to create a trigger in *SQL Server* is:

```
CREATE TRIGGER trigger name
      ON table name
            AFTER/INSTEAD OF
            INSERT/UPDATE/DELETE
AS
BEGIN
      SQL routine;
END;
```

Two basic types of triggers are available in SQL Server: the *AFTER* trigger and the *INSTEAD OF* trigger. As the name suggests, the *AFTER* trigger fires after an *INSERT*, *UPDATE* or *DELETE* operation has been executed on a table. The *INSTEAD OF* trigger, on the other hand, will fire instead of an *INSERT*, *UPDATE* or *DELETE* operation. What this means is that, if you try to execute an *INSERT/UPDATE/DELETE* statement, the trigger will skip the execution of the statement and only execute the trigger's routine.

We'll explain how and why the *INSTEAD OF* trigger does this a little later on. For now, know that when you create a trigger, *SQL Server* will provide you two special tables, *INSERTED* and *DELETED*, to access the new and old versions of a data row respectively. If you insert a row into a table, the *INSERTED* table will contain the row as well. If you update a row from a table, the *DELETED* table will contain the version of the row before your update operation and the *INSERTED* table will contain the version of the row after update operation. If you delete a row from a table, the *DELETED* table will contain the version of the row before delete operation.

Basic Syntax of Triggers in MySQL

The basic syntax to create a trigger in MySQL is like below:

```
DELIMITER delimiter character
CREATE TRIGGER trigger name
        BEFORE/AFTER
        INSERT/UPDATE/DELETE
    ON table name
        FOR EACH ROW
    BEGIN
        SQL routine;
    END delimiter character
DELIMITER ;
```

There are two basic types of triggers available in *MySQL*: the *BEFORE* trigger and the *AFTER* trigger. With the *BEFORE* trigger, if you execute an *INSERT/UPDATE/DELETE* statement, it will execute the trigger's routine first and then execute the SQL statement. In keeping with this logic, the *AFTER* trigger will fire after an *INSERT*, *UPDATE* or *DELETE* operation on the table, so if you execute an *INSERT/UPDATE/DELETE* statement, it will execute the statement first, then execute the *AFTER* trigger's routine. When you create a trigger in *MySQL* it will provide you two keywords, *NEW* and *OLD*, to access the new and old versions of the data row, respectively. If you insert a row into a table, the *NEW* keyword will contain the inserted row. If you update a row from a table, the *OLD* keyword will contain the version of the row before the update operation and the *NEW* keyword will contain the version of the row after the update operation. If you delete a row from a table, the *OLD* keyword will contain the version of the row before delete operation. As with stored procedures, you need to change the default delimiter character before your *CREATE TRIGGER* statement and be sure to change it back to a semicolon (;) after the *CREATE TRIGGER* statement.

How to Create a Trigger to Update Related Tables in SQL Server

When you add a row into the *SalesOrderProducts* table, the value of the *OrderedQuantity* column in the *Products* table must be incremented by the *ProductQuantity* column value of the newly added row. *SQL Server* will automatically update the *OrderedQuantity* column's value in the *Products* table if you create the trigger shown below on the *SalesOrderProducts* table:

```
CREATE TRIGGER UpdateOrderedQuantity_SalesOrderProducts
        ON SalesOrderProducts AFTER INSERT
AS
BEGIN
        UPDATE Products
            SET OrderedQuantity = OrderedQuantity + i.ProductQuantity
        FROM Products AS p
        INNER JOIN SalesOrderProducts AS sop ON p.ProductID = sop.ProductID
        INNER JOIN Inserted AS i ON sop.ProductID = i.ProductID;
END
```

This is an example of how the *AFTER* trigger will fire after an *INSERT* operation on the *SalesOrderProducts* table. The special table *INSERTED* will contain the value of *SalesOrderProducts* table's newly inserted row which will *INNER JOIN* with the *Products* table and update the corresponding product's *OrderedQuantity* column. To verify this *UpdateOrderedQuantity_SalesOrderProducts* trigger's activities, let's add a customer order using the *AddSalesOrderDetails* stored procedure that we created in *Lesson 16*:

Customer ID	5	Order Date	21/04/2017	Order Due Date	27/04/2017
Billing Address ID	8	Shipping Address ID	8	Credit Card ID	5

Product ID	Quantity	Unit Price	Unit Discount	Product Total	Product Discount Total
2	4	$100	$20	$400	$80
5	2	$20	$0	$40	$0
Order Total				$440	$80

You can execute the following SQL batch to add the sales order shown above:

```
-- Check the OrderedQuantity before adding new sales order
SELECT ProductID, OrderedQuantity FROM Products WHERE ProductID IN (2,5);

--Add a new sales order with Products 2 & 5
DECLARE @ReceiptNo INT;
EXECUTE AddSalesOrderDetails
      @OrderDate = '2017-04-21', @OrderDueDate = '2017-04-27', @CustomerID = 5, @OrderTotal = 440,
      @OrderDiscountTotal = 80, @OrderBillingAddressID = 8, @OrderShippingAddressID = 8, @OrderCreditCardID = 5,
      @ProductID1 = 2, @ProductQuantity1 = 4, @ProductUnitPrice1 = 100, @ProductUnitPriceDiscount1 = 20,
      @ProductID2 = 5, @ProductQuantity2 = 2, @ProductUnitPrice2 = 20, @ProductUnitPriceDiscount2 = 0,
      @SalesOrderID = @ReceiptNo OUTPUT;

-- Check the OrderedQuantity after adding new sales order
SELECT ProductID, OrderedQuantity FROM Products WHERE ProductID IN (2,5);
```

If you look at the result of the two *SELECT* statements, you will see that, as soon as the sales order's details have been entered into the *SalesOrderProducts* table, the *OrderedQuantity* of *ProductIDs 2 & 5* (in the *Products* table) have been increased by four & two, respectively. This has been done by the *UpdateOrderedQuantity_SalesOrderProducts* trigger.

How to Create a Trigger to Update Related Tables in MySQL

The MySQL version of the same trigger we just discussed for SQL Server will be like below:

```
DELIMITER //

CREATE TRIGGER UpdateOrderedQuantity_SalesOrderProducts
     AFTER INSERT ON SalesOrderProducts FOR EACH ROW
     BEGIN
          UPDATE Products
               SET OrderedQuantity = OrderedQuantity + New.ProductQuantity
          WHERE ProductID = New.ProductID;
     END //
DELIMITER ;
```

Similar to the process in SQL Server, the *AFTER* trigger in *MySQL* will fire after an *INSERT* operation on the *SalesOrderProducts* table, and through our *NEW* keywords we can then access all column values for the newly added rows. The *UPDATE* statement's *WHERE* clause matches the *ProductID* in the *Products* table with the newly added *ProductID (New.ProductID)* in the *SalesOrderProducts* table, then adds the new *ProductQuantity (New.ProductQuantity)* to the *OrderedQuantity* in the matching row. Similar to the previous topic, you can verify the trigger's activities by executing the SQL batch shown below:

```
-- Check the OrderedQuantity before adding new sales order
SELECT ProductID, OrderedQuantity FROM Products WHERE ProductID IN (2,5);

-- Add a new sales order with Products 2 & 5
CALL AddSalesOrderDetails ('2017-04-21','2017-04-27', 5, 440,80,8,8,5,2,4,100,20,5,2,20,0,@ReceiptNo);

-- Check the OrderedQuantity after adding new sales order
SELECT ProductID, OrderedQuantity FROM Products WHERE ProductID IN (2,5);
```

How to Create a Trigger to Log Data Manipulation in SQL Server

Changes to the values of the *StandardSalesPrice*, *SalesDiscountPercentage* and *SalesDiscountAmount* columns of the *Products* table can mean a significant impact on the database. For this reason, the company usually wants to be sure any changes to these sensitive data columns are logged. Let's create an audit table called *ProductChangeHistories* to log any price/discount changes for company products:

```
CREATE TABLE ProductChangeHistories(
        ProductHistoryID INT IDENTITY(1,1) NOT NULL PRIMARY KEY,
        ProductID INT NOT NULL,
        ColumnName VARCHAR(50) NOT NULL,
        OldValue DECIMAL(18,4) NOT NULL,
        NewValue DECIMAL(18,4) NOT NULL,
        UpdateDateTime DATETIME NOT NULL DEFAULT(GETDATE())
    );
```

Now, if you create the trigger you see below on the *Products* table, *SQL Server* will automatically add a row for the old value (before update) and the new value (after update) into the *ProductChangeHistories* table for each product as soon as it's *StandardSalesPrice/SalesDiscountPercentage/SalesDiscountAmount* changes:

```
CREATE TRIGGER LogProductPriceChanges_Products  ON  Products AFTER UPDATE
AS
BEGIN

    -- Log StandardSalesPrice changes
    INSERT INTO ProductChangeHistories (ProductID, ColumnName, OldValue, NewValue)
    SELECT p.ProductID, 'StandardSalesPrice' AS ColumnName, d.StandardSalesPrice AS OldValue,
        i.StandardSalesPrice AS NewValue
    FROM Products AS p
    INNER JOIN Inserted AS i ON p.ProductID = i.ProductID
    INNER JOIN Deleted AS d ON i.ProductID = d.ProductID
    WHERE d.StandardSalesPrice <> i.StandardSalesPrice;

    -- Log SalesDiscountPercentage changes
    INSERT INTO ProductChangeHistories (ProductID, ColumnName, OldValue, NewValue)
    SELECT p.ProductID, 'SalesDiscountPercentage' AS ColumnName, d.SalesDiscountPercentage AS OldValue,
        i.SalesDiscountPercentage AS NewValue
    FROM Products AS p
    INNER JOIN Inserted AS i ON p.ProductID = i.ProductID
    INNER JOIN Deleted AS d ON i.ProductID = d.ProductID
    WHERE d.SalesDiscountPercentage <> i.SalesDiscountPercentage;

    -- Log SalesDiscountAmount changes
    INSERT INTO ProductChangeHistories (ProductID, ColumnName, OldValue, NewValue)
    SELECT p.ProductID, 'SalesDiscountAmount' AS ColumnName, d.SalesDiscountAmount AS OldValue,
        i.SalesDiscountAmount AS NewValue
    FROM Products AS p
    INNER JOIN Inserted AS i ON p.ProductID = i.ProductID
    INNER JOIN Deleted AS d ON i.ProductID = d.ProductID
    WHERE d.SalesDiscountAmount <> i.SalesDiscountAmount;
END
```

This is an example of the *AFTER* trigger, which in this case will fire after an *UPDATE* operation on the *Products* table. The special table *DELETED* will contain the value of a row from the *Products* table just before the update operation. Meanwhile, the *INSERTED* table will contain the value of the same *Products* table row just after the update. We have created an *INNER JOIN* to link these two special tables to the *Products* table, and this is so that these tables will be returned before and after the columns are updated with new values. Note that the *WHERE* clause will include a row only if the new value of the column is different from the old value.

To verify this *LogProductPriceChanges_Products* trigger's activities, let's modify the *StandardSalesPrice* and *SalesDiscountPercentage* for *Product ID 5* using the below SQL batch and see what happens:

```
/* Check the audit table before price/discount update on Products table */
SELECT * FROM ProductChangeHistories;

/* Modify StandardSalesPrice and SalesDiscountPercentage for Product 5 */
UPDATE Products  SET StandardSalesPrice = 25, SalesDiscountPercentage = 5 WHERE ProductID = 5;

/* Check the audit table after price/discount update on Products table */
SELECT * FROM ProductChangeHistories;
```

If you look at the result of these two *SELECT* statements, you will notice that, as soon as the values of *StandardSalesPrice* and *SalesDiscountPercentage* are updated, one row has been added into *ProductChangeHistories* table for each column's change in value, so the trigger is working correctly.

How to Create a Trigger to Log Data Manipulation in MySQL

Here, we will create the same trigger, this time by using MySQL. The MySQL syntax to create the *ProductChangeHistories* table will look like:

```
CREATE TABLE ProductChangeHistories(
        ProductHistoryID INT AUTO_INCREMENT NOT NULL PRIMARY KEY,
        ProductID INT NOT NULL,
        ColumnName VARCHAR(50) NOT NULL,
        OldValue DECIMAL(18,4) NOT NULL,
        NewValue DECIMAL(18,4) NOT NULL,
        UpdateDateTime DATETIME NOT NULL DEFAULT NOW()
    );
```

The MySQL version of the same trigger of previous topic will be like below:

```
-- Change the default delimiter to //
DELIMITER //

CREATE TRIGGER LogProductPriceChanges_Products AFTER UPDATE ON Products FOR EACH ROW
BEGIN
    -- Log StandardSalesPrice changes
    IF Old.StandardSalesPrice <> New.StandardSalesPrice
      THEN
          INSERT INTO ProductChangeHistories (ProductID, ColumnName, OldValue, NewValue)
          VALUES ( New.ProductID, 'StandardSalesPrice', Old.StandardSalesPrice, New.StandardSalesPrice);
    END IF;

    -- Log SalesDiscountPercentage changes
    IF Old.SalesDiscountPercentage <> New.SalesDiscountPercentage
      THEN
          INSERT INTO ProductChangeHistories (ProductID, ColumnName, OldValue, NewValue)
          VALUES ( New.ProductID, 'SalesDiscountPercentage',Old.SalesDiscountPercentage, New.SalesDiscountPercentage);
    END IF;

    -- Log SalesDiscountAmount changes
    IF Old.SalesDiscountAmount <> New.SalesDiscountAmount
      THEN
          INSERT INTO ProductChangeHistories (ProductID, ColumnName, OldValue, NewValue)
          VALUES ( New.ProductID, 'SalesDiscountAmount', Old.SalesDiscountAmount, New.SalesDiscountAmount);
    END IF;
END //

-- Change the default delimiter back to ;
DELIMITER ;
```

In *MySQL*, the *AFTER* trigger will also fire after an *UPDATE* operation on the *Products* table. Through the *OLD* and *NEW* keywords, we can access column values before and after the update operation. Since *OLD* and *NEW* are not tables, we just need to use a simple *INSERT* statement here, however we do need to use an *IF* statement to ensure that the value will be added into the *ProductChangeHistories* only when a new value is different from the old one.

How to Create a Trigger to Archive Deleted Rows in SQL Server

When a customer provides abusive or offensive feedback for a product (which is completely inappropriate), companies often remove those feedbacks from their website. Even though deleted feedback is not displayed publicly on the website, you would be wise to keep any and all deleted rows for auditing purposes. Let's create a *DeletedCustomerFeedbacks* table for archiving the deleted rows from *CustomerFeedbacks*:

```
CREATE TABLE DeletedCustomerFeedbacks(
        DeletedFeedbackID INT IDENTITY(1,1) NOT NULL PRIMARY KEY,
        CustomerID int NOT NULL,
        ProductID int NOT NULL,
        CustomerFeedbackRating INT NOT NULL,
        CustomerFeedback VARCHAR(300) NULL,
        FeedbackDate DATETIME NULL,
        DeletedDate DATETIME NOT NULL DEFAULT(GETDATE())
    );
```

Now if you create a trigger *ArchiveDeletedCustomerFeedbacks_CustomerFeedbacks* on *CustomerFeedbacks* table, SQL Server will archive a row into *DeletedCustomerFeedbacks* before deleting from the *CustomerFeedbacks* table:

```
CREATE TRIGGER ArchiveDeletedCustomerFeedbacks_CustomerFeedbacks
    ON  CustomerFeedbacks AFTER DELETE
AS
BEGIN
    INSERT INTO DeletedCustomerFeedbacks(CustomerID, ProductID, CustomerFeedbackRating,
        CustomerFeedback,FeedbackDate)
    SELECT CustomerID, ProductID, CustomerFeedbackRating, CustomerFeedback, FeedbackDate
    FROM Deleted
END;
```

This is an example of the *AFTER* trigger, which in this case will fire after a *DELETE* operation on the *CustomerFeedbacks* table. The special table *DELETED* will contain the value of a row from the *CustomerFeedbacks* table just before the *DELETE* operation. This trigger simply retrieves the deleted row from the *DELETED* table, then inserts it into *DeletedCustomerFeedbacks* table.

To verify this *ArchiveDeletedCustomerFeedbacks_CustomerFeedbacks* trigger's activities, let's delete the feedback provided by *CustomerID 15* for *ProductID 5* using the below SQL batch and see what happens:

```
-- Check DeletedCustomerFeedbacks table before DELETE operation
SELECT * FROM DeletedCustomerFeedbacks;


-- Delete the feedback provided by CustomerID 15 for ProductID 5
DELETE FROM CustomerFeedbacks WHERE CustomerID=15 AND ProductID=5;


-- Check DeletedCustomerFeedbacks table after DELETE operation
SELECT * FROM DeletedCustomerFeedbacks;
```

If you look at the result of these two *SELECT* statements, you will notice that, as soon as you delete the feedback provided by *CustomerID 15* for *ProductID 5*, the deleted row has been inserted into *DeletedCustomerFeedbacks* table. So, the trigger is working correctly.

Creating a Trigger to Archive Deleted Rows in MySQL

Here, we will create the same trigger this time by using MySQL. The MySQL syntax to create the *DeletedCustomerFeedbacks* table will look like:

```
CREATE TABLE DeletedCustomerFeedbacks(
        DeletedFeedbackID INT AUTO_INCREMENT NOT NULL PRIMARY KEY,
        CustomerID INT NOT NULL,
        ProductID INT NOT NULL,
        CustomerFeedbackRating INT NOT NULL,
        CustomerFeedback VARCHAR(300) NULL,
        FeedbackDate DATETIME NULL,
        DeletedDate DATETIME NOT NULL DEFAULT NOW()
    );
```

The MySQL version of the same trigger from the previous topic will be like you see below:

```
-- Change the default delimiter to //
DELIMITER //

CREATE TRIGGER ArchiveDeletedCustomerFeedbacks_CustomerFeedbacks
    AFTER DELETE ON CustomerFeedbacks FOR EACH ROW

    BEGIN
        INSERT INTO DeletedCustomerFeedbacks(CustomerID, ProductID, CustomerFeedbackRating,
            CustomerFeedback,FeedbackDate)
        VALUES( Old.CustomerID, Old.ProductID, Old.CustomerFeedbackRating, Old.CustomerFeedback, Old.FeedbackDate);
    END //

-- Change the default delimiter back to ;
DELIMITER ;
```

Similar to the process in *SQL Server*, this *AFTER* trigger in *MySQL* will fire after a *DELETE* operation on the *CustomerFeedbacks* table, and through our *OLD* keyword we can then access all column values for the deleted rows. The *INSERT* statement will add all deleted rows from the *OLD* keyword into the *DeletedCustomerFeedbacks* table. Similar to the previous topic, you can verify the trigger's activities by executing the SQL batch shown below:

```
-- Check DeletedCustomerFeedbacks table before DELETE operation
SELECT * FROM DeletedCustomerFeedbacks;

-- Delete the feedback provided by CustomerID 15 for ProductID 5
DELETE FROM CustomerFeedbacks WHERE CustomerID=15 AND ProductID=5;

-- Check DeletedCustomerFeedbacks table after DELETE operation
SELECT * FROM CustomerFeedbacks;
```

How to Remove a Trigger

When you do not need a trigger, you need to remove it from your database. The basic syntax for removing a trigger is:

```
DROP TRIGGER trigger name;
```

If you want to remove the *ArchiveDeletedCustomerFeedbacks_CustomerFeedbacks* trigger, you can execute the SQL statement below:

```
DROP TRIGGER ArchiveDeletedCustomerFeedbacks_CustomerFeedbacks;
```

Lesson Summary

This lesson has briefly shown how triggers enable a database engine to perform additional tasks in the event of a data manipulation activity. You have also seen how triggers can be a very useful feature to ensure data integrities and logging activities:

- *CREATE/DROP TRIGGER* statements allow you to add/remove triggers from your database.
- SQL Server provides the *DELETED* and *INSERTED* special tables to access the before and after images of a row, MySQL provides the *OLD* and *NEW* keywords to access the before and after images of a row.
- Since the semicolon (;) is the default delimiter in MySQL, you now know how to use the *DELIMITER* keyword to change the delimiter for the stored procedure before a *CREATE TRIGGER* statement in order to avoid an issue with the RDBMS.
- Triggers can be used to update related tables, log data manipulation activities, archive deleted rows and enforce data validation before any data manipulation. Triggers perform all of these tasks automatically without any manual interaction from user.

Section E
Database Administration

Lesson 18
Improving query performance using indexes

Lesson Objective

You have learned all the necessary techniques to write and execute queries. Now it's time to improve query performance. This lesson will introduce you to a new database object called index that can run your query 10, 100, 1,000 or even 1,000,000 times faster.

Code Samples

For this lesson, you can find the example SQL codes at the following links:

SQL Server:
https://drive.google.com/open?id=11FFQ-ozKgVSjJbQRML9vsjZuzqhkXAF5

MySQL:
https://drive.google.com/open?id=1-lha5yY1p4KTBDO_0HTqfD9llFOcS6df

This lesson is all about improving the performance of your query. Although it may not seem that way, none of the tables we've created in our sample database have a large number of data. Therefore, before you start, we encourage you to create a new table *Customers_LargeTable* and insert data for 10,000 new customers into it. We have provided the code for this here:

SQL Server:
https://drive.google.com/open?id=1AtWjz-eH6CKYUX3z7zKagZmxUY6H1t6m

MySQL:
https://drive.google.com/open?id=1nu28RkflQxBgjZPgmEcuRBgINQ4W2c4Y

What is index?

An index is a database object that enables a query to perform a search of data quickly and efficiently. As you know, the best way to understand the index object is to see how it would work in a real-world example:

Let's assume that there was no chronological order of lessons and topics in this book, and you don't have the luxury of a *'search'* function to easily scan the text (as would be the case with any traditional hardcover book). In order to find the *'What is stored procedure?'* topic, you would need to start at the very first page and scan the pages until you found it. This would be very time-consuming and inefficient! Similarly, assume that the *Customers* table does not have a primary key, and the rows will be unsorted within the table. This is often called a *heap*. Trying to find the details of *CustomerID 20* in a database of 10,000 entries would probably be very frustrating. Imagine attempting the same task at a major corporation with millions of customers!

Now let's assume that the lessons and topics are in chronological order, but what if there wasn't an index? You could find a topic like *'What is stored procedure?'* very easily (e.g. by searching for the topic in the contents of the book to find the page number), but you'd still be forced to search the entire book if you wanted to find all the occurrences of the *INNER JOIN* keyword. You effectively need to read all the pages, line by line, which will be very slow.

Similarly, if the *Customers* table has a primary key (*CustomerID*), all the rows for the *Customers* table will be stored in chronological order by their *CustomerID*, and also there will be a summarized list of *CustomerIDs* and their location details of the actual rows. Therefore, if you want to look for the details of *CustomerID 20*, you can search for it in the summarized list and get the row location so you can directly retrieve the row from the location. Since you do not need to scan all the rows, it will be very fast. This whole data structure of the summarized key list along with the sorted detailed data rows is referred to as a *clustered index*. When you create a primary key for a table, most RDBMSs create a *clustered index* on the primary key column(s). However, if you want to see the details for all customers with the first name *'Rick'*, you do not have any ordered list by customer's first name. Hence, you need to scan all rows that will be very slow.

Of course, this book is professionally formatted with all the necessary components to make it easy to search for a lesson, section, or key term. It has:

- A table of contents at the beginning of the book
- Lessons and topics in chronological order
- An index of keywords and phrases is at the end of the book

If you want to read all topics that contain *INNER JOIN* keyword, you can search the *INNER JOIN* keyword in the index pages, then open all the related pages to read the topics. This will be very fast. The index object in SQL works quite the same way.

If you create an index on the *FirstName* column of *Customers* table, the RDBMS will duplicate all of the values of the *FirstName* column and their *CustomerID* into a separate data structure. This data structure does not store the actual data row. This is referred to as a *non-clustered index*. Now, as with a book index, if you want to see the details for all customers with the first name *'Rick'*, you do not need to search the whole table, you can simply seek it in the non-clustered index and get the corresponding *CustomerIDs* and then use a clustered key lookup to retrieve the data rows.

Needless to say, index is an invaluable tool for a database of any size, which is why we've dedicated this lesson to its usage. To understand how index can make your queries a million times faster, it is important to understand how an RDBMS stores data rows of a table inside the disk and how they retrieve data rows from the disk.

The storage data structure of a database

An RDBMS will divide the total disk space allocated for a database into pages. The page size depends on the RDBMS, and it varies between 4KB (kilobytes) and 64KB. If your RDBMS uses 8KB pages and your database's size is 8000KB, there will be 1000 pages in this database. The majority of these pages will be used to store data, while a small number of these pages will be used for page management (e.g. to identify the pages used by a given table). Each page contains a header and a data block. The header block contains summary information about the page as well as the navigation information (i.e. next and previous page pointers). When you create a new table, the RDBMS allocates a page (or a group of pages) for that table. When you start inserting data into the table, the RDBMS will fill up the first page to its maximum capacity, then go to fill the next page and so on. Each page has a pointer to the next page and the previous page in its group.

The storage data structure of a heap

When a table does not have a *primary key* (*cluster key*), it is often called as *heap*. When a table does not have a primary key, data will be inserted into data pages as it comes — there's no order to the column or group of columns.

Assume that you have already created the *Customers_LargeTable* table by executing the SQL provided at the beginning of this lesson. Each 8KB page will contain 10 rows of data. Therefore, the 10,000 rows of customer data will fill 1,000 pages. We have created the *Customers_LargeTable* table without any primary key, so the storage data structure for the table will be like you see in Fig 18.1.

Since the data are not storing in a particular order within a heap, even a simple query search of one row forces the storage engine to scan all 1,000 pages. Let's verify that to be true by executing some queries against the *Customers_largeTable* table.

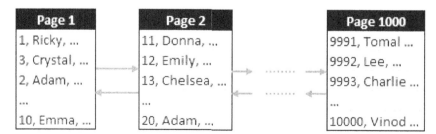

Fig 18.1: Storage data structure of a heap (Customers_LargeTable)

SQL Server:

If you execute *SET STATISTICS IO ON* before executing a query or a batch of queries, the *Messages* TAB will show the number of pages the storage engine has to scan to give the result of the query (you can find this number listed just after *'logical reads'* in the output as shown below). Let's retrieve all the rows from the *Customers_largeTable* table by executing the following query:

```
SET STATISTICS IO ON;
SELECT * FROM Customers_LargeTable;
```

Notice that the query has returned 10,000 rows, and the *Messages* TAB has shown:

```
 Results    Messages

(10000 row(s) affected)
Table 'Customers_LargeTable'. Scan count 1, logical reads 1118 physical reads 0, read-ahead reads 0,
lob logical reads 0, lob physical reads 0, lob read-ahead reads 0.
```

This indicates that the query scanned 1,118 pages. Notice that it has scanned 118 more pages than we thought. These are additional pages required to manage the pages, something we often call 'overhead'.

Let's retrieve a customer's details from the *Customers_largeTable* table. We'll search for *Charlie's* details by using his *CustomerID* in the *WHERE* clause:

```
SET STATISTICS IO ON;
SELECT * FROM Customers_LargeTable WHERE CustomerID = 9993;
```

Although the above query returned only one row, the *Messages* TAB will show exactly the same number of logical reads as the previous query: it scanned all 1,118 pages.

Now let's see if we'll have the same result by retrieving *Charlie's* details from *Customers_largeTable* table by using his *FirstName* in the *WHERE* clause:

```
SET STATISTICS IO ON;
SELECT * FROM Customers_LargeTable WHERE FirstName = 'Charlie';
```

As you may have suspected, the above query also returned one row and the *Messages* TAB showed us that the query scanned 1,118 pages to retrieve it.

MySQL:

In MySQL there is no quick way to find the number of pages. It entails using an advanced feature that is beyond the scope of this book (finding how many pages the storage engine has to scan to return the query result). There is a usable alternative, however. If we use the *EXPLAIN* keyword before a query, it will show how many estimated rows it has to examine to return the result. This will be a good indication of the performance of the query. Let's execute the three queries from the SQL Server section above with the *EXPLAIN* keyword:

```
EXPLAIN SELECT * FROM Customers_LargeTable;
EXPLAIN SELECT * FROM Customers_LargeTable WHERE CustomerID = 9993;
EXPLAIN SELECT * FROM Customers_LargeTable WHERE FirstName = 'Charlie';
```

We know the first query will return all rows and both of the other queries will return single rows. You might have noticed that all of the queries above have estimated the same number of rows (9,715). You can see the result in the *rows* column of the execution output:

id	select_type	table	partitions	type	possible_keys	key	key_len	ref	rows	filtered	Extra
1	SIMPLE	Customers_LargeTable	NULL	ALL	NULL	NULL	NULL	NULL	9715	100.00	NULL

The storage data structure of a clustered index

When a table has a *primary key*, the RDBMS will automatically create a *clustered index* for the table. As such, the data will be stored in the disk in the order of this *primary key*. In the real world, almost all database tables must have a primary key, and this is one excellent use for these keys.

When you create a clustered index, the RDBMS creates additional pages in order to organize the data into an ascending hierarchy that is easier and faster to search. This organized structure of non-data pages is known as *B-Tree*. Each additional page in a clustered index stores the primary keys and page pointers of the first rows of the data-containing pages in its *"cluster"*. This way, the RDBMS spends less time searching for a data row for a key.

If you create *CustomerID* as the primary key of the *Customers_LargeTable* table, the storage data structure for the table will be as you see in Fig 18.2 below:

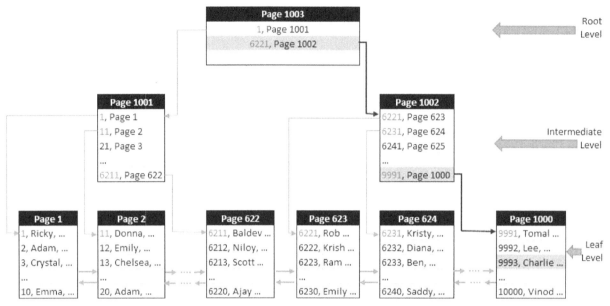

Fig 18.2: Storage data structure of a clustered index (Customers_LargeTable)

As shown in this diagram, the bottom level is the *'Leaf Level'*, above that are the *'Intermediate Levels'* and at the top is the *'Root Level'*. You may have noticed that the *leaf level* contains all the *data pages* that you would see in the *heap structure*, but here we have three more pages: two for the *intermediate level* and one for the *root level*. These three pages are called *index pages*. Each row of these pages stores only the primary key (*CustomerID*) of the first rows and page pointers (*page numbers*) of the entries on the next (below) level. Therefore, the row size of these index pages is very small. In our example, each of the 8KB index pages can store 622 rows. If you want to retrieve all of these rows, the RDBMS will scan the data pages from the leaf level (similar to the heap), but if you want to search single row (or few rows) by its primary key (*CustomerID*), the RDBMS will do the following actions:

1. First, it will look for the key in the root page, and then it will
2. get the page number and navigate down to the intermediate level,
3. look for the key again in the intermediate level page,
4. get the page number for the data page,
5. navigate down to the data page,
6. look for the key again in the data page and, finally,
7. it will return the data row.

So, for a *CustomerID* search the storage engine only needs to read three pages:

- The root page
- one intermediate page
- one data page

Here's a breakdown of what each of the index pages include:

Page 1001 (the first page of intermediate level):

This page contains 622 rows:
- The first row contains *CustomerID* from the first row of the first page, i.e. *1* and a page pointer i.e. *Page 1*.

- The second row contains *CustomerID* from the first row of the second page, i.e. *11* and a page pointer i.e. *Page 2.*
- The third row contains *CustomerID* from the first row of the third page, i.e. *21* and a page pointer i.e. *Page 3.*
- The last row (row 622) contains *CustomerID* from the first row of page 622 i.e. *6211* and a page pointer, i.e. *Page 622.*

Page 1002 (the second page of intermediate level):

This page contains 378 rows:
- The first row contains *CustomerID* from the first row of page 623 (*6221*) and a page pointer (*Page 623*).
- The second row contains *CustomerID* from the first row of page 624 (*6231*) and a page pointer (*Page 624*).
- The third row contains *CustomerID* from the first row of page 625 (*6241*) and a page pointer (*Page 625*).
- The last row (row 378) contains *CustomerID* from the first row of page 1000 (*9991*) and a page pointer (*Page 1000*).

You'll notice that page 1002 has some free space for more pages. We can still add 244 (*622 − 378 = 244*) rows if need be. The RDBMS can allocate 244 more pages of data without needing to allocate more pages at the intermediate level. When the number of customers grows to more than 12,440, the number of pages at the leaf level will exceed 1,244 and the RDBMS will allocate another page to the intermediate level and insert third row into *Page 1003*.

Page 1003 (root level page):

This page contains two rows:
- The first row contains *CustomerID* from the first row of first page of the next level (*page 1001*) i.e. *1* and a page pointer i.e. *Page 1001*.
- The second row contains *CustomerID* from the first row of second page of the next level (*page 1002*) i.e. *6221* and a page pointer i.e. *Page 1002*.
- This page has a lot of free spaces. We can still add 620 rows (*622 − 2 = 620*).

The root level will always have a single page and the intermediate level(s) will always have multiple pages. Let's assume that we do not have more than 6,220 customers. In this case, we do not need more than 622 pages, so there will be no need for the intermediate page 1002. The intermediate level will have only one page (i.e. *Page 1001*); hence this intermediate level become the root level. In this scenario the storage data structure will look like Fig 18.3.

Let's create a *primary key* for our *Customers_LargeTable* table by executing the statement shown below:

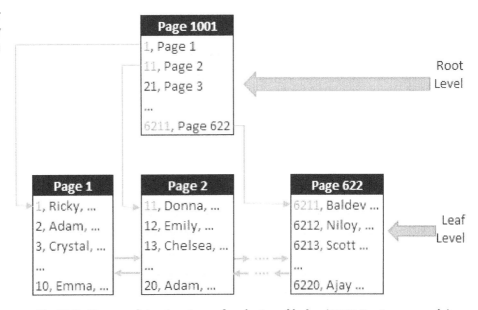

Fig 18.3: Storage data structure of a clustered index (6220 Customers only)

```
ALTER TABLE Customers_LargeTable
    ADD CONSTRAINT PK_Customers_LargeTable PRIMARY KEY (CustomerID);
```

Now let's see what happens when we execute the same queries we have executed for the heap (the *Customers_LargeTable* without a *primary key*).

SQL Server:
Queries:
```
SET STATISTICS IO ON;
SELECT * FROM Customers_LargeTable;
SELECT * FROM Customers_LargeTable WHERE CustomerID = 9993;
SELECT * FROM Customers_LargeTable WHERE FirstName = 'Charlie';
```

Output Messages:

```
    Results    Messages

    (10000 row(s) affected)
    Table 'Customers_LargeTable'. Scan count 1, logical reads 1007  physical reads 0, read-ahead reads 0,

    (1 row(s) affected)
    Table 'Customers_LargeTable'. Scan count 0, logical reads 3  physical reads 0, read-ahead reads 0, lot

    (1 row(s) affected)
    Table 'Customers_LargeTable'. Scan count 1, logical reads 1007  physical reads 0, read-ahead reads 0,
```

The first query has returned all (10,000) rows and read all (1,007) data pages. Therefore, when you want to return all rows, the heap and clustered index both perform similarly. You may have noticed that the same query has to read 1,118 data pages when the table did not have a primary key. This means that, when we add a primary key, the same data can be stored in slightly fewer pages (1,007).

The second query returned one row and scanned three pages (Page 1003, Page 1002 and Page 1000) instead of all the pages that was the case for the heap. When you search by *primary key* column, the clustered index performs much faster than heap.

The third query has also returned one row but scanned 1,007 pages (all of them, as with the heap). This query is searching for *FirstName*, but there is no *FirstName* in the root and intermediate levels. The storage engine did not find a quick way to navigate to the data row because table's data structure does not support that.

MySQL:

Below are the queries you should execute to see if the database engine searches the clustered index faster than the heap.

Queries:
```
EXPLAIN SELECT * FROM Customers_LargeTable;
EXPLAIN SELECT * FROM Customers_LargeTable WHERE CustomerID = 9993;
EXPLAIN SELECT * FROM Customers_LargeTable WHERE FirstName = 'Charlie';
```

Output Messages:

id	select_type	table	partitions	type	possible_keys	key	key_len	ref	rows	filtered	Extra
1	SIMPLE	Customers_LargeTable	NULL	ALL	NULL	NULL	NULL	NULL	9919	100.00	NULL

id	select_type	table	partitions	type	possible_keys	key	key_len	ref	rows	filtered	Extra
1	SIMPLE	Customers_LargeTable	NULL	const	PRIMARY	PRIMARY	4	const	1	100.00	NULL

id	select_type	table	partitions	type	possible_keys	key	key_len	ref	rows	filtered	Extra
1	SIMPLE	Customers_LargeTable	NULL	ALL	NULL	NULL	NULL	NULL	9919	10.00	Using where

You may have noticed that the first query has estimated it will examine 9,919 rows (i.e. all of them), which is fine because we are retrieving all rows. But the third query has also estimated it will examine all rows, which probably isn't optimal because we are retrieving only one row here. The second query estimated it will examine just one row, which is very fast compared to the heap query.

In Summary:

The first query will return all rows, as intended, so nothing can be done to improve performance.

The second query will return one row. Since this query is searching for the primary key, using a clustered index will significantly improve performance.

The third query will return one row but it still scans all rows. We will explore the techniques to improve this query's performance next.

The storage data structure of a non-clustered index

When you create a non-clustered index on a column (or a group of columns), the RDBMS will copy all the value for the column along with their *primary key* values, then store them to an additional set of pages in a particular order. This non-clustered index is often called simply an *index* and the column(s) used in the index are called *index keys*. When the storage engine needs more than one page to store all the index keys, it creates another page for the root level like the *B-Tree* we discussed earlier.

Let's explore this data structure with an example. If you create an index on the *FirstName* column of the *Customers_LargeTable* table, the RDBMS will create an additional storage data structure for the table, as demonstrated in Fig 18.4 below:

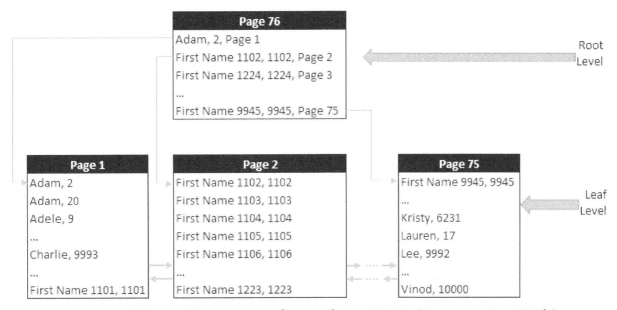

Fig 18.4: Storage data structure of a non-clustered index (Customers_LargeTable)

The leaf level pages of a non-clustered index store the index key (*FirstName*) and primary key (*CustomerID*). Here, the *FirstName* column is 50 characters long (it uses 50 bytes of storage) and the *CustomerID* column is an integer (it needs 4 bytes of storage). Therefore, each 8KB page can store approximately 134 rows. To store 10,000 rows, it will take 75 *(134 x 74 + 84)* pages (the last page will have only 84 rows).

When a query instructs the storage engine to return customers who have a particular *first name*, the storage engine will perform these steps:

- It will look for the *FirstName* in the root page, then navigate down to the leaf level page.
- Next, it will look for the *FirstName* in the leaf level page, get the corresponding *CustomerID*, then go to the *B-Tree* structure (*clustered index*) and get the corresponding rows.

The syntax for creating a non-clustered index is:

```
CREATE INDEX Index Name
    ON Table Name (
                    Column Name 1 ASC/DESC,
                    Column Name 2 ASC/DESC,
                    ............................................,
                    Column Name n ASC/DESC
            );
```

Let's create an index on the *FirstName* column of the *Customers_LargeTable* table by this statement:

```
CREATE INDEX idx_Customers_LargeTable_FirstName
    ON Customers_LargeTable (FirstName ASC);
```

Now let's execute the third query and review the output messages.

SQL Server:

Query:

```
SET STATISTICS IO ON;
SELECT * FROM Customers_LargeTable WHERE FirstName = 'Charlie';
```

Output Message:

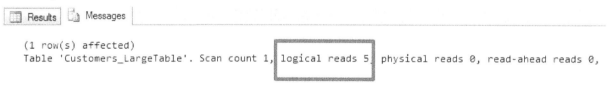

You may have noticed that the query has only scanned five pages (two pages from the non-clustered index and three pages from the clustered index).

MySQL:

Query:

```
EXPLAIN SELECT * FROM Customers_LargeTable WHERE FirstName = 'Charlie';
```

Output Message:

id	select_type	table	partitions	type	key	key_len	ref	rows	filtered	Extra
1	SIMPLE	Customers_LargeTable	NULL	ref	idx_Customers_LargeTable_FirstName	150	const	1	100.00	NULL

As the *'rows'* column shows, the query has estimated that it will only need to examine 1 row instead of 9,919 rows to find *Charlie's* data, because it is using the index key *idx_Customers_LargeTable_FirstName* instead of scanning the whole table.

Index's limitations

Hopefully, you can see how useful the index object is for speeding up your queries. With such a tool at your disposal, why not create indexes for every columns on every tables? There is one reason. You may have noticed that when you create an index, the RDBMS needs to create an additional storage structure for every index. As a result, when you insert a new row in the table, RDBMS has to add that row into multiple locations. Similarly, for any update on an index key column, the RDBMS has to update it in multiple locations as well. This means, the insert, update, and delete operations will be slower. Therefore, we urge you to create indexes wisely.

Lesson Summary

In this lesson we explained the index database object, how it can make queries run very fast, and what limitations you should consider before creating new indexes for your database.

Lesson 19

Backing up and restoring a database

NEW SQL STATEMENTS AND KEYWORDS COVERED IN THIS LESSON:

BACKUP DATABASE   RESTORE DATABASE
BACKUP LOG   RESTORE LOG
STOPAT

Lesson Objective

Data is the most valuable asset for any company, and disaster can happen any time. To protect your data from disastrous losses you need to have a recovery plan. The *backup* and *restore* process plays a vital role here. Disaster recovery is vast topic, so we will cover only the basics here:

- Why you need a backup
- Different types of backups
- How to create a database backup
- How to restore a database from backup
- How to restore a database in a specific point

Code Samples

You can find the SQL code solutions for the examples and business problems in this lesson at the following links:

SQL Server:
https://drive.google.com/open?id=1KlFhQULbMhtJmd1QGEV3FbsZS3dLVOTN

Why do we need to back up a database?

Preparing for the unexpected is always a good practice when your vital business assets are at stake. Here are just a few reasons why you'd be glad you backed up your database:

To recover from a disaster: A fire could break out in your office, a cyclone could hit the area, or worse, an earthquake could destroy the entire building. These are major, unpredictable events that could mean the loss of your entire database and, in some parts of the world, it's only a matter of time before it happens. Whatever the cause, your business needs to take precautions to avoid a total loss. That is why you need to back up your database so you can restore it to a different server and keep the business running.

To recover from human error: DBAs can accidentally drop a table from the database, delete critical data, or cause data loss in a multitude of other accidental (or non-accidental) ways. With a backup of your database, you'll be able to restore the database to the version just before the damage was done.

Copying a database from one environment to another: Preventing catastrophic loss is not the only reason to create a backup. Businesses often need a copy of its production database for testing and auditing purposes. To support this need, you need to back up the database from the production server and then restore it into the test/audit server.

Database backup types

There are several types of database backups that exist. Two of the most common are:

- Full
- Log

Full: As the name suggests, this type of backup entails copying the entire database.

Log: This type of backup copies any changes made since the last log backup. When you are backing up for the first time, it will copy changes made since last full backup.

So, why do a full backup instead of a log, and vice versa, and how often? This depends on your business requirements. For example, if company is willing to accept a maximum of one hour's data loss in the event of a fire in the datacentre, then the DBA must ensure the database is backing up once every hour. If the DBA decided to use the full backup method for every database in the datacentre every hour, it would require a huge amount of disks/tapes to store it all. A full backup may not be feasible or even needed, and that is where log backup become handy. The DBA could instead perform a log (changes since last backup) backup every hour, and only do the full database backup once every week or month.

The process of creating a database backup and restoring it in the same or a different server varies between RDBMSs. Next, we'll look at the steps of the process for *SQL Server*.

How to create a database backup in SQL Server

The basic syntax to create a full database backup is:

```
BACKUP DATABASE database name
    TO DISK = file name with full path
    WITH INIT;
```

Specifically, if you want to create a full backup file for our business case database *SalesOrderStore* in the *C:\Backup* folder with *SalesOrderStore_FullBackup.BAK* file name, you need to execute the SQL statement below:

```
BACKUP DATABASE SalesOrderStore
    TO DISK = 'C:\Backup\SalesOrderStore_FullBackup.BAK'
    WITH INIT;
```

The basic syntax to create a log backup for a database is:

```
BACKUP LOG database name
    TO DISK = file name with full path
    WITH INIT;
```

So, if you want to create a log backup file for our business case database *SalesOrderStore* in the *C:\Backup* folder with *SalesOrderStore_LogBackup.BAK* file name, you need to execute the SQL statement below:

```
BACKUP LOG SalesOrderStore
    TO DISK = 'C:\Backup\SalesOrderStore_LogBackup.BAK'
    WITH INIT;
```

How to restore a database from backup in SQL Server

Backing up databases is useless unless you know how to restore the backup when you need it. Let's look at the basic syntax to restore a database from a full backup:

```
RESTORE DATABASE database name
    FROM DISK = file name with full path;
```

Let's assume that, due to a fire, your database server has been destroyed. To simulate this event, please execute the SQL below to remove the *SalesOrderStore* database from your server (first make sure you've performed the backup as described in the section above):

```
DROP DATABASE SalesOrderStore;
```

Fortunately, the company has bought a new server and it's now time for you to restore the *SalesOrderStore* database from the backup file of *SalesOrderStore_FullBackup.BAK* that you stored in the *C:\Backup* folder. You can easily perform this task by executing:

```
RESTORE DATABASE SalesOrderStore
    FROM DISK = 'C:\Backup\SalesOrderStore_FullBackup.BAK';
```

Now, let's assume your test server has the *SalesOrderStore* database and you want to restore the latest production data from the earlier backup file on the test server. You may be thinking that you can copy the backup file to the test server and execute the *RESTORE* statement above, but it will return an error, because the database already exists in the server. You must instead execute the *DROP* statement first, then execute the *RESTORE* statement. Alternatively, instead of performing this two-step process, you can add the *WITH REPLACE* keyword at the end of the above *RESTORE* statement:

```
RESTORE DATABASE SalesOrderStore
    FROM DISK = 'C:\Backup\SalesOrderStore_FullBackup.BAK'
    WITH REPLACE;
```

How to restore a database from backup to a specific point in time in SQL Server

Human errors will always happen. Developers occasionally drop tables by mistake, deleting/updating data accidentally. In the event of such an incident, you as a DBA will need to restore the database to the point just before the accident. This is where restoring from a log backup becomes handy. Let's assume the current time is 10:00 am and some activities were performed in our *SalesOrderStore* database between 10:00 am and 10:20 am. Before we begin, note that we have indicated a specific time that each action occurred in our scenario. As you follow along, your SQL statements do not need to be executed at exactly the same time as ours, but you should keep careful track of the hour, minute, and second that each act was performed because you will be asked to indicate the specific time you added data to the statement later on in the simulation.

Here the steps to follow to simulate a *backup/loss/restore* of the *SalesOrderStore* database:

At 10:00 am: Create a sample customer table called *NewCustomers* in the *SaleOrderStore* database by executing this statement:

```
CREATE TABLE NewCustomers
    (
        CustomerID INT,
        Name VARCHAR(50)
    );
```

At 10:01 am: Now create an initial full backup of *SalesOrderStore*:

```
BACKUP DATABASE SalesOrderStore
    TO DISK = 'C:\Backup\SalesOrderStore_Initial_FullBackup.BAK'
    WITH INIT;
```

At 10:05 am: Add two new customers *(ID - 1, Name - Michelle* and *ID - 2, Name - Rick)* into the *NewCustomers* table by executing these statements:

```
INSERT INTO NewCustomers(CustomerID, Name) VALUES(1, 'Michelle');
INSERT INTO NewCustomers(CustomerID, Name) VALUES(2, 'Rick');
```

At 10:10 am: Create the first log backup by executing the following:

```
BACKUP LOG SalesOrderStore
    TO DISK = 'C:\Backup\SalesOrderStore_First_LogBackup.BAK'
    WITH INIT;
```

At 10:11 am: Remove the customer *Michelle* from *NewCustomers* table by executing this statement:

```
DELETE FROM NewCustomers WHERE CustomerID=1;
```

At 10:12 am: Add another new customer *(ID - 3, Name - Robert)* into the *NewCustomers* table by executing:

```
INSERT INTO NewCustomers(CustomerID, Name) VALUES(3, 'Robert');
```

At 10:13 am: Remove customer *Rick* from the *NewCustomers*:

```
DELETE FROM NewCustomers WHERE CustomerID=2;
```

At 10:14 am: Add another new customer *(ID - 4, Name - Mili)* into the *NewCustomers*:

```
INSERT INTO NewCustomers(CustomerID, Name) VALUES(4, 'Mili');
```

At 10:20 am: Create the second log backup by executing this statement:

```
BACKUP LOG SalesOrderStore
    TO DISK = 'C:\Backup\SalesOrderStore_Second_LogBackup.BAK'
    WITH INIT;
```

Great, you've made several changes to your database and taken precautions by backing up the database. Now let's assume that the customer you have removed from the *NewCustomers* table at 10:11am was a mistake and you want to restore the database to an earlier version at the time of 10:10am. You may recall we performed a full database backup at 10:01am, a log backup at 10:10am and another log backup at 10:20am. If you only restore the full backup, you will lose the two new customers that were added between 10:01am and 10:10am. But if you restore the full backup and then the first log backup, you will achieve your desired result. The *RESTORE DATABASE* statement you have just learned will make the database accessible immediately after the restore and someone else can add or remove data from the database the moment after the *RESTORE DATABASE* statement was executed. That is why *SQL SERVER* will not allow a user to restore a log backup on top of a full backup. To solve this issue, you need to keep the database inaccessible until you finish restoring the full backup and all required log backups. Once all the backups have been completed, you can make the database accessible for manipulation again.

To make a database inaccessible while you're restoring it, you need to add a *NORECOVERY* keyword in the *WITH* clause. After you finish restoring the full backup and all required log backups, you need to make the database accessible again by using a special *RESTORE* statement:

```
RESTORE DATABASE database name WITH RECOVERY;
```

Using this syntax, you can restore the database to a point up to 10:10am by executing the three *RESTORE* statements you see below (restore the full backup with *NORECOVERY*, then restore the first log backup with *NORECOVERY*, and finally, restore with *RECOVERY*):

```
-- Restoring from the FULL backup taken at 10:01am
RESTORE DATABASE SalesOrderStore
    FROM DISK = 'C:\Backup\SalesOrderStore_Initial_FullBackup.BAK'
    WITH REPLACE, NORECOVERY;

-- Restoring from the LOG backup taken at 10:10am
RESTORE LOG SalesOrderStore
    FROM DISK = 'C:\Backup\SalesOrderStore_First_LogBackup.BAK'
    WITH NORECOVERY;

-- Make the database accessible by restoring WITH RECOVERY
RESTORE DATABASE SalesOrderStore WITH RECOVERY;
```

Notes

Sometime you may receive an error like:

RESTORE cannot process database 'SalesOrderStore' because it is in use by this session

This means you or someone else is currently using the database. Whoever is currently using the database must end/close their session before you execute the *RESTORE* statement. Alternatively, they can change database context to a system database *Master* by executing the below statement:

```
USE Master;
```

If you are the only one using the database at this moment, simply execute the above *USE* statement just before the *RESTORE* statements.

Now let's assume that the customer you have removed at 10:11am was not removed by mistake, but the customer you have removed at 10:13am was a mistake and you want to restore the database up to 10:12am. If you recall, your second log backup was at 10:20am, but your incident happened at 10:13am. You won't be able to restore your database up to the point just before the accidental removal at 10:13 if you restore the second log backup after the first two *RESTORE* statements above. You need to restore the second log backup up to the point just before 10:13am (i.e. 10:12:59am). To do this, you need to add another keyword, *STOPAT*, which will allow you to specify the exact time. The *RESTORE* statement will restore only the activities happened up to that specified time. Therefore, you can perform your desired task by executing the *RESTORE* statements shown below:

```
USE Master;

-- Restoring from the FULL backup taken at 10:01am
RESTORE DATABASE SalesOrderStore
    FROM DISK = 'C:\Backup\SalesOrderStore_Initial_FullBackup.BAK'
    WITH REPLACE, NORECOVERY;

-- Restoring from the LOG backup taken at 10:10am
RESTORE LOG SalesOrderStore
    FROM DISK = 'C:\Backup\SalesOrderStore_First_LogBackup.BAK'
    WITH NORECOVERY;

-- Restoring up to 10:12:59am from the LOG backup taken at 10:20am
RESTORE LOG SalesOrderStore
    FROM DISK = 'C:\Backup\SalesOrderStore_Second_LogBackup.BAK'
    WITH NORECOVERY, STOPAT = '2018-03-20 10:12:59';

-- Make the database accessible by restoring WITH RECOVERY
RESTORE DATABASE SalesOrderStore WITH RECOVERY;
```

Lesson Summary

In this lesson, we explained the importance of keeping your database backed up, something that is a good practice no matter the size and purpose of the data. In addition to explaining the "*why*" of backing up and restoring data, we demonstrated the "*how*" performing a backup and restoring from that backup, including situations where you want to restore to a specific point in time.

Appendix A

Solutions to all of the Practice Business Problems of this book can be found in this Appendix.

Solutions to the Practice Business Problems of Lesson 4

Practice Business Problem 1 – SQL Server

```
CREATE TABLE Addresses
    (
        AddressID INT IDENTITY(1,1) NOT NULL PRIMARY KEY,
        StreetAddress VARCHAR(100) NOT NULL,
        City VARCHAR(25) NOT NULL,
        StateProvince VARCHAR(25) NULL,
        Country VARCHAR(25) NOT NULL,
        ZipOrPostalCode VARCHAR(20) NULL
    );
```

Practice Business Problem 1 – MySQL

```
CREATE TABLE Addresses
    (
        AddressID INT AUTO_INCREMENT NOT NULL PRIMARY KEY,
        StreetAddress VARCHAR(100) NOT NULL,
        City VARCHAR(25) NOT NULL,
        StateProvince VARCHAR(25) NULL,
        Country VARCHAR(25) NOT NULL,
        ZipOrPostalCode VARCHAR(20) NULL
    );
```

Practice Business Problem 2 – SQL Server

```
CREATE TABLE CreditCards (
        CreditCardID INT IDENTITY(1,1) NOT NULL PRIMARY KEY,
        CreditCardNumber VARCHAR(20) NOT NULL,
        CardHolderName VARCHAR(50) NOT NULL,
        CreditCardType VARCHAR(25) NOT NULL,
        CreditCardExpiryMonth INT NOT NULL,
        CreditCardExpiryYear INT NOT NULL
    );
```

Practice Business Problem 2 – MySQL

```
CREATE TABLE CreditCards (
        CreditCardID INT AUTO_INCREMENT NOT NULL PRIMARY KEY,
        CreditCardNumber VARCHAR(20) NOT NULL,
        CardHolderName VARCHAR(50) NOT NULL,
        CreditCardType VARCHAR(25) NOT NULL,
        CreditCardExpiryMonth INT NOT NULL,
        CreditCardExpiryYear INT NOT NULL
    );
```

Practice Business Problem 3

```
CREATE  TABLE Logins
    (
            UserID VARCHAR(50) NOT NULL PRIMARY KEY,
            Email VARCHAR(50) NOT NULL,
            Password NVARCHAR(50) NOT NULL,
            NoOfFailedAttempt INT NOT NULL DEFAULT 3,
            ChangePasswordInNextLogin BIT NOT NULL DEFAULT 1,
            IsLocked BIT NOT NULL DEFAULT 0,
            IsActive BIT NOT NULL DEFAULT 1
    );
```

Practice Business Problem 4

```
CREATE TABLE SalesOrderProducts
    (
            SalesOrderID INT NOT NULL,
            ProductID INT NOT NULL,
            ProductQuantity INT NOT NULL,
            ProductUnitPrice DECIMAL(18,4) NOT NULL,
            ProductUnitPriceDiscount DECIMAL(18,4) NOT NULL,
            ProductShipDate DATETIME NULL,
            ProductDeliveryDate DATETIME NULL,
            PRIMARY KEY (SalesOrderID, ProductID)
    );
```

Practice Business Problem 5

```
DROP TABLE Addresses;
```

Practice Business Problem 6

```
ALTER TABLE Logins ADD AdditionalNotes VARCHAR(300) NULL;
```

Practice Business Problem 7

```
ALTER TABLE Logins DROP COLUMN AdditionalNotes;
```

Solutions to the Practice Business Problems of Lesson 5

Practice Business Problem 1 – SQL Server

```
/* Adding employee's address details into Addresses table */
INSERT INTO Addresses (StreetAddress, City, StateProvince, Country, ZipOrPostalCode)
VALUES ('8888 Flinders Street', 'Brisbane', 'Queensland', 'Australia', '4000');

/* Assigning previously added identity number into @AddressID variable */
DECLARE @AddressID INT;
SELECT @AddressID = SCOPE_IDENTITY();

/* Adding employee's general details into Employees table */
INSERT INTO Employees(EmployeeFirstName, EmployeeLastName, EmployeeAddressID, EmployeePhoneNumber,
          EmployeeMobileNumber, EmployeeEmail, EmployeeDateOfBirth, EmployeeGender,
          EmployeeCommissionRatePercentage)
VALUES ('Tracey', 'Moore', @AddressID, '+61 3 222222222', '+61 4222222222', 'TraceyMoore@SaleOnYourOwn.com',
          '1980-01-01', 'Female', 25);

/* Adding employee's login details into Logins table */
INSERT INTO Logins(UserID, Password, ChangePasswordInNextLogin, Email)
VALUES ('TraceyMoore', 'Welcome123', 1, 'TraceyMoore@SaleOnYourOwn.com');
```

Practice Business Problem 1 – MySQL

```
/* Adding employee's address details into Addresses table */
INSERT INTO Addresses (StreetAddress, City, StateProvince, Country, ZipOrPostalCode)
VALUES ('8888 Flinders Street', 'Brisbane', 'Queensland', 'Australia', '4000');

/* Assigning previously added identity number into @AddressID variable */
SET @AddressID = LAST_INSERT_ID();

/* Adding employee's general details into Employees table */
INSERT INTO Employees(EmployeeFirstName, EmployeeLastName, EmployeeAddressID, EmployeePhoneNumber,
          EmployeeMobileNumber, EmployeeEmail, EmployeeDateOfBirth, EmployeeGender,
          EmployeeCommissionRatePercentage)
VALUES ('Tracey', 'Moore', @AddressID, '+61 3 222222222', '+61 4222222222', 'TraceyMoore@SaleOnYourOwn.com',
          '1980-01-01', 'Female', 25);

/* Adding employee's login details into Logins table */
INSERT INTO Logins(UserID, Password, ChangePasswordInNextLogin, Email)
VALUES ('TraceyMoore', 'Welcome123', 1, 'TraceyMoore@SaleOnYourOwn.com');
```

Practice Business Problem 2

```
UPDATE    Employees
    SET EmployeeLastName = 'William'
WHERE EmployeeEmail = 'TraceyMoore@SaleOnYourOwn.com';
```

Practice Business Problem 3

```
DELETE FROM    Employees
WHERE EmployeeEmail = 'TraceyMoore@SaleOnYourOwn.com';
```

Solutions to the Practice Business Problems of Lesson 6

Practice Business Problem 1 – SQL Server

```
SELECT    GETDATE() AS Today, DATEADD(dd, -3, GETDATE()) AS Date3DayAgo,
          DATEADD(dd, 3, GETDATE()) AS Date3DaysLater,
          DATEADD(wk, -3, GETDATE()) AS Date3WeekAgo,
          DATEADD(wk, 3, GETDATE()) AS Date3WeekLater,
          DATEADD(mm, -3, GETDATE()) AS Date3MonthAgo,
          DATEADD(mm, 3, GETDATE()) AS Date3MonthLater,
          DATEADD(yy, -3, GETDATE()) AS Date3YearAgo,
          DATEADD(yy, 3, GETDATE()) AS Date3YearLater;
```

Practice Business Problem 1 – MySQL

```
SELECT    CURRENT_DATE() AS Today, DATE_ADD(CURRENT_DATE(), INTERVAL -3 DAY) AS Date3DayAgo,
          DATE_ADD(CURRENT_DATE(), INTERVAL 3 DAY) AS Date3DaysLater,
          DATE_ADD(CURRENT_DATE(), INTERVAL -3 WEEK) AS Date3WeekAgo,
          DATE_ADD(CURRENT_DATE(), INTERVAL 3 WEEK) AS Date3WeekLater,
          DATE_ADD(CURRENT_DATE(), INTERVAL -3 MONTH) AS Date3MonthAgo,
          DATE_ADD(CURRENT_DATE(), INTERVAL 3 MONTH) AS Date3MonthLater,
          DATE_ADD(CURRENT_DATE(), INTERVAL -3 YEAR) AS Date3YearAgo,
          DATE_ADD(CURRENT_DATE(), INTERVAL 3 YEAR) AS Date3YearLater;
```

Practice Business Problem 2 – SQL Server

```
SELECT    FORMAT(GETDATE(), 'dd-MM-yyyy') AS Today,
          FORMAT(DATEADD(dd, -3, GETDATE()), 'dd-MM-yyyy') AS Date3DayAgo,
          FORMAT(DATEADD(dd, 3, GETDATE()), 'dd-MM-yyyy') AS Date3DaysLater,
          FORMAT(DATEADD(wk, -3, GETDATE()), 'dd-MM-yyyy') AS Date3WeekAgo,
          FORMAT(DATEADD(wk, 3, GETDATE()), 'dd-MM-yyyy') AS Date3WeekLater,
          FORMAT(DATEADD(mm, -3, GETDATE()), 'dd-MM-yyyy') AS Date3MonthAgo,
          FORMAT(DATEADD(mm, 3, GETDATE()), 'dd-MM-yyyy') AS Date3MonthLater,
          FORMAT(DATEADD(yy, -3, GETDATE()), 'dd-MM-yyyy') AS Date3YearAgo,
          FORMAT(DATEADD(yy, 3, GETDATE()), 'dd-MM-yyyy') AS Date3YearLater;
```

Practice Business Problem 2 – MySQL

```
SELECT    DATE_FORMAT(CURRENT_DATE(), '%d-%m-%Y') AS Today,
          DATE_FORMAT(DATE_ADD(CURRENT_DATE(), INTERVAL -3 DAY), '%d-%m-%Y') AS Date3DayAgo,
          DATE_FORMAT(DATE_ADD(CURRENT_DATE(), INTERVAL 3 DAY), '%d-%m-%Y') AS Date3DaysLater,
          DATE_FORMAT(DATE_ADD(CURRENT_DATE(), INTERVAL -3 WEEK), '%d-%m-%Y') AS Date3WeekAgo,
          DATE_FORMAT(DATE_ADD(CURRENT_DATE(), INTERVAL 3 WEEK), '%d-%m-%Y') AS Date3WeekLater,
          DATE_FORMAT(DATE_ADD(CURRENT_DATE(), INTERVAL -3 MONTH), '%d-%m-%Y') AS Date3MonthAgo,
          DATE_FORMAT(DATE_ADD(CURRENT_DATE(), INTERVAL 3 MONTH), '%d-%m-%Y') AS Date3MonthLater,
          DATE_FORMAT(DATE_ADD(CURRENT_DATE(), INTERVAL -3 YEAR), '%d-%m-%Y') AS Date3YearAgo,
          DATE_FORMAT(DATE_ADD(CURRENT_DATE(), INTERVAL 3 YEAR), '%d-%m-%Y') AS Date3YearLater;
```

Practice Business Problem 3 – SQL Server

```
SELECT    DATEPART(dd, GETDATE()) AS DayNumberOfMonth,
          DATENAME(dw, GETDATE()) AS DayNameOfWeek,
          DATEPART(mm, GETDATE()) AS MonthNumberOfYear,
          DATENAME(mm, GETDATE()) AS MonthNameOfYear,
          DATEPART(yyyy, GETDATE()) AS Year;
```

Practice Business Problem 3 – MySQL

```
SELECT   DAY(CURRENT_DATE()) AS DayNumberOfMonth,
         DAYNAME(CURRENT_DATE()) AS DayNameOfWeek,
         MONTH(CURRENT_DATE()) AS MonthNumberOfYear,
         MONTHNAME(CURRENT_DATE()) AS MonthNameOfYear,
         YEAR(CURRENT_DATE()) AS Year;
```

Practice Business Problem 4 – SQL Server

```
SELECT CONCAT('Sales Report for the Month of ', DATENAME(mm, GETDATE()), ' ', DATEPART(yyyy, GETDATE()));
```

Practice Business Problem 4 – MySQL

```
SELECT CONCAT('Sales Report for the Month of ', MONTHNAME(CURRENT_DATE()), ' ', YEAR(CURRENT_DATE()));
```

Solutions to the Practice Business Problems of Lesson 7

Practice Business Problem 1

```
SELECT ProductCategoryName
FROM ProductCategories;
```

Practice Business Problem 2

```
SELECT ProductSubCategoryName
FROM ProductSubCategories
ORDER BY ProductSubCategoryName ASC;
```

Practice Business Problem 3

```
SELECT VendorCategoryName, VendorMonthlyTarget, VendorCommissionRatePercentage
FROM VendorCategories;
```

Practice Business Problem 4

```
SELECT ProductID, ProductName, StandardSalesPrice, StockQuantity, ProductSubCategoryID
FROM Products
ORDER BY ProductSubCategoryID DESC;
```

Practice Business Problem 5

```
SELECT ProductID, ProductName, StandardSalesPrice, StockQuantity, ProductSubCategoryID
FROM Products
ORDER BY ProductSubCategoryID DESC, StockQuantity ASC;
```

Practice Business Problem 6

```
SELECT * FROM Products;
```

Practice Business Problem 7

```
SELECT   SalesOrderID AS OrderID, CustomerID, OrderDate, OrderDeliveryDate AS DeliveryDate,
         OrderTotal AS GrossValue, OrderDiscountTotal AS Discount, OrderTotal - OrderDiscountTotal AS NetValue
FROM SalesOrders;
```

Practice Business Problem 8

```
SELECT      ProductID, ProductName, StandardSalesPrice * 1.1 AS StandardUnitPrice,
            CASE WHEN SalesDiscountPercentage <> 0
                    THEN StandardSalesPrice * 1.1 * SalesDiscountPercentage/100
                ELSE SalesDiscountAmount
            END AS UnitDiscount,
            StandardSalesPrice * 1.1 - (CASE WHEN SalesDiscountPercentage <> 0
                                            THEN StandardSalesPrice * 1.1 * SalesDiscountPercentage/100
                                        ELSE SalesDiscountAmount
                                    END) AS NetUnitPrice
FROM Products;
```

Solutions to the Practice Business Problems of Lesson 8

Practice Business Problem 1

```
SELECT DISTINCT Country
FROM Addresses;
```

Practice Business Problem 2 – SQL Server

```
SELECT TOP 10 ProductID, ProductName, StandardSalesPrice AS StandardUnitPrice,
    CASE WHEN SalesDiscountPercentage <> 0
                THEN StandardSalesPrice * SalesDiscountPercentage/100
        ELSE SalesDiscountAmount
    END AS UnitDiscount,
    StandardSalesPrice -
        (CASE
                WHEN SalesDiscountPercentage <> 0
                THEN StandardSalesPrice * SalesDiscountPercentage/100
            ELSE SalesDiscountAmount
        END) AS NetUnitPrice
FROM Products;
```

Practice Business Problem 2 – MySQL

```
SELECT ProductID, ProductName, StandardSalesPrice AS StandardUnitPrice,
    CASE WHEN SalesDiscountPercentage <> 0
                THEN StandardSalesPrice * SalesDiscountPercentage/100
        ELSE SalesDiscountAmount
    END AS UnitDiscount,
    StandardSalesPrice -
        (CASE
                WHEN SalesDiscountPercentage <> 0
                THEN StandardSalesPrice * SalesDiscountPercentage/100
            ELSE SalesDiscountAmount
            END) AS NetUnitPrice
FROM      Products
LIMIT     10;
```

Practice Business Problem 3 – SQL Server

```
SELECT ProductID, ProductName, StandardSalesPrice AS StandardUnitPrice,
     CASE WHEN SalesDiscountPercentage <> 0
                    THEN StandardSalesPrice * SalesDiscountPercentage/100
          ELSE SalesDiscountAmount
     END AS UnitDiscount,
     StandardSalesPrice -
          (CASE
                WHEN SalesDiscountPercentage <> 0
                    THEN StandardSalesPrice * SalesDiscountPercentage/100
                ELSE SalesDiscountAmount
                END) AS NetUnitPrice
FROM     Products
ORDER BY NetUnitPrice DESC
OFFSET 0 ROWS FETCH NEXT 10 ROWS ONLY;
```

Practice Business Problem 3 – MySQL

```
SELECT ProductID, ProductName, StandardSalesPrice AS StandardUnitPrice,
     CASE WHEN SalesDiscountPercentage <> 0
                    THEN StandardSalesPrice * SalesDiscountPercentage/100
          ELSE SalesDiscountAmount
     END AS UnitDiscount,
     StandardSalesPrice -
          (CASE
                WHEN SalesDiscountPercentage <> 0
                    THEN StandardSalesPrice * SalesDiscountPercentage/100
                ELSE SalesDiscountAmount
                END) AS NetUnitPrice
FROM     Products
ORDER BY NetUnitPrice DESC
LIMIT 10 OFFSET 0;
```

Practice Business Problem 4

```
SELECT   EmployeeID, CONCAT(EmployeeFirstName, ' ', EmployeeLastName) AS Name,
         EmployeePhoneNumber AS Phone, EmployeeMobileNumber AS Mobile,
         EmployeeEmail AS Email, EmployeeGender AS Gender,
         EmployeeDateOfBirth AS BirthDate
FROM     Employees
WHERE    EmployeeGender = 'Female';
```

Practice Business Problem 5

```
SELECT   ProductID, ProductName, StandardSalesPrice
FROM     Products
WHERE    ProductID <= 15;
```

Practice Business Problem 6

```
SELECT   ProductID, ProductName, StandardSalesPrice
FROM     Products
WHERE    ProductID > 15;
```

Practice Business Problem 7 – SQL Server

```
SELECT    CustomerID, CONCAT(CustomerFirstName, ' ', CustomerLastName) AS Name,
          CustomerPhoneNumber AS Phone, CustomerMobileNumber AS Mobile,
          CustomerEmail AS Email, FORMAT(CustomerDateOfBirth, 'd MMM yyyy') AS BirthDate,
          CustomerGender AS Gender, FORMAT(CustomerJoinDate,'d MMM yyyy') AS JoinDate
FROM      Customers
WHERE     CustomerJoinDate >= DATEADD(yy, -5, DATEADD(dd,1,DATEDIFF(dd,0,GETDATE())));
```

Practice Business Problem 7 - MySQL

```
SELECT    CustomerID, CONCAT(CustomerFirstName, ' ', CustomerLastName) AS Name,
          CustomerPhoneNumber AS Phone, CustomerMobileNumber AS Mobile,
          CustomerEmail AS Email, DATE_FORMAT(CustomerDateOfBirth, '%d %b %Y') AS BirthDate,
          CustomerGender AS Gender, DATE_FORMAT(CustomerJoinDate,'%d %b %Y') AS JoinDate
FROM      Customers
WHERE     CustomerJoinDate >= DATE_ADD(DATE_ADD(CURDATE(), INTERVAL 1 DAY), INTERVAL -5 YEAR);
```

Practice Business Problem 8

```
SELECT    SalesOrderID AS OrderID, OrderDate, OrderDueDate AS DueDate,
          OrderDeliveryDate AS DeliveryDate,
          CustomerID, OrderTotal AS GrossValue,
          OrderDiscountTotal AS Discount,
          OrderTotal - OrderDiscountTotal AS NetValue
FROM      SalesOrders
WHERE     OrderTotal - OrderDiscountTotal BETWEEN 30000 AND 40000
ORDER BY  OrderDeliveryDate DESC, SalesOrderID DESC;
```

Practice Business Problem 9

```
SELECT    SalesOrderID AS OrderID, OrderDate, OrderDueDate AS DueDate,
          OrderDeliveryDate AS DeliveryDate,
          CustomerID, OrderTotal AS GrossValue,
          OrderDiscountTotal AS Discount,
          OrderTotal - OrderDiscountTotal AS NetValue
FROM      SalesOrders
WHERE     OrderDueDate IN ('2017-02-02','2017-02-03','2017-02-06')
ORDER BY  OrderDueDate ASC, SalesOrderID ASC;
```

Practice Business Problem 10

```
SELECT    CustomerID, CustomerFirstName, CustomerLastName,
          CustomerPhoneNumber, CustomerMobileNumber, CustomerEmail,
          CustomerGender
FROM      Customers
WHERE     CustomerLastName LIKE '%son';
```

Practice Business Problem 11

```
SELECT    SalesOrderID AS OrderID, OrderDate, OrderDueDate AS DueDate,
          OrderDeliveryDate AS DeliveryDate,
          CustomerID, OrderTotal AS GrossValue,
          OrderDiscountTotal AS Discount,
          OrderTotal - OrderDiscountTotal AS NetValue
FROM      SalesOrders
WHERE OrderDeliveryDate IS NULL;
```

Practice Business Problem 12

```
SELECT  CustomerID, CONCAT(CustomerFirstName, ' ', CustomerLastName) AS Name,
        CustomerGender AS Gender, YEAR(CustomerDateOfBirth) AS YearOfBirth
FROM    Customers
WHERE   YEAR(CustomerDateOfBirth) BETWEEN 1995 AND 2000
        AND CustomerFirstName LIKE 'R%'
ORDER BY CustomerID;
```

Practice Business Problem 13

```
SELECT  CustomerID, CONCAT(CustomerFirstName, ' ', CustomerLastName) AS Name,
        CustomerGender AS Gender, YEAR(CustomerDateOfBirth) AS YearOfBirth
FROM    Customers
WHERE   YEAR(CustomerDateOfBirth) BETWEEN 1995 AND 2000
        AND CustomerFirstName NOT LIKE 'R%'
ORDER BY CustomerID;
```

Practice Business Problem 14

```
SELECT  CustomerID, CONCAT(CustomerFirstName, ' ', CustomerLastName) AS Name,
        CustomerGender AS Gender, YEAR(CustomerDateOfBirth) AS YearOfBirth
FROM    Customers
WHERE   YEAR(CustomerDateOfBirth) BETWEEN 1995 AND 2000
        OR CustomerFirstName LIKE 'R%'
ORDER BY CustomerID;
```

Alternate Solution:

```
SELECT  CustomerID, CONCAT(CustomerFirstName, ' ', CustomerLastName) AS Name,
        CustomerGender AS Gender, YEAR(CustomerDateOfBirth) AS YearOfBirth
FROM    Customers
WHERE   YEAR(CustomerDateOfBirth) BETWEEN 1995 AND 2000

UNION

SELECT  CustomerID, CONCAT(CustomerFirstName, ' ', CustomerLastName) AS Name,
        CustomerGender AS Gender, YEAR(CustomerDateOfBirth) AS YearOfBirth
FROM    Customers
WHERE   CustomerFirstName LIKE 'R%'
ORDER BY CustomerID;
```

Index

About the Author

Hafizur Rahman

Hafizur Rahman is a senior data warehouse and business intelligent architect with more than 23 years of experience in relational database, data warehouse, reporting and analytics softwares. Since 1995, he has been involved in numerous projects as a key designer and architect in retail, financial and health industries. His passion is to help developers and business users solving day-to-day problems related to their data.

Made in the USA
Monee, IL
08 July 2022

99269093R00201